The Green Studio Handbook

DISCLAIMER

The information presented in this book has been assembled, derived, and developed from numerous sources including textbooks, standards, guidelines, professional firms, and the Internet. It is presented in good faith. The authors and the publisher have made every reasonable effort to ensure that the information presented herein is accurate; they do not, however, warrant (and assume no responsibility for) its accuracy, completeness, or suitability for any particular purpose or situation. The information is intended primarily as an aid to learning and teaching and not as a definitive source of information for the design of building systems by design professionals. It is the responsibility of all users to utilize professional judgment, experience, and common sense when applying information presented in this book. This responsibility extends to verification of local codes, standards, and legislation and assembly and validation of local climate data.

COPYRIGHTS AND TRADEMARKS

Numerous illustrations and tables in this book are reproduced with the express permission of a third-party copyright holder. These copyright holders are noted by citation immediately following the figure caption or table title. Tables and illustrations without such notation are copyright by the authors of this book.

Excerpts from *Time-Saver Standards for Landscape Architecture: Design and Construction Data*, 2nd ed., are used by permission of The McGraw-Hill Companies. McGraw-Hill makes no representations or warranties as to the accuracy of any information contained in the McGraw-Hill material, including any warranties of merchantability or fitness for a particular purpose. In no event shall McGraw-Hill have any liability to any party for special, incidental, tort, or consequential damages arising out of or in connection with the McGraw-Hill material, even if McGraw-Hill has been advised of the possibility of such damages.

LEED™ is a registered trademark of the U.S. Green Building Council

BREEAM and EcoHomes are registered trademarks of the Building Research Establishment, Ltd.

Living Machine® is a registered trademark of Living Machines, Inc.

ENVIRONMENT

All Architectural Press books are published by Elsevier which is part of the Reed Elsevier group. The Dow Jones Sustainability Index has classified Reed Elsevier as a Sustainability Leader citing a score "above the industry average with a good performance in environmental performance and reporting". Environmental best practice extends to all parts of our organization right down to its individual publications. Please see the Reed Elsevier website for further information on Reed Elsevier and the environment: http://www.reedelsevier.com/media/pdf/s/8/Environment06.pdf

The Green Studio Handbook

Environmental strategies for schematic design

Alison G. Kwok, AIA
and
Walter T. Grondzik, PE

AMSTERDAM • BOSTON • HEIDELBERG • LONDON • NEW YORK • OXFORD
PARIS • SAN DIEGO • SAN FRANCISCO • SINGAPORE • SYDNEY • TOKYO
Architectural Press is an imprint of Elsevier

Architectural
Press

Architectural Press is an imprint of Elsevier
Linacre House, Jordan Hill, Oxford OX2 8DP, UK
The Boulevard, Langford Lane, Kidlington, Oxford OX5 1GB, UK
84 Theobald's Road, London WC1X 8RR, UK
Radarweg 29, PO Box 211, 1000 AE Amsterdam, The Netherlands
30 Corporate Drive, Suite 400, Burlington, MA 01803, USA
525 B Street, Suite 1900, San Diego, CA 92101-4495, USA

First edition 2007

British Library Cataloguing in Publication Data
A catalogue record for this book is available from the British Library

Library of Congress Control Number: 2006933206

ISBN-13: 978-0-7506-8022-6
ISBN-10: 0-7506-8022-9

For information on all Architectural Press publications
visit our website at www.architecturalpress.com

Typeset by Charon Tec Ltd (A Macmillan Company), Chennai, India
www.charontec.com

Printed and bound in Italy
09 10 11   11 10 9 8 7 6 5

CONTENTS

PREFACE

The Green Studio Handbook was written to serve as a reference guide and source of inspiration for students in design studios and architects in professional practice. It is founded upon the premise that there would be more green buildings if the technics of green buildings—the underlying strategies that save energy, water, and material resources—were more accessible to the designer.

The student should find *The Green Studio Handbook* a useful introduction to green design strategies and the associated green design process. The architect, already convinced of the merits of green building and familiar with design process, can use the *Handbook* as an accessible supplement to augment his/her basic knowledge of green building strategies.

The Green Studio Handbook is not intended to serve as a green building checklist, nor as a textbook for environmental technology. Instead it provides the necessary information to make judgments about the appropriate use of green strategies and to validate design decisions regarding these strategies. It also provides tools for preliminary sizing of strategies and their components during the early stages of design. We hope designers will be able to realistically incorporate such strategies in schematic drawings. Aesthetics are left to the designer and project context, but examples of strategies are provided to trigger ideas and generate concepts.

Each strategy in *The Green Studio Handbook* includes a description of principle and concept, suggestions for integrating the strategies into a green building design, step-by-step procedures to assist with preliminary sizing of components, and references to standards and guidelines. Conceptual sketches and examples illustrate each strategy. To further the goal of integrative design, each strategy is linked to relevant complementary strategies.

The Green Studio Handbook is intended for use in university design studios and in professional office practice. Astute building owners might also use this book as a way of becoming better informed about green design projects. The focus is upon strategies that are of greatest interest to architectural designers; that have the greatest impact on building form; that must be considered very early in the design process. The book assumes that users have a basic knowledge of environmental technology concepts and of the design process and access to conventional design resources such as sun path diagrams, material R-values, thermal load calculation information, lighting standards, air quality guidelines, and the like.

ACKNOWLEDGMENTS

Similar to the design process, *The Green Studio Handbook* is very much a collaborative effort. There are many people to thank. That said, the authors are ultimately responsible for deciding what appears in this book and how information is organized and presented.

The internal production crew for this work included Kate Beckley and Sam Jensen-Augustine. Kate and Sam worked tirelessly to organize the nuts and bolts that hold a project such as this together. Kate also produced many of the drawings in the book and managed the database between sketching. Sam drafted and edited numerous strategies. We also thank Theodore J. Kwok for database streamlining and troubleshooting.

Most of the strategies in the book were first developed in a seminar course on the teaching of technical subjects in architecture offered at the University of Oregon. Alison Kwok was the faculty member in charge of that course—with assistance from Walter Grondzik. Students participating in this class included: Sam Jensen-Augustine, Juliette Beale, Kathy Bevers, Martha Bohm, Jessica Gracie Garner, Dan Goldstein, Jeff Guggenheim, Will Henderson, Daniel Meyers, Daniel Safarik, Alison Smith, Aaron Swain, Amelia Thrall, and Jason Zook. These initial strategies have been substantially morphed, tweaked, and transformed to their present form by numerous rounds of reviews and edits. Nicholas Rajkovich (Cornell University) and Emily Wright (Einhorn Yaffee Prescott Architecture and Engineering) developed several draft strategies to help fill gaps in coverage. Professor Donald Corner (University of Oregon) developed material for the Double Envelope design strategy. These were done under a tight deadline and competing time demands, so are especially appreciated.

The case studies presented in Chapter 5 were drafted by design professionals with direct knowledge of the projects. Bruce Haglund of the University of Idaho (who worked with Arup in London for a year) developed the Beddington Zero Energy Development, Arup Campus Solihull, and Druk White Lotus case studies. Emily Wright developed the case study of Lillis Hall, using her experience from working on the project with G.Z. Brown in the Energy Studies in Buildings Laboratory. Heidy Spaly, also a University of Oregon graduate and currently with Barker Rinker Seacat Architecture, developed the case study of the HRDC in Namibia (with input from the project's designer, Nina Maritz). Nicholas Rajkovich developed the case study of the Cornell Solar Decathlon House. The authors developed the case studies of The Helena Apartment Tower, National Association of Realtors Headquarters, and One Peking Road.

Two focused essays were prepared expressly for this work. Chapter 2 describing design and design process was prepared by Laura Briggs (Parsons: The New School for Design) and Jonathan Knowles (Rhode Island School of Design) of Briggs Knowles Design in New York City. Chapter 3 describing the green/integrated design process was prepared by David Posada (with GBD Architects in Portland, Oregon). These two essays have been edited by the authors of this book to reflect the needs of the book and our biases, but remain the essential product of the original contributors.

We would also like to thank Kathy Bevers, Martha Bohm, Christina Bollo (SMR Architects, Seattle, Washington), Bill Burke (Pacific Energy Center,

San Francisco, California), John Quale (University of Virginia), John Reynolds (professor emeritus, University of Oregon), Amelia Thrall, and Emily Wright (EYP) for their insightful comments on draft versions of this work. Their thoughtful concerns have helped improve the final product. As follow-up to his review of the draft manuscript, Bill Burke also wrote drafts of the "part-opener" summaries for the six topics that organize the strategies presented in Chapter 4.

The graphic design for this book—with which we are particularly pleased—was prepared by Noreen Rei Fukumori (Berkeley, California). Images throughout the book have been provided by numerous students, faculty, design professionals, and professional photographers. All images are credited immediately following the caption. Clearly, the images are an important aspect of the presentation of green design strategies, so these numerous contributions are greatly appreciated.

We also relied heavily on drawings from Jonathan Meendering and Amanda Hills (both in practice at Pivot Architecture, Eugene, Oregon). Greg Hartman (with Weber + Thompson Architects in Seattle) illustrated the topic openers and Kathy Bevers developed a number of system sizing graphs to replace complex equations. All four amazed us with their ease of depicting green technologies and data in a visually pleasing and inspiring graphic form.

We sincerely thank the staff at Architectural Press for seeing the value in this book and their diligent efforts to get it produced and into your hands in the form that you see. Special thanks go to Jodi Cusack, Commissioning Editor, Laura Sacha, Editorial Assistant, Margaret Denley, Project Manager, and Barbara Massam, Subeditor.

Alison G. Kwok and Walter T. Grondzik

What is This Book?

The purpose of *The Green Studio Handbook* is to provide enough information about the What, How, and How Big of various green design strategies to permit a "go or no-go" decision regarding the appropriateness and viability of a given strategy to be made during schematic design. It is not unusual for students—and practicing designers—to have the best of intentions about developing a green building, only to have lack of information about specific strategies get in the way of decision making.

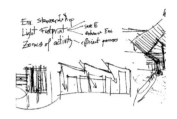

1.1 Exploring intentions with an initial gestural sketch. ALEX WYNDHAM

The intent of this book is to provide a concise catalog of information for a range of green strategies. The information is specifically intended to help the designer understand what each strategy actually does, what data are needed to make a preliminary estimate of its appropriateness, general guidelines to permit preliminary sizing, and pointers to related strategies.

The fundamental premise of this book is that if appropriate strategies are not included during the schematic design phase they will never be included. This is generally true, as many such strategies are demandingly form-giving. Once fundamentally bad decisions regarding building orientation, massing, and interior layout have been made it is nearly impossible to come back and incorporate working daylighting, passive heating, or passive cooling systems. Opportunities for green architectural strategies are rife in the conceptual and schematic design phases. They are sparse during design development.

This book includes both active and passive strategies. There are, however, many more passive strategies. These require early implementation in the design process and are typically more form-shaping. The overall focus is upon those strategies that would (or should) be implemented during schematic design. Many green design strategies are not included. Low-VOC paints, for example, are not included as they have virtually no impact on schematic design decisions. This is not a catalog of green design strategies—it is a catalog of green strategies for schematic design.

Following this chapter's introductory discussion, Chapter 2 reflects upon the nature of the design process and Chapter 3 discusses the green/integrated design process.

Chapter 4 presents 40 strategies. Each strategy has a brief description of principle and concept, a discussion of architectural and implementation issues, a procedure (typically with associated tables and charts) to assist with preliminary design sizing, key issues to be aware of when implementing a given strategy, and pointers to sources for further information (including WWW sites, books, and manuals). Conceptual sketches and photographic examples illustrate each strategy.

A concluding chapter with case studies of nine green building projects provides further examples of the strategies presented and their incorporation into integrated building designs. Although the strategies can be perused and applied in isolation that is not the intent of this book. Green design is not simply about picking parts from a catalog. It is about ensuring that an ecological design intent is achieved.

Some Context and Approach

This book is structured around a view of the design/construction process that involves the following phases: Pre-Design, Conceptual Design, Schematic Design, Design Development, Construction Documents, Construction, and Occupancy. The exact nature of these phases varies from project to project and from designer to designer. Nevertheless there is some general consistency.

Pre-Design. This phase involves the development of the program (or brief) for the project. The owner's project requirements are developed. Ideally, the design team will be involved with this phase, although this information is often developed by a separate specialist consultant. If green design is not clearly stated as an objective at the end of this phase, the green design task becomes more difficult—perhaps more of a sales effort than a design effort.

Conceptual Design. An outline of one or more proposed design solutions is developed during conceptual design. The primary purpose of conceptual design is to obtain buy-in from the client and design team on a solution that will be further pursued. Form-giving green design strategies (such as direct gain passive solar heating, cross ventilation, daylighting) must be included (if only conceptually) and shown in plans, sections, and elevations developed during this phase. Otherwise the buy-in will not include key green design strategies. The examples of strategies presented in Chapter 4 will be of use during conceptual design.

Schematic Design. This phase of design is essentially the proof-of-concept phase. The project directions outlined in conceptual design are verified as being technically feasible, within budget, and able to deliver on design intents. Hopes meet reality during schematic design. A roof-mounted PV array, for example, that was expected to provide the building's electricity becomes the array that provides 45% of the building's electricity. This book was written primarily for the schematic design phase—when concept becomes reality.

Design Development. Design development might be best described as the analysis and production phase of a project. Schematic design decisions are validated, systems are optimized, details are developed, specific equipment selected, and drawings and specifications initiated. Each strategy in this book includes a "Beyond Schematic Design" discussion that addresses some of the many implementation issues likely to be encountered during design development (and beyond).

Construction Documents. Construction documents are the construction drawings, specifications, and related documents that convey the aspirations of the owner and design team to the contractor. These become a major part of the contract between an owner and a contractor and are the basis for construction.

Construction. During construction, the architect-client-contractor team converts the construction documents to physical reality. Sometimes requests for substitutions occur during bidding and construction. Such requests should be carefully reviewed for their impact on design intent and green design strategies. Construction is not the time to abandon design intent and criteria. The commissioning of green projects is highly recommended. Commissioning-related testing and verification of systems performed during construction can be exceptionally useful for unconventional and/or interdisciplinary building systems.

Occupancy. On most projects, the design team has historically had little (if any) interaction with the occupied building. This, however, is a really bad idea for a green building. Many passive (or unconventional active) systems require informed operators (who are often the building occupants). Design team development of User's Manuals to help ensure proper system operation is strongly recommended.

Active or Passive?

Chapter 4 presents active and passive design strategies. Most larger-scale green buildings include both types of systems. Simply put, a passive system:

- uses no purchased energy (no electricity, natural gas, …);
- uses components that are part of another system (windows, floors, …);
- is closely integrated into the overall building fabric (not tacked on).

An active system has essentially the opposite characteristics. Active and passive strategies have no inherent goodness or badness—they are simply means to an end. The design team and owner, however, can place value on the means. This book, and many green designers, value passive strategies above active. This valuing must be tempered by practicality, and by an understanding of what the various systems can and cannot rationally accomplish in general and in the context of a particular building.

Design Intent, Criteria, and Method

The terms intent, criteria, method are used throughout this book. As concepts, they are critical to successful completion of the design process. An intent is a general statement of expected outcome, for example: a green building, a low-cost building, an efficient building, a comfortable building, a building with good air quality. All parties involved with a project will understand the gist of such statements, even though they are rather vague. The importance of design intent is in their statement—not their specificity. The proposed destination of a project should be explicit, not implicit.

A design criterion is a benchmark that sets minimum acceptable performance targets for the issues addressed in intent statements. What is meant by a "green" building, a "comfortable" building? Criteria define the general terms used in intent statements. "Green" may be defined by performance on a particular rating scheme, "comfortable" by adherence to ASHRAE Standard 55. Saying "blue" carpet is fine for design intent, but "blue" must really be more clearly defined before the carpet is selected and installed. Green buildings demand clear and comprehensive intent statements and well-defined criteria for each intent.

A method is a means of accomplishing intent and meeting criteria. The strategies presented herein are methods. None of these strategies should be treated as intent or criteria. Although this may seem an odd thing to have to state, methods are sometimes seen as intents ("we need daylighting"). Such a situation short-circuits the design process and avoids addressing the owner's true needs.

This book was intentionally titled *The Green Studio Handbook*—not *The Sustainable Studio Handbook*. The terms "green" and "sustainable" seem to be used synonymously by many. This is not a good idea. A green building will be energy-efficient, water-efficient, and resource-efficient and address on-site as well as off-site impacts on the environment. This is contributory to sustainability, but not identical with sustainability. We believe that sustainability implies having no net negative impacts on the environment. Paraphrasing the Brundtland (*Our Common Future*) report: sustainability is meeting the needs of the current generation without impairing the ability of future generations to meet their needs. Green design is a precursor to, a component of, a positive step toward sustainable design. Green design is a means—but not the end. We should surely do no less than green, but also must do more.

One of the most critical challenges now facing designers—and one of the aspects of "doing more" that must be actively considered—is the problem of climate change fueled by greenhouse gas emissions. Carbon dioxide is a key greenhouse gas and is a major product of our current building design, construction, and operation practices. While green design focuses upon reducing the environmental impacts of energy, water, and material usage (including, presumably, carbon emissions), truly informed designs must *explicitly* reduce the carbon dioxide emissions from buildings. Present-day green design efforts may reduce carbon emissions—but not in a manner that is easily quantified, nor open to accountability. There is little information currently available to help guide designers toward the use of quantifiably carbon-neutral products and processes and unfortunately, the time to seriously begin dealing with carbon-neutral design outcomes appears to have been yesterday. Given this quandary, and until such time as clear-cut carbon-neutral design guidance is available, the prudent course seems to be to "green" every building and to go deeper green than lighter on every green project.

How to Use This Book

Although this is a book of strategies, the strategies need to be applied in the context of a well-organized design process. Please read Chapters 2 and 3 before delving into Chapter 4 (the strategies chapter). A review of the cases studies in Chapter 5 is also recommended.

Each strategy is a package of information believed to be important to the application of that strategy during conceptual or schematic design. An introductory paragraph describes what the strategy can and cannot be expected to do. Photos and diagrams provide a sense of what the strategy looks like in application and the components that make up a complete system. A discussion of architectural and other implementation issues provides a sense of how the strategy fits into the bigger picture of building design.

A preliminary design procedure is provided (where applicable) to allow the estimation of system size in the context of a given project. The design procedure is illustrated via a worked sample problem. These procedures are approximate and intended for use in estimating the size of system (or component) with limited input information—a situation often representative of schematic design.

Solar orientation descriptions in this book have been given from a Northern Hemisphere perspective. This is not to ignore those designing for the Southern Hemisphere, but to attempt to simplify the wording of the text (equatorial-facing sounds a bit awkward). For projects in the Southern Hemisphere, "south-facing" should be taken to mean "north-facing."

Sources of further information are provided for each strategy. A "Beyond Schematic Design" paragraph suggests future steps to be taken if a strategy proves to be viable and feasible during schematic design. More accurate system sizing, systems optimization, commissioning, and development of a User's Manual are recurring themes.

This book is purposely not a comprehensive manual on building science. It assumes that users have a fundamental understanding of building design and conventional building systems. Sizing procedures for many green strategies require estimates of building heat loss or gain or information regarding illuminance values, solar position, or climate data. It is assumed that this information will be obtained from other resources (there are many available).

This book is also not a "how-to-get-a green-rating" handbook. There are many green building rating schemes available today. Each of these schemes (such as the U.S. Green Building Council's LEED program and the British Building Research Establishment's BREEAM program) has a well-defined process under which a building achieves "acceptance." LEED Links are provided, however, for each strategy as a means of identifying what section(s) of the LEED-NC (New Construction) rating system are most connected to a particular strategy. The nature of the BREEAM system precludes such a cross-referencing for BREEAM.

The Challenge

There are many ways for a building to obtain green building status. It is possible for a green building to perform well primarily as a result of active strategies implemented by a consulting engineer during design development. It is also possible for a green building to become so primarily as a result of passive systems incorporated during conceptual and schematic design. Although the bottom line accounting (the end) of these two approaches may be equivalent, the means are not. And the means are architectural design. That is the challenge. Architects must be active participants in shaping green buildings—through early, reasoned, and appropriate integration of green design strategies. As educators, we believe that this process must happen in the design studio where students can learn, test, and be critiqued. Then it will flow into practice. Students will be the agents of change.

NOTES

"The specialist in comprehensive design is an emerging synthesis of artist, inventor, mechanic, objective economist and evolutionary strategist. He bears the same relationship to Society in the new inter-active continuities of world-wide industrialization that the architect bore to the respective remote independencies of feudal society."
Buckminster Fuller, Comprehensive Designing,
in *Ideas and Integrities*

Design is a multifaceted pursuit. It is at once cultural, technical, formal, and programmatic. An emphasis on one or another of design's facets affects the outcome of the pursuit and its resulting architectural expression. A comparison of two buildings by two Italian architects practicing in the early 20th century reveals striking differences emerging from design emphasis. Luigi Nervi's work is defined by structural logic wherein force diagrams become the form, while Gio Ponte draws upon a compositional logic that prioritizes the development of the surface. While Ponte's buildings also have a structural logic and Nervi's are always also compositional, the unique inflection is clear in their works.

Does a focus on ecological design similarly change a building's articulation or does this focus only change the underlying values? This is a question unique to each design team and speaks to the degree to which techniques are concealed or revealed, drawn out or underplayed, and whether the concerns of ecology are primary or secondary emphases. Nonetheless, the process of design, particularly in the early schematic stages, is by necessity transformed by an ecological focus. Ironically, a focus on environmental performance requires the pursuit of an expanded set of issues. The process, therefore, requires the architect to assume a greater than normal degree of expertise as naturalist, material scientist, lighting designer, or engineer to be able to converse with specialists in creative ways. The architect's role is transformed from a specialist of form to a generalist of building performance—perhaps a reversion to the earlier days of design. This focus represents an opportunity for innovation and greatly affects our understanding of design.

Defining the Problem

Schema. The first stage of design includes the moments when the project is conceptualized, the intention is elaborated, and a geometric logic is settled upon—whether that logic is strict, internalized, or drawn as a gesture. The formal and the abstract must hold together. The first design moves are a graphic sketch or outline, a plan of action, a systematic or organized framework. They provide the opportunity to define goals and to set criteria. This moment is but part of the larger process of design. It is a time to set a direction for form and to gather ideas and concepts. It is not a time, however, to close possibilities or crystallize all relationships. It is the beginning phase and, as such, it is open. The outlines formed in the mind fall on the blank sheet of paper. While it is useful to articulate intent before starting to draw, it is also useful to clarify and sharpen ideas through trial and error. The process of drawing/modeling slowly, tentatively, hypothetically unfolds the direction of the design. While the paper may be blank, the mind itself never is. Behind the first sketch are values, attitudes, assumptions, and sets of knowledge.

2.1 Process sketch for an entry to a school classroom. JONATHAN MEENDERING

2.2 Early thoughts about circulation, structure, and daylight sketched in plan, section, and perspective. KATE BECKLEY

For better or worse, arbitrariness, inspiration, and other influences seep in when least expected.

Intention. At the beginning moments of a project, it is important to define the expectations for building performance. It should be decided whether the building will perform to minimum standards (as embodied in building codes) or will strive to surpass them—which must be the case for a green building. What kind of performance will be emphasized: energy efficiency, quality of light, or air quality? What degree of green design is to be considered? A zero-energy building, a reduction of energy usage, a mimic of nature, or a "wild" architecture that, according to the architect Malcolm Wells, is regenerative in its nature? The intention must be clear because it points to the kind of process, the type of team, and potential strategies and technologies that will be most appropriate for a given project. This process of design requires the architect to be equally pragmatic and speculative.

Criteria. Project criteria are the standards by which judgments and decisions are tested. They are often established by an authority, custom, or general consent; but for innovative projects they are often internally established. What is really meant by green? Who decides? Criteria can be based upon quantitative standards (such as energy efficiency) or upon qualitative criteria (such as a type of lighting effect). Criteria should be realistic so they can be met; they should also be stringent enough to provide a challenge and meet design intent.

Validation. One must be conscious of the types of issues to be framed and the appropriate design methods and strategies to use. The way a designer frames a set of issues speaks to the outcomes. The method used implies a feedback loop. A knowledge-based profession reflects upon previous efforts and specifically learns from successes and failures. During the construction of Chartres, collapses occurred. Calculations and formulations about how materials work under the forces of gravity were rethought and the famous cathedral was rebuilt. This is also true with environmental forces, although they are often more subtle, complex, and variable than gravity. A different type of feedback loop is required, not one due to collapse, but one that is part of the larger discipline—learning from others and learning from analysis. The analysis of an existing project becomes a hypothesis of how things should work.

Prioritizing. Finally, it is important to give order to intentions and goals. Prioritizing goals helps the designer and client to understand what is most important, what can be discarded, and how flexible are proposed solutions. As with any design process, one works through sets of ideas to get to a clarification of goals. This is particularly important because one strategy can negate or conflict with another.

Project Data

Collection. Photographs of the office of Charles and Ray Eames depict large cabinets and walls that display beautiful objects. These displays frame a space more like a museum than a place of work. The airy room was filled with a marvelous collection of things (in addition to work in progress), all emanating something provocative (i.e. geometric orders and skeletal structures). The image encapsulates an important moment in the design process, which is research.

The Eames's research involved collecting and interpreting a curious assembly of elements that ranged in scale and function. As "copy artists," they drew happily from their surroundings. Their work was as much about research into the way things work as it was the creation of things. Their images were an inspiration. With ecological design, each project requires its own archive. What one chooses to research affects the way one sees the project and, therefore, what he or she makes of it and what can be done. Ecologies work on many scales, therefore research starts with the collection of data at different scales.

Site analysis. The designer must look at the site up close and from afar. One must read the site, and learn from what is apparent, invisible, and ephemeral. The effects of the earth's tilt cause the gradients of sun angles as well as atmospheric stirrings that produce wind. Some data, such as wind speed or solar insolation, can usually be found synthesized and packaged on the Internet or in a library. Other data, such as noise levels or circulation patterns, must be observed on site. The essence of site analysis is finding the resources and identifying the problems of a site in the context of the project and the designer's values.

It is also useful to look at vernacular architecture, which, of necessity, used the envelope and materials to mitigate climate impacts on a building. Knowledge of an appropriate climate response is implicit in many traditional ways of building and in the living patterns of the occupants. Great projects are sometimes a case of understanding and applying traditional modes of building.

Site selection. Through its interactions with its surroundings (or the lack thereof) every building modifies an external as well as internal climate. Any project creates its own microclimate and has an effect on the conditions subsequently experienced on the site. A new building affects slope, vegetation, soil type, and obstructions. Understanding the effects of various elements of a site, it is then possible to manipulate these elements to modify the microclimate for various purposes. For instance, the planting of a shade tree or the building of a simple wall can positively transform the thermal qualities of a portion of a site. The site selection process emphasizes the relation of building to localized ecological phenomena, but the logic of climate optimization also extends to the scale of the urban as well as to the building plan.

Form Givers

Daylighting. Light has famously been understood as a form giver throughout the history of architecture. In the Pantheon, Hadrian's architect dramatically captured light from an enormous oculus; all of Alvar Aalto's buildings use light scoops to steal the low sun of the far northern hemisphere. Traditional solar design uses a celebration of southern glazing in combination with thermal mass to provide passive heating. Windows, however, must be carefully sized and arranged to provide a balance between the correct amount of light, well-insulated walls, and solar collection. To arrive at a lighting strategy, appropriate lighting levels should be determined based upon the functions and needs of the various spaces, then potential solutions tested and evaluated using daylighting models or other tools. The effects of light also can be easily studied through ray diagrams expressing the sun's path. The results of such studies should provide for distinct lighting effects—and a distinct building form.

Passive and active strategies. Solar buildings are often characterized by an "either/or" of passive or active techniques. Passive systems strategically use walls, window placement, and overhangs to capture and control solar gain, whereas active systems deploy pumps, piping, and manufactured devices to collect, store, and redistribute the sun's energy. The choices are often complex and may result in adopting a hybrid of the two approaches.

Passive design means that nature (and the architect) does the work. Passive strategies adjust to environmental conditions primarily through the architecture and should be considered before active. This means that the architect must be strategic. It means using the resources on site rather than importing energy from a remote source. The careful placement of walls, windows, and overhangs can help to "green" a project; otherwise mechanical equipment (and engineering consultants) will be forced to do the job.

Hybrid systems often create a symbiosis between the building envelope and the heating and cooling systems, each working to mitigate the use of energy. Building components that are traditionally static may move (through computerized servos and biological means), while elements of a mechanized system that appear visually inert convey fluids internally. A hybrid system allows the occupant to engage the variability of the surrounding natural environment in unique ways.

It is important to realize when and how often the variability of the site climate goes beyond the comfort zone and thereby begins to define the direction of a project—its logical mix of passive and active.

Feedback Loops

A number of design tools can be deployed to predict a building's performance before it is built; these include hand calculations, computer simulations, and drawing (mapping). The performance of an environmental system is more difficult to evaluate than the performance of structure, material, or envelope. One can often envision the effects of weather and stress on materials, but it is difficult to see the movement of tempered air through a room. Powerful predictive computer tools are now available, such as Energy-10, DOE-2, Energy Scheming, ECOTECT, eQUEST, and EnergyPlus. These tools can help a designer to visualize how heat moves in and around the spaces and form of a building. One must be trained to use these programs, however, to know what to "see"—as the power of the programs can be overwhelming.

Drawings and diagrams, documenting the changing phenomena of light and wind, can tangibly attest to what a given site can provide. Each site is unique and has unique characteristics. It is possible to sketch where the sun is, how it changes throughout the day, and the potential for shadows. Sun charts and diagrams may be used to quickly gain information about sun angles. Dynamic computer models provide a relatively new way to track the position of the sun. Lighting levels can be tested mathematically with various daylighting design methods or through daylighting models.

Buildings should be commissioned by an independent authority with the active involvement of the design team. The goal of commissioning is to verify that building equipment and systems have been installed correctly and are working as intended and designed. Post-occupancy evaluation (POE) is a related feedback tool. It is critical to build a database of POE information (likely as case studies) to be used in the future. Lessons learned from direct experience with system performance in a successful project can be applied to more general situations. Quality diagnostic research captured for use and publicly shared would advance the discipline of environmental design.

Building Organization

The architectural program developed by the architect and client determines the underlying potential for building performance. Based upon layout and orientation, the forms implicit in every potential building bear within themselves the possibility of responding well or poorly to a given climate. Reyner Banham in his book *The Architecture of the Well-Tempered Environment* (2nd ed., University of Chicago Press, 1984) points out the clever way Frank Lloyd Wright manipulated form to provide comfort through the use of overhangs, bay windows, and the hearth. The building organization can gather light in the winter, collect and channel wind, and provide shade. The form and shape of the building can guide the flow of natural phenomena. Simple tenets include arranging buildings and vegetation so that solar access is possible during the heating season and placing taller buildings to the north, to avoid overshadowing lower ones.

Transitional Spaces

In simple terms, a transitional space is a connection between two environments. A revolving door or a double-doored vestibule are the most common examples. These devices are useful but have but one purpose. Much more sophisticated concepts of transitional spaces can be seen in the work of Louis Kahn, who mastered the idea that an environmental response can also be architecturally rich. His projects for the Salk Library (unbuilt), the Indian Institute of Management, and the Assembly Hall in Dhaka all use transitional spaces for circulation and to bounce daylight throughout the buildings. These double shell constructions are used for corridors and stairs and are thermally neutral. They are used infrequently and require less energy; at the same time, they separate the heat of the sun from its daylight.

Structure

Structure is form-giving. Different systems allow for different opportunities but also have inherent consequences. For instance, a load-bearing masonry wall provides a thermal mass that can be used to passively modulate the temperature of a building in both hot and cold climates. Lightweight construction such as wood frame is much more susceptible to abrupt temperature swings and must be effectively insulated, yet is a good choice in climates with little diurnal temperature change.

Envelope

Material. To design a building detail is to test a hypothesis; but the difference between idea, intention, and the actuality of the full-scale artifact can be immense. The infinite specificity of the real makes it difficult to anticipate exactly how materials will come together, correspond, and behave. For this reason, the conception of a project must be constantly examined throughout its development and grounded in a rigorous process and intuition about the behavior of materials. Material choice and relationships reinforce the spatial organization and the legibility of the idea and vice versa. A detail must have constructional purpose and critical content. Of primary interest is the way in which the building envelope (wall, roof, floor, and openings) plays a critical role alongside mechanical systems in providing visual and thermal comfort. The conscientious and rigorous development of a detail becomes more complex as the building itself assists in mitigating the variability and extremes of weather. Material choice deals directly with the interrelated nature of structure, construction, and environmental systems in pursuit of the integration of these technologies into the architectural idea.

Insulation. Attention to a well-insulated envelope allows the designer to reduce the size of climate control systems. The exterior walls, floors, and roof of a structure should be insulated to a level consistent with climate and codes. Walls, floors, roofs, and fenestration of a green building should exceed code-minimum performance requirements. Infiltration must be controlled; this means air cannot move through unplanned openings in the envelope. Windows and glazed doors should be selected and specified to contribute to the goals of the project—whether this be through solar admittance, daylighting, and/or solar rejection.

A green roof can provide many advantages. It plays an aesthetic role by extending the form of the project and creating a place of refuge. Species of grasses and plants should be selected because they require minimal water and maintenance, will shade the project when full grown in the summer, and can provide produce (flowers/herbs) of use in the building. Lightweight soil can provide extra insulation and absorb water runoff. Rainwater can be used for irrigating the garden or used in a greywater system. The garden thus extends the usable living space of the project in area and in spirit.

Climate Control Systems

Basic advantages of green heating and cooling systems over conventional heating and cooling technologies include using natural ambient conditions to the fullest extent to provide heating and cooling for a building. These ambient energies are typically renewable and non-polluting. Passive strategies have the capacity to deliver heating and cooling strictly from environmental resources on site. A climate control system should be designed to be simple, both in operation and installation.

In Summary

The design process is never "conventional," although the means by which a building takes form generally fall into specific phases and include idea generation, testing, and working at multiple scales. Integrating of technologies is often viewed as an unwanted task and/or delegated to consulting engineers—instead of being viewed as an ongoing design opportunity. Working with environmental strategies is more than assembling parts, or the choosing of systems as if selecting from a menu. Like a great collage, it is important for the parts to blend. In addition, they can be executed with infinite variation.

To assist designers in achieving a synthesis of ecological design principles, Chapter 3 presents factors considered to be of importance to a truly integrated design process.

Each strategy outlined in Chapter 4 is like a hook. But using one strategy alone does not make a project green. This becomes clear if one considers the strategies outlined. For instance, in sizing a photovoltaic (PV) system without first using energy-efficiency strategies, one would have an untenable PV strategy—not an environmentally-responsive solution. A whole roof of PVs may only be able to provide 20% of the electricity needs of a project. One must balance the quantitative and qualitative. It is important to work with the strategies as part of a defined intention in order to close the loop.

The best way to use the strategies is to understand their basis in physics, ecology, and chemistry and to match the technology with the need. Avoid using high-end technologies for low-grade tasks. Don't use purified water to flush a toilet or photovoltaic electricity for a hair dryer. It is important to seek common solutions to disparate problems. This is called functional redundancy and is the basis of green design and this book.

Laura Briggs and Jonathan Knowles, New York City

Context

Design is a means to an end. Unfortunately, neither the ends nor the means are necessarily always clear. This is especially true today as society faces the challenges of global warming, peak oil, and water scarcity.

Green building and sustainable design are terms that are often used to describe the final result of a building project—how much energy a building will save, how much less pollution it will produce, what sort of materials were chosen, and what affect on the health and comfort of the occupants is expected. *They are better used to describe process.* "Green" and "sustainable" are often used interchangeably to describe similar goals or design responses such as the use of daylight, natural ventilation, solar energy, and non-toxic building materials. *This is terribly incorrect.*

We strongly suggest that sustainability is broader in its reach, addressing the long-term impacts of the built environment on future generations and demanding an examination of the relationship between ecology, economics, and social well-being. Implicit in this notion of a "triple bottom line" is the suggestion that the design process will seek to examine and address issues beyond the scope of the traditional design process.

This book does not presume to address sustainable design. This is, however, OK. Green design and green buildings are a step toward sustainable design and sustainability—and may, honestly, be the best that can be accomplished on a large scale in today's societal context. The need (and demand) for green buildings has become increasingly clear. The means for defining specific goals and measurable achievements for green buildings have also been refined through the development of programs such as the U.S. Green Building Council's LEED; the Building Research Establishment's BREEAM; and Smart Homes, Built Smart, EcoHomes, etc.

Still, the means for achieving green design goals remain elusive or at least challenging. In some cases a project team may have an intuitive sense for what feels like "the right thing to do," but lack the tools to make a clear argument for why the approach would be effective. At other times a designer may be faced with a bewildering choice of green design strategies and not have a clear picture of how to proceed. A committed design team may have a number of promising options on the table but concerns about technical viability or budget prevent implementing them. Oftentimes the timing and sequence of the design process do not leave adequate time to explore the necessary options or examine enough alternatives. The goals remain clear, but are often just out of reach.

Integrated design provides a process for achieving these goals. The specifics of a project may vary, but the means of achieving them are consistent. Recent years have seen great improvements in our technical understanding of energy use in buildings and systems for making better use of solar heat, light, air, and materials. Numerous buildings have shown vast improvements over conventional standards of energy consumption, human comfort, and environmental impact. The process by which these buildings get built shows that not only are our building forms, materials, and systems evolving, but so is the means by which we design and build them.

3.1 Courtyard sketch—bringing daylight into adjacent rooms. DANIEL JOHNSON

3.2 View of the transitional spaces at entry to an off-the-grid elementary school. JONATHAN MEENDERING

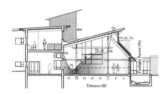

3.3 Schematic drawing showing daylight factors for an interpretive center—measured using a physical daylighting model. JONATHAN MEENDERING

Integrated Design Defined

Integrated design is a process that applies the skills and knowledge of different disciplines and the interactions of different building systems to synergistically produce a better, more efficient, and more responsible building—occasionally for lower first cost, but more typically for lower life-cycle cost. Integrated design considers the relationships between elements that have often been seen as unrelated. Habitat, water quality, deforestation, and light pollution were often seen as abstract issues far removed from the task of the designer.

Design is a process of inquiry. Every project is unique—presenting a unique response to the particular combinations of site, climate, user, budget, and program that define context. Every building design is a hypothesis about what represents an acceptable, a good, or an outstanding response to these contextual elements. There is much we still don't know or fully understand about building performance and many elements of equipment, materials, and systems that can contribute to green solutions are only recently emerging from the ongoing and growing research into the performance of constructed green buildings.

Design is a process of collaboration. No single person, no single profession has all of the knowledge or skills required to understand all of the details. The best design solutions reflect an in-depth understanding developed through the contributions of many disciplines.

Design is a process of integration. Abundant knowledge must be filtered and the most relevant and applicable principles teased out of the mix. This must be done by a group of people with different backgrounds, expertise, and personalities through the congested channels of meetings, e-mail, voicemail, contracts, and work schedules. It helps if all players are working from a common value set.

Integrated design may be defined by a comparison with what it is not.

It is not high-tech design. The technological era has resulted in increased specialization and fragmentation of knowledge. When very specialized knowledge was applied to problems the results often led to worse problems—following the law of unintended consequences. While high-tech knowledge is not unwelcome in integrated design, the process tries to understand the functioning of the whole system instead of just one technical response. Many people see the conventional design process as an inevitable outgrowth of the industrial revolution, as the application of mechanistic ways of seeing how a narrowly defined system behaves. The "machine for living in" has not delivered on its promise; some would say it has made our situation worse.

It is not sequential design. The conventional design process is often described as "baton passing" from one specialty to another; from designer to drafter to engineer to contractor to subs. Costs increase when one party makes decisions without the input of others, and opportunities for combined benefits are missed. Conventional design can be thought of as "knowledge applied in series." Integrated design is "knowledge applied in parallel."

It is not design by committee. Input from team members is sought as a way to test design ideas on a rapid cycle and to look for multiple benefits from unexpected alternatives. It is a way of increasing the overall design intelligence applied to a problem and providing quick reality checks and course corrections. Design leadership is still required, but those leaders need to be sincere in soliciting and integrating the input of other team members.

It is not the same old process applied under a different set of rules. Design teams are understandably prone to applying the methods and approaches they have used in the past. Only by stepping back from a situation and examining the underlying assumptions and rules can a solution be made visible. A contemporary parallel can be seen in Amory Lovins's "philosophy" that people want hot showers and cold beer—not sticky, black goo. Owners want productivity, occupants want comfort—not HVAC systems or light shelves.

It is not a point-chasing game. The requirements of rating systems such as LEED can produce, in some cases, a mentality where strategies are adopted not because of their opportunities for long-term benefits but for the short-term goal of certification. LEED requirements can also take on the appearance of an additional layer of code requirements and, in the effort to meet the requirements, teams can lose sight of the original intent of the project. The Americans with Disabilities Act requirements have been seen as burdensome or limiting, but they have also opened up designers' eyes to solutions that improved the qualities of a space for all users.

It is not easy. Habits, conventions, contracts, and regulations all evolved in response to a system that grew out of a particular view of what was expected or required. The existing system is designed to address things in a piecemeal fashion. To make buildings, communities, and cities that produce energy, support human health and activity, and improve rather than degrade the environment we cannot apply a design process that created just the opposite.

Integrated design looks at the ways all parts of the system interact and uses this knowledge to avoid pitfalls and discover solutions with multiple benefits.

Stepping Toward Integrated Design

Establishing commitment. Desire and commitment should start with the owners or clients, since they ultimately direct and pay for the work of the design team. Their perseverance and desire for innovation can persuade reluctant members of the team to keep moving forward. This does not suggest that the design team is a neutral observer of project values. Sometimes a charismatic designer can convert an owner to green commitment. Normally the owner and the design team share similar values and objectives. It is great, however, if the owner is the go-getter on the team.

Team formation and setting of goals. A design team ideally would be made up of people with the experience and expertise to quickly identify new opportunities and solutions. But if it were this easy, we'd already all be doing it. A lack of experience or knowledge can be offset by a willingness to explore new territory and to let go of prior assumptions and habits.

Information gathering. Each discipline needs to gather information not just dealing with their conventional area of expertise, but expanding the search to see how their realm of experience interacts with and affects other parts of the system. By looking for interactions and foreseeing problems and opportunities, one can identify potential solutions. Brainstorming these solutions provides a starting point for collaborative discussion.

Conceptual and schematic design. The conceptual and schematic design phases are where the design team typically first engages the owner's program (or brief). During conceptual design the owner is convinced that the design team has a vision worth pursuing. During schematic design the design team convinces itself that the vision sold to the owner is in fact feasible. Rarely do any big ideas (or big strategies) creep into the design process after these initial phases. Many green design strategies will be lost forever if not incorporated during schematic design.

Testing. Once a number of options are on the table, the design team can test the energy, cost, and material consequences of the options. Software models can simulate building energy use; financial models, life-cycle costing, and pro forma can test the economic implications for both long- and short-term costs and returns; the availability, costs, and implications of materials and systems can be explored. This leads to refinement of the developing design. Problems inevitably arise that force the team to re-evaluate the strategies being considered—sometimes the original intent and criteria of the project. If the team has "done its homework" by thoroughly examining the resources and constraints of the site, climate, program, and budget it will be easier and faster to find alternate solutions. Design intent and criteria should be vigorously defended (unless obviously flawed)—they represent the original project aspirations. This is where owner commitment is critical.

Design development. The end of the design development phase typically culminates in the preparation of construction documents (drawings and specifications) that become the basis for the general contractor's bidding and hiring of subcontractors. If the contractor joins the design team at this late point, he/she would have little knowledge of the intent and commitment behind the documents, and thus will be more likely to propose substitutions or changes that might alter the original intent.

Construction. The contractor should be part of the design team from early on; he/she would then be familiar with the project intents and would have a chance to suggest changes to the design based upon the constraints and opportunities inherent in the construction process. This part of the process can be either trying or informative depending upon the mindset of the involved parties.

Assessment and verification. A number of steps can be taken to ensure that an owner "gets what they have paid for." Commissioning is becoming a common means of verifying that building systems are functioning as intended and required. Commissioning is not a construction-phase process; it starts in pre-design and continues through occupancy. A thorough post-occupancy evaluation (POE) is also often warranted.

Guidance

If integrated design is the means to the end of green design, what is the means to the end of integrated design? What ideas can we use for guidance in implementing this new kind of design process?

Different conceptual ideas have been used to describe this design process—using the language and insights of different fields. A philosopher might see this discussion as an extension of ethics, expanding the circle of populations or issues considered worthy of ethical treatment. Green design, for example, typically involves looking at off-site impacts on people not directly connected to the project developer. A biologist might see a biophiliac approach. Systems Thinking, Learning Organizations, The Natural Step, The Triple Bottom Line, Whole Building Systems—all are different ways of describing a similar process and goal. The process is based upon an understanding of how the components of complex systems interact; the goal is driven by what some call "purposeful" intent, which often has a moral or ethical component.

The notion of "systems thinking" arose in the mid 20th century and has been applied to many different disciplines from the social sciences, human resources, and biological sciences to software development and military planning. It is fundamentally different from the Cartesian world view, which studies an object or function in isolation, trying to minimize the interactions of other forces to understand its essential function. Systems thinking realizes that nothing ever occurs in a vacuum. Every element and event is seen as being a part of, and interacting with, a larger system, and that system in turn is part of an even larger system of interactions. Rather than ignore these interactions, systems thinking instead describes the different subsystems and super-systems and clarifies the boundaries that separate one system from the next.

Applying these ideas to building design is sometimes done metaphorically. Integrated design is often facilitated by looking to biological models for guidance. The interaction of many organisms in a biotic environment is akin to the ways that humans interact with their physical and social environments. Biological models can help explain the interactions between different components or the web of relationships and make it easier to see how the parts of the building and social system can interact.

Author and farmer Wendell Berry (*The Gift of Good Land: Further Essays Cultural and Agricultural*, North Point Press, New York, 1982) describes the notion of "Solving for Pattern," in which good solutions tend to solve many problems simultaneously, and at many different scales. A large-scale monoculture farm deals with pests by applying greater amounts of pesticides; the side effects become as troubling as the initial problem. Solving for pattern sees the problem as one of scale: by bringing the scale of the farm back to what one farmer can oversee, it becomes possible to cultivate a variety of crops and use techniques that reduce pests without large-scale chemical applications. The smaller farm can also contribute to a wider pattern of farmers' markets or local commerce that yields benefits to the family and community as well.

An example of solving for pattern in architectural design can be seen when using building forms that maximize the use of daylight. Not only are electric loads lessened (through appropriate controls), but human comfort and productivity improve, heat gains are lessened, natural ventilation becomes easier, greater articulation of the building form and aesthetic values can result, and circulation and use patterns more conducive to social well-being may evolve.

The ability to understand the patterns of energy, light, water, and air as they apply to the built environment is a step toward developing integrated design skills. For some people thick books or long lectures help to explain these patterns, but for many the quickest route may be to apply appropriate strategies to design problems using quick ballpark estimates, back-of-the-envelope calculations, or general guidelines. Examples of such schematic approaches for many strategies follow.

On an integrated design team, one would ideally be able to turn to an expert and ask: "How do we do this?" This book attempts to be that knowledgeable companion. Rather than long-drawn-out explanations, integrated design requires concise suggestions of how to begin. This helps form an initial hypothesis of how a building may work. Getting a "thumbs-up" regarding proposed strategies during schematic design allows the design team to make their first moves their "best" moves. Thus, schematic design can provide the proof-of-concept for green design ideas. In-depth modeling, more drawing or testing can evaluate these formative hypotheses during the next design iteration.

David Posada, Portland, Oregon

CHAPTER 4

The green strategies in this chapter are organized into six major topics and include those strategies that most influence schematic design. Each strategy describes an underlying green principle or concept. Sidebar links suggest related strategies and larger design issues to consider. The essence of each strategy is a step-by-step design procedure to guide the preliminary sizing of building and system components. Where a strategy is more conceptual than physical, the design procedure provides guidance to help incorporate the concept during schematic design. Conceptual sketches illustrate each strategy to reinforce the fundamentals and photographs show strategies applied to built projects.

DESIGN STRATEGIES

ENVELOPE

LIGHTING

HEATING

COOLING

ENERGY PRODUCTION

WATER & WASTE

NOTES

ENVELOPE

Building envelope considerations begin with the siting of the building and placement of windows and skylights. Orienting a building on an east-west axis while placing the bulk of window openings on the north and south elevations makes solar control and daylighting easier to achieve.

Insulation is a crucial part of any green building project. Because reducing energy use is a high priority in a green building, a thick layer of a not-quite-green insulation is almost always preferable to an inadequate thickness of a green insulation. That said, presuming adequate insulation values and quality of installation can be achieved, choose a green insulation over a non-green one.

When selecting materials for structure and envelope, less is often more. Using materials more efficiently conserves resources, reduces waste, and helps reduce construction costs. If using wood framing, make sure spacing and detailing are optimized for resource efficiency. Forest Stewardship Council (FSC) certified framing and/or engineered wood products should be considered. If using concrete, design for efficient use of the material and reduce cement content by incorporating fly ash. For steel, develop insulation details that avoid thermal bridging.

During schematic design, consider the benefits of admitting or rejecting solar heat and begin to think about glazing with a solar heat gain coefficient (SHGC) to best address solar concerns. Glazing selection is shaped by many factors. A wise choice for one project may not be appropriate in another. Overhangs and shading devices can reduce or eliminate the need for solar control glazing.

Consider alternative materials—such as strawbales for commercial or residential buildings in appropriate climates. Roofing presents several options. A green roof offers many benefits, reducing the urban heat island effect, potentially providing high insulation values, reducing rainwater runoff, and possibly offering habitat for local flora and fauna. If a green roof is not an option, cool roofing materials are preferable in cooling dominated climates. Cool roofing can lessen solar loads on the building and extend the life of the roof by reducing expansion and contraction of materials.

Materials that last longer will reduce the demand for resources and in many cases involve lower embodied energy. They also reduce maintenance costs and thus may be cheaper from a life-cycle perspective even if they involve higher first costs.

STRATEGIES

Insulation Materials
Strawbale Construction
Structural Insulated Panels
Double Envelopes
Green Roofs

NOTES

INSULATION MATERIALS

INSULATION MATERIALS have traditionally played a vital role in building design for climate control. Their impact on energy efficiency (and thus energy savings) can be substantial. Many insulation materials, however, contain polluting and/or non-biodegradable substances that could seriously decrease the greenness of a project. This strategy provides suggestions on selecting insulation materials that have reduced negative environmental impacts and also provides guidelines on what to watch for regarding thermal insulation during the schematic design phase of a project.

4.1 Installation of faced, formaldehyde-free batt insulation. JOHNS MANVILLE, INC.

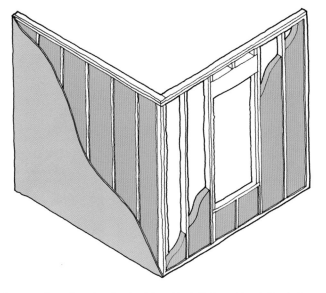

4.2 Wood frame wall section showing traditional installation of insulation between studs. Rigid insulation/sheathing is applied as needed to meet project objectives. NICK RAJKOVICH

Numerous types of insulation materials are available, including:

Plastic foam board (rigid board) insulation. Comprising products such as beadboard (molded expanded polystyrene—MEPS) and foamboard (extruded expanded polystyrene—XEPS), this category of materials can contain VOCs (volatile organic compounds) and is not biodegradable.

Spray-applied foam insulation (spray-in cavity-fill). Some open-cell polyurethane insulation products are produced with soy oil comprising about 40% of their "poly" components, resulting in foam that is about 25% soy and 75% petrochemically derived. Although these products do not have R-values as high as those of closed-cell polyurethane, they are three to four times as resource-efficient.

Magnesium silicate or cementitious foam (Air Krete®). This product provides CFC- and HCFC-free insulation alternatives. Although it is more expensive than products that use CFCs and HCFCs, it is fire-resistant and has no indoor air quality impact. Its weakest point is its fragility—which may soon be addressed by adding plastics to the mix to reduce brittleness.

INTENT
Energy efficiency, thermal comfort, environmental resource conservation

EFFECT
Reduced heating/cooling loads, improved mean radiant temperatures

OPTIONS
Insulation type, thickness, and location

COORDINATION ISSUES
All aspects of building envelope design

RELATED STRATEGIES
Structural Insulated Panels, Double Envelopes, Green Roofs

LEED LINKS
Energy & Atmosphere, Materials & Resources, Innovation & Design Process

PREREQUISITES
Applicable building code requirements, design intent

ENVELOPE

LIGHTING

HEATING

COOLING

ENERGY PRODUCTION

WATER & WASTE

Cellulose insulation. Installed loose-fill, sprayed damp, or densely packed, cellulose insulation is made from 75–85% recycled newsprint. Embodied energy is about 150 Btu/lb [0.09 kWh/kg]. This insulation contains non-toxic chemical additives that are within U.S. Consumer Product Safety Commission fire-retardancy requirements. There are no significant indoor air quality issues if this product is properly installed, although there are potential risks resulting from dust inhalation during installation and VOC emissions from the incorporated printing inks.

Fibrous batt and board insulation. These materials are an insulation mainstay; unfortunately many of these products use formaldehyde as a primary component. Glass fiber products usually use phenol formaldehyde as a binder, which is less likely to emit harmful pollutants than urea formaldehyde. Some major manufacturers have elected not to use formaldehyde binders in their fibrous insulation products.

Loose-fill fiber. Loose-fill glass fiber or blowing wool that does not contain formaldehyde is readily available in applications with R-values ranging from 11 to 60 [RSI 1.9 to 10.6].

Mineral wool. Often used for fire protection of building structural elements, this material is made from iron ore blast-furnace slag (an industrial waste product from steel production that has been classified by the U.S. Environmental Protection Agency as hazardous) or from rock such as basalt.

Cotton insulation. Batt insulation that is made from recycled denim scraps. Some products use 85% recycled fiber saturated with a borate flame retardant or a combination of borate and ammonium sulfate flame retardants.

Radiant barriers (bubble-backed, foil-faced polyethylene foam, foil-faced paperboard sheathing, foil-faced OSB). These are thin, reflective foil sheets (available in a range of configurations) that reduce the flow of heat by radiant transfer. They are effective only if the reflective surface of the barrier faces an airspace. Proper installation is a key to the success of this type of insulation. Recycled polyethylene products containing 20–40% post-consumer recycled content are available.

Perlite. This is a siliceous rock that forms glass-like fibers. Perlite is usually poured into cavities in concrete masonry units (or similar assemblies). It is non-flammable, lightweight, and chemically inert. Perlite generates very little pollution during manufacturing and poses a minor threat for dust irritation during installation. Its main drawback is its limited range of applications due to its "fluid" character.

Structural insulated panels (SIPs). Comprising "structural" and insulation materials in one assembly, SIPs generally outperform other insulation/construction compositions in terms of R-value per assembly thickness. Building envelopes constructed with SIPs are also virtually airtight when properly installed. (See the Structural Insulated Panels strategy.)

Key Architectural Issues

The primary early design phase implications of thermal insulations involve necessary building envelope assembly thickness and unconventional

4.3 Application of open-cell polyurethane produced using water as a blowing agent. ICYNENE INC.

4.4 "Spider" is a lightweight glass fiber insulation bound with a non-toxic, water-soluble adhesive that also binds to cavity surfaces for gap-free coverage. JOHNS MANVILLE, INC.

4.5 Cotton insulation made from 85% recycled denim and cotton fibers. BONDED LOGIC, INC.

construction approaches—either of which may impact the building footprint and/or the relationships between building planes and openings. In practical terms, a better-insulated envelope is usually a thicker-than-normal envelope. An exceptionally well-insulated envelope may substantially reduce the required size of passive and/or active heating systems, providing opportunities for first and life-cycle cost savings.

Implementation Considerations

Provide the highest feasible insulation levels. Remember that codes typically require only minimum acceptable insulation values—not optimum values—and that the cost of energy generally escalates (making more insulation more cost-effective over time). When the use of low-R-value materials makes sense from another perspective, increase the material thickness to produce reasonable U-factors.

Given comparable R-value and performance, always choose high-recycled-content insulation materials over alternatives made from virgin materials. Require that scrap insulation generated on site be recycled. Select/specify extruded polystyrene (XPS) products with low to no ozone-depleting potential. Except when moisture is an issue, use polyisocyanurate instead of XPS or EPS. Rigid mineral insulation works well as a foundation insulation due to its good drainage properties.

4.6 Retrofitting an old uninsulated attic with 12 in. [300 mm] of R-38 [6.7] glass fiber batt insulation improved comfort and reduced heating bills by 40%.

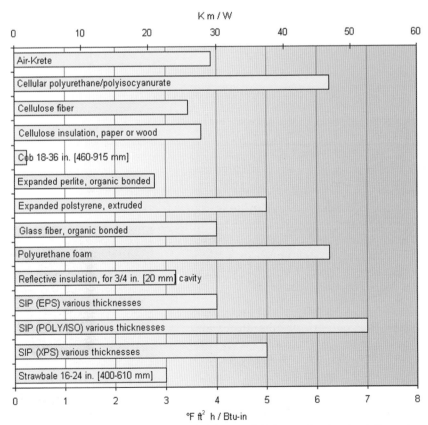

4.7 Thermal resistance (R) values for a 1 inch [1 meter] thickness of various insulation and alternative building materials (thickness noted in the figure describe the installation context).

KATHLEEN BEVERS

When necessitated by the choice of structural system or detailing, minimize thermal bridging by enclosing highly conductive framing elements with a layer of appropriate insulation. A thermal bridge is an uninsulated or poorly insulated path between interior and exterior environments.

What is considered an environmentally acceptable thermal insulation material varies from country to country. Be sure to be aware of local restrictions and incentives intended to steer selection decisions toward preferred materials.

Design Procedure

1. Determine the minimum acceptable insulation R-value (or assembly U-factor) permitted by applicable building codes.

2. This minimum requirement will seldom be appropriate for a green building. Determine whether this minimum insulation requirement meets the intents of the client and design team. If not, establish more appropriate (demanding) insulation values using design guides, client directives, and/or life-cycle cost analysis.

3. Determine whether any likely-to-be-implemented insulation approaches will require unconventional construction or materials assemblies that will impact schematic design. If so, incorporate these considerations into the proposed design solution.

4. Move on with design—remembering the impact that better than minimum insulation may have on system sizing and equipment space requirements.

Examples

4.8 Loose-fill glass fiber insulation being blown into a new attic. This insulation is also used in existing homes because of its ease of application in difficult-to-reach areas.

SAMPLE PROBLEM
A single-story strip commercial building is being designed for Hoboken, New Jersey. The building will have a sloped roof with attic and use steel stud wall construction. Hoboken has 6572 HDD65 [3651 HDD18] and 2418 CDD50 [1343 CDD10].

1. Using ASHRAE Standard 90.1 as a benchmark, Hoboken is in climate zone B-13. The minimum roof insulation for an attic construction is R-30 [5.3]. The minimum wall insulation for metal framing is R-13 [2.3]. The minimum floor slab edge insulation is R-7.5 [1.3].

2. Considering the green design intent for this project and the fact that envelope loads will play a big role in building thermal performance, 30% higher R-values are selected. Thus, the roof will be insulated to R-40 [7], the walls to R-17 [3], and the floor slab edge to R-10 [1.8].

3. The attic can be insulated using loose-fill blown-in insulation with no impact on construction details. The wall insulation can be accommodated using batt insulation and 6 in. studs or batt insulation with 4 in. studs and rigid insulation sheathing. The latter is chosen as a means of reducing thermal bridging. The slab insulation can be easily accommodated with two layers of conventional rigid board insulation.

4. The impact of the increased envelope resistance will be considered when calculating heating and cooling loads.

ENVELOPE

LIGHTING

HEATING

COOLING

ENERGY PRODUCTION

WATER & WASTE

4.9 Installation of cotton batt insulation does not require special clothing or protection.
BONDED LOGIC, INC.

4.10 Installation of Air Krete foam, an inert, inorganic, cementitious product made from magnesium oxide (from seawater and ceramic talc). AIR KRETE® INC.

Further Information

Air Krete, Inc. www.airkrete.com/

Allen, E. and J. Iano. 2003. *Fundamentals of Building Construction,* 4th ed. John Wiley & Sons, New York.

Bonded Logic, Inc. www.bondedlogic.com/

BREEAM EcoHomes Developer Sheets (Building Research Establishment, Garston, Watford, UK). www.breeam.org/pdf/EcoHomes2005DeveloperSheets_v1_1.pdf

Building Green. www.buildinggreen.com/

Icynene Inc. www.icynene.com/

Johns Manville. www.johnsmanville.com/

Mendler, S., W. Odell and M. Lazarus. 2005. *The HOK Guidebook to Sustainable Design*, 2nd ed. John Wiley & Sons, Hoboken, NJ.

North American Insulation Manufacturer's Association. www.naima.org/

Wilson, A. 2005. "Insulation: Thermal Performance is Just the Beginning." *Environmental Building News*, Vol. 14, No. 1, January.

Structural Insulated Panel Association. www.sips.org/

BEYOND SCHEMATIC DESIGN

Detailing of enclosure elements during design development will be critical to the overall success of building envelope performance—particularly with respect to thermal bridging and vapor retarders.

STRAWBALE CONSTRUCTION

STRAWBALE CONSTRUCTION is a strategy for building energy-efficient, low environmental impact buildings. Dry strawbales are set upon a moisture-protected foundation, stacked in a running bond, and secured with rebar or bamboo sticks. The bale wall is then post tensioned with cables or rope to prevent extreme settling. Wire mesh is applied to the constructed bale walls and the resulting assembly is finished with several layers of plaster, spray-applied concrete, or stucco.

4.11 Drilling to place rebar into a strawbale.

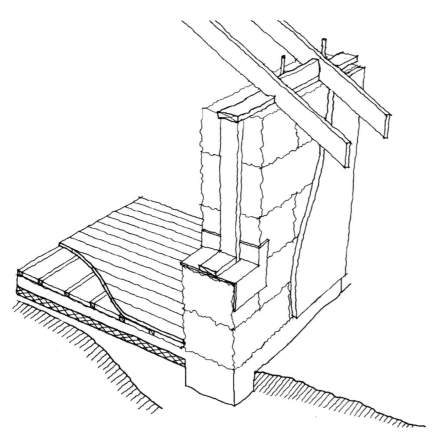

4.12 Diagram showing typical strawbale wall construction. JONATHAN MEENDERING

Early settlers in Nebraska (USA) pioneered strawbale construction methods when faced with a limited timber supply. Many of these century-old structures still stand today as a testament to the viability and durability of strawbale construction.

Straw is a renewable agricultural waste product that is abundantly available, inexpensive, and simple to work with. Bales are typically priced between 1–4 US$ each. They may be used as a structural component of a building as in "Nebraska Style" construction or coupled (as infill) with wood, metal, or concrete framing. "Nebraska Style" is a stressed skin panel wherein the assembly derives its strength from the combined action of bales and a plaster or stucco finish. Used as infill, strawbales carry no appreciable loads (which are borne by an independent structural system). A hybrid system may be adopted to satisfy specific local building code requirements.

INTENT
Climate control, energy efficiency, resource efficiency

EFFECT
Reduced energy consumption for heating/cooling, reduced use of non-renewable building materials, improved interior environmental quality

OPTIONS
Strawbales used as structural elements or as infill, bale characteristics and thicknesses

COORDINATION ISSUES
Climate and site conditions, interior and exterior finishes, heating/cooling systems

RELATED STRATEGIES
Insulation Materials, Cross Ventilation, Stack Ventilation, Direct Gain, Indirect Gain, Isolated Gain, daylighting strategies

LEED LINKS
Energy & Atmosphere, Materials & Resources, Innovation & Design Process

PREREQUISITES
Available material resources, amenable codes

Strawbale walls lend themselves to passive solar structures. With R-values generally between R-35 and R-50 [RSI 6.2–8.8], the inherent insulating value of straw is a valuable tool in passive heating and cooling design. With a wall thickness of 16 in. [400 mm] or greater providing a substantially massive envelope, strawbale construction can also serve as an effective sound barrier.

Although ideally suited for dry climates, strawbale buildings can be constructed in any area where straw is available, provided careful measures are taken to eliminate moisture infiltration. Misconceptions exist regarding the fire resistance of strawbale construction; a well-constructed wall assembly can have a fire resistance rating higher than that of a typical wood frame building.

Key Architectural Issues

During schematic design the most important issue to consider is likely to be wall thickness. Substantially thicker than normal walls that result from strawbale construction must be dealt with in terms of building footprint. Keeping water away from the strawbale construction (via siting, grading, and overhangs) is also a schematic design concern.

Many important architectural design issues involving detailing will be dealt with later in design. They are noted here because of their overall importance. Water resistance is the key to the long-term success of a strawbale structure. Cracks and holes in the weather skin must be avoided and roof overhangs suitably designed to provide good rain protection. Fenestration elements are susceptible to water penetration and require careful attention to detail. The base of the wall, top plate, and sill should incorporate a moisture barrier. Large wall areas should not be covered with a vapor retarder as it may retain moisture rather than assist with keeping the wall dry.

Foundations should be constructed to limit the exposure of bales to water by providing a generous elevation above the ground surface and, if possible, above interior floor height. Like any wall system, the insulating value of strawbale walls can be weakened by thermal bridging. Care should be taken to ensure that structural members in a strawbale infill system have minimal thermal bridging capacity. This can be accomplished by insulating the structural elements or encasing structural members within the strawbale assembly (not easy due to the thickness of the bales, which must be retained for thermal performance).

Roof systems are constructed in conventional fashion using a range of systems and materials. When a hybrid wall system is utilized, traditional top plates (adjusted for wall width) support the roof. With Nebraska Style construction, a box frame is common. In either case, the weight of the roof should be distributed to the center of the wall (and not at the edge) to prevent bowing.

Implementation Considerations

Strawbales are typically available in two- and three-string bindings (wire-bound bales are recommended). Two-string bale dimensions are

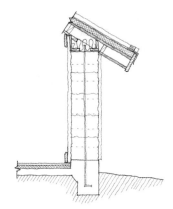

4.13 Section through a strawbale wall. JONATHAN MEENDERING

4.14 Strawbale bicycle shelter project under construction in Moscow, Idaho. BRUCE HAGLUND

4.15 A truth window is often installed in strawbale walls to show their construction. WILLIAM HOCKER

ENVELOPE

LIGHTING

HEATING

COOLING

ENERGY PRODUCTION

WATER & WASTE

STRAWBALE CONSTRUCTION **33**

ENVELOPE

LIGHTING

HEATING

COOLING

ENERGY PRODUCTION

WATER & WASTE

usually 14 in. [350 mm] high, 30–40 in. [760–1020 mm] long, and 18–20 in. [460–500 mm] wide. Three-string bales measure 14–17 in. [350–430 mm] high, 32–48 in. [810–1220 m] long, and 23–24 in. [580–610 mm] wide. Consider bale dimensions when choosing a foundation type. Bale setting should begin at least 8 in. [200 mm] above grade.

Bale tightness and moisture content are of primary importance when choosing an appropriate source of materials. A good strawbale (for construction) will have a density of 7–8 lb/ft^3 [112–128 kg/m^3]. Bales compacted much beyond 8 lb/ft^3 [112 kg/m^3] have limited air spaces and thus begin to lose thermal resistance. A maximum 20% moisture content is suggested to reduce the danger of mold, mildew, and decomposition within the wall. A moisture meter can help in determining this value for bales under consideration.

Published information on the thermal resistance of strawbales shows a wide range of values (or, put another way, a range of potential discrepancies). Be cautious when using R-values from the literature. Use values that are most appropriate both technically and contextually; consider local experiences and performance reports.

When selecting individual bales, consistent size is a key criterion. Avoid lopsided bales that will make leveling difficult. Chopped straw bales should be avoided; long-stalk bales provide superior strength. Bales must be free of grain seed that may attract pests. Dry, seedless straw possesses no nutritional value and ensures that the walls are not attractive to insects or rodents. Ask the bale supplier about pesticide and chemical use, if this is of concern (as should be the case with green building design).

All piping, wiring, and plumbing run within bales should be encased in sleeves (insulated as appropriate) for safety.

Design Procedure

1. Establish the general feasibility of strawbales in the context of the proposed project. Are bales readily available? Are they permitted by building code? What size bales are generally available? Are they a generally green product (or do they require extensive irrigation and/or transportation)? Will strawbales provide the intended thermal performance?

2. Ensure that the proposed site is appropriate for strawbale construction relative to water-flow characteristics. Select a building location on site that minimizes potential water problems (i.e. well drained soil, slopes that carry water away from the foundation).

3. Select a structural approach that works in the context of the project and prevailing codes—infill, structural bales, or a hybrid system. Consider the seismic requirements of the locale.

4. Select a foundation type (slab on grade, block, pier, etc.) that best suits the soil characteristics, frost line, and loads.

5. Allow for increased wall thickness when laying out interior spaces, the roof system (including generous overhangs to protect against rain wetting), and fenestration openings.

4.16 Structural timber framing and strawbales are supported on poured-in-place concrete foundations that are the full width of the bales and rise 15–18 in. [380–460 mm] above any water.
FREEBAIRN-SMITH & CRANE ARCHITECTS

4.17 At Ridge Vineyard's Lytton Springs Winery in Healdsburg, California, a "breathing" (non-cementitious) earthplaster allows water vapor to pass through the strawbale walls. The plaster was mixed at the site and blown and hand-troweled onto the bales.
FREEBAIRN-SMITH & CRANE ARCHITECTS

SAMPLE PROBLEM

The design of a strawbale building entails the design of an entire building system. For schematic design, the initial steps described in the design procedure and knowledge of the available bale size will allow the designer to begin with well-reasoned envelope dimensions.

Examples

4.18 Ridge Vineyard's Lytton Springs Winery in Healdsburg, California used over 4000 rice-bales and integrates several green strategies including photovoltaics, shading devices (including vines), and daylighting. WILLIAM HOCKER

4.19 At the Lytton Springs Winery, non-load-bearing rice-bale walls are 20–24 ft [6–7 m] tall. The walls serve as infill within a frame of non-treated glulam timber columns and beams. The bales are secured by wire mesh cages (see Figure 4.16). The bales and steel strap seismic cross-bracing were later plastered. FREEBAIRN-SMITH & CRANE ARCHITECTS

ENVELOPE

LIGHTING

HEATING

COOLING

ENERGY PRODUCTION

WATER & WASTE

4.20 The entrance to the wine tasting room (left) and other wall openings at the Lytton Springs Winery are shaded by deep roof eaves and vine-covered trellises. Door and window frames are further shaded by recessing them into the 24 in. [600 mm] depth (right) of the strawbale walls. FREEBAIRN-SMITH & CRANE ARCHITECTS

4.21 The Lytton Springs Winery has a daylit tasting room with smooth earthplastered strawbale walls and maple cabinetry and woodwork. MISHA BRUK, BRUKSTUDIOS.COM

ENVELOPE

LIGHTING

HEATING

COOLING

ENERGY PRODUCTION

WATER & WASTE

ENVELOPE

LIGHTING

HEATING

COOLING

ENERGY PRODUCTION

WATER & WASTE

Further Information

California Straw Building Association. www.strawbuilding.org/

Commonwealth of Australia. Technical Manual: *Design for Lifestyle and the Future*. www.greenhouse.gov.au/yourhome/technical/fs34e.htm

Jones, B. 2002. *Building With Straw Bales—A Practical Guide for the UK and Ireland*. Green Books, Totnes, Devon, UK.

Magwood, C. and P. Mack. 2000. *Straw Bale Building—How to Plan, Design and Build with Straw*. New Society Publishers, Gabriola Island, BC.

Steen, A. 1994. *The Straw Bale House*. Chelsea Green Publishing Company, White River Junction, VT.

The Straw Bale Building Association (for Wales, Ireland, Scotland, and England). strawbalebuildingassociation.org.uk/

BEYOND SCHEMATIC DESIGN

Most of the design of a strawbale building is "beyond schematic design." Once deemed feasible in schematic design, the real effort of designing and detailing to ensure structural stability, weather integrity, thermal performance, and acceptable aesthetics begins. This is really no different from other building types—except for the less conventional nature of the fundamental building material and its associated requirements.

ENVELOPE

LIGHTING

HEATING

COOLING

ENERGY PRODUCTION

WATER & WASTE

STRUCTURAL INSULATED PANELS

STRUCTURAL INSULATED PANELS (SIPs) consist of an insulating core element sandwiched between two skins. In this structural assembly, the skins act in tension and compression while the core handles shear and buckling forces. SIPs are commonly composed of an expanded polystyrene (EPS) core with adhesive-attached oriented-strand board (OSB) facings. Alternatives to EPS as a core include extruded polystyrene (XPS), polyurethane, polyisocyanurate, and straw. The advantages and disadvantages of these materials, as well as many construction details, are presented by Michael Morley in *Building with Structural Insulated Panels (SIPS)*.

4.22 Residential construction using SIPs roof panels in Idaho.
BRUCE HAGLUND

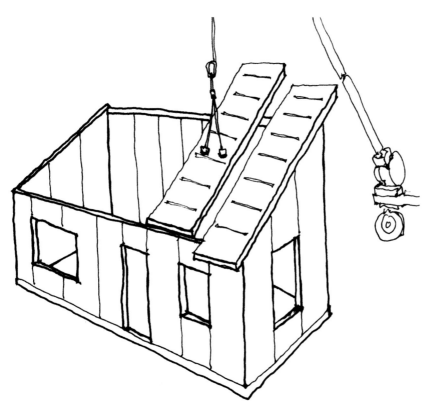

4.23 Conceptual diagram showing the use and assembly of structural insulated panels.
KATE BECKLEY

INTENT
Energy efficiency, efficient use of materials, structural integrity, making use of prefabrication

EFFECT
Good overall thermal performance, reduced infiltration, reduced site waste

OPTIONS
Skin and core materials vary, dimensions vary

COORDINATION ISSUES
Site conditions, heating/cooling loads, fenestration, ventilation

RELATED STRATEGIES
Energy conservation strategies, Air-to-Air Heat Exchangers, Energy Recovery Systems

LEED LINKS
Energy & Atmosphere, Materials & Resources, Innovation & Design Process

PREREQUISITES
A convenient supplier of panels (to reduce transportation requirements) and simplify coordination

Building with structural insulated panels has proven to be an energy-efficient alternative to stick-frame construction primarily because of the limited need for heat-conducting (thermal bridging) studs. The structural strength of this construction method is also superior. Homes built with SIPs have survived tornados in North America and an earthquake in Japan. Another benefit is resource efficiency. Wood for OSB typically originates from tree farms and EPS is produced without ozone-damaging CFCs or HCFCs. A quiet interior in a building that is solidly built is a valuable, though often overlooked, asset that fits with green design intent. Due to their potential for rapid assembly, SIPs are a good choice for a project on a tight schedule. Because manufacturers work with the designer and contractor in the production of panels, customization is not difficult as long as it falls within the capacity of a manufacturer's machinery.

From a disassembly and recycling perspective, the EPS and polyurethane components of SIPs are generally recyclable, but foam and adhesive residue on the OSB panels will probably prevent their beneficial reuse. The amount and type of VOCs emitted by SIPs can vary from manufacturer to manufacturer. Some data suggest that SIPs emit lower levels of formaldehyde than standard wooden residential construction (some SIPs may not emit any) but may emit higher levels of other chemicals.

Key Architectural Issues

SIPs may be used in conjunction with timber framing, stick-framing, steel, and other materials. Typically SIPs are used for exterior walls and/or bearing walls, with stick framing used for interior partitions. Interior gypsum board, a finished ceiling surface, and a fire-retarding finish are some of the options that may be incorporated into a SIPs assembly at the factory, rather than on site. Cement tile backerboard for stucco, cementitious plank, and other materials may be factory-applied on the exterior skin.

SIPs may be used for walls, roofs, and/or floors. Top and bottom plates, headers, and trimmers are still necessary to enclose the foam core, thus sealing the envelope. Non-structural panels are available for use in conjunction with timber or steel framing systems—with a range of options for interior and exterior facings. Because these framing systems are not as energy-efficient, some builders have used SIPs to enclose conventional structural frames.

Implementation Considerations

To reduce field costs and resource wastage, a building designer using SIPs must consider the modular nature of these panels and work with the dimensions to minimize field cutting. To simplify construction, site access for a crane to unload, raise, and place the panels is necessary.

When using SIPs in long-span floors or roofs, creep may cause the SIPs facings to pull away from the core. To avoid this problem, confirm the viability of intended applications with the panel manufacturer and/or project structural engineer.

Gypsum board (drywall) facings may be required in order to meet fire code ratings. Verify requirements with the local jurisdiction. A pest control barrier should be provided to prevent carpenter ants and termites from nesting in the insulating core of the SIPs. The use of stick framing behind kitchen sinks (and similar locations) will simplify plumbing installation.

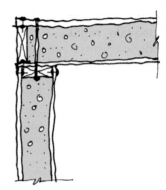

4.24 SIP corner assembly detail. KATE BECKLEY

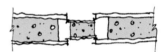

4.25 SIP spline connection detail. KATE BECKLEY

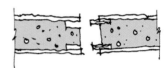

4.26 SIP connection using a foam block. KATE BECKLEY

4.27 SIP connection using a wood spline. KATE BECKLEY

STRUCTURAL INSULATED PANELS **39**

ENVELOPE

LIGHTING

HEATING

COOLING

ENERGY PRODUCTION

WATER & WASTE

Because SIPs construction can greatly reduce infiltration, ensure that adequate ventilation (active or passive) is provided for acceptable indoor air quality. (See, for example, the strategy addressing Air-to-Air Heat Exchangers.) Select a SIPs manufacturer who has had panel performance tested (and reported) by a third party.

Design Procedure

1. Determine the dimensions of panels that are readily and locally available. Dimensions for SIPs vary between manufacturers. A typical panel is 4 or 8 ft [1.2 or 2.4 m] wide and 8 to 24 ft [2.4 to 7.3 m] long, usually available in 2 ft [0.6 m] increments. Other dimensions are often available, as are curved panels. Openings are most efficiently done at the manufacturing plant using computerized layout tools; a precision of 1/8 in. [3 mm] is common. A factory is also more likely to have a waste materials recycling program than a job site.

2. Determine the minimum R-value (or maximum U-factor) permitted by building code for those envelope elements to be assembled of SIPs. These requirements will usually be different for wall, roof, and floor assemblies. Select panels of appropriate thickness and composition to meet code minimums—or more typically to exceed them. The R-value of a SIP increases as panel thickness increases. Standard thicknesses for SIPs, including the insulating core and standard OSB facings, are 4.5, 6.5, and 8.25 in. [115, 165, and 210 mm]. Thicker panels (10.25 and 12.25 in. [260 and 312 mm]) are also available.

3. Investigate building framing and enclosure. A study model is suggested as a means of validating roof panel layouts and addressing complex assembly geometries.

The Structural Insulated Panel Association (www.sips.org/) provides a listing of North American SIPs manufacturers. Manufacturers will typically provide information regarding:

- permissible loadings (axial and transverse)

- available R-values

- standard dimensions

- assembly and connection details

- third-party test results

- consultation services available.

SAMPLE PROBLEM
The design of a building using SIPs involves the design of an entire building system. For schematic design, the initial steps are described in the design procedure and the selected SIP sizes will allow the designer to estimate envelope dimensions.

ENVELOPE

LIGHTING

HEATING

COOLING

ENERGY PRODUCTION

WATER & WASTE

Examples

4.28 These apartment buildings (under construction in Massachusetts) are close to an airport. SIPs and triple glazing were selected to provide the necessary noise control.
AMELIA THRALL

4.29 Combining SIPs (to the right) and conventional interior framing—to use the respective assets of each method to best advantage. AMELIA THRALL

ENVELOPE

LIGHTING

HEATING

COOLING

ENERGY PRODUCTION

WATER & WASTE

4.30 The Not-So-Big Showhouse in Orlando, Florida used SIPs. Visit www. notsobigshowhouse.com/2005/virtualtour/ to view a video that includes footage shot in a SIPs factory and a crane setting the dormer of the home into place.

4.31 Zion National Park Visitor's Center under construction; the roof uses structural insulated panels. PAUL TORCELLINI, DOE/NREL

ENVELOPE

LIGHTING

HEATING

COOLING

ENERGY PRODUCTION

WATER & WASTE

Further Information

Build It Green Structural Insulated Panel.
www.buildit-green.co.uk/about-SIPs.html

Morley, M. 2000. *Building with Structural Insulated Panels (SIPS)*. The Taunton Press, Newtown, MA.

Sarah Susanka's Not So Big Showhouse 2005.
www.notsobigshowhouse.com/2005/

Structural Insulated Panel Association. www.sips.org/

BEYOND SCHEMATIC DESIGN

Much of the effort involved in designing a SIPs-based building will occur after schematic design, during detailing and specification. The key issue relative to SIPs during schematic design is applicability. Planning for SIPs must start early in the design process; detailing for SIPs can come later.

DOUBLE ENVELOPES

DOUBLE ENVELOPES, as described in this strategy, are multiple-leaf wall assemblies used in the transparent or largely transparent portions of a building facade. They range, in configurations, from the time-honored storm window to a recurring modernist ideal, the all-glass facade. Double envelopes consist of an outer facade, an intermediate space, and an inner facade. The outer leaf provides weather protection and a first line of acoustic isolation. The intermediate space is used to buffer thermal impacts on the interior. Through the use of open slots and operable elements in the glass planes it is possible to ventilate the interstitial space on warm days and admit partially conditioned air to adjacent rooms on cool days. In most cases sunshades are placed in the intermediate zone where they can operate freely, but with reasonable access for maintenance. Double glazing of the inner facade provides an optimum thermal barrier (for most climates), while single glazing of the outer facade is sufficient to create the buffer space.

4.32 Buffer zone within the double envelope at the Westhaven Tower in Frankfurt, Germany. DONALD CORNER

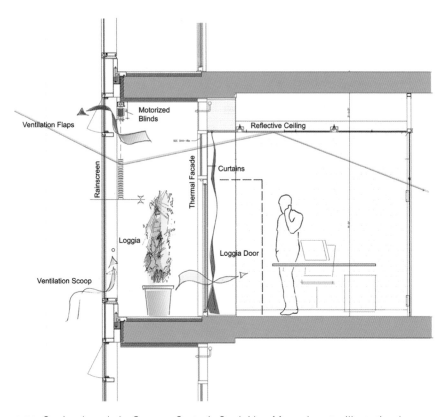

Ventilation Flaps
Motorized Blinds
Reflective Ceiling
Rainscreen
Thermal Facade
Curtains
Loggia
Loggia Door
Ventilation Scoop

4.33 Section through the Genzyme Center in Cambridge, Massachusetts, illustrating the corridor facade configuration of a double skin facade. BEHNISCH ARCHITEKTEN

Double envelopes present the building designer with an extraordinary array of options. The selection of an appropriate system proceeds through the following considerations:

- relationship of the glazing to the overall facade
- performance objectives of the transparencies

INTENT
Climate control, daylighting, acoustic isolation

EFFECT
Natural ventilation, daylighting, thermal insulation, aesthetic impact

OPTIONS
Configurations: box, shaft-box, corridor, multistory

COORDINATION ISSUES
Passive cooling, passive heating, active heating/cooling, acoustics, sunshading, building/facade orientation, building footprint, internal partitions

RELATED STRATEGIES
Direct Gain, Indirect Gain, Cross Ventilation, Stack Ventilation, Light Shelves, Shading Devices

LEED LINKS
Energy & Atmosphere, Indoor Environmental Quality, Innovation & Design Process

PREREQUISITES
A clear understanding of design intent and how use of a double envelope can contribute to meeting such intent

ENVELOPE

LIGHTING

HEATING

COOLING

ENERGY PRODUCTION

WATER & WASTE

- construction strategies, and

- maintenance requirements.

Relationship of the glazing to the overall facade. Traditional facades usually have punched openings or horizontal bands of glass surrounded by solid wall elements. Structural loads are collected in the solid portions and the principal glass plane is often drawn back into the depth of the wall. In such cases it is relatively easy to add a second glazing plane flush with the exterior face and attached to the same structure. Examples include the traditional storm window and its modern counterpart, the "box window" as shown in Figure 4.34. A second facade type consists of an outer glazing mounted a considerable distance in front of only selected portions of the facade. Examples include oriel windows, glazed loggias, and attached sunspaces (shown in Figure 4.35). An inner leaf of glass allows the captured space to act as a double envelope and develops an intermediate zone that is large enough to be a useful space under the right conditions. Finally, double envelopes may consist of an outer leaf of glass across the entire surface of the facade, shown in Figure 4.36. This general type can range from a glass "re-wrap" of an existing structure to a free standing glass box with one or more buildings sheltered inside. Included in this type are the closely-coupled glass double facades that have become popular in Europe since the mid 1990s.

Performance goals at the transparencies. Double envelopes can be further characterized by the tasks they are asked to perform. These requirements determine whether ventilation openings are to be developed in one or both glass leaves and what elements are to be placed inside the captured space. Most double envelopes are designed to maximize daylight while controlling solar gain—a condition typical of office buildings dominated by internal heat gains. The interstitial space is used first and foremost as a protected enclosure for operable shading devices that might otherwise suffer from wind damage and weather exposure. Solar energy absorbed by the shading devices is returned to the exterior environment by free ventilation of heated air through paired openings in the outer leaf or by stack ventilation of the entire facade. Second among typical performance attributes is acoustic isolation in urban environments. The best examples of successful solutions use an unbroken outer leaf of glass with ventilation air for the cavity coming from a remote source or through a sound-baffled inlet system. Double envelope installations that are considered to be effective performers are usually motivated by one or both of these two factors.

Additional performance benefits include the opportunity to ventilate occupied spaces through the inner leaf with the buffer zone acting to mitigate air temperature contrasts in the winter or adverse wind effects in tall buildings. Double envelopes mitigate the surface temperature of the interior glass, reducing the mechanical intervention required to provide comfortable conditions under both heating and cooling modes. The interstitial space can be used as a solar collector to warm the building directly or to move incident energy from a sunny exposure to a shaded exposure. The space can also be used to preheat fresh air for introduction to spaces via the mechanical system in buildings not

4.34 Box-windows within the double skin facade of the GAAG Architecture Gallery in Gelsenkirchen, Germany.
DONALD CORNER

4.35 Glazed balconies in Venice, Italy. DONALD CORNER

4.36 Outer glazing covers the entire surface of the facade at the Arup offices in London, UK.
DONALD CORNER

DOUBLE ENVELOPES **45**

ENVELOPE

LIGHTING

HEATING

COOLING

ENERGY PRODUCTION

WATER & WASTE

ventilated directly through the skin. Thermal siphon effects generated in a double facade can be used to draw air out of a building, although other forms of stack ventilation are more cost-effective.

Construction strategies. One configuration of double envelope consists of a single layer of glass attached to the cantilevered edges of the floor plates with a thermally insulated, infill system standing on each floor an appropriate distance toward the interior. The name "corridor facade" (Figures 4.33, 4.37, and 4.38) is given to this and any configuration in which the intermediate space is divided floor by floor. Often the outer layer is a curtain wall, while the protected inner leaf is a much less expensive storefront system provided by a different vendor.

To maximize usable floor area, the outer glass leaf may be suspended beyond the edge of the primary structure using struts, cables, or trusses. In its pure form, this approach leads to the "multistory facade" in which the cavity is ventilated through large openings at the base and the parapet. Conceptually, this is a transformation of the heavy external shading systems popular in the 1980s. By adding monumental glass panels to the outside face, fixed shades can be replaced with lighter-weight operable units that can respond to changes in sun angle and intensity without having to resist external weather forces.

For large projects it is often desirable to prefabricate the double envelope as a unitized curtain wall system. Complete assemblies, with inner and outer glass leaves installed, can be lifted into place in one step. The units may be self-contained "box windows" with air intake and exhaust ports for cavity ventilation. Alternatively, they may be connected to adjacent units to reduce the number of ventilation ports and separate the intake and exhaust locations across the facade. Typically this is a "corridor facade" with staggered vents. A continuous vertical cavity can be used as a thermal chimney to exhaust the individual units on either side in what is called a "shaft-box facade." Any technique that joins facade modules across multiple interior rooms may improve airflow and reduce costs, but raises concerns about fire spread and sound transmission from room to room through the facade cavity.

Maintenance requirements. The ultimate configuration of a double envelope will be greatly influenced by the need to get inside the cavity to clean the glass surfaces and maintain ventilation controls and shading devices. Large-scale corridor facades meet this requirement without disturbing the workspaces, but at the cost of significant floor area around the building perimeter that is likely to be underutilized. Multistory facades often incorporate service walkways of metal grating into the cantilevered structure of the interstitial zone.

In Europe, especially Germany, building codes and cultural traditions require that a high percentage of the inner glazing leaf be operable to allow for individual control over outdoor air in the workspace. If operable glass can provide access into each facade unit, the depth of the intermediate cavity can be reduced from a matter of feet [meters] to a matter of inches [millimeters]. This greatly improves the material efficiency of a unitized production system, particularly if the cost of the operable units is offset by a reduction in mechanical plant capacity due to increased use of natural ventilation.

4.37 Curtain wall of the Genzyme Center in Cambridge, Massachusetts. DONALD CORNER

4.38 Within the corridor-facade of the Genzyme Center in Cambridge, Massachusetts. DONALD CORNER

ENVELOPE

LIGHTING

HEATING

COOLING

ENERGY PRODUCTION

WATER & WASTE

In the North American market, unitized curtain wall strategies generally utilize fixed insulating glass in the outer leaf with a hinged plate of glass added to the inside face of the mullions to create a thin double envelope. Service access is from the interior. This is a revival of the "exhaust window" concept in which a percentage of stale interior air is drawn through the facade cavity to remove heat absorbed by shading louvers. This strategy has a low first cost, but only a limited air volume is available to flush the cavity as compared to systems that ventilate freely through the outside glazing plane.

Key Architectural Issues

The primary architectural issue related to double envelope construction is the fact that building appearance and thermal and lighting performance are essentially defined by the success of the facade. It is imperative that the designer have clear design intent, explicit design criteria, and a sense that the intended envelope design can deliver what is expected. Unfortunately, a double envelope facade is a very complex system that may not behave totally intuitively.

Implementation Considerations

The effectiveness of double envelope systems is widely debated and difficult to summarize. A simple comparison of facade costs has little meaning without also comparing the floor space available for use, the cost of a compatible structural system, the size and complexity of the mechanical plant, total building energy flows, and the cost of long-term maintenance. One must also examine the qualitative benefits to building occupants and the ecological impacts of the materials required. Some of the most effective double envelope applications are "re-wraps" of existing building envelopes that are poor energy performers.

Generally, double envelopes should not be the first green strategy adopted. They should be considered when and if they complement other steps taken in pursuit of overall environmental quality and energy efficiency. Many of the benefits associated with double envelopes can be achieved through means that have far less design and cost impact. Passive ventilation, for instance, can be integrated using trickle vents through a single leaf skin. Openings in a facade should be designed to optimize the harvesting of daylight and provide meaningful connections to the outdoor environment. Too often double envelopes are used to control gains and losses through areas of glass that are much larger than can be justified by these fundamental performance considerations.

Design Procedure

1. Develop a narrative to express design intent and related design criteria for the building envelope that will be affected by a double envelope facade—especially thermal and visual comfort, energy efficiency, and climate control systems. For example: provide quality daylighting; a minimum daylight factor of 5% will be provided in all exterior offices; a double skin facade will assist in achieving this by _____.

2. Consider the various types of double envelope systems and construction strategies and sketch a building plan and a wall section that has the elements necessary to deliver the intended performance. Address issues such as whether the interstitial space will be occupiable, whether individual control of light, air, and view is intended, whether acoustic isolation is required.

3. Do a reality check on the implications inherent in the above narrative. How is daylighting performance enhanced by a double envelope? How will a double envelope reduce winter heat losses? How will ventilation air flow through a double envelope? The purpose of this check is not to reject a double envelope strategy, but rather to validate the assumptions inherent in projections of system performance.

4. Reiterations of the conceptual sketches are made as models (physical and simulation) and are used to analyze various building systems.

Examples

4.39 Glass "wrap" facade (left) and close up of glass panels (right) used as shingles and hung from the facade of the Kuntshaus Art Gallery in Bergenz, Austria. DONALD CORNER

SAMPLE PROBLEM
As can be seen in the adjacent design procedure, there is no simple or single means of sizing or verifying the feasibility of a double envelope facade proposal. The spatial implications of the double envelope strategy selected will need to incorporate specific building systems desired by the design criteria. For example, the corridor facade shown in previous examples might need to be wide enough for people to pass or for other uses. The depth of the external glazing system and internal walls will depend on the components selected.

ENVELOPE

LIGHTING

HEATING

COOLING

ENERGY PRODUCTION

WATER & WASTE

ENVELOPE

LIGHTING

HEATING

COOLING

ENERGY PRODUCTION

WATER & WASTE

4.40 The double envelope facade of Bayerische Vereinsbank building in Stuttgart, Germany is a "re-wrap" or reconstruction of an existing building in which an operable leaf of glass louvers has been added in front of a system of operable strip windows. There are shades in the cavity.
DONALD CORNER

Further Information

Boake, T.M. 2003. "Doubling Up." *Canadian Architect,* Vol. 48, No. 7, July.

Boake, T. M. 2003. "Doubling Up II." *Canadian Architect,* Vol. 48, No. 8, August.

Diprose, P. and G. Robertson. 1996. "Towards a Fourth Skin? Sustainability and Double-Envelope Buildings." www.diprose.co.nz/WREC/WREC.htm

Herzog, T., R. Krippner and W. Lang. 2004. *Facade Construction Manual.* Birkhauser, Basel, Switzerland.

Oesterle, E. et al. 2001. *Double-Skin Facades: Integrated Planning.* Prestel, Munich.

BEYOND SCHEMATIC DESIGN

It has been said that "the devil is in the details." That saying clearly applies to double envelope facades. Much of the design work on a double envelope will occur during design development—including extensive modeling of the system's performance. Proposed configurations may be tested through physical mockups or computer simulations (including computational fluid dynamics analyses) to optimize ventilation performance and understand overall thermal performance.

GREEN ROOFS can be used to provide for rainwater detention or retention, to increase the thermal resistance and capacitance of a building roof, to reduce the urban heat island effect, and to provide green space for animals and people on what would otherwise be a hard-surfaced area. Green roofs are of two basic types: extensive and intensive.

Extensive green roofs have a relatively shallow soil base, making them lighter, less expensive, and easier to maintain than intensive green roofs. Extensive roofs usually have limited plant diversity, typically consisting of sedum (succulents), grasses, mosses, and herbs. They are often not accessible by building tenants, but may provide for "natural" views from adjacent rooms or neighboring buildings.

4.41 Green roof in Norway.

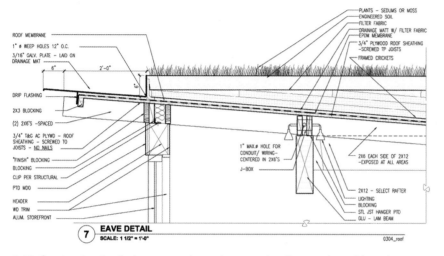

4.42 Construction detail of a green roof over the garage/studio area of a residence in Seattle, Washington. MILLER/HULL PARTNERSHIP

Extensive green roofs can work at slopes of up to 35°, although slopes above 20° require a baffle system to prevent soil slump. These can be used in both urban and rural settings, are applicable to a wide variety of building types, and can be used in both new and existing construction.

From 2 to 6 in. [50–150 mm] of some kind of lightweight growing material (often a mineral-based mixture of sand, gravel, and organic matter) is required for an extensive green roof. In addition to the growing medium, a drainage system for excess rainwater and a protective barrier for the roof membrane are required. Because plant roots bond to underlayment fabrics to create a unified whole, there is no need to provide additional ballast against roof uplift unless the roof is located in an unusually high wind area, such as on a high-rise building or in a coastal area.

Intensive green roofs have a deeper soil base than extensive green roofs. They are not limited in terms of plant diversity (as are shallower extensive green roofs) and often feature the same kinds of landscaping as local gardens. Intensive green roofs can provide park-like accessible open spaces, and often include larger plants and trees as well as walkways, water features, and irrigation systems. The deeper soil base required for these roofs and the weight of the plants combined with the

INTENT
Site enhancement, climate control

EFFECT
Stormwater retention/detention, improved envelope performance, reduced urban heat island effect, creation of a green space, water and air quality mitigation

OPTIONS
A range of strategies—from a minimal, non-accessible extensive green roof to a large, fully-accessible forested intensive green roof

COORDINATION ISSUES
Structural system, roof insulation, storm drainage, roof access, irrigation system (if required), rooftop elements (such as plumbing vents, exhaust fans)

RELATED STRATEGIES
Water Reuse/Recycling, Pervious Surfaces, Insulation Materials

LEED LINKS
Sustainable Sites, Water Efficiency, Innovation & Design Process

PREREQUISITES
An appropriate roof area, the potential to access the roof for maintenance

ENVELOPE

LIGHTING

HEATING

COOLING

ENERGY PRODUCTION

WATER & WASTE

weight of water that may saturate the soil make them much heavier than extensive green roofs or conventional roofs. This extra weight requires a substantial building structure, and results in a roof that is more expensive to build. Intensive green roofs are feasible only on flat-roofed buildings.

While intensive green roofs involve more cost, design time, and attention than other roofs, this approach provides the broadest palette by which the roof can become an exciting and vibrant environment. A great diversity of habitats can be created, including those with trees. These types of roofs are often accessible to people for recreation, for open space, even for growing food. Intensive green roofs are more energy-efficient than extensive green roofs, and their roof membranes are typically more protected and last longer. The deeper soil base provides greater stormwater retention capacity. Growing media depth for intensive green roofs is typically 24 in. [600 mm].

The layers of a green roof can vary depending upon the specific type of green roof selected. Generally, insulation will be placed on top of the roof deck. Above this will be a waterproof membrane, a root barrier, a

4.43 Green roof on Seattle City Hall in Seattle, Washington. BRUCE HAGLUND

4.44 2005 Rhode Island School of Design Solar Decathlon House with a green roof for outdoor dining.

4.45 Sketch showing an extensive roof proposal for a low-rise building. KATE BECKLEY

4.46 Extensive green roof and eating area on the 2005 Rhode Island School of Design Solar Decathlon House. JONATHAN KNOWLES

4.47 Experimental green roof on a building (left) at Yokohama National University, Yokohama, Japan. The left side of the roof has pallets of clover, the right side is a conventional exposed roof surface. Infrared thermography (right) shows the effect of the green roof on surface temperatures. ECOTECH LABORATORY

drainable layer, a filter membrane, and finally growing media for the plants. Drainable insulation planes are also commonly used, where the waterproofing is located at the structural surface. Depending upon the weight of the soil base and plants, additional structure may be needed on top of the insulation layer. Careful attention should be given to vapor retarder location.

Key Architectural Issues

Successful green roofs require a building massing that provides appropriate solar exposure for the intended types of vegetation. Shading from adjacent buildings or trees can have a big impact on the success of rooftop plantings. Building massing can also be used to create rooftop surfaces that are relatively protected from wind. Building form will also determine how building occupants can interact with a green roof. A green roof is a user amenity only if it is at least visible to occupants. If it is also accessible to building occupants, greater integration of the green roof with appropriate interior spaces is desirable. Structural system design, careful detailing of drainage systems, irrigation systems, and penetrations of the roof membrane are key concerns.

Implementation Considerations

Hardy, drought resistant, low-height plants should be selected for extensive green roofs. Plants on such a roof experience higher wind speeds, more solar radiation, have a thinner soil base, and much less access to groundwater resources than plants in conventional locations. As a result, plants on a green roof experience high evapotranspiration losses, making drought resistant plants most suitable to conditions. Windburn is also a concern. In North American frost zones 4–8 (see www.emilycompost. com/zone_map.htm), at least half of the plants on extensive green roofs should be sedums. In colder climates, grass dominated covers are recommended. Many extensive green roof plantings turn brown in the winter, and this color change should be anticipated.

Although extensive green roofs are generally not open (other than to maintenance personnel), a safe and viable means of access should be provided to simplify construction and encourage maintenance. A safety railing should be provided at the roof perimeter.

Intensive green roofs create an opportunity to incorporate trees into the roofscape. Trees and other heavy elements should be placed directly over columns or main beams. The area directly underneath a tree can be deepened if necessary. Rooftops experience higher wind velocities than found at ground level. To protect plants and occupants, roof gardens should include both a windbreak and a railing (perhaps provided by a parapet wall). Trees must be anchored against the wind, while avoiding stakes that might puncture the roof membrane. Tension cables are sometimes attached to the root ball and to the roof structure below the soil surface. Pavers should be as light as possible to reduce the dead load on the roof.

4.48 Lecture hall located below an experimental green roof at Yokohama National University. ECOTECH LABORATORY

4.49 Thermograph taken at 3:00 PM in classroom below the green roof. Temperatures average 90 °F [32 °C]. ECOTECH LABORATORY

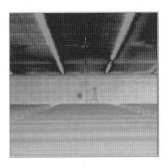

4.50 Thermograph taken at 3:00 PM in classroom without a green roof. Temperatures average 100°F [38 °C] in the seating area and 108 °F [42 °C] at the ceiling. ECOTECH LABORATORY

Design Procedure

1. Determine the desired function(s) of the green roof with respect to project design intents. Typical functions include:
   - providing a visual amenity for building occupants
   - providing an occupiable green space
   - reducing building energy consumption
   - stormwater retention/detention.

2. Determine if an intensive or an extensive green roof is most appropriate to achievement of the design intents and desired functions.

3. Determine the amount of sun and shade that the proposed green roof area will receive during the year. A sunpeg chart and simple massing model are recommended as easy-to-use tools. Adjust location of the green roof area as necessary to achieve adequate solar exposure.

4. Determine the types of plantings desired, taking into consideration sun/shade patterns, available rainfall, and likely wind speeds. Consultation with a local landscape specialist is recommended.

5. Determine the soil depth required to support the desired plantings—see Table 4.1 for minimum depths for various planting types.

6. Estimate the dead weight of the proposed green roof (assuming a fully saturated condition) to permit an estimate of the size (depth) of the supporting structural system (see Tables 4.1 and 4.2).

7. If the green roof approach seems feasible, adopt this strategy and proceed with design. Consider how to incorporate access for maintenance and irrigation (if required).

TABLE 4.1 Minimum soil depths for green roof planting. *TIME-SAVER STANDARDS FOR LANDSCAPE ARCHITECTURE*, 2ND ED.

PLANTING	MINIMUM SOIL DEPTH[a]
Lawns	8–12 in. [200–300 mm]
Flowers and ground covers	10–12 in. [250–300 mm]
Shrubs	24–30 in. [600–750 mm][b]
Small trees	30–42 in. [750–1050 mm][b]
Large trees	5–6 ft [1.5–1.8 m][b]

[a] above filter fabric and drainage medium
[b] dependent upon ultimate plant size

SAMPLE PROBLEM

An ecological housing co-op in North Carolina is interested in a green roof for its communal dining building. The roof is approximately 30 by 20 ft [9.1 by 6.1 m], with a south-facing 20° slope.

1. The roof will be visible from the ground but not accessible by residents. It should retain stormwater, mitigate heat island effects, and serve as a symbol of the community's commitment to green solutions.

2. An extensive green roof is appropriate for the sloped, inaccessible, low-maintenance roof desired and fits the client's budget.

3. The building is surrounded by low buildings, a lawn, and a parking area. Little shading of the roof is likely and solar exposure will be similar to that of ground plantings.

4. Plantings are selected considering climate. The site experiences over 100 sunny days per year. Winters are generally mild, with occasional frosts and snow. Summers are long, hot and humid. Yearly rainfall is approximately 50 in. [130 cm]. Considering the above and the thin soil layer in an extensive green roof, succulents and drought resistant plants are selected.

5. A preliminary soil depth of 10 in. [250 mm] of lightweight medium is selected, to be placed atop a 4 in. [100 mm] drainage layer.

6. The estimated roof dead load due to the green roof elements is: $(10/12)(70) + (4/12)(120) = 98\ \text{lb/ft}^3\ [1570\ \text{kg/m}^3]$. The weight of the structure and insulation plus live loads must be added to this value.

7. This green roof approach is considered feasible.

TABLE 4.2 Approximate weights of green roof materials. *TIME-SAVER STANDARDS FOR LANDSCAPE ARCHITECTURE,* 2ND ED.

MATERIAL	DRY lb/ft^3 [kg/m^3]	WET lb/ft^3 [kg/m^3]
Sand or gravel	90 [1440]	120 [1929]
Cedar shavings with fertilizer	9.3 [149]	13 [209]
Peat moss	9.6 [154]	10 [166]
Redwood compost and shavings	15 [2387]	22 [357]
Fir and pine bark humus	22 [357]	33 [535]
Perlite	6.5 [104]	32 [521]
Topsoil	76 [1216]	78 [1248]
Concrete		
Lightweight	90 [1400]	—
Precast	130 [2080]	—
Reinforced	150 [2400]	—
Steel	490 [7840]	—

Examples

4.51 Green roof on the Roddy/Bale garage/studio in Seattle, Washington has a variety of native plants and ground cover. MILLER/HULL PARTNERSHIP

ENVELOPE

LIGHTING

HEATING

COOLING

ENERGY PRODUCTION

WATER & WASTE

4.52 A green roof covers the restaurant at the Eden Project near St. Austell in Cornwall, UK.

Further Information

British Council for Offices. 2003. Research Advice Note: "Green Roofs." www.bco.org.uk/

Centre for the Advancement of Green Roof Technology. commons.bcit.ca/greenroof/

Earth Pledge. 2004. *Green Roofs: Ecological Design and Construction.* Schiffer Publishing, Atglen, PA.

Green Roofs for Healthy Cities. www.greenroofs.net/

Harris, C. and N. Dines. 1997. *Time-Saver Standards for Landscape Architecture,* 2nd ed. McGraw-Hill, New York.

Oberlander, C.H., E. Whitelaw and E. Matsuzaki. 2002. *Introductory Manual for Greening Roofs for Public Works and Government Services Canada,* Version 1.1. ftp.tech-env.com/pub/SERVICE_LIFE_ASSET_ MANAGEMENT/ PWGSC_GreeningRoofs_wLinks.pdf

Osmundson, T. 1997. *Roof Gardens: History, Design, and Construction.* W.W. Norton, New York.

Velazquez, L. 2005. "Organic Greenroof Architecture: Design Consideration and System Components" and "Organic Greenroof Architecture: Sustainable Design for the New Millennium," *Environmental Quality Management,* Summer.

BEYOND SCHEMATIC DESIGN

During design development, a green roof will be optimized and detailed. A landscape architect will likely be involved to ensure the survivability, compatibility, and vibrancy of plantings. The roof structure will be analyzed and detailed. If the building (or roof, due to height) is in a high wind area detailed wind studies may be done to estimate wind speeds on the roof and to determine the best placement of windbreaks and walls and tree anchorage requirements.

ENVELOPE

LIGHTING

HEATING

COOLING

ENERGY PRODUCTION

WATER & WASTE

ENVELOPE

LIGHTING

HEATING

COOLING

ENERGY PRODUCTION

WATER & WASTE

LIGHTING

The controlled distribution of daylight in buildings is a cornerstone of green design. Daylighting is a key to good energy performance, as well as occupant satisfaction, productivity, and health. Daylighting must be addressed early in schematic design because requirements for successful daylighting usually have major implications for building massing and zoning of activities.

Toplighting (daylighting through skylights, roof monitors, etc.) and sidelighting (daylighting through vertical windows at the building perimeter) lead to different sets of coordination issues for designers. Toplighting allows even levels of diffuse light to be distributed across large areas of a building. For this reason, successful toplighting is typically easier to achieve and requires less complex electric lighting controls. Sidelighting tends to be more complex. Size, location, visual transmittance, and energy performance characteristics of glazing must be carefully refined. Glare control, involving window overhangs, interior light shelves, glazing choices, as well as interior shades or blinds, is critical. Because daylight illuminance drops off with distance from the windows, electric lighting controls become more complex.

It is important to distinguish between sunlight and daylight. In most situations, direct sunlight brings excessive heat and light leading to visual and thermal discomfort. Skylights designed to provide daylighting should contain diffusing (rather than clear) glazing. Controlling solar gain through skylights is critical to building energy efficiency. Vertical glazing design must include glare and heat control. Large areas of unprotected glass do not result in well-daylit buildings.

The importance of viable and working controls for electric lighting cannot be overstated. Unless electric lighting is dimmed or switched off, there are no savings of electricity or reductions in cooling load. Without controls, even a well-designed daylighting system will require the use of more, not less, energy.

Interior finishes and furnishing are very important in a daylit building. Ceilings and walls should be light colored with high reflectance. Office partitions and cubicles should be as low as possible while meeting privacy needs. These requirements must be communicated to the client and interior designer or the architect's intentions for daylighting may not be achieved.

If a project is to be certified under the USGBC LEED-NC rating system, note that the credits for daylight and views under Indoor Environmental Quality address daylight as an amenity for building occupants, not as an energy-efficiency strategy. A well-designed and controlled daylighting system will reduce energy use. Thus, daylighting can result in additional points under the Energy & Atmosphere category.

STRATEGIES
Daylight Factor
Daylight Zoning
Toplighting
Sidelighting
Light Shelves
Internal Reflectances
Shading Devices
Electric Lighting

ENVELOPE

LIGHTING

HEATING

COOLING

ENERGY PRODUCTION

WATER & WASTE

NOTES

DAYLIGHT FACTOR

ENVELOPE

LIGHTING

HEATING

COOLING

ENERGY PRODUCTION

WATER & WASTE

DAYLIGHT FACTOR (DF) is a numerical ratio used to describe the relationship between indoor and outdoor daylight illuminances (typically under overcast sky conditions). In order to make sense of daylighting system performance and the many design strategies used to deliver daylight, it is critical to understand this key measurement that is universally used to quantify and assess daylight illuminance.

Because sky conditions are always changing, daylight illuminance is exceptionally variable throughout a typical day/month/year. It is not, therefore, possible to flatly state that the daylight illuminance at some point in a building will be "x" footcandles [lux]. Whatever value for "x" is stated will be incorrect most of the time (under different exterior conditions). Absolute values of daylight illuminance are often not a useful metric for design. As a ratio (a relative measure) daylight factor is generally stable across time and therefore much more useful and usable as a design tool—although at some point in the design process a daylight factor will typically need to be related to an illuminance value.

4.53 Exterior view of a typical daylighting study model.

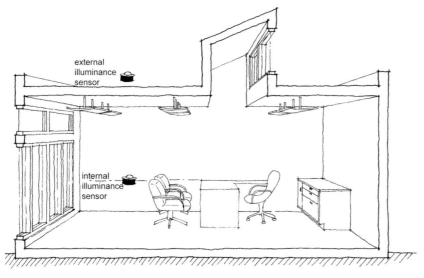

4.54 The fundamental concept of daylight factor—the relationship between indoor and outdoor daylight illuminances. JONATHAN MEENDERING

As suggested in Figure 4.54, daylight factor equals the internal daylight illuminance at a specific point divided by a reference external daylight illuminance. DF is dimensionless (the illuminance units cancel) and is expressed either as a percentage (for example, 2.5%) or as a decimal (0.025). Daylight factor is position-specific; there will be a range of daylight factors in any given space. Daylight factor literally represents the efficiency of the entire daylighting system in delivering daylight from the exterior environment to a specific point within a building.

Daylight factor is used both as a design criterion (a design target) and as a measure of actual system performance. As a design criterion DF may be set to meet an internally established client goal, to meet some externally mandated or suggested minimum performance, or to meet

INTENT
Used as a daylighting performance quantifier

EFFECT
Normalizes variations in daylight illuminance over time

OPTIONS
Expressed as either a percentage or decimal value

COORDINATION ISSUES
Not applicable

RELATED STRATEGIES
Sidelighting, Toplighting, Light Shelves, Shading Devices, Internal Reflectances

LEED LINKS
Indoor Environmental Quality

PREREQUISITES
Not applicable

ENVELOPE

LIGHTING

HEATING

COOLING

ENERGY PRODUCTION

WATER & WASTE

an explicit energy efficiency or passive system contribution threshold. Recommendations for minimum daylight factors may be obtained from numerous resources.

Key Architectural Issues

The daylight *factor* experienced at a given point in a particular building space depends upon a number of design factors including:

- size of daylight apertures (windows, skylights, etc.);

- location of daylight apertures (sidelighting, toplighting, etc.);

- access to daylight (considering the site, building, and room contexts);

- room geometry (height, width, and depth);

- location of the point of interest relative to apertures;

- visible transmittance (VT) of glazing;

- reflectances of room surfaces and contents;

- reflectances of exterior surfaces affecting daylight entering the aperture;

- the effects of daylighting enhancements (such as light shelves).

The daylight *illuminance* experienced at any given point in a building depends upon the factors noted above and:

- the building's global location and prevailing climate;

- the time of day/month/year;

- the current sky conditions.

Having information about the daylight factor at some location within a building allows a designer to estimate daylight illuminance on the basis of available exterior illuminance. For example, the expected illuminance (E) at point "A" in some room at 10:00 A.M. on March 25 is found as follows:

$$E = (DF \text{ at point "A"}) (\text{exterior illuminance})$$

where the "exterior illuminance" is the design exterior illuminance likely to prevail at the building site at 10:00 A.M. on March 25.

The actual daylight illuminance experienced at point "A" in this room at 10:00 A.M. on any specific March 25 will be modified by the weather conditions existing at that time.

ENVELOPE

LIGHTING

HEATING

COOLING

ENERGY PRODUCTION

WATER & WASTE

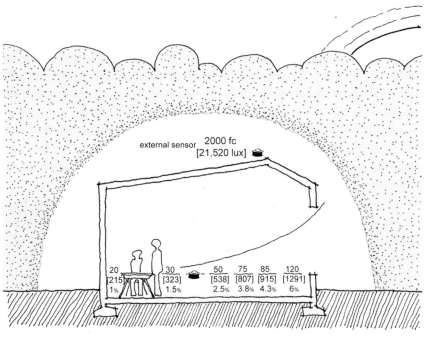

4.55 Daylight factor versus illuminance as a measure of daylighting. The illuminance values will change throughout the day, while the daylight factors will be reasonably constant throughout the day (under similar sky conditions). KATE BECKLEY

Implementation Considerations

As a design criterion. Using daylight factor as a design target is straight-forward. Simply set DF criteria for various spaces (and/or locations within spaces) that are appropriate to the design context—remembering that a given DF target will represent different illuminances in different climates and at different times. These targets may come from the client, from codes, from standards or guidelines, or from the environmental or economic values of the design team. DF criteria are often expressed as minimum targets (for example, a DF of no less than 4%). DF criteria may also be derived from a design intent to displace (wholly or in part) electric lighting. In this case, a target DF would be established on the basis of required design illuminance values. Stated another way: sometimes DF criteria will be set based upon a general sense that this or that DF represents a "good" or "reasonable" effort. In other cases, DF targets are explicitly linked to a specific outcome (such as no use of electric lighting between the hours of 10:00 A.M. and 4:00 P.M.).

The U.S. Green Building Council's LEED NC-2.1 system established a minimum DF of 2% (with conditions) as the threshold for a LEED day-lighting credit. The British Research Establishment's EcoHomes pro-gram requires a minimum 2% average DF in kitchens and a 1.5% minimum average DF in living rooms, dining rooms, and studies. Other minimum daylight factor requirements or recommendations can be found in the building codes or lighting standards of many countries. In the absence of other criteria, Table 4.3 provides general recommendations for target daylight factors that have been extracted from several North American and United Kingdom sources.

From a subjective perspective, the following user responses to daylight factors have been suggested:

- With a DF of less than 2%, a room will seem gloomy. Electric lighting will be required for most of the daylight hours.

- With a DF between 2% and 5%, a room will feel that it is daylit, although supplementary electric lighting may be needed.

- With a DF greater than 5%, a room will feel vigorously daylit. Depending upon the task at hand, electric lighting may not be necessary during daylight hours.

TABLE 4.3 Suggested daylight factor criteria (under overcast skies)

SPACE	AVERAGE DF	MINIMUM DF
Commercial/Institutional		
Corridor	2	0.6
General Office	5	2
Classroom	5	2
Library	5	1.5
Gymnasium	5	3.5
Residential		
Dining Room/Studio	5	2.5
Kitchen	2	0.6
Living Room	1.5	0.5
Bedroom	1.0	0.3

As a performance predictor. There are a number of analog, digital, and correlational methods that can be used to predict the daylight factor likely to be experienced at some point in a building under design. These methods generally include:

- Scale models (daylighting models) that attempt to physically represent a proposed design—predicted DF is measured in an appropriate setting with paired illuminance meters.

- Computer simulations that attempt to represent a proposed design numerically—predicted DF is given as a numerical or graphic output.

- A range of performance guidelines for use in the early stages of design that attempt to correlate a proposed design with the measured performance of previously built spaces. These methods typically give rough feedback on whether a daylight strategy can meet established performance criteria. The 2.5 H rule that suggests usable daylight will penetrate a space to 2.5 times the window head height is an example of this type of method.

As a measure of constructed performance. Daylight factor is easily measured in a completed building with the use of paired illuminance meters. The measurement of in-situ DF values would be an expected element of any serious post-occupancy evaluation (POE) of a daylit building.

4.56 Daylight factor can be measured in the field (such as in this residence) using paired illuminance meter readings.

4.57 Scale models (such as of the residence shown above) can be used to predict daylight factor during design. Surface reflectances must be carefully modeled for accurate predictions.

4.58 A computer simulation, such as Radiance, can provide daylight factor predictions and facilitate qualitative evaluation of a proposed design. GREG WARD

Design Procedure

1. Based upon recommendations or requirements that are most applicable to the context of the project, establish daylight factor criteria for the various spaces in the building being designed. These will typically be minimum values, rather than point-specific targets.

2. Select the daylighting approach or combination of approaches most likely to provide performance to match the criteria established in Step 1. Daylighting approaches include sidelighting, toplighting, and special designs involving light pipes or guides. See the Toplighting and Sidelighting strategies that follow.

3. Size daylighting apertures using available schematic design guidance or trial and error.

4. Model the daylighting performance (including daylight factors) of the proposed daylighting system. Modeling tools include physical scale models, computer simulations, and hand calculations.

5. Adjust selected daylighting design parameters (aperture size, glazing transmittance, surface reflectances, light shelves, etc.) as necessary to achieve established daylight factor criteria.

6. Revalidate daylighting design using modified parameters; iterate as necessary to meet design criteria.

Examples

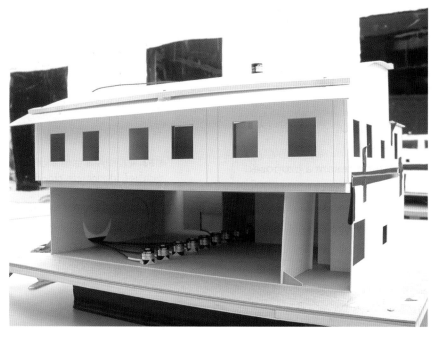

4.59 Daylight model placed in an artificial sky with several interior photosensors and a single exterior sensor (on roof) to measure illuminances and determine daylight factors. The model is "unglazed" and the additional daylight this admits will be corrected for when calculating DF.
ROBERT MARCIAL

SAMPLE PROBLEM
The design team for a small stand-alone dentist's office in Alpine, Texas intends to daylight the building in accordance with LEED NC-2.1 requirements.

1. The LEED connection leads to specific daylight factor criteria: a minimum DF of 2% for 75% of the normally occupied spaces.

2. A sidelighting approach is selected as views are also considered important by the design team.

3. Using available design guidelines (see, for example, Sidelighting) windows are sized to provide the target daylight factor. Building layout is critical to the success of this daylighting approach.

4. A physical daylighting model is used to test the proposed daylighting design.

5. The proposed design provides minimum DFs of over 2.5% in all spaces except for two, where the minimum is below 2%. The aperture sizes in these spaces are increased.

6. Retesting confirms that the minimum daylight factor is provided in 80% of all occupied spaces.

ENVELOPE

LIGHTING

HEATING

COOLING

ENERGY PRODUCTION

WATER & WASTE

4.60 Daylight model being tested outdoors under an overcast sky with an interior and exterior photosensor to measure illuminances and calculate daylight factor.

Further Information

British Standards. 1992. *Lighting for Buildings: Code of Practice for Daylighting* (BS 8206-2). BSI British Standards, London.

Brown, G.Z. and M. DeKay. 2001. *Sun, Wind & Light: Architectural Design Strategies*, 2nd ed. John Wiley & Sons, New York.

IESNA. 1999. *Recommended Practice of Daylighting* (RP-5-99). Illuminating Engineering Society of North America, New York.

Moore, F. 1993. *Environmental Control Systems: Heating, Cooling, Lighting*. McGraw-Hill, Inc., New York.

Square One Research. www.squ1.com/daylight/daylight-factor.html

Stein, B. et al. 2006. *Mechanical and Electrical Equipment for Buildings*, 10th ed. John Wiley & Sons, Hoboken, NJ.

BEYOND SCHEMATIC DESIGN

Although daylight factor plays an important role in benchmarking daylighting during schematic design, it is equally valuable as a performance indicator during design development and post-occupancy evaluations. Several green building rating systems use a minimum daylight factor as a threshold for daylighting credits.

ENVELOPE

LIGHTING

HEATING

COOLING

ENERGY PRODUCTION

WATER & WASTE

DAYLIGHT ZONING is the process of grouping various spaces in a building with similar luminous requirements into a daylighting zone, thereby enabling design and control cost savings. Daylighting schemes can be developed and tailored to meet the particular needs and conditions of associated spaces with similar daylighting needs—thus optimizing the design strategy for each zone.

Several rooms with similar characteristics with respect to lighting might be grouped to form a zone, or a single room might be treated as a zone. Combining spaces into daylight zones is commonly done by considering three characteristics of a space:

- *Function:* The type of visual activities that predominate within a space will establish the lighting requirements that will permit the activity to be performed to a level of quality as defined by design intent.

- *Usage schedule:* The primary time(s) of use of a space and how those times relate to daylight availability will determine daylight potential and influence zoning.

- *Location and orientation:* The location of a space relative to the daylight source (e.g. next to an exterior wall, within an interior atrium, etc.) and the orientation of the space (e.g. a space with an aperture facing north versus a west-facing aperture) will help to determine how daylight can be used.

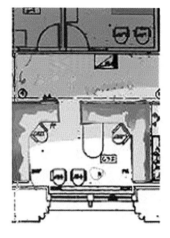

4.61 Isolux plot of measured daylight zones in an office building.

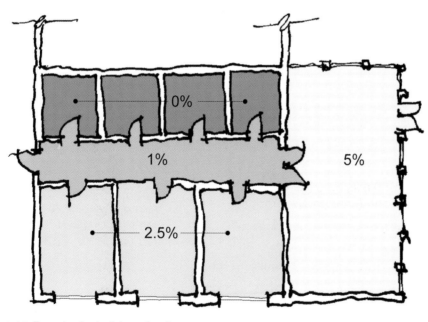

4.62 Example of a daylight zoning diagram. KATE BECKLEY

While function and usage schedule are primarily determined by the building program, the designer has control over the location and orientation of a space and can use these decisions to optimize the effectiveness of daylighting schemes. In addition, related factors that may be

INTENT
Optimized daylighting design

EFFECT
Energy efficiency, building organization, potential for coordination with electric lighting

OPTIONS
Not applicable

COORDINATION ISSUES
Daylighting strategy, daylight factor, electric lighting, glazing, shading devices, ceilings, finishes

RELATED STRATEGIES
Daylight Factor, Internal Reflectances, Shading Devices, Light Shelves, Electric Lighting

LEED LINKS
Indoor Environmental Quality, Energy & Atmosphere

PREREQUISITES
Building program, preliminary spatial layout, lighting design criteria

ENVELOPE

LIGHTING

HEATING

COOLING

ENERGY PRODUCTION

WATER & WASTE

important to consider in the zoning process include visual comfort, thermal comfort, fire and smoke control, and building automation opportunities and requirements.

Key Architectural Issues

Daylight zoning can dramatically affect a building's orientation, massing, plan layout, and section and should be a guiding factor during schematic design. Optimizing daylight access for zones where lighting needs can be largely met by daylighting suggests maximizing the building perimeter and the use of toplighting for critical interior spaces. The use of atria and/or light courts may also be appropriate. Daylighting decisions often result in a building with a higher skin-to-volume ratio than a typical compact (electrically lit) building.

Implementation Considerations

The building program or schedule of usage may complicate daylight zoning efforts because the particular mix of space types and/or times of usage does not accommodate a logical assemblage of daylit spaces. Sometimes what makes sense from a daylight zoning point of view does not work from a functional point of view. The design team will need to resolve any such conflicts.

Site conditions may constrict solar access such that it is not possible to utilize daylighting as much as desired or to accommodate a desired zoning scheme while addressing required design adjacencies and circulation needs.

Glazing, light shelves, and shading devices should be selected and designed to reinforce proposed daylight zoning schemes. Interior partition arrangement can have a dramatic impact on daylight distribution and thus on daylighting zones.

Design Procedure

1. List and define the types of spaces that will be present in the building.

2. Determine required ambient and task illuminance values for the various space types based upon the visual activities that will be performed. Recommended illuminance levels may be found in the *IESNA Lighting Handbook* and similar resources.

3. Outline an anticipated schedule of usage and daylighting potential for each space type in a table (as per the example in Table 4.4).

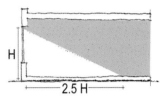

4.63 Illustration of the 2.5 H daylighting guideline. KATE BECKLEY

4.64 The 15/30 daylighting guideline—although not linked to a specific window height, there is a presumption that an adequate and appropriate sidelighting aperture has been provided. KATE BECKLEY

SAMPLE PROBLEM
The use of daylight zoning is illustrated in Figure 4.62. Application of the 2.5 H and 15/30 rules is illustrated in the Sidelighting strategy.

TABLE 4.4 Example illuminance and usage schedule analysis

SPACE TYPE	ILLUMINANCE EXPECTATIONS		USAGE SCHEDULE	DAYLIGHTING POTENTIAL
	AMBIENT	TASK		
Retail	High	High	10 A.M.–5 P.M.	Little
Meeting Room	Low	High	8 A.M.–5 P.M.	Ambient
Restroom	Low	Low	10 A.M.–5 P.M.	Ambient and Task
Office	Low	High	8 A.M.–6 P.M.	Ambient
Gallery	Low	High	10 A.M.–5 P.M.	Ambient

4. Group rooms into zones based upon similar lighting needs (considering ambient and task needs), complementary schedules, corresponding uses, and thermal comfort requirements.

5. Arrange building massing, plans, and sections to allow these zones to optimize daylighting potential by placing zones with higher illuminance needs nearest daylighting apertures and zones with lower illuminance needs further from daylighting apertures.

6. Verify the potential performance of daylighting strategies for each of the different daylight zones. Two general guidelines—the 2.5 H rule and the 15/30 rule—are useful tools in this regard during the schematic design phase (as explained below).

Most rooms in a large building have, at most, one exterior wall with access to daylight. Windows along an exterior wall constitute the most commonly used daylighting strategy—sidelighting. With sidelighting, daylight levels in a room will tend to be higher on the aperture side of the room and decrease moving away from the aperture wall. The 2.5 H guideline (as shown in Figure 4.63) can be used to estimate how far into a room usable daylight derived from sidelighting will reach. This rule suggests that significant levels of daylight will only reach into the room a distance of 2.5 times the height of the aperture window.

In large, multistory buildings the ability to utilize daylighting wisely is often a result of the shape of the plan and the adjacency of a particular space to an exterior wall. Figure 4.64 shows a relatively common situation leading to the 15/30 guideline that is also useful for schematic design. This rule suggests that with good window design, on average a 15-ft [4.6 m] deep zone next to a window can be illuminated chiefly by daylighting, and a secondary 15-ft [4.6 m] deep zone (between 15 and 30 ft [4.6 and 9.1 m] from the window) can be illuminated by daylighting supplemented by electric lighting. Spaces farther than 30 ft [9.1 m] from a window will need to be lit entirely by electric lighting, if there is no opportunity for toplighting or sidelighting from a second source.

ENVELOPE

LIGHTING

HEATING

COOLING

ENERGY PRODUCTION

WATER & WASTE

Examples

4.65 Daylit computer area in the Queen's Building at DeMontfort University in Leicester, UK, showing coordination of electric lighting fixtures with sidelighting zones. THERESE PEFFER

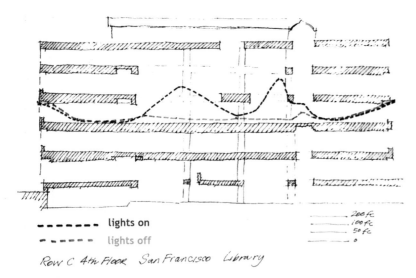

– – – – – **lights on**

– – – – – lights off

————— 200 fc
————— 100 fc
————— 50 fc
————— 0

Row C 4th Floor San Francisco Library

4.66 Illuminance measurements taken throughout the San Francisco Public Library in San Francisco, California with the electric lighting on and off suggest the designer zoned particular spaces for daylighting from windows and skylights.

4.67 Three distinct daylight zones—reading cubicles, corridor, and stack area—in the Mt. Angel Abbey Library in St. Benedict, Oregon.

Further Information

Ander, G.D. 2003. *Daylighting Performance and Design*, 2nd ed. John Wiley & Sons, New York.

Baker, N., A. Fanchiotti and K. Steemers (eds). 1993. *Daylighting in Architecture: A European Reference Book*. Earthscan/James & James, London.

Bell, J. and W. Burt. 1996. *Designing Buildings for Daylight*. BRE Press, Bracknell Berkshire, UK.

Brown, G.Z. and M. DeKay. 2001. *Sun, Wind & Light: Architectural Design Strategies*, 2nd ed. John Wiley & Sons, New York.

CIBSE. 1999. *Daylighting and Window Design*. The Chartered Institution of Building Services Engineers, London.

CIBSE. 2004. *Code for Lighting*. The Chartered Institution of Building Services Engineers, London.

Guzowski, M. 2000. *Daylighting for Sustainable Design*. McGraw-Hill, New York.

Moore, F. 1985. *Concepts and Practice of Architectural Daylighting*. Van Nostrand Reinhold, New York.

Rea, M.S. ed. 2000. *IESNA Lighting Handbook*, 9th ed. Illuminating Engineering Society of North America, New York.

BEYOND SCHEMATIC DESIGN

During design development, careful consideration and design of daylighting controls—time clocks, photocontrols (open loop versus closed loop), and switching versus dimming—is critical to an energy-saving daylighting system. Open loop controls sense incoming daylight and raise electric lighting to a predetermined level to augment the daylight. Closed loop controls sense the combined effect of daylight and electric light in the space, and raise the electric lighting until a target illuminance is met. Open loop systems are cheaper and easier to commission. If a building doesn't require a complex control system, simpler is better. Industrial, and many retail, buildings can use switching strategies instead of dimming. Switching is cheaper and the controls are simpler.

ENVELOPE

LIGHTING

HEATING

COOLING

ENERGY PRODUCTION

WATER & WASTE

NOTES

TOPLIGHTING is a daylighting strategy that uses apertures located at the roof plane as the point of admission for ambient daylight. Any system that delivers daylight onto a horizontal task plane generally from above is considered a toplighting strategy—a few of which include skylights as the daylight aperture, sawtooth roof glazing arrangements, or clerestories located high within a space often in concert with a reflecting ceiling plane.

Toplighting allows for the consistent introduction of daylight into a space while allowing for reasonably easy control of direct glare. Any toplighting strategy must address the control of direct solar radiation, as such intense radiation/light can cause glare and adds unnecessary heat gains to a space. Toplighting is an ideal strategy under overcast sky conditions because overcast skies have a greater luminance at the zenith (overhead) than at the horizon. Toplighting is usually easily coordinated with electric lighting systems.

4.68 Skylight with large splayed distribution surfaces at Mt. Angel Abbey Library in St. Benedict, Oregon.

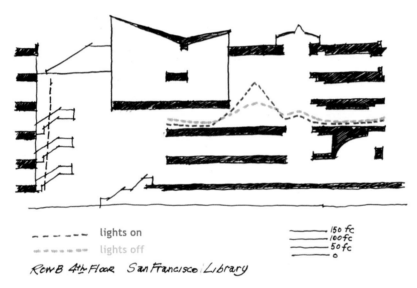

lights on
lights off

150 fc
100 fc
50 fc
0

Row B 4th Floor San Francisco Library

4.69 Conceptual diagram of a toplighting system at the San Francisco Public Library in San Francisco, California. Illuminance measurements with the electric lighting on and off show the light distribution through the space and the influence of daylight from the skylights.

Key Architectural Issues

Toplighting liberates the walls of a space. Daylighting from above, rather than the sides, allows for greater latitude in how the walls of a space are used. Additionally, light scoops, clerestories, roof monitors, and skylights all provide opportunities for architectural expression in the building form. An inherent limitation to toplighting is single story construction (or toplighting only the uppermost floor of a multistory building). A toplit building can, however, have great depth—as lighting access is not limited to the walls (and is freed of the 2.5 H rule). Toplighting encourages the activation of the ceiling plane, an area often forgotten in the design process.

INTENT
Task visibility, energy efficiency, occupant satisfaction

EFFECT
Reduced consumption of electricity, a high likelihood of improved occupant satisfaction, potentially reduced cooling loads

OPTIONS
Numerous options for apertures and their integration into roof forms, various shading devices and techniques

COORDINATION ISSUES
Design intent, spatial functions and tasks, building/aperture orientation, solar heat gain, electric lighting system controls

RELATED STRATEGIES
Daylight Factor, Daylight Zoning, Sidelighting, Electric Lighting, Internal Reflectances, cooling strategies, building envelope strategies, Shading Devices

LEED LINKS
Energy & Atmosphere, Indoor Environmental Quality

PREREQUISITES
Design intent, preliminary spatial layout, daylight factor criteria

ENVELOPE

LIGHTING

HEATING

COOLING

ENERGY PRODUCTION

WATER & WASTE

Implementation Considerations

Proper detailing is essential in toplighting strategies. No amount of daylight will convince users that a leaky roof is acceptable. Direct solar radiation must also be addressed. Toplighting could exacerbate solar gain in the summer by allowing high altitude sun angles entry into a space—if not properly shaded (e.g. using a skylight versus a sawtooth monitor). Direct solar radiation can cause substantial visual discomfort due to excessive contrast. While a "dazzle" effect is sometimes desirable, it is inappropriate for tasks on the work surface. Finally, consider that most building users want a visual connection to the outdoors regardless of interior illuminance, which will not be provided by translucent skylights.

Design Procedure

This procedure presumes that the merits of toplighting versus sidelighting have been considered and toplighting selected as the approach of interest. This does not preclude the use of combined toplighting and sidelighting systems. Illuminances are additive, such that the contribution of one system can be added to that of another system.

1. Establish target daylight factors for the various spaces and activities to be toplit. See the Daylight Factor strategy for suggested daylight factors.

2. Arrange the building spaces and floor plan layouts such that those areas to be toplit have a roof exposure.

3. Determine what type of toplighting aperture (e.g. skylight, clerestory, sawtooth, light scoop, roof monitor) is most appropriate for the space, building orientation, sky conditions, and climate. This is a complex design issue and there is no single best answer (although horizontal skylights should generally be avoided in hot climates).

4. Evaluate different glazing options for the aperture. In general the glazing should have a high visible transmittance (VT) value to maximize daylight entry. In hot climates a low solar heat gain coefficient (SHGC) is generally desirable to minimize solar heat gains. Often a compromise between VT and SHGC is in order. Manufacturers' catalogs are suggested as a valuable source of current information.

5. Estimate the size of daylighting apertures required to provide the target daylight factors as follows (derived from Millet and Bedrick, 1980):

$$A = ((DF_{avg})(A_{floor})) / (AE)$$

where,
A = required area of aperture, ft^2 $[m^2]$

SAMPLE PROBLEM

A 4500 ft^2 [418 m^2] ball-bearing factory in Brazil will be toplit to lower energy costs and provide a more pleasant working environment.

1. A daylight factor of 4–8% is considered appropriate for fine machine work. The designer selects a 6% DF.

2. The factory is a single story building; all spaces have roof exposure.

3. The design team decides to use a vertical roof monitor aperture to more easily control the intense direct solar radiation that occurs in this climate.

4. A high VT glass is chosen because the aperture will be shaded by external shading devices (rather than by the glazing itself).

5. For a vertical monitor the area of glazing is estimated as: (DF) (floor area) / AE

$$A = (0.06)(4500 \, ft^2) / (0.2)$$
$$= 1350 \, ft^2 \, [125 \, m^2]$$

1350 ft^2 [125 m^2] of monitor glazing will be distributed evenly across the roof to facilitate a balanced distribution of daylight.

DF_{avg} = target daylight factor
A_{floor} = illuminated floor area, ft^2 [m^2]
AE = aperture effectiveness factor (see Table 4.5)

TABLE 4.5. Toplighting aperture effectiveness (AE) factors

APERTURE TYPE	AE FACTOR
Vertical monitors/clerestories	0.20
North-facing sawtooth	0.33
Horizontal skylights	0.50

Note the inherent luminous efficiency of horizontal skylights expressed in the above values (while remembering their potential for heat gain).

6. Arrange surfaces adjacent to the toplighting apertures to diffuse entering light to reduce contrast (a potential cause of glare) and more evenly distribute daylight throughout the space.

7. Evaluate the need for shading for the toplighting apertures and design appropriate devices to provide the necessary shading. The assumption that daylighting provides more energy-efficient illumination than electric lighting is dependent upon the exclusion of direct solar radiation from daylighting apertures. Failure to provide appropriate shading will result in increased cooling loads and the potential for glare.

Examples

6. The roof form is designed to improve the diffusion and distribution of daylight—to the extent practical in schematic design.

7. A shading device to block direct solar radiation during the summer is designed; the device also facilitates a more diffuse distribution of light.

4.70 A clerestory "oculus" provides toplighting (integrated with electric lighting) at the Ryan Library at Point Loma Nazarene University in San Diego, California. ED GOHLICH

4.71 Pod monitor skylight at the Arup Campus Solihull in Blythe Valley Park, Solihull, UK. One of the dual-function roof pods as seen from the roof (left) and from the floor below (right). ARUP ASSOCIATES | TISHA EGASHIRA

ENVELOPE

LIGHTING

HEATING

COOLING

ENERGY PRODUCTION

WATER & WASTE

ENVELOPE

LIGHTING

HEATING

COOLING

ENERGY PRODUCTION

WATER & WASTE

4.72 Multiuse room with toplighting and sidelighting to provide even daylight distribution at the Christopher Center at Valparaiso University, Indiana. © PETER AARON/ESTO

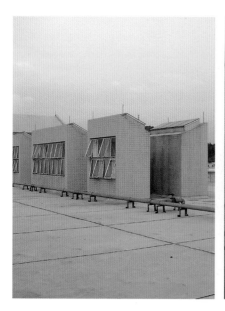 

4.73 Skylight and clerestory monitors on the roof (left) of the administration building at Guandong Pei Zheng Commercial College in Huadu, China; resulting toplighting distributed by light wells (right) provides illumination for four floors along a circulation corridor.

4.74 The Hood River Public Library (left) in Hood River, Oregon uses daylight and natural ventilation strategies; a long, clerestory monitor (right) illuminates the main reading area in the Library addition. FLETCHER FARR AYOTTE, INC.

4.75 A glass canopy over the Great Court spans between the old and new portions of the British Museum in London, UK and provides delightful toplighting.

ENVELOPE

LIGHTING

HEATING

COOLING

ENERGY PRODUCTION

WATER & WASTE

ENVELOPE

LIGHTING

HEATING

COOLING

ENERGY PRODUCTION

WATER & WASTE

4.76 Toplighting washes brick walls with light in an interior courtyard in Montepulciano, Italy.

Further Information

Evans, B. 1981. *Daylight in Architecture*. Architectural Record Books, New York.

International Energy Agency. 2000. *Daylight in Buildings*. Lawrence Berkeley National Laboratory, Berkeley, CA.

Millet, M. and J. Bedrick. 1980. *Graphic Daylighting Design Method*. U.S. Department of Energy/Lawrence Berkeley National Laboratory, Washington, DC.

Moore, F. 1985. *Concepts and Practice of Architectural Daylighting*. Van Nostrand Reinhold, New York.

Stein, B. et al. 2006. *Mechanical and Electrical Equipment for Buildings*, 10th ed. John Wiley & Sons, Hoboken, NJ.

Whole Building Design Guide, "Daylighting."
www.wbdg.org/design/daylighting.php

BEYOND SCHEMATIC DESIGN

The preliminary sizing of apertures undertaken during schematic design will be verified by more accurate modeling studies during design development. Aperture details (including shading and diffusing elements) will be finalized during design development, along with integration of daylighting and electric lighting controls. Commissioning of daylighting-related controls is strongly recommended.

SIDELIGHTING is a daylighting strategy that uses apertures located in the wall planes as the point of admission for ambient daylight. Any system that delivers daylight onto a horizontal task plane generally from the side is considered sidelighting. Sidelighting approaches often utilize windows as the daylight aperture—but glass block, low clerestories, and vertical openings into light courts or atria would also be considered sidelighting approaches.

4.78 Conceptual diagram of a sidelighting system showing typical light distribution pattern in a space and attention to aperture detail. KATE BECKLEY

The same windows that allow daylight into a building can provide a visual connection to the outside. The relationship of window height (and hence ceiling height) to room depth is an important consideration with respect to daylight factor. Window height is also a key determinant of views (along with site conditions). Sidelighting systems often involve two distinct apertures—a lower view and daylight window and an upper daylight-only window associated with a light shelf.

Most daylighting systems are designed assuming that no direct solar radiation enters the building through the apertures. First, the direct solar component is not needed to provide adequate daylight factors (illuminance) in most climates during most of the day. Second, direct solar radiation brings unwanted heat gain—which if admitted into a building will greatly decrease the luminous efficacy of daylight. Third, direct solar radiation admittance greatly increases the potential for direct glare experiences. Thus, some form of shading should be used in conjunction with sidelighting—the exception being north-facing windows. Admittance of solar radiation via sidelighting apertures as part of a direct gain passive heating system is an exception to the direct solar radiation exclusion discussed above.

4.77 Sidelighting a corridor using glazed recessed doors; the Hearst Memorial Gymnasium, University of California Berkeley, Berkeley, California.

INTENT
Task visibility, energy efficiency, occupant satisfaction, views

EFFECT
Reduced consumption of electricity, improved occupant satisfaction, potentially reduced cooling loads, visual relief

OPTIONS
Numerous options for apertures, shading devices, light shelves, light courts, and atria

COORDINATION ISSUES
Design intent, spatial functions and tasks, building/facade orientation, solar heat gain, electric lighting system controls

RELATED STRATEGIES
Daylight Factor, Daylight Zoning, Toplighting, Light Shelves, Direct Gain, Shading Devices, Internal Reflectances, Electric Lighting, cooling strategies, building envelope strategies

LEED LINKS
Energy & Atmosphere, Indoor Environmental Quality

PREREQUISITES
Design intent, preliminary spatial layout, daylight factor criteria

ENVELOPE

LIGHTING

HEATING

COOLING

ENERGY PRODUCTION

WATER & WASTE

ENVELOPE

LIGHTING

HEATING

COOLING

ENERGY PRODUCTION

WATER & WASTE

Key Architectural Issues

Windows have a rich architectural history, from Gothic cathedrals to the modern glass curtain wall or double envelope. Windows, however, are not synonymous with sidelighting. How a given window sees the sky (or not), how it is detailed, how it relates to the task plane and bounding room surfaces, and the type of glazing used are all important to a daylighting system. Sidelighting favors tall, shallow rooms. Sidelighting is a very visible design strategy because apertures have a dominant presence. Windows often define the character of a building facade.

The relationship between windows and interior surfaces is an important design consideration, as such surfaces act as secondary light sources and assist with distribution and diffusion of daylight.

Implementation Considerations

Glazing selection is important to toplighting, but is especially so to sidelighting. Daylight aperture glazing should have a high visible transmittance (VT) value, but also often needs to meet building/energy code requirements for solar heat gain coefficient (SHGC). Large areas of glazing can affect mean radiant temperatures in perimeter spaces, so an appropriate U-factor to mitigate glazing surface temperatures is another consideration.

A daylighting system will save no energy unless it displaces electric lighting. It is thus critical that the daylighting and electric lighting systems in a space be closely coordinated and that appropriate controls to dim or turn off unnecessary electric lamps be provided. Continuous dimming controls have proven to be well accepted by users, but difficult to properly implement and maintain in practice.

Design Procedure

This procedure presumes that the merits of sidelighting versus toplighting have been considered and sidelighting selected as the approach of interest. This does not preclude the use of combined sidelighting and toplighting systems. Illuminances are additive, such that the contribution of one system can be added to that of another system.

The design of a sidelighting system is not a purely linear process. Several iterations are often necessary to determine the most appropriate implementation.

1. Establish target daylight factors for each space and activity. Recommended daylight factors for various spaces can be found in the Daylight Factor strategy.

2. Arrange program elements into a footprint that maximizes wall area (surface area to volume ratio)—using, for example, U-shaped buildings, courtyards/atria, long thin building plans. Maximize opportunities for daylighting without direct solar radiation by focusing upon the north and south orientations as prime locations

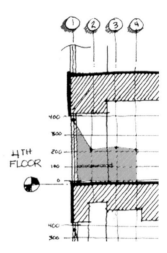

4.79 Illuminance measurements taken at increments from a window in the reading area of the San Francisco Public Library in San Francisco, California.

for daylight apertures. East and west apertures require careful consideration of shading devices to reduce the potential for direct glare and unwanted solar gains.

3. Organize the building floor plan with spaces that will benefit the most from daylighting located along the perimeter of the building. Spaces with a lesser need for daylight (or lower illuminance requirements) can be placed in the interior and arranged to borrow light from perimeter spaces.

4. Determine the depth of the space to be daylit, as required by programmatic needs. Depth is the distance inward from the perimeter wall.

5. Divide the depth of the room by 2.5 to determine the minimum top-of-window (head) height needed to effectively sidelight a space of this depth.

6. Verify that the required window head height (measured from the floor) is acceptable (or feasible). Not all of the window height needs to be "view" window. Areas above a reasonable view height can be glazed solely for daylight admittance. When this approach is taken, the two window elements are often separated by a light shelf (see the strategy on Light Shelves).

7. Multiply the proposed window width by 2 to determine the extent of horizontal (parallel to the window plane) light penetration. Ensure that the window width is adequate to provide daylight coverage across the full room width. (This approximation assumes an even distribution of glazing across the width of the window wall.)

8. Modify the proposed glazing width and head height as required to work within the above constraints.

9. Determine the required area of daylighting aperture by using the following estimates (derived from Millet and Bedrick, 1980):

$$A = ((DF_{target}) (A_{floor})) / (F)$$

where,
A = required area of aperture, ft^2 [m^2]
DF_{target} = target daylight factor
A_{floor} = illuminated floor area, ft^2 [m^2]
F = 0.2 if the target is an average daylight factor *OR*
　　0.1 if the target is a minimum daylight factor

Note: any window area below task height is of little use for daylighting.

10. Refine the design to maximize the effectiveness of daylight admitted via sidelighting. Arrange primary building structural elements to maximize light penetration into the space. For example, primary beams should run perpendicular to the fenestration plane. Verify appropriate visual connections with the exterior via any view windows. Analyze the potential for glare. Design shading as required by the orientation of the window (see the Shading Devices strategy).

4. A depth of 20 ft [6.1 m] is proposed for the open-plan workspaces.

5. (20 ft / 2.5) = 8 ft [2.4 m] is the required height of the top of the window.

6. Local building ordinances make floor-to-floor height a limiting design factor. A maximum window height of 8 ft [2.4 m] is feasible. A task of height of 30 in. [760 mm] makes the usable window height 5.5 ft [1.7 m].

7. A window more or less the width of the space (less mullions) is proposed, so window width is not a limiting factor.

8. No adjustments to proposed window width are required.

9. Considering a unit width (1 ft or 1 m) of floor, the required area of aperture to obtain a *minimum* DF of 2.5% is:

A = (0.025) (20) / (0.1)
　 = 5 ft^2 [0.5 m^2]

The proposed window area is feasible and fits within the constraints of the design, while providing the target daylight factor.

10. Refine elements of the proposed design to minimize glare, control direct solar gain, and beneficially diffuse daylight.

ENVELOPE

LIGHTING

HEATING

COOLING

ENERGY PRODUCTION

WATER & WASTE

ENVELOPE

LIGHTING

HEATING

COOLING

ENERGY PRODUCTION

WATER & WASTE

Examples

4.80 Bilateral sidelighting from view windows and clerestories in a computer lab at the Global Ecology Research Center at Stanford University, Palo Alto, California. © PETER AARON/ESTO

4.81 A lounge in the Christopher Center at Valparaiso University, Indiana, demonstrates a "wall washing" daylighting technique with the glazing aperture directly adjacent to a light-colored wall. © PETER AARON/ESTO

4.82 Sidelighting through tall windows (left) and toplighting via a skylight (right) at the Raffles Hotel in Singapore.

4.83 North-facing clerestories and operable windows at reading areas provide diffuse sidelighting at the Mt. Angel Abbey Library in St. Benedict, Oregon.

ENVELOPE

LIGHTING

HEATING

COOLING

ENERGY PRODUCTION

WATER & WASTE

Further Information

Evans, B. 1981. *Daylight in Architecture*. Architectural Record Books, New York.

International Energy Agency. 2000. *Daylight in Buildings*. Lawrence Berkeley National Laboratory, Berkeley, CA.

Millet, M. and J. Bedrick. 1980. *Graphic Daylighting Design Method*, U.S. Department of Energy/Lawrence Berkeley National Laboratory, Washington, DC.

Moore, F. 1985. *Concepts and Practice of Architectural Daylighting*. Van Nostrand Reinhold, New York.

Stein, B. et al. 2006. *Mechanical and Electrical Equipment for Buildings*, 10th ed. John Wiley & Sons, Hoboken, NJ.

Whole Building Design Guide, "Daylighting." www.wbdg.org/design/daylighting.php

BEYOND SCHEMATIC DESIGN

Preliminary estimates of sidelighting performance will be refined via more detailed analysis during design development. Glazing, shading, and distribution elements will be considered, selected, and specified. Electric lighting and control systems will be addressed during design development. Controls for integrating daylighting and electric lighting must be commissioned.

ENVELOPE

LIGHTING

HEATING

COOLING

ENERGY PRODUCTION

WATER & WASTE

LIGHT SHELVES

ENVELOPE

LIGHTING

HEATING

COOLING

ENERGY PRODUCTION

WATER & WASTE

LIGHT SHELVES are used to more evenly distribute daylight entering a building through sidelighting apertures (typically windows). Light bounces off the reflective surfaces of the shelf and subsequently off the ceiling and creates a more even illuminance pattern than would occur without a shelf. The form, material, and position of a light shelf determine the distribution of incoming daylight. A light shelf may be placed on the exterior or interior of a building or both; the defining element is that there is glazing directly above the plane of the shelf. The glazing above a light shelf is solely for daylighting. Glazing below a light shelf can provide for view, as well as daylighting.

4.84 Conceptual sketch of a light shelf in an office. GREG HARTMAN

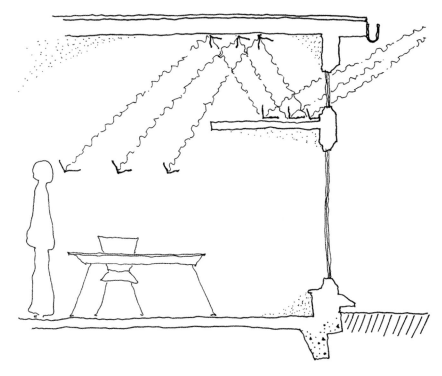

4.85 Section through an exterior wall with sidelighting apertures, showing typical placement of a light shelf. KATE BECKLEY

By redirecting incoming daylight and increasing light diffusion, a well-designed light shelf will add to the physical and visual comfort of a space and reduce the use of electric lighting by increasing daylight factors away from the aperture and reducing contrast caused by daylighting within a space. An exterior light shelf may also serve as a sunshading device for lower glazing areas, thereby reducing cooling loads by reducing solar gains.

Light shelves are often used in offices and schools where an even distribution of daylight is desirable for visual comfort and a more even distribution of daylight can reduce electric lighting costs.

Key Architectural Issues

A light shelf does not need to look like a shelf. With an understanding of sky conditions, the path of the sun and its seasonal variations, and the use

INTENT
More even and somewhat deeper distribution of daylight, reduction of glare potential

EFFECT
Reduced electrical lighting usage, potential for reduced cooling load

OPTIONS
Exterior, interior, or continuous shelves; fixed or adjustable

COORDINATION ISSUES
Ceiling design, daylighting aperture, glazing, internal partitions, orientation, shading, heat gain

RELATED STRATEGIES
Daylight Factor, Internal Reflectances, Shading Devices

LEED LINKS
Energy & Atmosphere, Indoor Environmental Quality

PREREQUISITES
Preliminary room layout (geometry), information on room orientation, site latitude, sun angles, site obstructions

ENVELOPE

LIGHTING

HEATING

COOLING

ENERGY PRODUCTION

WATER & WASTE

and layout of a space, creative options can enhance the facade of a building. Light shelves should be considered in conjunction with the type, size, and placement of daylight apertures, reveals, walls, ceilings, materials, and furniture. Designing in section—and with consideration of these related elements—it should be possible to maximize the amount and optimize the placement of light that is redirected by a light shelf.

A light shelf is often an appropriate solution to the problem of providing a reasonably even distribution of daylight in a building with unilateral sidelighting. In some situations (such as very deep spaces or where ceiling height is restricted) other methods of redirecting daylight, such as light scoops, light pipes, prismatic devices, and anidolic zenithal collectors may be more appropriate. A bilateral aperture arrangement is very appropriate for deep spaces.

Implementation Considerations

Orientation. Light shelves can be effective shading devices on south-facing facades in the northern hemisphere. Light shelves will typically capture additional direct solar radiation for redistribution when located on a south facade; this benefit must be tempered, however, against the additional cooling load contributed by this captured solar radiation.

Shelf height and angle. Light shelves should be located above eye level to reduce the potential of glare from the reflective upper shelf surface. Depending upon the use of the area adjacent to the windows, light shelves may also need to be above head height. Horizontal light shelves are very common because they can provide a balance of light distribution, glare control, shading performance, and aesthetic potential. Tilted light shelves, however, may provide better performance (a design decision to be verified during design development).

Ceiling. A high ceiling is desirable for light shelf applications. If floor-to-floor height is tight, sloping the ceiling upward toward the window aperture may prove useful (although the effect of this move is disputed).

Windows. Higher windows allow daylight to penetrate deeper into a space. Above a light shelf, clear, double-paned glazing is recommended for most climates. A horizontal louvered shading device may be installed between the panes. If there is glazing below a light shelf for view, make a climate-appropriate, view-appropriate, selection.

Shading. Use horizontal blinds for the glazing above a light shelf as necessary to block direct solar radiation and (when oriented at roughly 45°) to direct light to the ceiling. Design a separate shading solution to protect glazing below the light shelf from solar gain.

Finishes. Consider splaying window reveals and frames to reduce contrast. A specular (mirror-like) finish on a light shelf may increase daylight levels, but can also become a potential source of glare. A semi-specular (but still quite reflective) finish is generally preferable. A matte finish will also provide more diffuse light distribution (Figure 4.86). The ceiling and walls of a daylit space should be smooth and reflective, but not so much that they become a source of glare. Consider the effect that partition design, furniture layout, and interior finishes will have on

4.86 A matte, light-colored finish on the top of this light shelf diffuses daylight in multiple directions. Fluorescent lighting fixtures are integrated along the edge of the shelf.

increasing daylight penetration and reducing glare. Consider the interrelated effect of all interior design decisions.

Maintenance. Consider how interior and/or exterior light shelves might be maintained. Dust and debris reduce the reflectivity of a light shelf. Interior light shelves can be designed to fold down for easy maintenance. For exterior light shelves, consider rain runoff, snow collection, and disruption of potentially beneficial airflow patterns along the facade.

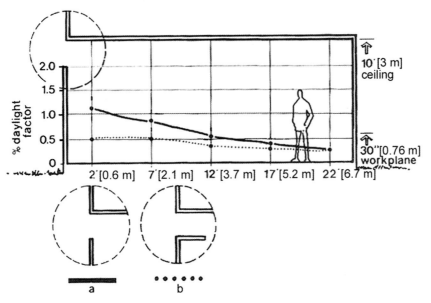

4.87 Effect of the position of a white-colored light shelf on interior illuminance (daylight factor), with clear glazing and overcast sky. No light shelf (a) and interior light shelf (b). FULLER MOORE

Design Procedure

1. Determine if an external, internal, or dual light shelf is more appropriate for the intended use of the space. An exterior light shelf can even out daylight levels in a space while providing protection from solar gain through the lower glazing. An interior light shelf may decrease daylight levels, particularly in the window vicinity, but provide a more even light distribution with less contrast within a space (see Figure 4.87).

2. Sketch the proposal in section. For an exterior south-facing light shelf, estimate the depth as roughly equal to the difference between the height of the shelf and the work plane. For an interior light shelf, estimate the depth of the shelf as roughly equal to the height of the glazing above it. The top surface of a light shelf should be at least 2 ft [0.6 m] from the ceiling. The ceiling height should be at least 9 ft [3 m].

3. Create a daylighting model to test a proposed design. The model must be large enough to evaluate the rather subtle effects of light shelves and to allow distinct measurements to be made in the space of most interest. See Moore or Evans for recommendations on preparing daylighting models.

SAMPLE PROBLEM
Sidelighting will be used with a 50 ft × 100 ft [15.3 × 30.5 m] open office space in a four-story building in Boca Raton, Florida. A window faces south. Ceiling height is 10 ft [3.1 m]; window height is 6 ft [1.8 m] with 2 ft [0.6 m] above the light shelf and 4 ft [1.2 m] below with a 3 ft [0.9 m] sill height.

1. The initial light shelf design proposes a dual (interior and exterior) light shelf.

2. Using the preliminary depth rules, the interior light shelf depth is proposed as 2 ft [0.6 m] and the exterior extension as (4 + 3 − 2.5) = 4.5 ft [1.4 m].

3. Study the performance of this proposed design using either

ENVELOPE

LIGHTING

HEATING

COOLING

ENERGY PRODUCTION

WATER & WASTE

ENVELOPE

LIGHTING

HEATING

COOLING

ENERGY PRODUCTION

WATER & WASTE

Examples

4.88 Light shelf in a classroom at Ash Creek Intermediate School, Independence, Oregon. Over time, teachers placed items on top of the light shelves, which interfered with the daylighting effectiveness.

4.89 Specular reflectors (another way of thinking about light shelves) at the top of an atrium in the Hong Kong Shanghai Bank, Hong Kong, direct daylight to floors below.

physical models or appropriate computer simulations. Adjust the design as suggested by the modeling studies and intended performance.

Further Information

Evans, B. 1981. *Daylight in Architecture*. Architectural Record Books, New York.

IEA. 2000. *Daylight in Buildings: A Source Book on Daylighting Systems and Components*. International Energy Agency. Available at: gaia.lbl.gov/iea21/ieapubc.htm

LBL. 1997. "Section 3: Envelope and Room Decisions," in *Tips for Daylighting With Windows*. Building Technologies Program, Lawrence Berkeley National Laboratory. Available at: windows.lbl.gov/daylighting/designguide/designguide.html

LRC. 2004. "Guide for Daylighting Schools." Developed by Innovative Design for Daylight Dividends, Lighting Research Center, Rensselaer Polytechnic Institute, Troy, NY. Available at: www.lrc.rpi.edu/programs/daylightdividends/pdf/guidelines.pdf

Moore, F. 1985. *Concepts and Practice of Architectural Daylighting*. Van Nostrand Reinhold, New York.

NREL. 2003. "Laboratories for the 21st Century: Best Practices" (NREL Report No. BR-710-33938; DOE/GO-102003-1766). National Renewable Energy Laboratory, U.S. Environmental Protection Agency/U.S. Department of Energy. Available at: www.nrel.gov/docs/fy04osti/33938.pdf

BEYOND SCHEMATIC DESIGN

The performance of a light shelf (as estimated during schematic design) will be verified and optimized during design development. Controls are the key to reducing energy use in a daylit building. Photosensor control for each row of lights, running parallel to the light shelf, is recommended. A light shelf must not interfere with sprinkler operation, diffuser performance, or natural ventilation airflows. Occupants will need to learn how (and should be trained via a User's Manual) to use any operable sun control devices. Establish a reasonable and documented maintenance schedule and routine.

ENVELOPE

LIGHTING

HEATING

COOLING

ENERGY PRODUCTION

WATER & WASTE

NOTES

ENVELOPE

LIGHTING

HEATING

COOLING

ENERGY PRODUCTION

WATER & WASTE

The INTERNAL REFLECTANCES of a space are governed by two primary surface characteristics of the bounding materials—color and texture. Color determines the quantity of light reflected from a surface. Dark-colored materials absorb light, whereas light-colored materials reflect light. Texture determines the quality of light leaving a surface. Rough textured surfaces, sometimes referred to as matte, create diffused reflected light. Smooth or glossy surfaces create specular reflected light. When lighting a space, diffuse light is preferable because specular reflections can lead to glare. In order to maximize the amount of light in a space it is important to choose light-colored finishes.

The dimensions of a space have a great influence over the internally reflected component of daylight (and also electric light). The further away a surface is from a light source, the more light that will be lost en route via interreflections: thus, the less light that will be available for illumination. A larger space has more opportunity for interreflections (losses) than a smaller space. This is true when designing in both plan and section.

4.90 Origami pieces at Haneda Airport in Japan provide filtered (and animated) light that enhance the space by internal reflectances.

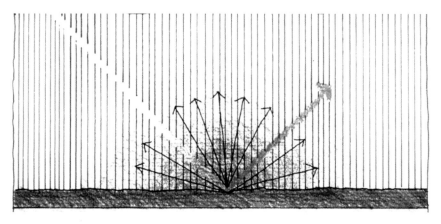

4.91 Light reflects off a specular surface at approximately the angle of incidence. Light disperses diffusely off a matte surface. VIRGINIA CARTWRIGHT

Key Architectural Issues

The reflectances of interior materials, the dimensions of the space, and the location of window apertures play key roles in determining the daylight factor at any given point within a space. The importance of having reflective finishes within a room becomes greater with increasing distance between the area to be lit and the source of light illuminating it.

Implementation Considerations

Inform both the client and interior architect/designer of the architectural intentions and assumptions concerning distribution of light in a space. A client's choice of colors and furnishings can reduce the effectiveness of even the best daylighting design.

Dirt accumulation and wear and tear will reduce surface brightness over time—an effect captured in a value called "light loss" or "maintenance"

INTENT
Optimized lighting effectiveness

EFFECT
Energy efficiency, visual comfort

OPTIONS
Numerous materials, finishes, and reflectances

COORDINATION ISSUES
Client's preferred finish materials and colors, tasks related to the space, visual comfort, furnishings, windows, electric lighting

RELATED STRATEGIES
Toplighting, Sidelighting, Daylight Factor, Light Shelves

LEED LINKS
Energy & Atmosphere, Indoor Environmental Quality

PREREQUISITES
This "strategy" is essentially a prerequisite for successful daylighting

ENVELOPE

LIGHTING

HEATING

COOLING

ENERGY PRODUCTION

WATER & WASTE

ENVELOPE

LIGHTING

HEATING

COOLING

ENERGY PRODUCTION

WATER & WASTE

factor. One (of several) key light loss factors is the room surface dirt depreciation factor, which is a function of room dimensions, atmospheric dirt conditions, and an estimate of cleaning/refurbishment intervals. This factor can reasonably range from 0.50 (terribly dirty environment) to 0.95 (pristine, well-maintained environment). The effect of dirt depreciation must be considered during the design process and results in a need for greater initial illuminance (so that an acceptable maintained illuminance is available over time). This relationship between initial, maintained, and design illuminance is as follows (where design illuminance represents the design criterion): initial illuminance $\geq$ maintained illuminance $\geq$ design illuminance.

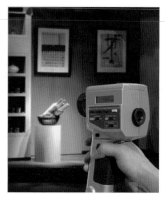

4.92 A precision luminance meter can be used to accurately measure the amount of light leaving a surface (i.e. surface brightness) in cd/m^2 or ft-L.
© PACIFIC GAS AND ELECTRIC COMPANY

4.93 An illuminance meter can be used to roughly estimate luminance. Measure the illuminance at the surface (left) and then measure the amount of light leaving (reflected from) the surface (right). The quantity of reflected light divided by the quantity of incident light is the surface reflectance. (Make sure that self-shadowing does not unduly interfere with the measurements.)

Design Procedure

1. Make sure that the window jamb and sill have a high reflectance, as they can make excellent reflectors. Splay deep jambs away from the window. Both of these design recommendations will increase daylight throughput as well as decrease the contrast between the interior and exterior environments (reducing glare potential).

2. The ceiling is the most important surface for daylighting. Choose a ceiling paint or tile that has a reflectance of 90% or higher to optimize light distribution within the space. Recommended minimum surface reflectances for energy-efficient lighting design are shown in Table 4.6. Use the upper limits of the reflectance ranges for spaces with more difficult daylighting constraints or requiring higher design illuminances.

3. Angling the ceiling toward the source of incoming light can increase the amount of light that is reflected. This works especially well with daylight coming from clerestory windows. Assuming that light is reflected at an angle equal to its incidence angle can assist in making decisions regarding ceiling surface angles.

SAMPLE PROBLEM
The adjacent procedure is best applied through use of a physical model.

TABLE 4.6   Recommended reflectances for interior surfaces in different spaces. *IESNA LIGHTING HANDBOOK*, 9TH ED.

SURFACE	RECOMMENDED REFLECTANCES		
	OFFICES	CLASSROOMS	RESIDENCES
Ceilings	>80%	70–90%	60–90%
Walls	50–70%	40–60%	35–60%
Floors	20–40%	30–50%	15–35%
Furnishings	25–45%	30–50%	35–60%

4. Choose light-colored furniture, fixtures, and equipment as they can significantly affect light distribution within a space (see Tables 4.7 and 4.8 for typical reflectances).

TABLE 4.7 Reflectances of common building and site materials. EXCERPTED FROM HOPKINSON ET AL. AND ROBBINS

MATERIAL	REFLECTANCE
Aluminum	85%
Asphalt	5–10%
Brick	10–30%
Concrete	20–30%
Gravel	20%
Plaster, white	40–80%
Water	30–70%
Vegetation	5–25%

TABLE 4.8 Reflectances of typical paint colors

COLOR	REFLECTANCE
White	80–90%
Pale blue	80%
Canary yellow	75%
Lemon yellow	65%
Dark cream	60%
Light blue	55%
Light green	50%
Light brown	50%
Apricot	45%
Apple green	40%
Medium brown	35%
Red-orange	30%
Dark red, blue, gray	15%
Black	5%

There is a great deal of variance among paint colors, names, and reflectances; the above are rough approximations.

ENVELOPE

LIGHTING

HEATING

COOLING

ENERGY PRODUCTION

WATER & WASTE

ENVELOPE

LIGHTING

HEATING

COOLING

ENERGY PRODUCTION

WATER & WASTE

Examples

4.94 Translucent and tinted side apertures introduce daylight and modify its color as it falls on concrete floors and ceilings at the Laban Centre in London, UK. DONALD CORNER

4.95 Colored walls within the light-capturing aperture in the St. Ignatius Chapel in Seattle, Washington reflect "borrowed" color onto otherwise white walls.

4.96 On-site luminance measurements (cd/m²) in the San Francisco Public Library with the electric lighting off (left) and the electric lighting on (right). Part of a study to examine the influence of light-reflective surfaces in daylit zones.

Further Information

Brown, G.Z and M. DeKay. 2001. *Sun, Wind and Light: Architectural Design Strategies,* 2nd ed. John Wiley & Sons, New York.

Hopkinson, R., P. Petherbridge and J. Longmore. 1966. *Daylighting.* Heinemann, London.

Rea, M. ed. 2000. *The IESNA Lighting Handbook*, 9th ed. Illuminating Engineering Society of North America, New York.

Robbins, C. 1986. *Daylighting: Design and Analysis.* Van Nostrand Reinhold, New York.

Stein, B. et al. 2006. *Mechanical & Electrical Equipment for Buildings,* 10th ed. John Wiley & Sons, Hoboken, NJ.

BEYOND SCHEMATIC DESIGN
Schematic design phase assumptions regarding reflectances of surfaces and furnishings must be passed on to the design development phase. Failure to communicate this critical information could result in decisions that degrade intended system performance. The importance of maintaining surface reflectances after occupancy should be conveyed to the building owner.

ENVELOPE

LIGHTING

HEATING

COOLING

ENERGY PRODUCTION

WATER & WASTE

ENVELOPE

LIGHTING

HEATING

COOLING

ENERGY PRODUCTION

WATER & WASTE

NOTES

SHADING DEVICES

ENVELOPE

LIGHTING

HEATING

COOLING

ENERGY PRODUCTION

WATER & WASTE

SHADING DEVICES can significantly reduce building heat gains from solar radiation while maintaining opportunities for daylighting, views, and natural ventilation. Conversely, carefully designed shading can admit direct solar radiation during times of the year when such energy is desired to passively heat a building. While the window (or skylight) is often the focus of shading devices, walls and roofs can also be shaded to help reduce heat gains through the opaque building envelope.

4.97 Movable shading devices on the Royal Danish Embassy, Berlin, Germany. CHRISTINA BOLLO

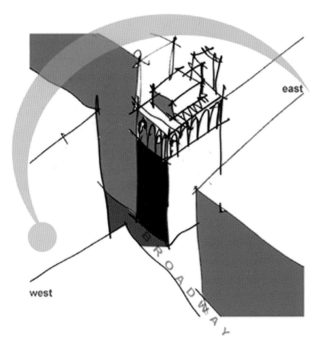

4.98 Appropriate shading design is dependent upon a number of physical variables, such as the path of the sun, nearby obstructions, time of day, orientation, and latitude.

Radiation is an energy form that does not require a material medium through which to travel. Energy from the sun reaches the earth entirely through radiation. Solar radiation consists of visible (light), ultraviolet, and infrared radiation components. When solar radiation strikes a surface, the radiation may be reflected, absorbed, or transmitted depending upon the nature of the surface. For example, a fair percentage of solar radiation passes through a typical window, while some of that transmitted solar radiation striking a floor will be absorbed (as heat) and some will be reflected.

The percentage of solar radiation that passes through a window and into a building depends upon the properties of the glass and the window assembly. Solar heat gain coefficient (SHGC) is a dimensionless number (generally falling between 0 and 1) that gives an indication of how much of the solar radiation incident upon a glazing assembly reaches the inside of a building. An SHGC of 1 means that 100% of incident solar radiation passes through the window or skylight. An SHGC of 0.2 indicates that 20% of the incident solar radiation is passed into the interior of the building. (It is important to remember that a window also transmits heat via conduction and convection.) Shading coefficient (SC)

INTENT
Energy efficiency (through screening of solar radiation when not needed and admitting it when desired), visual comfort

EFFECT
Reduced cooling load, solar access when desired, reduced glare

OPTIONS
Devices internal, integral, or external to the building envelope, operable or fixed

COORDINATION ISSUES
Building orientation and footprint, passive and active heating and cooling, natural ventilation

RELATED STRATEGIES
Sidelighting, Toplighting, Cross Ventilation, Direct Gain, Indirect Gain, Isolated Gain

LEED LINKS
Energy & Atmosphere, Indoor Environmental Quality

PREREQUISITES
Site latitude, window/wall orientation, skylight tilt/orientation, massing of neighboring buildings and trees, a sense of building heating and cooling loads

is an alternative (and more historic) measure used to quantify shading. Shading coefficient is the ratio of radiant heat flow through a particular window relative to the radiant heat flow through 1/8 in. [3.2 mm] thick, double strength, clear window glass. Shading coefficient only applies to the glazed portion of a window or skylight; solar heat gain coefficient applies to the glazing–frame combination.

Shading building envelope elements from direct radiation can dramatically lower heat gains during the cooling season. If the shading is from an internal device (like a blind, Figure 4.99, top), solar radiation gain through the window can be reduced on the order of 20%. However, if the shading is provided by an external device (as in Figure 4.99, bottom), the heat gain can be reduced by up to 80%. The preferred hierarchy for shading device placement is: external to the glazing, integral with the glazing, and then internal to the glazing.

Knowing the applicable sun paths at different times of the year allows the designer to create a shading device that provides shade when it is desirable to do so. Some shading devices use adjustable movable parts for the time of day or the year to optimize shading effects. Louvers can be moved to admit light or to block it, depending upon time of day, season, or orientation (Figure 4.100). Fixed shading devices are generally positioned for the difference between the high summer and low winter sun positions for shade in summer and sun in winter.

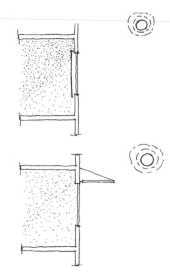

4.99 Internal (top) and external (bottom) shading devices.
KATE BECKLEY

Key Architectural Issues

The massing and orientation of a building are key determinants in designing a building that can be easily shaded. The east and west sides of a building are difficult to shade because of the low altitude of the rising and setting sun in the eastern and western skies. A building with long north and south facades and short east and west facades is much easier to shade. The north side of a building generally receives little direct solar radiation while the south side of a building sees high solar altitude angles during the summer months and low angles during the winter months.

A shading device should not compromise the other amenities that a window can provide—namely daylighting, views, and breezes. External shading devices do not necessarily have to be separate objects attached to a building exterior. Recessed window openings and facade geometry can allow a building to act as its own shading device.

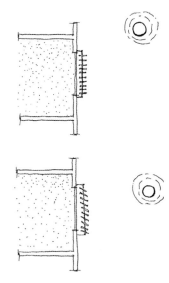

4.100 Movable shading device adjusts for high solar altitude (top) and low altitude (bottom).
KATE BECKLEY

Design Tools

Several tools are available for analyzing the extent and pattern of shade that will be provided by a particular shading device at varying latitudes, orientations, and times of the year. A sun path chart (or Sun Angle Calculator) can quickly provide the sun's altitude and azimuth angles for any specific latitude, month, day, and time of day. This manual tool will also provide the profile angle, the key angle for determining the extent of shading that a device will provide. The percentage of a window shaded on various dates can be determined.

The solar transit (Figure 4.101) is a device that can trace the path of the sun in the sky for any particular day of the year, on site. This is useful for determining the hours of sun available at a particular spot on a site. The solar transit method automatically takes into consideration obstructions to the sun such as neighboring buildings and/or trees. Various computer software packages will simulate the effects of solar radiation on three-dimensional virtual models. A simple massing model of a house (Figure 4.102), for example, clearly shows patterns of shade and direct sunlight on building surfaces and the adjacent site. At the site scale, a fisheye lens can be used to take a picture of the skydome at a particular point on a site. A sun path chart placed on the picture can determine the times during the year when that portion of the site will be shaded by obstructions (Figure 4.103).

A three-dimensional physical model and a sunpeg chart can be a powerful means to quickly study shading at various times of the year. The sunpeg chart is affixed to the physical model with the proper orientation (north arrow on the sunpeg chart pointing to north on the model). The model can be rotated and tilted under a direct light source while the sunpeg chart indicates the date and time the shading seen would actually be produced.

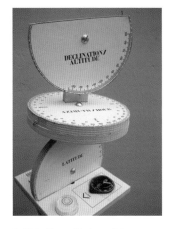

4.101 The solar transit is a useful device to trace the sun's path across the sky and create horizon shading masks for a particular location.

4.103 Sun path chart overlain onto a fisheye photo of the sky. ROBERT MARCIAL

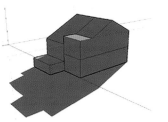

4.102 Cast shadows provided by a simple computer rendering of a massing model reveal patterns of solar irradiation and shading on a building and its site.

Implementation Considerations

Reflective surfaces on the top side of strategically placed horizontal sunshades can reflect light (and other radiation components) into a building. This can be used to bring more daylight into a building while simultaneously shading the majority of a window.

Plant shading can often be more effective than from a fixed shading device because sun angles do not always correlate to ambient air temperature (and a resulting need for heating or cooling). For example, the sun angles on the spring equinox (March 21) are identical to the sun angles on the fall equinox (September 21). However, in the northern

ENVELOPE

LIGHTING

HEATING

COOLING

ENERGY PRODUCTION

WATER & WASTE

ENVELOPE

LIGHTING

HEATING

COOLING

ENERGY PRODUCTION

WATER & WASTE

hemisphere, it is typically much warmer in late September than it is in late March, requiring more shading in September than in March. Deciduous plants respond more to temperature than to solar position. Leaves may not be present in early March, allowing sun to warm a building, while they are still on the trees in September, providing shading.

Design Procedure

1. Determine the shading requirements. Shading requirements are building- and space-specific and are dependent upon many variables including climate, building envelope design, building/space functions, visual comfort expectations, thermal comfort expectations, and the like. It is impossible to make generic statements about this first critical step in the design procedure.

2. Determine whether shading will be interior, exterior, or integral to glazing; whether movable or fixed. The project budget, facade design intents, importance of views and daylighting (among other considerations) will help determine which is most appropriate.

3. Develop a trial design for the shading device. Examples of shading devices and their applications (as richly given in *Solar Control and Shading Devices*) can greatly assist in this step.

4. Check the performance of the proposed shading device—using shading masks, computer simulations, or scale models as most appropriate to the project context and designer's experiences.

5. Modify the shading device design until the required performance is obtained and the design is considered acceptable with respect to other factors (daylighting, ventilation, aesthetics, etc.).

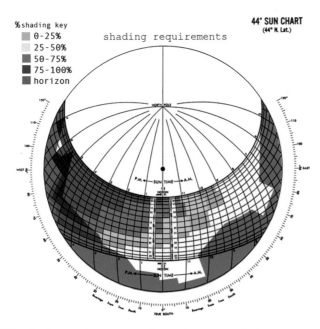

4.104 Building shading requirements superimposed on a sun path chart. RUSSELL BALDWIN, DOUGLAS KAEHLER, ZACHARY PENNELL, BRENT STURLAUGSON

SAMPLE PROBLEM
An office building in Eugene, Oregon with a south facade experiences high summer solar heat gains. An analysis of climate, internal heat gains, and building envelope yields the shading requirements shown in Figure 4.104. A bay of the south facade was modeled with a sunpeg chart used to check the performance of a proposed shading device at two opposite times of the year (Figures 4.105 and 4.106).

4.105 Performance of proposed shading device at 3:00 P.M. on June 21.

4.106 Performance of proposed shading device at 1:00 P.M. on December 21.

Examples

4.107 South-facing shaded outdoor balcony at Arizona State University School of Architecture, Tempe, Arizona.

4.108 South-facing facade with horizontal shading louvers on the Burton Barr Central Library in Phoenix, Arizona.

4.109 North-facing facade of the Burton Barr Central Library with "sail-fins" to shade against early morning and late evening sun during the summer months.

ENVELOPE

LIGHTING

HEATING

COOLING

ENERGY PRODUCTION

WATER & WASTE

ENVELOPE

LIGHTING

HEATING

COOLING

ENERGY PRODUCTION

WATER & WASTE

4.110 Newly planted wisteria vines will provide additional shading at Casa Nueva. RYAN JORDAN

4.111 Vertical fins provide shading from the western sun at Casa Nueva, Santa Barbara County Office Building in Santa Barbara, California. WILLIAM B. DEWEY

4.112 1 Finsbury Square (left) in London, UK uses classic, stout shading overhangs attached to a glass curtain wall and the Menara Mesiniaga (right) in Kuala Lumpur, Malaysia has horizontal shading bands to block the high equatorial sun. DONALD CORNER | ALISON KWOK

Further Information

Olgyay, A. and V. Olgyay. 1957. *Solar Control & Shading Devices.* Princeton University Press, Princeton, NJ.

Pacific Energy Center, Application Notes for Site Analysis, "Taking a Fisheye Photo." www.pge.com/pec/ (search on "fisheye")

Pilkington Sun Angle Calculator. Available through the Society of Building Science Educators. www.sbse.org/resources/index.htm

Solar Transit Template. Available through the Agents of Change Project, University of Oregon. aoc.uoregon.edu/loaner_kits/index.shtml

BEYOND SCHEMATIC DESIGN
Refined calculations of building heating and cooling loads, which impact the extent and timing of desired shading, will typically be made during design development. Ease of maintenance, cleaning of shading elements (birds like them), thermal breaks as appropriate, structure, and detailing to avoid trapping heat will be addressed.

ELECTRIC LIGHTING systems are one of the most energy-intensive components of modern buildings. A recent International Energy Agency report (Waide 2006) indicates that lighting accounts for around 19% of global electrical energy consumption and contributes carbon dioxide emissions equivalent to 70% of that caused by passenger vehicle emissions. The same report suggests that using compact fluorescents in place of incandescent lamps, using high-efficiency instead of low-efficiency ballasts, and replacing mercury vapor HID (high intensity discharge) lamps with more efficient alternatives would reduce global lighting demand by up to 40%—with a concomitant impact on global electricity use.

4.113 Daylight-integrated electric lighting controlled by photosensors in a classroom at Clackamas High School in Clackamas, Oregon.

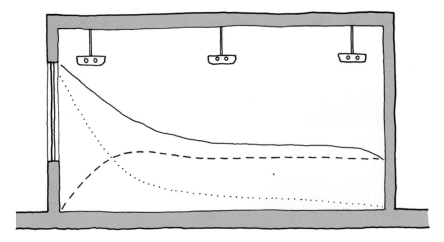

4.114 The conceptual basis of energy efficiency in electric lighting system design (use only what is needed). NICHOLAS RAJKOVICH

A "green" electrical lighting system will reduce lighting energy consumption, can (and most likely will) reduce energy consumption for space cooling, and should improve the visual comfort environment of a building—relative to a less efficient system. To maximize efficiency, electric lighting should be treated as a supplement to, not a replacement for, daylighting. A wide range of techniques is available to maximize the efficiency and quality of electric lighting systems. Technologically-based strategies include the selection of appropriate lamps, luminaires, and lighting controls. Architecturally-based strategies include the design of appropriate spatial geometries; the selection of appropriate surface finishes; and the thoughtful positioning of luminaires relative to spatial geometries, other system elements (such as ductwork), and sources of daylight.

Several key indices are used to express various efficiency aspects of electric lighting systems. These include:

Luminous efficacy. A measure (in lumens/watt) of the luminous (light) output of a lamp per watt of electrical input. The higher the luminous efficacy, the more light produced per watt of consumption. Luminous efficacies of commercially available lamps range from a low of around 20 to a high of around 120—a six-to-one ratio (see Figure 4.115). All else being equal, select the lamp with the highest luminous efficacy that will

INTENT
Visual performance, visual comfort, ambience, energy efficiency

EFFECT
Illuminance, luminance

OPTIONS
Innumerable combinations of lamps, luminaires, spatial geometries, and controls; daylight integration

COORDINATION ISSUES
Daylighting design, furniture and partition layout, automatic control systems

RELATED STRATEGIES
Daylight Factor, Internal Reflectances, Toplighting, Sidelighting

LEED LINKS
Energy & Atmosphere, Indoor Environmental Quality

PREREQUISITES
Established design intent and criteria, local lighting codes/standards (if applicable)

ENVELOPE

LIGHTING

HEATING

COOLING

ENERGY PRODUCTION

WATER & WASTE

ENVELOPE

LIGHTING

HEATING

COOLING

ENERGY PRODUCTION

WATER & WASTE

meet all project design criteria (color rendering, lamp lumen depreciation, life-cycle cost, etc.).

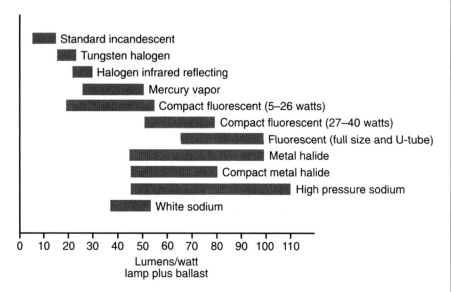

4.115 Luminous efficacies of common electric lamps. *IESNA LIGHTING HANDBOOK*, 9TH ED.

Fixture (or luminaire) efficiency. A measure of the ability of a luminaire to deliver light from a lamp; this is a dimensionless ratio of the lumens actually emitted from a luminaire to the lumens emitted by the lamp(s) installed in the luminaire. A higher luminaire efficiency is generally better—all else being equal.

Ballast factor (BF). A measure of the effectiveness of a given ballast–lamp combination relative to the performance of the same lamp operated with an ANSI-standard ballast (for that lamp type). This is a dimensionless index and higher is generally better—all else being equal.

Luminaire efficacy rating (LER). A measure of the efficacy of a lamp–ballast–luminaire combination. LER is calculated by dividing the product of luminaire efficiency times lamp lumens times ballast factor by the luminaire electrical input wattage. LER is expressed as lumens/watt and higher is generally better—all else being equal.

Coefficient of utilization (CU). A measure of the ability of a particular luminaire, installed in a particular spatial geometry with particular surface reflectances, to deliver light to a defined task plane. CU is dimensionless (essentially delivered lumens/lamp lumens) and is the most important metric of a lighting system's efficiency (although luminous efficacy is also certainly important). All else being equal, select the combination of elements (luminaire, room geometry, and reflectances) with the highest CU that will meet all project design criteria (illuminance, surface luminance, maintainability, life-cycle cost, etc.).

On conventional (non-green) projects, the above considerations are often not addressed until well into design development. In many designs, electric lighting is not even considered during schematic design (consider, for example, the typical university design studio project). When

ENVELOPE

LIGHTING

HEATING

COOLING

ENERGY PRODUCTION

WATER & WASTE

this is the case, some critical aspects of lighting design (such as spatial geometry) are decided (locked into place) without consideration of their impact on lighting system efficiency.

A truly energy-efficient electric lighting system is one that operates only when, and to the extent, required to meet design criteria. Unoccupied spaces do not generally need activated electric lighting systems; well-daylit spaces do not need electric light that increases illuminances beyond design criteria values. Controls are critical to efficient system operation. Lighting controls can also impact user satisfaction with an electric lighting system. Lighting controls fall into three general categories: manual, automatic, and hybrid. Manual controls are the most common and lowest first-cost means for controlling electric lighting in a space. Automated systems (using photosensitive dimming and switching to vary lamp intensity to maintain a constant illuminance in a space with fluctuating daylight availability and increasing light loss factors) can be the lowest life-cycle-cost means of control. Automatic occupancy sensors and timers can ensure that lamps are turned off when a space is unoccupied. Hybrid systems combine the energy efficiency of automation with some degree of manual user control—but must be accompanied by user education to avoid misuse/abuse.

Key Architectural Issues

The variability and adaptability of electric lighting systems allow their integration into a variety of architectural forms. These forms and their reflective/absorptive characteristics play a big role in the distribution of light from source to task. Ceiling height and view angles (the dimensions and shape of a space) will affect—and be affected by—electric lighting strategies and will also affect the potential for direct and reflected glare.

The location and sizing of windows will predetermine the electric lighting operation schedule (and resultant energy consumption) of a space.

Luminaire type and location are often a major architectural consideration. Luminaires (and their patterns) typically become highly visible design elements in a space as a result of their relative brightness and prominent locations.

Implementation Considerations

Electric lighting design for a green building cannot be deferred until design development. The impact of schematic design decisions on the need for and efficiency of electric lighting systems must be addressed during schematic design.

Design Procedure

1. Establish a comprehensive daylighting strategy for the building (see the daylighting strategies). Conceptualize how the

SAMPLE PROBLEM
As outlined in the adjacent procedure, considering lighting during schematic design involves

daylighting and electric lighting systems will interact and complement each other—especially via integrated controls.

2. Establish electric lighting system design intents and criteria. Such criteria will typically include appropriate requirements for task illuminances and surface luminances for the various visual tasks and space types and also express expectations for spatial ambience.

3. Establish needs and requirements for non-task-related lighting, including mood lighting, decorative lighting, and emergency lighting.

4. Select lamp types and associated luminaires to maximize light generation and delivery efficiency, while satisfying design intent relative to color rendering, glare control, first cost, and integration with daylighting systems. Lamp and luminaire selection are both important—as both contribute to the overall efficiency of an electric lighting system. Energy-efficient ballasts should be selected and provision made for controls that will permit lamps to be easily turned off or dimmed when not required. Selection of lamps, luminaires, and space finishes that will minimize light losses over time (as quantified via light loss factor—LLF) is critical. Over-lamping to mitigate lighting system degradation due to aging and dirt collection can easily add 25–40% to the energy demands of an electric lighting system.

Examples

4.116 Indirect fluorescent luminaires (lighting fixtures) direct light to a reflective ceiling recess in a computing center at the Christopher Center at Valparaiso University, Indiana.
© PETER AARON/ESTO

numerous variables. Offering a sample problem would not do justice to the individuality and complexity of electric lighting design.

4.117 Luminous ceiling in a computer area of the library in the Christopher Center, Valparaiso University, Indiana. © PETER AARON/ESTO

4.118 General lighting from recessed luminaires in a lecture auditorium at the Christopher Center, Valparaiso University, Indiana. © PETER AARON/ESTO

ENVELOPE

LIGHTING

HEATING

COOLING

ENERGY PRODUCTION

WATER & WASTE

4.119 Integrated electric lighting and daylighting in a reading area of the Christopher Center at Valparaiso University, Indiana. © PETER AARON/ESTO

Further Information

The European Greenlight Programme. www.eu-greenlight.org/

International Organization for Energy-Efficient Lighting. www.iaeel.org/

Rea, M. ed. 2000. *The IESNA Lighting Handbook*, 9th ed. Illuminating Engineering Society of North America, New York.

U.S. Department of Energy, Energy Efficiency and Renewable Energy, Lighting. www.eere.energy.gov/EE/buildings_lighting.html

Waide, P. 2006. "Light's Labour Lost." International Energy Agency, Paris.

Whole Building Design Guide, Energy Efficient Lighting. www.wbdg.org/design/efficientlighting.php

BEYOND SCHEMATIC DESIGN

The entire design of electric lighting systems is often undertaken during design development—in many cases by a consultant (lighting designer or electrical engineer). During design development, lamps, luminaires, and controls are selected, coordinated, and specified. Commissioning of all types of automatic lighting controls is strongly recommended—as they seem notoriously prone to poor installation and/or calibration.

ENVELOPE

LIGHTING

HEATING

COOLING

ENERGY PRODUCTION

WATER & WASTE

HEATING

In thinking schematically about heating a building, an understanding of the extent of the heating loads is critical. In single-family homes, heating loads tend to be larger than cooling loads (except in very mild or hot climates). Larger (internal load dominated) buildings tend to have significant cooling loads due to occupancy, lighting, and equipment—along with a low surface-to-volume ratio. It is not unusual for a large office building to be in permanent cooling mode at the building core, with heating required only at the perimeter—and with a high-performance facade it is possible to virtually eliminate perimeter heating. Thus, the heating strategies covered in this book are most appropriate for residential or small-scale commercial/institutional buildings.

The simplest way to heat a building is with direct solar gain, admitting solar radiation during the heating season and storing it in thermally massive materials. Direct gain is very effective in a well-insulated building with good windows. It can bring glare, however, and cause deterioration of interior finishes and furnishings. It is best suited where occupants can move about as conditions change over the course of the day, such as in a residence or library reading room. Direct gain heating is problematic in offices, where workers typically are not free to move to another workspace.

With indirect gain, a massive assembly (such as a Trombe wall or roof pond) absorbs solar radiation without directly admitting the sun into the occupied space. The collected heat gradually conducts through the thermal mass, and radiates and convects to the occupied spaces later in the day. Indirect gain can be combined with direct gain to balance heating over the course of a day.

STRATEGIES

Direct Gain
Indirect Gain
Isolated Gain
Active Solar Thermal Energy Systems
Ground Source Heat Pumps

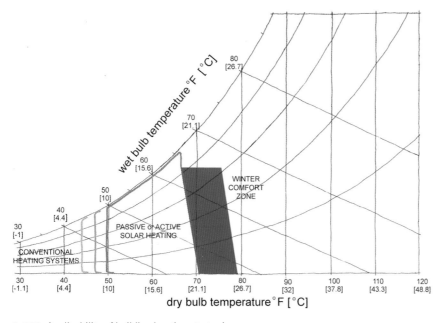

4.120 Applicability of building heating strategies. ADAPTED FROM *ENERGY CONSERVATION THROUGH BUILDING DESIGN*

ENVELOPE

LIGHTING

HEATING

COOLING

ENERGY PRODUCTION

WATER & WASTE

A sunspace absorbs and stores solar heat that can be drawn off for use in occupied spaces as needed. Usually the thermal storage space is not occupied, so temperatures need not be maintained in the comfort zone. In fact, the sunspace may be most effective in providing heat if temperatures rise (and drop) well beyond the comfort zone.

Ground source heat pumps are an active strategy using the refrigeration cycle to move heat from one location to another. A ground source heat pump uses the soil as a source of heat during the heating season and as a heat sink during the cooling season. Because the ground temperature is warmer than the outside air during the winter (and cooler during the summer) a ground source heat pump is more efficient than an air source heat pump (which in turn is more efficient than most other active alternatives).

DIRECT GAIN systems are generally considered to be the most basic, simple, and cost-effective means of passive solar heating. During the heating season, solar radiation enters south-facing glazing and is then absorbed by and heats interior mass. Properly sized storage mass can provide steady and reliable heating performance. During the cooling season, solar radiation can be blocked with appropriate shading devices (including landscaping). The defining design and operational feature of a direct gain system, seen in Figure 4.122, is the fact that occupants inhabit the building heating system.

4.121 The concrete floor and stone fireplace absorb solar radiation from window and skylight apertures at the Bundy Brown residence in Ketchum, Idaho. BRUCE HAGLUND

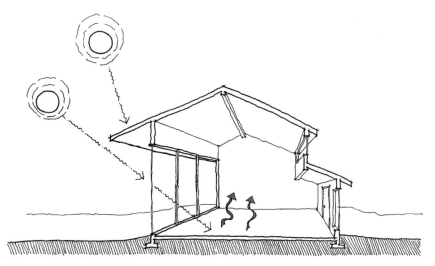

4.122 A direct gain system uses thermal mass to absorb and store solar energy to heat a building. Shading devices control unwanted summer sun. KATE BECKLEY

Key Architectural Issues

Although direct gain systems perform surprisingly well in a variety of climates and building types, cloudless winters and smaller, skin-load dominated buildings make for an ideal application of this strategy.

The building axis for a direct gain system should run generally east-west to maximize solar exposure on the south-facing aperture. As long as the aperture is within 15° of true south (or north, in the southern hemisphere), the building will receive within 90% of optimal winter solar heat gains. Shifting the aperture to the east or west will somewhat shift the timing of these heat gains.

The distribution of functional spaces (Figure 4.123) in a direct gain building is an important consideration. South-facing rooms will benefit from direct solar heating, while north-facing ones will not. Those areas with direct gain aperture will also receive more daylight than rooms with primarily opaque walls. Placing lesser-used spaces (i.e. closets, bathrooms, circulation, service spaces) along the north wall can provide a buffer on the under-heated northern facade, and reduce the need to transfer heat from the southern spaces.

INTENT
Climate control (heating), thermal comfort

EFFECT
Use of a renewable resource, passive heating, energy efficiency

OPTIONS
One fundamental approach, but with numerous options for individual elements (aperture, collection, storage, distribution, control)

COORDINATION ISSUES
Passive cooling, active heating, daylighting, interior furnishings, occupant controls

RELATED STRATEGIES
Night Ventilation of Mass, Indirect Gain, Isolated Gain, Shading Devices

LEED LINKS
Energy & Atmosphere, Indoor Environmental Quality

PREREQUISITES
Suitable climate, suitable site, suitable building type, appropriate design intent

ENVELOPE

LIGHTING

HEATING

COOLING

ENERGY PRODUCTION

WATER & WASTE

Night ventilation of mass for passive cooling in the summer is a logical complement to a direct gain passive heating system. Coordination of prevailing summer (cooling) wind directions with the elongated southern solar exposure is necessary if this combination of systems is to succeed.

It is important to recognize that a direct gain system will have large glazing areas, therefore it is also important to take steps to mitigate glare and reduce nighttime heat losses. Using light-colored surfaces and furnishings near windows can help reduce glare potential by reducing contrast. The use of some type of movable insulation or high-performance glazing can help reduce nighttime heat losses. Furniture and carpets in the path of direct sunlight may fade if not selected with this exposure in mind— they will also interfere with the absorption and storage of solar energy.

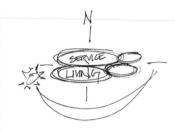

4.123 Unoccupied or service spaces can be placed along the cooler non-solar facade, leaving the warmer side for living spaces.
KATE BECKLEY

Implementation Considerations

Sloped glazing is often considered as a way to maximize solar exposure. Left unshaded, however, this solution may increase unwanted summer gains. Shading tilted glazing is more difficult than shading vertical glazing. Deciduous vegetation can be used to control seasonal heat gains. Remember that even bare trees provide some shading effect that may reduce system performance.

The color of the absorber surface/thermal mass is an important consideration. Dark colors (with an absorptance of 0.5–0.8) work best. Most unpainted masonry materials will perform reasonably well. Because even reflected radiation can contribute to heating, low thermal-mass surfaces (ceilings, partitions) should be painted a light color in order to reflect radiation onto the identified thermal storage surfaces.

TABLE 4.9 Thermal properties of various materials

MATERIAL	SPECIFIC HEAT		DENSITY		HEAT CAPACITY	
	Btu/lb°F	kJ/kg K	lb/ft^3	kg/m^3	Btu/ft^3°F	kJ/m^{3}K
Water	1.0	4.18	62.4	998	62.4	4172
Brick	0.22	0.92	120	1920	26.4	1766
Concrete	0.19	0.79	150	2400	28.5	1896
Air	0.24	1.00	0.075	1.2	0.018	1.2

As the simplest passive solar heating approach, direct gain systems have certain limitations. Sunnier than average conditions, for example, can lead to overheating—as the heat storage capacity of the building is exceeded. The opposite can occur during cloudy periods. Because of this, it is important to include a certain degree of occupant control (i.e. movable shades or operable exhausts to temper overheating). A backup active (mechanical) heating system is commonly required—both to provide for heating loads that cannot be met passively with a reasonably sized system and for use during periods of extreme (cold or cloudy) weather.

Thermal storage mass should generally not exceed a thickness of 4–5 in. [100–125 mm]. Any additional mass required to provide adequate storage should be provided by additional surfaces. Increasing thickness is progressively less effective and distributed storage can help keep a room evenly heated. Because the absorber surface is also the top of the thermal storage in most direct gain systems, locating storage mass is constrained by solar exposure. Secondary storage (not receiving direct solar radiation) is much less effective in controlling overheating. Any mass should be exposed as much as possible, so limit the use of rugs or carpets (which act as insulators).

South glazing should have an SHGC (solar heat gain coefficient) of 0.60 or higher (the higher the better, as shading is best provided by other means) and a U-factor of 0.35 [2.0] or less. Non-solar glazing should be selected to optimize building envelope performance. To help keep heat from migrating out of windows at night, use insulating shades or panels to cover the glazing at night.

In a building subdivided into rooms (most buildings), the direct gain heating system only heats the rooms with a solar aperture—unless serious efforts are made to ensure the distribution of heat to adjacent or distant non-aperture rooms. This can place severe limitations on the applicability of direct gain systems in larger buildings or where there are complex room arrangements.

Design Procedure

The purpose of the procedure outlined herein is to establish the general sizes of system components during the schematic design phase of a project. These rough estimates will be refined and optimized during design development.

The first, and most important, step in the design of a passive solar heating system is to minimize the rate of heat loss through non-south-facing envelope components (including infiltration losses). This is a design concern that is typically addressed in later phases of design—as specific components are selected and specified. Some opportunities to minimize losses, however, will be lost if not made during schematic design— earth berming, building form, and orientation, for example. The bottom line is that it makes little sense to attempt to heat a leaky or poorly insulated building with solar energy (or any form of energy for that matter). This step of the design process has been described as providing "insulation before insolation."

1. Estimate the required size of solar apertures (glazing). Use the ranges given below logically—a value toward the higher end being appropriate for a moderately well-insulated building, a colder climate, and/or a climate with limited solar resources.
   - For a cold to temperate climate, use a solar glazing ratio of between 0.2 and 0.4 ft^2 [0.02–0.04 m^2] of south-facing, appropriately-glazed aperture for each ft^2 [m^2] of heated floor area. In mild to temperate climates, use between 0.10 and 0.20 ft^2 [0.01–0.02 m^2] of similar aperture for each ft^2 [m^2] of heated floor area.

2. Estimate the amount of thermal storage required to support the proposed glazing. A general rule is to provide a concrete mass of

ENVELOPE

LIGHTING

HEATING

COOLING

ENERGY PRODUCTION

WATER & WASTE

SAMPLE PROBLEM

A 1000 ft^2 [93 m^2] building located in Minneapolis, Minnesota will be heated by a direct gain passive solar heating system.

1. For this cold climate building a glazing area ratio of 0.4:1 is considered appropriate. Thus, the estimated glazing area is:

   (1000 ft^2) (0.4) = 400 ft^2 [37 m^2]

2. Each unit area of glazing requires 3 unit areas of thermal mass for heat storage:

   (400 ft^2) (3) = 1200 ft^2 [112 m^2]

   This exceeds the floor area of the building. Assuming that 700 ft^2 [65 m^2] of the floor area could be used as thermal storage, then (1200 − 700) or 500 ft^2 [47 m^2] of equivalent mass must be provided in walls, partitions, or other storage objects. Using a 2:1 multiplier for indirect or secondary thermal mass (to account for its inefficiency), this equates to 1000 ft^2 [93 m^2] of non-floor mass.

ENVELOPE

LIGHTING

HEATING

COOLING

ENERGY PRODUCTION

WATER & WASTE

4–6 in. [100–150 mm] thickness that is about 3 times the area of the solar glazing. This assumes the mass is directly irradiated by solar radiation. A ratio of 6:1 is generally recommended for mass that receives only reflected radiation.

3. Estimate the "non-south" building envelope and infiltration heat loss rate (excluding conduction/convection losses through solar apertures)—per degree of temperature difference. Multiply this hourly unit heat loss by 24 to obtain the total heat loss per day (essentially heat loss per day per degree day); this value is called the net load coefficient (NLC).

4. Divide the overall NLC by the total floor area, and check the unit NLC against the data presented in Table 4.10.

TABLE 4.10 Overall heat loss criteria for a passive solar heated building. BALCOMB, J.D. ET AL. *PASSIVE SOLAR DESIGN HANDBOOK*, VOL. 2

ANNUAL HEATING DEGREE DAYS Base 65 °F [18 °C]	TARGET NLC Btu/DDF ft² [kJ/DDC m²]
Less than 1000 [556]	7.6 [155]
1000–3000 [556–1667]	6.6 [135]
3000–5000 [1667–2778]	5.6 [115]
5000–7000 [2778–3889]	4.6 [94]
Over 7000 [3889]	3.6 [74]

5. If the estimated NLC is greater than the target NLC listed above, then improvements in building envelope performance are necessary to reduce heat loss.

Examples

4.124 Concrete floors absorb solar radiation in the direct gain dining hall of IslandWood Campus on Bainbridge Island, Washington.

Assuming building dimensions of 50 ft by 20 ft [15.3 by 6.1 m], the interior surface area of non-south exterior walls would be around: (8 ft) (20 + 50 + 20) = 720 ft² [(2.4)(6.1 + 15.3 + 6.1) = 66 m²]. Thus, around 720 ft² [66 m²] of secondary storage might be available just using these walls (if of high mass construction, readily exposed to the space, and well insulated on the exterior of the mass). Additional internal storage mass would need to be provided to reach the 1000 ft² [93 m²] design target.

Again assuming a 50 ft [15.3 m] long south facade, the glazing would need to be (400 ft²/50 ft) or 8 ft high [37/15.3 = 2.4 m]. Without a sloped ceiling/roof, the south facade would be all glass. This is possible, but will dramatically affect facade design and building appearance.

3. The building has an estimated design heat loss of 3.5 Btu/ft² DD F [72 kJ/m² DD]. Heating degree days = 7981 65 °F [4434 18 °C].

4. The estimated NLC of 3.5 [72] is below (though just barely) the target value of 3.6 [74] from Table 4.10.

4.125 Classic example of solar apertures, solar control, and thermal mass in the Shaw residence in Taos, New Mexico.

Further Information

Balcomb, J.D. et al. 1980. *Passive Solar Design Handbook, Vol. 2, Passive Solar Design Analysis*, U.S. Department of Energy, Washington, DC.

Fosdick, J. 2006. Whole Building Design Guide: "Passive Solar Heating." Available at: www.wbdg.org/design/psheating.php

Greenbuilder.com. A Sourcebook for Green and Sustainable Building: "Passive Solar Guidelines." Available at: www.greenbuilder.com/sourcebook/PassSolGuide1-2.html

Mazria, E. 1979. *The Passive Solar Energy Book*. Rodale Press, Emmaus, PA.

Stein, B. et al. 2006. *Mechanical and Electrical Equipment for Buildings*, 10th ed. John Wiley & Sons, Hoboken, NJ.

BEYOND SCHEMATIC DESIGN

Schematic design is the phase in which a direct gain system must pass proof-of-concept. The decisions regarding footprint, elevations, orientation, and spatial layout required for a successful system must be made as early as possible. During design development, these decisions will be adjusted to optimize system performance—but radical changes in the basic system elements will be hard to make as these elements are really the building itself.

ENVELOPE

LIGHTING

HEATING

COOLING

ENERGY PRODUCTION

WATER & WASTE

ENVELOPE

LIGHTING

HEATING

COOLING

ENERGY PRODUCTION

WATER & WASTE

NOTES

An INDIRECT GAIN system is a passive solar heating system that collects and stores energy from the sun in an element that also acts to buffer the occupied spaces of the building from the solar collection process. Heating effect occurs as natural radiation, conduction, and/or convection redistributes the collected energy from the storage element to the building spaces. Conceptually speaking, occupants reside right next to an indirect gain system—whereas they reside in a direct gain system and near an isolated gain system. As is the case with most passive systems, an indirect gain system will exert substantial influence on the form of the building as a whole.

There are three basic types of indirect gain passive solar heating systems: thermal storage walls using masonry (also called Trombe walls), thermal storage walls using water storage (sometimes called water walls), and thermal storage roofs (roof ponds).

4.126 View of Trombe wall at Zion National Park Visitor's Center in Springdale, Utah. THOMAS WOOD, DOE/NREL

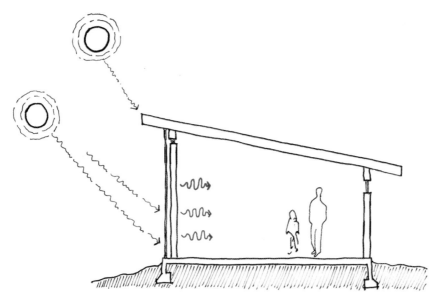

4.127 Schematic diagram of an indirect gain heating system showing the collection of solar energy in a south-facing thermal storage wall, which then transfers heat into the occupied space. KATE BECKLEY

A thermal storage wall is a south-facing glazed wall with an appropriate storage medium (such as heavy masonry or substantial water) located immediately behind the glass. Solar radiation passes through the glass and is absorbed by, and subsequently warms, the storage element. The collected heat is conducted slowly through the masonry or water to the interior face of the element and then into the occupied spaces. Vents are often placed in the top and bottom of a Trombe wall to permit additional heat transfer through convection (tapping into a mini stack effect). In water walls, convective currents in the water wall enable heat transfer to the interior, improving the efficiency of heat transfer into and through the storage element.

A thermal storage roof is similar in concept to a thermal storage wall, except that the storage mass is located on the roof. The thermal mass is either masonry (rare), water in bags, or a shallow pond of water. Movable insulation is opened and closed diurnally, exposing the storage mass to solar

INTENT
Climate control (heating), thermal comfort

EFFECT
Use of a renewable resource, passive heating, energy efficiency

OPTIONS
Thermal storage wall (masonry or water), thermal storage roof

COORDINATION ISSUES
Active heating, passive cooling, daylighting, interior furnishings, occupant controls

RELATED STRATEGIES
Night Ventilation of Mass, Direct Gain, Isolated Gain, Shading Devices

LEED LINKS
Energy & Atmosphere, Indoor Environmental Quality

PREREQUISITES
Suitable climate, suitable site, suitable building type, appropriate design intent

ENVELOPE

LIGHTING

HEATING

COOLING

ENERGY PRODUCTION

WATER & WASTE

radiation during the day and insulating it at night to reduce heat losses. The same roof system can provide passive cooling during the summer by tapping into the cooling potential of the night sky.

TABLE 4.11 Plan and section requirements and heating characteristics of indirect gain systems

SYSTEM TYPE	PLAN/SECTION REQUIREMENTS	HEATING CHARACTERISTICS
Masonry thermal storage wall (Trombe wall)	South-facing wall and glazing required. Storage wall should be within 25 ft [7.6 m] of all occupied spaces	System is slow to warm up and slow to cool in the evening, with small temperature swings
Water thermal storage wall (water wall)	South-facing wall and glazing required. Storage elements should be within 25 ft [7.6 m] of all occupied spaces	System is slow to warm up and slow to cool in the evening, with small temperature swings
Thermal storage roof (roof pond)	Flat or low slope (<3:12) roof required. Skylights are discouraged. Additional structural support required for the roof	Low temperature swings, can provide heating in winter and cooling in summer

Key Architectural Issues

The designer must consider site climate, building orientation, and solar access potential when considering a passive solar heating system. The form of a solar building will tend to strongly reflect its role as a solar collector and heat distributor. An indirect gain heating system must be integrated with plan and section decision making. The placement of glazing (solar apertures) and absorber/storage elements must be considered in concert with decisions regarding the building envelope.

There is no substantial performance penalty if the solar glazing faces within 5° of true south. Glazing facing 45° from true south, however, incurs a reduction in performance of more than 30%. Direct gain systems are sometimes intentionally shifted in orientation to give preference to morning or afternoon warm-up; such shifts make less sense in an isolated gain system where there is an inherent time delay built into the entry of solar effect into the space.

The design of solar glazing must include provision for shading as a means of seasonal performance control. The building design as a whole should consider ventilation in summer, both for general comfort cooling and for mitigation of potential overheating from the solar system. Design to provide for easy operations and maintenance, especially for the cleaning of glazing.

Adequate space/volume and structural support must be provided for thermal mass (masonry or water). This is especially true for a roof-based indirect gain system. Structural solutions that minimize additional costs are ideal. A backup or auxiliary heating system will be required in many projects to meet design intent.

ENVELOPE

LIGHTING

HEATING

COOLING

ENERGY PRODUCTION

WATER & WASTE

Implementation Considerations

Early in the design process, determine the most applicable system type (thermal storage wall, water wall, or thermal storage roof) and its general impact upon the plan and section of the building. An appropriate system type will match the climate, program, and schedule of use of the building. In addition, the system type will be seen as working with (even complementing) the intended form and aesthetic of the building.

Anticipated needs for daylighting and cooling should be coordinated with the selection of the passive solar heating system type. Consider the provision of adequate shading and ventilation to prevent and/or mitigate summertime overheating.

A backup heating system will be required in most climates. Space must be allocated for this equipment.

The following issues are worthy of consideration during schematic design:

- Overheating: Inadequate thermal storage capacity will cause overheating. Match thermal storage capacity with system type and the proposed collector area.

- Lag time: Excessive thermal storage capacity will cause overly long lag times in system response, impeding system performance. Appropriate lag time depends upon building type, diurnal weather patterns, and design intent.

- Leakage/storage failure: Absorber surfaces and storage media are subject to large, daily shifts in temperature, increasing opportunities for failure. Routine, preventive maintenance can prevent a catastrophic failure—especially critical when water is the storage medium. Provide adequate space and access for maintenance and repair during schematic design, including provisions for normal and emergency drainage.

- Maintenance: In addition to maintenance access for water storage elements, provide adequate space and access for periodic cleaning of glazing and absorber surfaces.

Design Procedure

The purpose of the procedure outlined herein is to establish the general sizes of system components during the schematic design phase of a project. These rough estimates will be refined and optimized during design development.

The first, and most important, step in the design of a passive solar heating system is to minimize the rate of heat loss through non-south-facing envelope components (including infiltration losses). This is a design concern that is typically addressed in later phases of design—as specific components are selected and specified. Some opportunities to minimize losses, however, will be lost if not made during schematic design—earth berming, building form, orientation, for example. The bottom line is that it makes little sense to attempt to heat a leaky or poorly insulated building with solar energy (or any form of energy for that matter). "Insulation before insolation," often describes this step.

SAMPLE PROBLEM
The Not-Real-Big Competition House is a 640 ft² [60 m²] home located in Lansing, New York.

1. A range of from 0.40 to 1.0 ft² [0.04–0.09 m²] of south-facing Trombe wall aperture is recommended for each unit of floor area. Therefore, between 260 and 640 ft² [24–60 m²] of aperture would be required. Because of Lansing's rather dreary winter climate, a value near the high end is appropriate—using 600 ft² [56 m²].

ENVELOPE

LIGHTING

HEATING

COOLING

ENERGY PRODUCTION

WATER & WASTE

ENVELOPE

LIGHTING

HEATING

COOLING

ENERGY PRODUCTION

WATER & WASTE

1. Estimate the required size of solar apertures (glazing). Use the ranges given below logically—a value toward the higher end being appropriate for a moderately well-insulated building, a colder climate, and/or a climate with limited solar resources.
   - For a Trombe wall (masonry storage) in a cold climate, use between 0.40 and 1.0 ft^2 [0.04–0.09 m^2] of south-facing, double-glazed aperture for each ft^2 [m^2] of heated floor area. In moderate climates, use between 0.20 and 0.60 ft^2 [0.02–0.056 m^2] of similar aperture for each ft^2 [m^2] of heated floor area.
   - For a water wall in a cold climate, use between 0.30 and 0.85 ft^2 [0.029–0.079 m^2] of south-facing, double-glazed aperture for each ft^2 [m^2] of floor area. In moderate climates, use between 0.15 and 0.45 ft^2 [0.015–0.04 m^2] of similar aperture for each ft^2 [m^2] of floor area.
   - Roof ponds are not recommended for cold climates. For a moderate climate, use between 0.6 and 0.9 ft^2 [0.056–0.084 m^2] of appropriately "glazed" pond with night insulation for each ft^2 [m^2] of floor area.

2. Estimate the amount of thermal storage required to support the proposed glazing. General rules are as follows, with the presumption that these thicknesses are for storage elements that are the same area as the solar aperture. As with glazing area estimates, apply these ranges logically; thicker storage elements provide greater heat capacity, but also increase time lag:
   - For a Trombe wall (masonry mass) allow for 8–12 in. [200–300 mm] of adobe (or similar earthen product), 10–14 in. [250–350 mm] of brick, and 12–18 in. [300–460 mm] of concrete.
   - For a water wall allow for a minimum of 6 in. [150 mm] "thickness" of water storage.
   - For a roof pond allow for a water (thermal storage) depth of between 6 and 12 in. [150–300 mm].

3. Estimate the "non-south" building envelope and infiltration heat loss rate (excluding conduction/convection losses through solar apertures)—per degree of temperature difference. Multiply this hourly unit heat loss by 24 to obtain the total heat loss per day (essentially heat loss per day per degree day); this value is called the net load coefficient (NLC).

4. Divide the overall NLC by the total floor area, and check the unit NLC against the data presented in Table 4.12.

TABLE 4.12 Overall heat loss criteria for a passive solar heated building. BALCOMB, J.D. ET AL. *PASSIVE SOLAR DESIGN HANDBOOK*, VOL. 2

ANNUAL HEATING DEGREE DAYS Base 65 °F [18 °C]	TARGET NLC Btu/DDF ft^2 [kJ/DDC m^2]
Less than 1000 [556]	7.6 [155]
1000–3000 [556–1667]	6.6 [135]
3000–5000 [1667–2778]	5.6 [115]
5000–7000 [2778–3889]	4.6 [94]
Over 7000 [3889]	3.6 [74]

For a water wall, from 0.30 to 0.85 ft^2 [0.04–0.09 m^2] of south-facing aperture is required for each unit of floor area. Therefore, between 200 and 545 ft^2 [20– 50 m^2] of aperture would be required. Again, considering climate, a value of around 500 ft^2 [46 m^2] is considered appropriate.

A roof pond would not be a reasonable option for the cold Lansing climate.

2. A concrete storage wall would be most appropriate for this building context, with a 16 in. [400 mm] thickness used as a starting point for design. If using water storage, an 8 in. [200 mm] thick element would be a good starting point.

3. U-factors for all of the non-south-aperture envelope elements are estimated, along with anticipated infiltration. The estimated total (non-south glazing) heat loss for the house is 90 Btu/h °F [48 W/°C].

   The Net Load Coefficient is (24) (90) = 2160 Btu/DDF [4102 kJ/DDC].

4. Normalizing this loss for building floor area, 2160 Btu/DDF/640 ft^2 = 3.375 Btu/DDF ft^2 [68 kJ/ DDC m^2].

   Lansing, New York experiences 7182 65 °F [3990 18 °C] annual heating degree days; therefore a reasonable NLC target is 3.6 Btu/DDF ft^2 [74 kJ/DDC m^2].

5. The Not-Real-Big Competition House is thus adequately insulated (does not exceed the target heat loss).

5. If the estimated NLC is greater than the target NLC listed above, improvements in building envelope performance are necessary to reduce heat loss.

Examples

4.128 Thermal storage (Trombe) walls behind the glazed facades of this retail building in Ketchum, Idaho collect solar energy. BRUCE HAGLUND

4.129 Circular inlet opening at the bottom of the Ketchum Trombe wall (left) brings warm air up through the cavity into a second-story office via the circular outlet (right). BRUCE HAGLUND

ENVELOPE

LIGHTING

HEATING

COOLING

ENERGY PRODUCTION

WATER & WASTE

ENVELOPE

LIGHTING

HEATING

COOLING

ENERGY PRODUCTION

WATER & WASTE

4.130 Zion National Park Visitor's Center in Springdale, Utah showing a Trombe wall and clerestory (direct gain) windows. ROBB WILLIAMSON, DOE/NREL

Further Information

Balcomb, J.D. et al. 1980. *Passive Solar Design Handbook, Vol. 2, Passive Solar Design Analysis*, U.S. Department of Energy, Washington, DC.

Brown, G.Z. and M. DeKay. 2001. *Sun, Wind & Light: Architectural Design Strategies*, 2nd ed. John Wiley & Sons, New York.

Mazria, E. 1979. *The Passive Solar Energy Book.* Rodale Press, Emmaus, PA.

Stein, B. et al. 2006. *Mechanical and Electrical Equipment for Buildings*, 10th ed. John Wiley & Sons, Hoboken, NJ.

BEYOND SCHEMATIC DESIGN

More accurate (and complex) analysis methods will validate the decisions made in schematic design. Numerous energy modeling programs are available to assist in better understanding building energy demands, integrating passive systems, and reducing annual energy use. These programs, such as Energy Scheming, DOE-2, or EnergyPlus, can be of great assistance in "right-sizing" solar apertures versus thermal storage.

A User's Manual should be developed to provide occupants with an outline of their role in the operation and performance of a passive heating system—and giving them a sense of what conditions might be expected in a passive building.

ISOLATED GAIN

ENVELOPE

LIGHTING

HEATING

COOLING

ENERGY PRODUCTION

WATER & WASTE

An ISOLATED GAIN system is a passive solar heating system that collects and stores energy from the sun in a building element thermally separated from the occupied spaces of the building. A sunspace (attached greenhouse) is the most common example, although there are other configurations, including convective loops. Heating effect occurs as solar energy captured in the collector element is redistributed from a storage component to the occupied building spaces through natural radiation, conduction, and/or convection. As opposed to a direct or indirect gain system, where occupants reside in or right next to the passive heating system, an isolated gain system provides thermal and spatial separation between the occupancy and heat collection functions. An isolated gain system will substantially influence the form of the building as a whole.

4.131 Sunspace in a residence in Dublin, New Hampshire. ALAN FORD, DOE/NREL

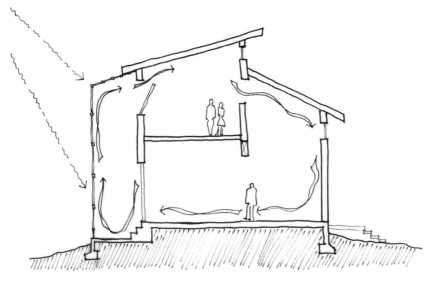

4.132 Conceptual diagram of an isolated gain passive solar heating system. KATE BECKLEY

A sunspace can fit into the overall building floor plan in many ways—including adjacency with the main building along one side of the sunspace, adjacency with the main building along two sides, or adjacency along three sides (where the building embraces the sunspace). A sunspace could also be an internal element, such as an atrium, but solar access and heat distribution would be more difficult in such a configuration. Convective loop systems employ a collector element located below the elevation of the building proper; heat flows to the occupied building by air circulating in a convective loop via the stack effect. Thermal storage components of an isolated gain system include masonry floors and/or walls, water tubes or barrels, or a rock bed when using a convective loop.

Key Architectural Issues

A key issue to consider relative to sunspace systems is that thermal functions dictate the role of the space; functioning as comfortably occupiable space is a secondary role. During the course of heat collection and discharge, a sunspace will likely reach temperatures substantially above and below the comfort zone. This is both natural and necessary. Use of

INTENT
Climate control (heating), thermal comfort

EFFECT
Use of a renewable resource, passive heating, energy efficiency

OPTIONS
Sunspace, convective loop

COORDINATION ISSUES
Active heating, passive cooling, daylighting, interior furnishings, occupant controls, secondary use of space

RELATED STRATEGIES
Night Ventilation of Mass, Direct Gain, Indirect Gain, Shading Devices

LEED LINKS
Energy & Environment, Indoor Environmental Quality

PREREQUISITES
Suitable climate, suitable site, suitable building type, appropriate design intent

the space (for people or plants) must accommodate these temperature swings. A working sunspace will generally make a bad dining room or conservatory.

The designer must consider site climate, building orientation, and solar access potential when considering a passive solar heating system. The form of a passive solar building will tend to reflect strongly its role as a solar collector and heat distributor. This is especially true of isolated gain systems, which involve substantial areas of glazing that are not quite part of the building proper.

Solar glazing should generally face within 5° of true south. Glazing facing 45° from true south incurs a substantial reduction in performance. As with direct gain systems, isolated gain apertures can be intentionally oriented to give preference to morning or afternoon warm-up—although the lag of storage and thermal separation make implementation less simple.

The design of solar glazing must include provision for shading as a means of seasonal performance control. This is especially true for sunspaces, which tend to include substantial glazing, often tilted from the vertical. Shading is fundamental to system success on a year-round basis. Natural ventilation often mitigates summer overheating in a sunspace. Design to provide for easy operation and maintenance, especially for the cleaning of sloped glazing.

Implementation Considerations

Determine the most applicable system type (sunspace or convective loop) early in the design process. Convective loop systems work best when there is a natural elevation change on site that can be used to advantage. Establish how the collector element will integrate with the main building. An isolated gain heating system can drive the aesthetics of a small building.

The distribution of heat from the isolated gain collector area to the occupied spaces is a major design challenge. By its very nature an isolated gain system removes the heating function from the vicinity of the occupied spaces. Natural heat transfer must convey the heat from its collection point to where it is needed.

Two fundamental options exist with an attached greenhouse (sunspace) system: (1) the connecting wall between the collector and the occupied building is insulated and all heat transfer occurs by convection (this is a truly isolated gain system), or (2) the connecting wall is uninsulated and provides both heat storage and transfer functions (like an oversized Trombe wall arrangement). This is a decision that can be deferred until design development and detailed simulations.

A backup heating system for the occupied building will be required in most climates. It is important to allocate space for this equipment.

Design Procedure

The purpose of this procedure is to establish general sizes of components during the schematic design phase of a project (see the Indirect

SAMPLE PROBLEM
A 2500 ft² [230 m²] homeless shelter is proposed for Vancouver, British Columbia.

Gain strategy for notes and commentary regarding this procedure). This procedure applies only to sunspace systems; convective loop systems are too specialized to generalize (although similar thermal principles apply).

1. Estimate the required size of solar apertures (glazing). Use the ranges given below—a value toward the higher end being appropriate for a moderately well-insulated building, a colder climate, and/or a climate with limited solar resources.
   - In a cold climate, use between 0.65 and 1.5 ft² [0.06–0.14 m²] of south-facing, double-glazed aperture for each ft² [m²] of heated floor area.
   - In moderate climates, use between 0.30 and 0.90 ft² [0.03–0.085 m²] of similar aperture for each ft² [m²] of heated floor area.

2. Estimate the amount of thermal storage required to support the proposed glazing. General rules follow, with the presumption that these thicknesses are for storage elements that are collectively roughly the same area as the solar aperture. As with glazing area estimates, apply these ranges logically; thicker storage elements provide greater heat capacity, but also increase time lag.
   - For a sunspace, allow for 8–12 in. [200–300 mm] of adobe (or similar earthen product), 10–14 in. [250–350 mm] of brick, or 12–18 in. [300–460 mm] of concrete.
   - For water-based storage, allow for a minimum of 8 in. [150 mm] "thickness" of water storage.

3. Estimate the "non-solar" building envelope and infiltration heat loss rate (excluding conduction/convection losses through solar apertures)—per degree of temperature difference. Multiply this hourly unit heat loss by 24 to obtain the total heat loss per day (essentially heat loss per day per degree day); this value is called the net load coefficient (NLC).

4. Divide the overall NLC by the total floor area, and check the unit NLC against the data presented in Table 4.13.

TABLE 4.13 Overall heat loss criteria for a passive solar heated building. BALCOMB, J.D. ET AL. *PASSIVE SOLAR DESIGN HANDBOOK*, VOL. 2.

ANNUAL HEATING DEGREE DAYS Base 65 °F [18 °C]	TARGET NLC Btu/DDF ft² [kJ/DDC m²]
Less than 1000 [556]	7.6 [155]
1000–3000 [556–1667]	6.6 [135]
3000–5000 [1667–2778]	5.6 [115]
5000–7000 [2778–3889]	4.6 [94]
Over 7000 [3889]	3.6 [74]

5. If the estimated NLC is greater than the target NLC listed above, then improvements in building envelope performance are necessary to reduce heat loss.

1. For a temperate climate, use recommendation of 0.30 to 0.90 ft² [0.03–0.085 m²] of south-facing sunspace aperture for each unit of floor area. So, between 750 and 2250 ft² [70–210 m²] of aperture would be required. A value nearer the high end is appropriate (desire to minimize the use of active heating and the cloudy climate)—select 2000 ft² [186 m²]. This is too much glazing for this size building. Select a different heating system or reduce performance expectations.

2. Assuming a smaller system was acceptable, a concrete storage wall is appropriate for this building context, with a 16 in. [400 mm] thickness used as a starting point. The floor of the sunspace would also be used for thermal storage (at a lesser thickness), which would reduce the required area of storage wall proportionately.

3. U-factors for all of the non-solar aperture envelope elements were established, along with anticipated infiltration. The estimated total (less solar glazing) heat loss for the shelter is 385 Btu/h °F [205 W/°C].

   The Net Load Coefficient is (24) (385) = 9240 Btu/DDF [17,548 kJ/DDC].

4. Normalizing this loss for building floor area, 9240 Btu/DDF/ 2500 ft² = 3.7 Btu/DDF ft² [76 kJ/DDC m²].

5. Vancouver experiences around 3000 65 °F [1667 18 °C] annual heating degree days; and a reasonable NLC target is 5.6 Btu/DDF ft² [115 kJ/DDC m²]. The proposed shelter is thus adequately insulated (does not exceed the target heat loss).

ENVELOPE

LIGHTING

HEATING

COOLING

ENERGY PRODUCTION

WATER & WASTE

Examples

4.133 An adobe residence with an attached sunspace in Santa Fe, New Mexico.

4.134 Dining and outdoor-ish activities in a residential sunspace in the Beddington Zero Energy Development in Beddington, Sutton, UK. GRAHAMGAUNT.COM

4.135 Ecohouse in Oxford, England integrates a number of strategies including an attached sunspace, roof integrated photovoltaic panels, and flat plate collectors for solar water heating.

4.136 The sunspace of the Ecohouse opens to a sitting area and English garden beyond.

ENVELOPE

LIGHTING

HEATING

COOLING

ENERGY PRODUCTION

WATER & WASTE

Further Information

Balcomb, J.D. et al. 1980. *Passive Solar Design Handbook, Vol. 2, Passive Solar Design Analysis.* U.S. Department of Energy, Washington, DC.

Brown, G.Z. and M. DeKay. 2001. *Sun, Wind & Light: Architectural Design Strategies,* 2nd ed. John Wiley & Sons, New York.

Mazria, E. 1979. *The Passive Solar Energy Book.* Rodale Press, Emmaus, PA.

Stein, B. et al. 2006. *Mechanical and Electrical Equipment for Buildings,* 10th ed. John Wiley & Sons, Hoboken, NJ.

U.S. Department of Energy, Energy Efficiency and Renewable Energy, "Isolated Gain (sunspaces)." www.eere.energy.gov/consumer/your_home/designing_remodeling/index.cfm?mytopic=10310

BEYOND SCHEMATIC DESIGN

More accurate (and complex) analysis methods (see Further Information) will validate, and help to adjust and optimize, early design decisions. Energy modeling programs, such as Energy Scheming, DOE-2, or EnergyPlus, can be of great assistance in "right-sizing" solar apertures versus thermal storage.

A User's Manual should be developed to provide occupants with an outline of their role in the operation and performance of a passive system—and give them a sense of what conditions might be expected in a passive building.

ACTIVE SOLAR THERMAL ENERGY SYSTEMS utilize energy from the sun for domestic water heating, pool heating, preheating of ventilation air, and/or space heating. The most common application for active solar thermal energy systems is heating water for domestic use. The major components of an active solar thermal system include a collector, a circulation system that moves a fluid from the collectors to storage, a storage tank (or equivalent), and a control system. A backup heating system is typically included.

There are four basic types of active solar thermal systems: thermosiphon systems, direct circulation systems, indirect circulation systems, and air-water systems.

ENVELOPE

LIGHTING

HEATING

COOLING

ENERGY PRODUCTION

WATER & WASTE

ACTIVE SOLAR THERMAL ENERGY SYSTEMS

4.137 Evacuated tube solar collectors at the 2005 University of Texas-Austin Solar Decathlon House.

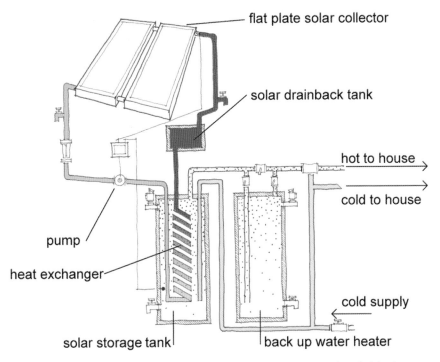

flat plate solar collector

solar drainback tank

hot to house

cold to house

pump

heat exchanger

cold supply

solar storage tank

back up water heater

4.138 Solar thermal system components and their general arrangement in a drainback configuration.

In a thermosiphon system, the collector heats water (or an antifreeze fluid), which causes the fluid to rise by convection to a storage tank. Pumping is not required, but fluid movement and heat transfer are dependent upon the temperature of the fluid. A thermosiphon system is a good option for climates with good solar radiation resources and little chance of low outdoor air temperatures.

A direct circulation system pumps water from a storage tank to collectors during hours of adequate solar radiation. Freeze protection is addressed either by recirculating hot water from the storage tank through the collectors or by draining the water from the collectors when freezing conditions occur.

INTENT
Energy efficiency

EFFECT
Reduced use of purchased energy resources, water heating, space heating

OPTIONS
Thermosiphon, direct circulation, indirect circulation, air-water configurations

COORDINATION ISSUES
Active heating and cooling systems, plumbing system, orientation and tilt of potential collector mounting surfaces, provision for mechanical space

RELATED STRATEGIES
Energy Recovery Systems

LEED LINKS
Energy & Environment

PREREQUISITES
Building heating and cooling requirements, domestic hot-water requirements, design heating and cooling data, site climate data

An indirect circulation system circulates an antifreeze fluid through a closed loop. A heat exchanger transfers heat from this closed collector loop to an open potable water circuit. Freeze protection is achieved either by specification of an antifreeze fluid or by draining the collectors when freezing conditions occur. Glycol-based solutions are the most commonly used fluids for closed loop freeze protection.

The collector in an air-water system heats air. A fan moves the heated air through an air-to-water heat exchanger. The efficiency of an air-to-water heat exchanger is generally in the range of 50 to 60%. Air-based solar systems, while not as efficient as water systems, are an option if the inherent freeze protection provided by air is a key point of interest. Solar heated air can also directly heat a space, with heat storage occurring in a rock-bed storage bin.

There are four common types of solar collectors: batch collectors, flat plate collectors, evacuated tube collectors, and transpired collectors.

A batch (or breadbox) collector includes an insulated storage tank, lined with glass on the inside and painted black on the outside. The collector is mounted on a roof (or on the ground) in a sunny location. Cold inlet water comes from the building's potable water system. The breadbox is the collector, absorbing and retaining heat from the sun. An outlet at the top of the insulated storage tank supplies the building with heated water. Direct and thermosiphon systems often employ batch collectors.

The flat plate collector is the most common collector type. A flat plate collector is a thin, rectangular box with a transparent or translucent cover, usually installed on a building's roof. Small tubes run through the box carrying either water or an antifreeze solution to a black absorber plate. The absorber plate absorbs solar radiation and quickly heats up; the heat is transferred to the circulating fluid. A small pump (or gravity) moves the fluid into the building. Direct, indirect, and thermosiphon systems commonly use flat plate collectors.

Evacuated tube collectors consist of parallel rows of transparent glass tubes each containing an absorber tube with a selective surface coating (high absorbtivity, low emissivity). Solar radiation enters the tube, strikes the absorber, and heats a freeze-protected liquid flowing through the absorber. The tubes are vacuum-sealed, which helps them achieve extremely high temperatures with reasonably high efficiencies (due to reduced heat losses). Such collectors can provide solar heat on days with limited amounts of solar radiation. Evacuated tube collectors are used only with indirect circulation systems.

A transpired collector is a south-facing exterior wall covered by a dark sheet metal collector. The collector heats outdoor air, which is drawn into the building through perforations in the collector. The heated air can heat a space or be used to precondition ventilation air.

Key Architectural Issues

The designer must consider climate, orientation, solar access, and the loads being served when integrating an active solar thermal system into a project. Consider collector location in the context of the overall design

4.139 Typical batch solar thermal collector. FLORIDA SOLAR ENERGY CENTER

4.140 Flat plate solar thermal collectors at the Woods Hole Research Center in Falmouth, Massachusetts.

of the building envelope, although the optimum location is usually on a south-facing wall or roof. Placement of collectors should include provisions for operations and maintenance access, especially for cleaning of collector surfaces and checking for leaks.

System components located inside the building (typically circulation, storage, and control components) require adequate space, including room for maintenance and repair.

Implementation Considerations

Freeze protection is a critical component of all water-based solar systems. When designing for a climate where freezing is possible, three basic methods can be employed to avoid damage.

- Design an indirect system with an antifreeze solution that will not freeze at the lowest temperature likely to occur at the site.

- Design an indirect system with a drainback mode, to drain the fluid from the collectors when freezing conditions are expected.

- Design a drain-down system so that water can be drained from the collectors when freezing temperatures occur. This type of freeze protection should only be used in climates where freezing temperatures are infrequent.

Determine if a low-temperature or high-temperature domestic water heating system is necessary by reviewing project needs, climate data, and groundwater temperatures. A low-temperature solar water-heating system can preheat water in locations with low groundwater temperatures; when hot water is needed, the preheated water is boosted to full temperature with a conventional hot-water system.

A high-temperature solar domestic hot-water system can provide ready-to-use hot water. A conventional gas or electric backup system is operated only when there is limited solar radiation for an extended period of time. A high-temperature system can provide greater energy savings than a low-temperature system—but the tradeoff is equipment that is more expensive.

In addition to freeze protection, consider the following for systems using water as the distribution medium:

- Overheating: If water stagnates in a solar collector, very high temperatures result, which can rupture the system from overpressure. Pressure venting or continuously circulating fluid through the collector will avoid stagnation.

- Hard water: In areas with hard water, calcium deposits can clog passages or corrode seals in collectors. Direct circulation systems are especially vulnerable. A water softener or the use of buffering chemicals should be considered in such areas.

ENVELOPE

LIGHTING

HEATING

COOLING

ENERGY PRODUCTION

WATER & WASTE

ENVELOPE

LIGHTING

HEATING

COOLING

ENERGY PRODUCTION

WATER & WASTE

- Leakage: Seals, piping, and storage media will at some point leak. Routine, preventive maintenance can prevent a catastrophic failure, but well-placed drains are a good idea.

- Pumping: Electric pumps can use a significant amount of parasitic energy, and each pump installed requires a control that increases the cost of the system. Failure of a pump (often difficult to detect) can result in stagnation or freezing damage to an entire system.

Design Procedure

1. Select an appropriate system type for the climate and projected loads from among the thermosiphon, direct circulation, indirect circulation, and air-based options. Select an appropriate collector type for the system chosen.

2. Estimate the required solar collector area according to the following design guidelines:
   - Domestic hot-water systems: 10 to 20 ft^2 [0.9 to 1.8 m^2] of collector area per person being served by the system.
   - Pool heating systems: 0.6 to 1.1 ft^2 [0.06 to 0.1 m^2] of collector area per ft^2 [m^2] of pool surface area. Use a higher value for year-round pool heating.
   - Space heating systems: a solar collector area equal to 10 to 30% of the heated floor area.

   Use the lower value in the above estimates in warm climates and/or areas with good (and reliable) solar radiation resources. Use the higher value in the opposite situation.

3. Estimate an appropriate storage tank size based upon load and needs. The tank must be large enough to meet the peak hourly hot-water demands of a domestic water system or to assist meaningfully with space heating loads. For domestic water heating, a 60-gallon [230 L] storage tank is usually reasonable for one or two people. An 80-gallon [300 L] storage tank is recommended for three to four people. Use a larger tank for more than four people. Providing adequate storage capacity reduces overheating on good collection days. An alternative estimating guideline suggests 1.5 to 2.0 gallons [61 to 82 L] of storage for each square foot [square meter] of collector area— generally applicable to both space heating and domestic water systems.

4. Select a backup approach or system to provide hot water/space heating when adequate solar radiation is not available.

Solar thermal systems can also provide space cooling via connection to an absorption chiller. Although intriguing from an energy perspective, this solar application is rare. No general sizing guidelines exist for active solar cooling systems.

SAMPLE PROBLEM
A small, off-grid residence in Ithaca, New York will collect all of its energy using photovoltaics and active solar thermal collectors.

1. Because of extended periods of overcast sky and extremely cold winter conditions, consider an indirect circulation system for the domestic water heating system, using evacuated tube solar collectors.

2. With four occupants, at 20 ft^2 [1.8 m^2] per occupant the estimated collector area is 80 ft^2 [7.4 m^2]. The higher end of the estimate range was used due to the climate.

3. An 80 gal [300 L] storage capacity is recommended by one guideline and (1.5)(80) = 120 gal [450 L] by another guideline. The larger capacity is more appropriate due to the off-grid nature of the building (demanding greater self-sufficiency).

4. Because the building is off-grid, does not have access to a natural gas line, and propane is not acceptable to the client, a wood stove backup water heating system is selected.

Examples

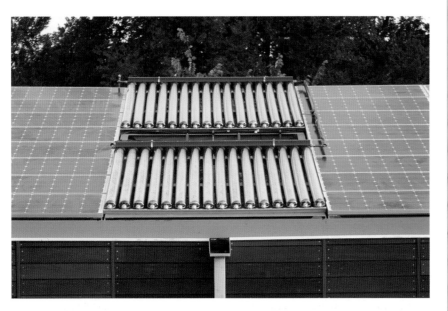

4.141 Evacuated tube solar thermal collectors (surrounded by photovoltaic panels) mounted on the roof of the 2005 Cornell University Solar Decathlon competition entry.
NICHOLAS RAJKOVICH

4.142 Flat plate solar thermal collectors (two panels on the left) integrate well with the photovoltaic modules (the array to the right) on the roof of the 2005 Cal Poly San Luis Obispo Solar Decathlon competition entry.

ENVELOPE

LIGHTING

HEATING

COOLING

ENERGY PRODUCTION

WATER & WASTE

ENVELOPE

LIGHTING

HEATING

COOLING

ENERGY PRODUCTION

WATER & WASTE

Further Information

Brown, G.Z. et al. 1992. *Inside Out: Design Procedures for Passive Environmental Technologies*, 2nd ed. John Wiley & Sons, New York.

Grumman, D.L. ed. 2003. *ASHRAE GreenGuide.* American Society of Heating, Refrigerating and Air-Conditioning Engineers, Atlanta, GA.

U.S. Department of Energy, A Consumer's Guide to Energy Efficiency and Renewable Energy, "Water Heating." www.eere.energy.gov/ consumer/your_home/water_heating/index.cfm/mytopic=12760

U.S. Department of Energy, Solar Hot Water and Space Heating & Cooling. www.eere.energy.gov/RE/solar_hotwater.html

BEYOND SCHEMATIC DESIGN

Detailed design of an active solar thermal system requires the expertise of a qualified mechanical engineer or solar consultant—who will be involved during design development to verify preliminary system sizing decisions and develop the final design of the system, including equipment selection and specification and consideration of controls and systems integration. Skillful detailing of collector supports and piping penetrations through the building envelope is critical to long-term owner satisfaction.

All solar thermal systems should be commissioned and a User's Manual prepared to assist the owner with system operations and maintenance.

GROUND SOURCE HEAT PUMPS use the mass of the earth to improve the performance of a vapor compression refrigeration cycle—which can heat in winter and cool in summer. Ground temperature fluctuates less than air temperature. The enormous mass of soil at even moderate depths also contributes to a seasonal temperature lag, such that when air temperatures are extreme (summer and winter), the ground temperature is comparatively mild. The price of the improved efficiency of a ground source heat pump is higher equipment cost.

GROUND SOURCE HEAT PUMPS

ENVELOPE

LIGHTING

HEATING

COOLING

ENERGY PRODUCTION

WATER & WASTE

4.143 Ground source heat pump using a vertical ground loop. KATE BECKLEY

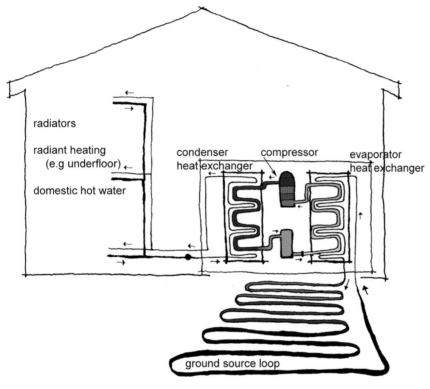

4.144 Schematic diagram of a water heating ground source heat pump. The majority of the components are conventional vapor compression system components (except for the ground source tubing and heat exchanger). Three options for use of the hot water are shown (radiator/baseboard convector, radiant heating, and domestic hot water heating). KATE BECKLEY

A basic ground source heat pump system includes a vapor compression cycle that produces the basic heating/cooling effect, air or water distribution of the heating/cooling effect, and a pump/tubing subsystem to obtain or reject heat to the soil or groundwater. The heat exchange fluid in the tubing (usually water) is circulated through a pipe field (or well) that is located outside of the building. The tubes—usually made of a high-density 3/4-in. [20 mm] polyethylene—allow the fluid to absorb heat from the surrounding soil during winter months, or dump heat to the soil during summer months. The amount/length of tubing depends upon the configuration of the system, the soil conditions, and the heating/cooling capacity required. A heat exchanger is used to transfer heat from the refrigerant in the heat pump cycle to air or water that is then circulated

INTENT
Energy-efficient heating and cooling, thermal comfort

EFFECT
Reduced energy consumption, lower utility bills

OPTIONS
Open loop versus closed loop, horizontal versus vertical loop, air or water delivery

COORDINATION ISSUES
Site planning, water heater integration, mechanical spaces and location

RELATED STRATEGIES
Various passive heating and cooling strategies

LEED LINKS
Energy & Atmosphere, Indoor Environmental Quality

PREREQUISITES
Site area that is large enough for desired configuration and capacity, an annual average ground temperature of 55–65 °F [13–18 °C]

throughout the building for climate control. A deep well may substitute for horizontally buried tubing.

Because of the thermal advantage provided by the more benign below-ground environment, this strategy presents an energy-efficient alternative to conventional heat pumps—and a great advantage over electric resistance heating systems.

Ground source heat pumps can be used in many types of buildings in virtually any climatic condition. The cost of a ground source heat pump system is dependent upon the depth of the frost line; the deeper the frost line, the deeper the tubing needs to be buried to benefit from a buffered ground temperature.

Various configurations have been used for the ground source component—closed horizontal loops are very common (these are pipe fields running parallel to the plane of the ground a few feet below the surface that require minimum excavation), closed vertical loops (similar to an enclosed well) can overcome deep frost lines and the constraints of small sites, open loop systems (such as an open well) can reduce costs in areas where acceptable groundwater is plentiful and connection to the aquifer is permitted.

Key Architectural Issues

Ground source heat pumps are a virtually invisible technology. The ground elements are underground (or underwater) and the associated mechanical equipment is practically identical in size to conventional active heating/cooling equipment. As a result, site planning is the most important factor when considering a ground source heat pump. Landscaping and paving may need to be designed to provide access to or protection for the tubing system. Landscaping can be used to provide soil shading, shielding the ground from solar gains (if this is climatically desirable). Landscaping may also be planned to highlight or illustrate the loop system occurring underground.

4.145 Typical configurations of ground source heat pumps. KATE BECKLEY

Implementation Considerations

- **Excavation.** Not only is excavation expensive, it can also be difficult and/or dangerous, with utilities (electric, cable, telephone, sewer, and water lines) often running below ground. A thorough analysis of the site and existing infrastructure will indicate how difficult (costly) excavation will be. If other systems require excavation at the same time, however, this can reduce the combined expense of the systems through a common burial.

- **Future site planning.** Because a ground source heat pump system can last between 35 and 50 years, planning for the future development of a site is critical. Depending upon site constraints, installation of a horizontal ground loop may make future development difficult or impractical. System sizing should take into account future loads expected due to expansion or change of function that may occur during the life of the system.

ENVELOPE

LIGHTING

HEATING

COOLING

ENERGY PRODUCTION

WATER & WASTE

- **Frost depth/ground temperature.** The economics of a ground source heat pump are seriously affected by prevailing ground temperatures—as this variable affects required excavation depth and the thermal efficiency of the system.

Design Procedure

The sizing of a ground source heat pump is a specialized and technical issue. For schematic design purposes, however, here are some guidelines for estimating the extent of the exterior "source" components that will be required.

Guideline for horizontal loops. Assume a loop capacity of 400–650 ft/ton of heating or cooling [35–60 m/kWh]. Trenches are normally 4–6 ft [1.2–1.9 m] deep and up to 400 ft [120 m] long, depending upon how many pipes are in a trench. Most horizontal loop installations use trenches about 6 in. [150 mm] wide.

A well-insulated 2000 ft^2 [185 m^2] home would need about a 3-ton [10.5 kW] system with 1500–1800 ft [460–550 m] of pipe. Non-residential building loads can be estimated using appropriate guidelines.

Guideline for vertical loops. The typical vertical loop will be 150–450 ft [45–140 m] deep. About 100 to 200 ft^2 of contact area will supply about 1 ton [3.5 kW] of heating/cooling.

Guideline for flow rates. Average ground loop flow rates should be about 2–3 gal per min/ton of heating or cooling [0.36–0.54 L/s per kW].

Examples

SAMPLE PROBLEM
What size horizontal ground loop will be required for a small office building in a temperate climate with an estimated cooling load of 10 tons [35 kW]?

Using 500 ft per ton [45 m per kW] as a guide (toward the low end of the range considering the temperate climate), the horizontal loop would be 500 × 10 = 5000 ft [45 × 35 = 1575 m] in length. Remembering that the purpose of the loop is to exchange heat with the soil, this length must be developed without too much crowding or overlap of tubes.

4.146 Installation of a large-scale horizontal ground loop in Arkansas. HYDRO-TEMP CORPORATION

4.147 Eight miles [12.9 km] of piping, staged for placement in a river—in a water-based ground source application. HYDRO-TEMP CORPORATION

ENVELOPE

LIGHTING

HEATING

COOLING

ENERGY PRODUCTION

WATER & WASTE

4.148 Ground source loops being installed in a 3-ft [0.9-m] deep trench at a school in Mississippi. HYDRO-TEMP CORPORATION

4.149 Aerial image showing preparation of trenches for ground source heat pump loops adjacent to a new house in Missouri. HYDRO-TEMP CORPORATION

Further Information

ASHRAE. 1997. *Ground Source Heat Pumps: Design of Geothermal Systems for Commercial & Institutional Buildings.* American Society of Heating, Refrigerating and Air-Conditioning Engineers, Atlanta, GA.

Econar Energy Systems. 1993. *GeoSource Heat Pump Handbook.* Available at: www.wbdg.org/ccb/DOE/TECH/geo.pdf

Geothermal Heat Pump Consortium. www.geoexchange.org/

Hydro-Temp Corporation. www.hydro-temp.com/

International Ground Source Heat Pump Association. www.igshpa.okstate.edu/

Oregon Institute of Technology, Geo-Heat Center. geoheat.oit.edu/

Stein, B. et al. 2006. *Mechanical and Electrical Equipment for Buildings,* 10th ed. John Wiley & Sons, Hoboken, NJ.

Water Furnace International. www.wfiglobal.com/

BEYOND SCHEMATIC DESIGN

During design development, detailed calculations of heating and cooling loads will be undertaken. These loads will be used to select appropriate equipment and distribution components. Similarly detailed calculations of required loop capacity and capability would be undertaken to finalize design of the below-ground system components.

ENVELOPE

LIGHTING

HEATING

COOLING

ENERGY PRODUCTION

WATER & WASTE

NOTES

ENVELOPE

LIGHTING

HEATING

COOLING

ENERGY PRODUCTION

WATER & WASTE

COOLING

The most effective method to lessen energy use for mechanical cooling is to eliminate the need for it through climate-adapted design. While this is not always possible, climate-based design strategies can reduce the run-time and/or the size of mechanical cooling systems. Identifying an appropriate cooling strategy for a particular building during schematic design requires an understanding of three things: climate, building type, and pattern of operation.

Monthly climate data, plotted on a bioclimatic chart, provides a visual indication of possible cooling strategies. In a hot desert climate, high thermal mass with night ventilation can provide comfort even with high daytime temperatures because of low relative humidity and large diurnal temperature swings. No amount of direct ventilation, however, can produce comfort under such daytime conditions. Similarly, no amount of thermal mass can produce comfort under a combination of high air temperature and high relative humidity. The first design requirement is to match the cooling strategy to the climate.

Buildings can be broadly grouped into two thermal types, skin-load dominated and internal-load dominated. Skin-load dominated buildings (most residences and small commercial buildings) do not generate much internal heat. Their cooling requirements are largely determined by exterior climate and design of the building envelope. Internal-load dominated buildings (such as large office buildings) have occupant, lighting, and equipment heat loads that are not driven by exterior conditions. The second design requirement is to match the cooling strategy to the building type.

COOLING

STRATEGIES
Cross Ventilation
Stack Ventilation
Evaporative Cool Towers
Night Ventilation of Thermal Mass
Earth Cooling Tubes
Earth Sheltering
Absorption Chillers

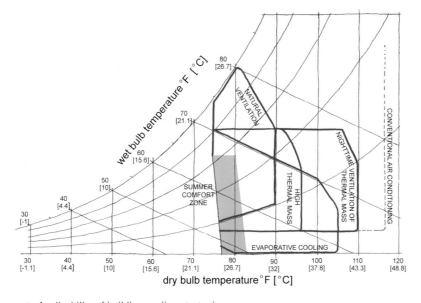

4.150 Applicability of building cooling strategies. ADAPTED FROM *ENERGY CONSERVATION THROUGH BUILDING DESIGN*

A designer must also understand patterns of building operation. A facility that is not open during the hottest time of day or year needn't be designed to provide comfort during those periods. For example, an elementary school that closes during summer months need not provide comfort under early August conditions. Additionally, if a school closes at 2:30 P.M., window shading and cooling requirements may be very different than for a school that closes at 4:30 P.M. The third design requirement is to understand the patterns of building usage.

ENVELOPE

LIGHTING

HEATING

COOLING

ENERGY PRODUCTION

WATER & WASTE

CROSS VENTILATION establishes a flow of cooler outdoor air through a space; this flow carries heat out of a building. Cross ventilation is a viable and energy-efficient alternative to mechanical cooling under appropriate climate conditions. The design objective may be direct cooling of occupants as a result of increased air speed and lowered air temperature or the cooling of building surfaces (as with nighttime flushing) to provide indirect comfort cooling. The effectiveness of this cooling strategy is a function of the size of the inlets, outlets, wind speed, and outdoor air temperature. Air speed is critical to direct comfort cooling; airflow rate is critical to structural cooling.

4.151 A café in Bang Bao, Koh Chang, Thailand utilizes high ceilings and windows for cross ventilation combined with thatched overhangs for shading. KATE BECKLEY

1 night spray radiant cooling
2 sunshades
3 high-performance glazing
4 efficient ventilation with heat recovery
5 radiant slab heating + cooling
6 lightshelves
7 naturally-ventilated top floor
8 spectrally-selective roofing
9 on-site water detention
10 fully daylit interiors with lighting controls

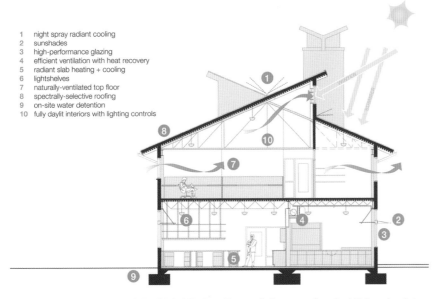

4.152 Schematic section of the Global Ecology Research Center at Stanford University, Palo Alto, California showing the integration of several strategies, including orientation to the prevailing winds to maximize cross ventilation potential on the second floor. EHDD ARCHITECTURE

Cross ventilation cooling capacity is fundamentally dependent upon the temperature difference between the indoor air and outdoor air. Cross ventilation cooling is only viable when the outdoor air is at least 3 °F [1.7 °C] cooler than the indoor air. Lesser temperature differences provide only marginal cooling effect (circulating air at room temperature, for example, cannot remove space heat or reduce space temperature). Outdoor airflow rate is another key capacity determinant. The greater the airflow, the greater the cooling capacity.

Wind pressure is the driving force behind cross ventilation. The greater the wind speed the greater the cross ventilation cooling potential. Prevailing wind direction often changes with the seasons, and may shift throughout the day. Wind speed is usually variable daily and seasonally—and typically very weak at night in the absence of solar heating of the ground. If no air enters the inlet of a cross ventilation system the system does not work.

Buildings are typically best naturally ventilated when they are very open to the breezes yet shaded from direct solar radiation. Building materials in a cross ventilated building may be light in weight, unless night ventilation

INTENT
Climate control (cooling), thermal comfort

EFFECT
Passive cooling

OPTIONS
Comfort cooling, structural cooling

COORDINATION ISSUES
Active heating and cooling, security, acoustics, air quality, orientation, footprint, internal partitions

RELATED STRATEGIES
Sidelighting, Stack Ventilation

LEED LINKS
Energy & Atmosphere, Indoor Environmental Quality

PREREQUISITES
Prevailing wind direction and design average wind speed (monthly), outdoor air temperatures (monthly, hourly), estimated design cooling load, desired indoor air temperature

ENVELOPE

LIGHTING

HEATING

COOLING

ENERGY PRODUCTION

WATER & WASTE

ENVELOPE

LIGHTING

HEATING

COOLING

ENERGY PRODUCTION

WATER & WASTE

of mass is intended—in which case thermally massive materials are necessary.

Key Architectural Issues

Successful cross ventilation requires a building form that maximizes exposure to the prevailing wind direction, provides for adequate inlet area, minimizes internal obstructions (between inlet and outlet), and provides for adequate outlet area. An ideal footprint is an elongated rectangle with no internal divisions. Siting should avoid external obstructions to wind flow (such as trees, bushes, or other buildings). On the other hand, proper placement of vegetation, berms, or wing walls can channel and enhance airflow at windward (inlet) openings.

Implementation Considerations

Cross ventilation for occupant comfort may direct airflow through any part of a space if the outdoor air temperature is low enough to provide for heat removal. At high outdoor air temperatures, cross ventilation may still be a viable comfort strategy if airflow is directed across the occupants (so they experience higher air speeds). Cross ventilation for nighttime structural cooling (when adequate wind speed exists) should be directed to maximize contact with thermally massive surfaces. A

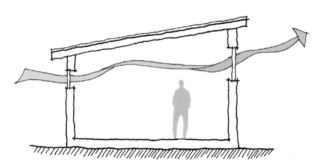

4.153 High inlets and outlets provide structural cooling but no air movement at occupant level. KATE BECKLEY

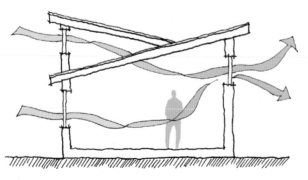

4.154 Clerestories do not assist in occupant level air movement. Cross ventilation through lower inlets provides occupant level air movement. Orientation of the building to the prevailing winds will maximize airflow. KATE BECKLEY

ENVELOPE
LIGHTING
HEATING
COOLING
ENERGY PRODUCTION
WATER & WASTE

design caution: high outdoor relative humidity may compromise occupant comfort even when adequate sensible cooling capacity is available.

Outside air is flushed through the building to provide cooling, allowing anything in the air to be introduced to the building. For this reason, careful consideration to the location of intake openings and ambient air quality is important. This strategy can also easily introduce noise into a building. Attention should be paid to nearby noise sources. Openings can be located to minimize the effect of noise on occupied spaces.

Design Procedure

Cross ventilation should normally be analyzed on a space-by-space basis. An exit opening equal in size to the inlet opening is necessary. This procedure considers only sensible loads and calculates the size of the inlet (assuming an equal sized outlet).

1. Arrange spaces to account for the fact that building occupants will find spaces near inlets (outdoor air) to be cooler than spaces near outlets (warmed air). Substantial heat sources should be placed near outlets, not near inlets.

2. Estimate design sensible cooling load (heat gain) for the space(s)—including all envelope and internal loads (but excluding ventilation/infiltration loads). *Btu/h or W*

3. State the design cooling load on a unit floor area basis. *Btu/h ft² or W/m²*

4. Establish the ventilation inlet area (this is free area, adjusted for the actual area of window that can be opened and the estimated impact of insect screens, mullions, shading devices) and the floor area of the space that will be cooled. The inlet area may be based upon other design decisions (such as view) or be a trial-and-error start to cooling system analysis. *ft² or m²*

5. Determine the inlet area as a *percentage* of the floor area: (inlet area/floor area) × 100.

6. Using Figure 4.155, find the intersection of the inlet area percentage (Step 5) and the design wind speed (from local climate data). This intersection gives the estimated cross ventilation cooling capacity—assuming a 3 °F [1.7 °C] indoor-outdoor air temperature difference. Design wind speed should represent a wind speed that is likely to be available during the time of design cooling load.

7. Compare the estimated cooling capacity (Step 6) with the required cooling capacity (Step 3).

8. Increase the proposed inlet area as required to achieve the necessary capacity; decrease the proposed inlet area as required to reduce excess cooling capacity.

This design procedure addresses "worst case" design conditions when outdoor air temperatures are usually high. Extrapolation beyond the

Assume a 4500 ft² [418 m²] small commercial building located in a temperate European climate.

1. A spatial layout anticipated to maximize cooling effectiveness for the occupants is established.

2. The estimated design cooling load is 120,000 Btu/h [35,170 W].

3. Given the 4500 ft² [418 m²] floor area, then:

    120,000/4500 = 26.7 Btu/h ft²

    [35,170/418 = 84.1 W/m²]

4. Assume 250 ft² [23 m²] of free inlet area as an initial trial.

5. Finding inlet area/floor area times 100 gives:

    (250/4500) × 100 = 5.6%

    [(23/418) × 100 = 5.6%]

6. With a design wind speed of 7 mph [3.1 m/s] the estimated cooling capacity is 45 Btu/h ft² [142 W/m²].

7. The available cooling capacity is greater than the required cooling capacity (45 > 26.7) [142 > 84.1].

8. The inlet area could be reduced to

    (26.7/45) × 250 = 148 ft²

    [(84.1/142) × 23 = 13.6 m²]

    and still provide adequate cross ventilation capacity.

ENVELOPE

LIGHTING

HEATING

COOLING

ENERGY PRODUCTION

WATER & WASTE

values in Figure 4.155 for a greater Δt is not recommended as a means of sizing openings. On the other hand, greater temperature differences will exist during the cooling season permitting a reduction in inlet and outlet size under such conditions. Extrapolation for higher wind speeds is not recommended due to potential discomfort from too-high indoor air speeds. Also, wind speeds at airport locations can be very different than at the city center or in suburban areas, depending upon the terrain. During schematic design, adjustments can be made to account for the variation by comparing "local" and airport wind speed data. As a rough estimate, urban wind speeds are often only a third of airport wind speeds; suburban wind speeds two-thirds of airport speeds.

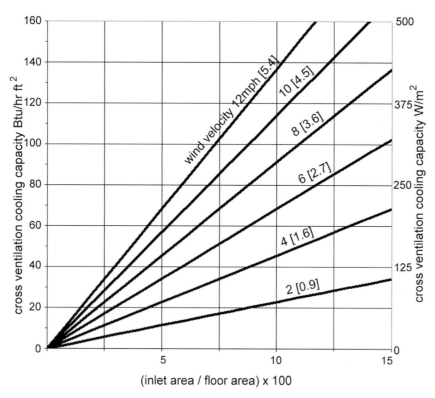

4.155 Cross ventilation cooling capacity. Heat removed per unit floor area (based upon a 3 °F [1.7 °C] temperature difference) as a function of size of inlet openings and wind speed.
KATHY BEVERS; DERIVED FROM EQUATIONS IN *MECHANICAL AND ELECTRICAL EQUIPMENT FOR BUILDINGS*, 10TH ED.

Examples

4.156 Operable windows along a corridor (left) allow air movement through a classroom building at IslandWood Campus, Bainbridge Island, Washington. Dog-trot house on Kauai, Hawaii (right) with cross ventilation through wrap-around porches used for indoor and outdoor living.

4.157 Café at the Honolulu Academy of Arts, Honolulu, Hawaii uses floor-to-ceiling sliding doors and ceiling fans to enhance air movement.

ENVELOPE

LIGHTING

HEATING

COOLING

ENERGY PRODUCTION

WATER & WASTE

ENVELOPE

LIGHTING

HEATING

COOLING

ENERGY PRODUCTION

WATER & WASTE

Further Information

Brown, G.Z. and M. DeKay. 2001. *Sun, Wind & Light: Architectural Design Strategies*, 2nd ed. John Wiley & Sons, New York.

National Climatic Data Center. www.ncdc.noaa.gov/oa/ncdc.html

Olgyay, V. 1963. *Design with Climate*. Princeton University Press, Princeton, NJ.

Royle, K. and C. Terry. 1990. *Hawaiian Design: Strategies for Energy Efficient Architecture*, Diane Publishing Co., Collingdale, PA.

Square One. www.squ1.com/site.html

Stein, B. et al. 2006. *Mechanical and Electrical Equipment for Buildings*, 10th ed. John Wiley & Sons, Hoboken, NJ.

BEYOND SCHEMATIC DESIGN

Validation of cross ventilation effectiveness during design development requires the use of sophisticated computer simulation or physical modeling tools. Computational fluid dynamics (CFD) is typically used for numerical simulations. Wind tunnel tests are typically used for physical simulations. Both involve steep learning curves, considerable technical expertise, and appropriate software/ laboratory facilities.

STACK VENTILATION is a passive cooling strategy that takes advantage of temperature stratification. It relies on two basic principles: (1) as air warms, it becomes less dense and rises; (2) ambient (hopefully cooler) air replaces the air that has risen. This system of natural convection creates its own air current, where warmer air is evacuated at a high point, and cooler outdoor air is brought in at a lower level. Stack ventilation will only work for thermal comfort conditioning when outside air temperature is cooler than the desired inside temperature. In order to function effectively (i.e. generate a substantial airflow), the difference between ambient indoor and outdoor air temperatures needs to be at least 3 °F [1.7 °C]. A greater temperature difference can provide more effective air circulation and cooling. Because it creates its own air current, stack ventilation is only minimally affected by building orientation. Air won't flow properly, however, if an outlet faces the windward direction.

4.158 Solar chimneys at the Building Research Establishment offices, Garston, Hertfordshire, UK. THERESE PEFFER

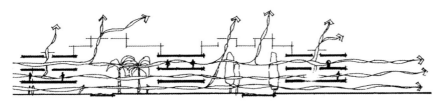

4.159 Schematic competition entry for the IBN-DLO Institute for Forestry and Nature Research in Wageningen, The Netherlands. Cooler outdoor air enters at the building perimeter, is warmed as it moves through the building, and then rises and exits through openings in the roof. BROOK MULLER

One way to achieve a greater temperature difference is to increase the height of a stack—the higher the stack, the greater the vertical stratification of temperatures. Because of the need for height to achieve effective air stratification, stack ventilation is often designed in section. See Figure 4.160 for a few common stack ventilation design strategies.

Another way to increase the temperature difference between entering and exiting air is to use solar energy to heat the air. In the BRE building (Figure 4.158) in the UK, ventilation stacks are located along the southern face of the buildings. These stacks are glazed with a translucent material so that solar radiation heats the air in the stack, causing an increase in airflow within the building.

As seen in the projects illustrating this strategy, the use of stack ventilation brings with it some interesting design possibilities. For example, in the BRE building the stacks are given greater height than the rest of the building, providing an architectural feature that highlights the significance of these devices to the functioning of the building.

Key Architectural Issues

To work well, a stack needs to generate a large temperature difference between exhaust air and incoming air. This can be done in several ways, including increasing stack height. A typical stack will provide effective ventilation for areas within the lower half of its total height. This implies that stacks be double the height of the building if they are

INTENT
Climate control (cooling), indoor air quality, thermal comfort

EFFECT
Reduced energy usage/costs, improved indoor air quality

OPTIONS
Central versus distributed stacks, stack height, number of stacks

COORDINATION ISSUES
Active heating and cooling, security, acoustics, air quality, orientation, footprint, internal partitions, fire and smoke control

RELATED STRATEGIES
Cross Ventilation, Night Ventilation of Mass, Evaporative Cool Towers, Double Envelope

LEED LINKS
Energy & Atmosphere, Indoor Environmental Quality, Innovation & Design Process

PREREQUISITES
Substantial height available for stack, potential for properly sized and located air inlets and outlets, solar access (for solar-assisted stacks only)

ENVELOPE

LIGHTING

HEATING

COOLING

ENERGY PRODUCTION

WATER & WASTE

to serve all floors of a building, or that they only serve a portion of the total floor area.

Stacks may be integrated or exposed. This is a question of expression: placing a stack on the building perimeter for solar access or integrating it into an atrium are very different architectural solutions. This decision will hinge not only upon aesthetics, but also upon climate conditions, cooling loads, and zoning and building codes. Exterior finishes and landscaping (plants, misting, and ground covers) can lower the incoming air temperature. Inlet (and outlet) sizing is critical to system performance. Inlet location, quantity, and size can affect building security, building facade appearance, and the quality of the incoming air (inlets should not be located near loading docks or in parking garages).

Implementation Considerations

Stacks tend to "blur" thermal zones, favoring spaces lower on the "ventilation chain"—in other words, providing more air movement (ventilation) at lower levels of a stack. Modular and separated stacks can address this problem, but an abundance of stacks is costly and requires more openings, which may not be possible for a variety of reasons; security, location, adjacencies, etc. Zoning by function and occupancy needs (both in plan and section) should be a primary schematic design consideration. Additionally, vertical stacks may need to be integrated with HVAC and structural systems to ensure effective utilization of space. Although stack ventilation will generally work in most climates, those with large diurnal temperature ranges are ideal.

Outside air is flushed through the building to provide cooling, allowing anything in the air to be introduced to the building. For this reason, careful consideration to the location of intake openings and ambient air quality is important. This strategy can also easily introduce noise into a building. Attention should be paid to nearby noise sources. Openings can be located to minimize the effect of noise on occupied spaces.

Design Procedure

A trial-and-error process will typically be required to zero-in on a workable design that balances system capabilities with cooling requirements.

1. Establish a workable stack height for the project. An effective stack will usually be twice as tall as the height of the tallest space it is ventilating. It is common to zone buildings such that only the lower floors are served by a stack (allowing for stack ventilation without exceptionally tall stack protrusions).

2. Size the stack openings (inlet, outlet, and throat area). The smallest of the following areas will define system performance: the total free area of inlet openings, the total free area of outlet openings, or the horizontal cross-sectional area (the "throat area") of the stack.

3. Using Figure 4.161, estimate the cooling capacity of the stack ventilation system on the basis of stack height and stack-to-floor area ratio (where floor area is the area served by the stack or stacks).

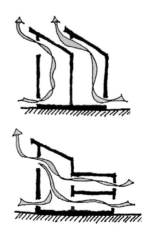

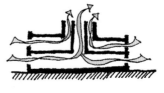
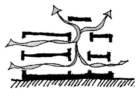

4.160 Various stack ventilation configurations. KATE BECKLEY

SAMPLE PROBLEM
A two-story building has a large atrium, 30 ft [9.1 m] in height.

1. The first floor of the building will be ventilated using the stack, providing an effective stack height of around 20 ft [6.1 m].

2. The openings at ground level and the top of the stack (atrium) are 200 ft² [18.6 m²] each; throat area is not a limiting factor.

3. The floor area to be ventilated via the stack is 2000 ft²

ENVELOPE

LIGHTING

HEATING

COOLING

ENERGY PRODUCTION

WATER & WASTE

4. Adjust stack openings and/or height as necessary to obtain desired cooling capacity.

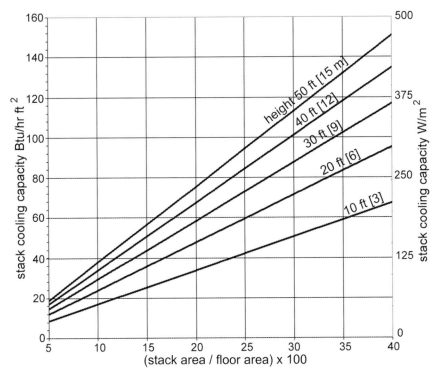

4.161 Stack ventilation capacity. Heat removed per unit floor area (based upon a 3 °F [1.7 °C] temperature difference) relative to stack size and height. KATHY BEVERS; DERIVED FROM EQUATIONS IN *MECHANICAL AND ELECTRICAL EQUIPMENT FOR BUILDINGS*, 10TH ED.

Examples

4.162 The Logan House (left), Tampa, Florida, a well-studied example of stack effect ventilation. Bubble-testing a model of the Logan House (right) to determine stack performance and examine alternative window configurations. ALISON KWOK | CHRISTINA BOLLO

[186 m^2]. The stack-to-floor area ratio is: (200/2000) (100) = 10. From Figure 4.161, the estimated cooling capacity of a 20-ft [6.1 m] stack with a ratio of 10 is about 24 Btu/h ft^2 [76 W/m^2]. This capacity assumes a 3 °F [1.7 °C] temperature difference between indoor and outdoor air (a reasonable assumption during a summer day).

4. This cooling capacity would be compared to the cooling load of the spaces being ventilated to determine whether it is adequate. As seen in Figure 4.161, capacity can be increased by increasing stack height (unlikely in this example) or by increasing stack opening area.

ENVELOPE

LIGHTING

HEATING

COOLING

ENERGY PRODUCTION

WATER & WASTE

ENVELOPE

LIGHTING

HEATING

COOLING

ENERGY PRODUCTION

WATER & WASTE

4.163 Windows open into the solar stack in an office space at the Building Research Establishment. The undulating ceiling provides a channel for cross ventilation across the building for night ventilation of thermal mass. THERESE PEFFER

4.164 South facade features photovoltaic panels, solar chimneys (with glass block to assist) and a stack ventilated top floor at the Building Research Establishment offices, Garston, Hertfordshire, UK. THERESE PEFFER

4.166 Stack ventilation towers exhaust warm air at Lanchester Library at Coventry University, Coventry, UK.

4.165 Lanchester Library features a large central vertical well that provides air supply and exhaust.

ENVELOPE

LIGHTING

HEATING

COOLING

ENERGY PRODUCTION

WATER & WASTE

4.167 Thermal chimneys on the north side of the Natural Energy Laboratory of Hawaii Authority building exhaust hot interior air through a void under the copper roofing. FERRARO CHOI AND ASSOCIATES LTD.

4.168 The Natural Energy Laboratory of Hawaii Authority, Kona, Hawaii integrates numerous green strategies, including photovoltaics, stack ventilation, use of seawater for space cooling, condensation collection for irrigation, and native plantings. This project is LEED-NC Platinum certified. FERRARO CHOI AND ASSOCIATES LTD.

Further Information

Grondzik, W. et al. 2002. "The Logan House: Signing Off," *Proceedings of 27th National Passive Solar Conference—Solar 2002* (Reno, NV). American Solar Energy Society, Boulder, CO.

Stein, B. et al. 2006. *Mechanical and Electrical Equipment for Buildings*, 10th ed. John Wiley & Sons, Hoboken, NJ.

Whole Building Design Guide, "Natural Ventilation." www.wbdg.org/design/naturalventilation.php

BEYOND SCHEMATIC DESIGN

The estimated sizing and performance evaluation of stack ventilation made during schematic design will be verified during design development. Such validation is not easy, and might include the use of computer simulation tools or physical models to optimize the effectiveness of potential design configurations.

NOTES

EVAPORATIVE COOL TOWERS use the principles of direct evaporative cooling and downdraft to passively cool hot dry outdoor air and circulate it through a building. The resulting cooler and more humid air can be circulated through a building using the inertia inherent in the falling cool air. Cool towers are sometimes referred to as reverse chimneys.

Hot dry air is exposed to water at the top of the tower. As water evaporates into the air inside the tower, the air temperature drops and the moisture content of the air increases; the resulting denser air drops down the tower and out of an opening at the base. The air movement down the tower creates a negative (suction) pressure at the top of the tower and a positive pressure at the base. Air exiting the base of the tower enters the space or spaces requiring cooling.

4.169 Evaporative cool tower at the Center for Global Ecology, Stanford University, Menlo Park, California.

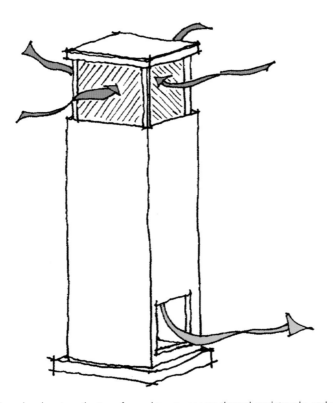

4.170 Warm dry air enters the top of a cool tower, passes through moist pads, and exits the base of the tower as cooler and more humid air. KATHLEEN BEVERS

An evaporative cool tower can provide a very low-energy alternative to active (mechanical) cooling for a building in a hot and dry climate. The sole energy input (required only in low water pressure situations) is for a pump to circulate water. A cool tower does, however, consume water—which may be a concern in an arid climate.

In theory (and generally in practice) an evaporative cooling process exchanges sensible cooling for latent heating along a constant enthalpy (heat content) line. As the process proceeds, dry bulb and wet bulb air temperatures converge. Theoretically the air emerging from the evaporation process would have a dry bulb temperature equal to the

INTENT
Climate control (cooling), thermal comfort

EFFECT
Passive cooling, humidification

OPTIONS
Number and location of towers

COORDINATION ISSUES
Effective thermal envelope, spatial layout, generally unimpeded interior airflow

RELATED STRATEGIES
Night Ventilation of Mass, Water Reuse/Recycling, Water Catchment Systems

LEED LINKS
Energy & Atmosphere, Indoor Environmental Quality, Innovation & Design Process

PREREQUISITES
Hot dry climate, available height for towers, water source

ENVELOPE

LIGHTING

HEATING

COOLING

ENERGY PRODUCTION

WATER & WASTE

wet bulb temperature. In practical applications the process results in a dry bulb temperature that is about 20 to 40% higher than the wet bulb (Givoni 1994).

Evaporative cool tower performance is dependent upon the wet bulb depression (the difference between dry and wet bulb air temperatures). The greater the wet bulb depression the greater the potential difference between the ambient outdoor air temperature and the temperature of the cooled air exiting the tower. The airflow rate from the base of the cool tower is dependent upon the wet bulb depression and the design of the tower—specifically the height of the tower and the area of the wetted pads at the top of the tower.

Key Architectural Issues

Cool towers can add architectural interest to a building. The cool tower at the Visitor Center in Zion National Park in Utah was designed to echo the form of the dramatic high canyon walls along the river in the park. The base of the tower in the Visitor Center's interior invokes the feeling of a massive hearth.

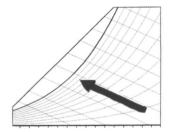

4.171 Evaporative cooling as a psychrometric process.

Evaporative cool towers work best with open floor plans that permit the cooled air to circulate throughout the interior without being impeded by walls or partitions. Cool towers do not rely upon wind for air circulation and require minimal energy input. Cool towers do require that the evaporative pads be continuously kept wet and increase the relative humidity of the ambient air. Cool towers also involve fairly large airflow volumes that must be accommodated. This above-normal airflow can be a plus relative to indoor air quality and occupant satisfaction with the thermal environment.

Because a cool tower involves wetted pads (or misting) and regions of high relative humidity, biological growth (mold) is a potential. Ready access for inspection and maintenance of the wetted areas should be provided.

Consideration of a dual-function tower may be warranted in some climates—operating as an evaporative cool tower during the day and a stack ventilator during the night.

Implementation Considerations

Evaporative cool towers work best under dry, hot conditions. Under these conditions (in an arid climate) the wet bulb depression is high so the cooling effect is maximized. Also, the increase in relative humidity of the exiting air is not a problem (and is likely a benefit). The effectiveness of a cool tower does not depend upon wind, so cool towers can be used in areas with little or no wind resources (Givoni 1994) and on sites with limited or no wind access.

Givoni (1994) developed formulas for estimating the effectiveness of an evaporative cool tower based upon exit temperature and airflow. He found that wind speed had little impact on exit temperature. These formulas are based upon a limited amount of data for towers with wetted pads at the top, but are considered appropriate for schematic design.

ENVELOPE

LIGHTING

HEATING

COOLING

ENERGY PRODUCTION

WATER & WASTE

Design Procedure

1. Establish design conditions. Find the design ambient dry bulb (DB) and mean coincident wet bulb (WB) temperatures for the hottest time of the year for the building site. The wet bulb depression is the difference between the dry bulb and wet bulb temperatures.

2. Find the approximate exiting air temperature to determine feasibility. Using the wet bulb depression and the ambient outdoor dry bulb temperature, estimate the exiting air temperature using Figure 4.172. If this temperature is low enough to provide cooling, continue to Step 3.

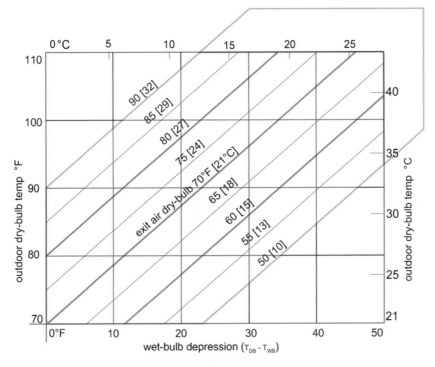

4.172 Exiting evaporative cool tower air temperature as a function of wet-bulb depression and outdoor dry-bulb air temperature. KATHLEEN BEVERS; DERIVED FROM *MECHANICAL AND ELECTRICAL EQUIPMENT FOR BUILDINGS*, 10TH ED.

3. Determine the necessary airflow rate. Determine the quantity of exiting airflow (at the leaving dry bulb temperature) required to offset the space/building sensible cooling load.

$$Q = q/(F)(\Delta t)$$

where,
Q = airflow rate, cfm [L/s]
q = design sensible cooling load, Btu/h [W]
Δt = temperature difference between supply (cool tower exiting) air and room air, °F [°C]
F = conversion factor, 1.1 [1.2]

4. Determine tower height and area of wetted pads. Based upon the required airflow rate, use the graph in Figure 4.173 to determine an appropriate tower height and wetted pad area.

SAMPLE PROBLEM
Determine if an evaporative cool tower would cool a 4000 ft^2 [372 m^2] office building in Boulder, Colorado with an estimated cooling load of 15 Btu/h ft^2 [47.3 W/m^2].

1. Boulder has a design DB of 91 °F [32.8 °C] and a mean coincident WB of 59 °F [15 °C]—giving a wet bulb depression of (91−59 °F) = 32 °F [17.8 °C]. Looking at Figure 4.172 this falls well within the conditions appropriate for evaporative cooling.

2. The wet bulb depression is (91−59 °F) = 32 °F [17.8 °C]. From Figure 4.172, an exiting air temperature of about 65 °F [18.3 °C] is predicted.

3. Determine the amount of supply air at T_{exit} required to offset the cooling load.

   $Q = q/(1.1)(\Delta t)$

   q = (15 Btu/h ft^2) (4000 ft^2) = 60,000 Btu/h

   Δt = (78–65) = 17 °F

   Q = 60,000/(1.1)(17)

   Q = 3210 cfm [1515 L/s]

   A flow rate of about 3200 cfm [1510 L/s] of 65 °F [18.3 °C] exiting tower air will offset the cooling load of 15 Btu/h ft^2 [47.3 W/m^2].

4. From Figure 4.173, a wet-bulb depression of 26 °F [14.4 °C] and a flow rate of 3200 cfm [1,510 L/s] suggests that a 25-ft [7.6 m] tower with a 48 ft^2 [4.5 m^2] total pad size will cool the office building at an exiting temperature of 65 °F [18.3 °C].

ENVELOPE

LIGHTING

HEATING

COOLING

ENERGY PRODUCTION

WATER & WASTE

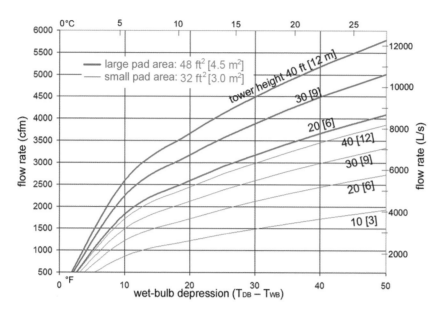

4.173 Recommended cool tower height and wetted pad area as a function of required airflow rate and wet-bulb depression. KATHLEEN BEVERS; DERIVED FROM *MECHANICAL AND ELECTRICAL EQUIPMENT FOR BUILDINGS*, 10TH ED.

Examples

4.174 Evaporative cool towers at Zion National Park Visitor's Center, Zion, Utah. HARVEY BRYAN

4.175 Evaporative cool tower at the Global Ecology Research Center at Stanford University, Menlo Park, California. © PETER AARON/ESTO

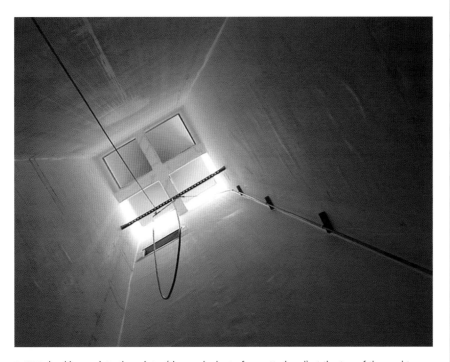

4.176 Looking up into the mister (the equivalent of a wetted pad) at the top of the cool tower of the Global Ecology Research Center. ROBERT MARCIAL

ENVELOPE

LIGHTING

HEATING

COOLING

ENERGY PRODUCTION

WATER & WASTE

4.177 Exit opening—located in the lobby area—of the cool tower at the Global Ecology Research Center. © PETER AARON/ESTO

Further Information

Chalfoun, N. 1997. "Design and Application of Natural Down-Draft Evaporative Cooling Devices," *Proceedings 1997 Conference of ASES*. American Solar Energy Society, Boulder, CO.

Givoni, B. 1994. *Passive and Low Energy Cooling of Buildings.* Van Nostrand Reinhold, New York.

Givoni, B. 1998. *Climate Considerations in Building and Urban Design.* Van Nostrand Reinhold, New York.

Global Ecology Research Center, Stanford University. globalecology. stanford.edu/DGE/CIWDGE/CIWDGE.HTML (select "Building")

Thompson, T., N. Chalfoun and M. Yoklic. 1994. "Estimating the Thermal Performance of Natural Draft Evaporative Coolers," *Energy Conversion and Management*, Vol. 35, No. 11, pp. 909–915.

U.S. Department of Energy, Office of Energy Efficiency and Renewable Energy, High Performance Buildings, Zion National Park Visitor Center. www.eere.energy.gov/buildings/highperformance/zion/

BEYOND SCHEMATIC DESIGN

If shown to be feasible during schematic design, the technical details and architectural detailing of the cool tower(s) would occur during design development. At that time the use of alternative sources of water (perhaps a cistern) or pumping energy (perhaps PV) can be solidified.

ENVELOPE

LIGHTING

HEATING

COOLING

ENERGY PRODUCTION

WATER & WASTE

NIGHT VENTILATION OF THERMAL MASS takes advantage of the capacitive properties of massive materials to maintain comfortable space temperatures. The mass materials moderate air temperature, reducing extreme swings of alternating hot and cold temperatures. During the day, when temperatures are warmer and solar radiation and internal loads act to increase interior temperatures, the building mass absorbs and stores heat. At night, when outdoor air temperatures are cooler, outdoor air is circulated through the building. The heat that was absorbed during the day is released from the mass to the cooler air circulated through the space and then discharged outdoors. This cycle allows the mass to discharge, renewing its potential to absorb more heat the following day. During colder months the same mass may be used to help passively heat the space (see Related Strategies).

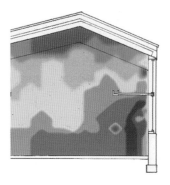

4.178 Isothermal rendering of a thermally massive partition wall.
WENDY FUJINAKA

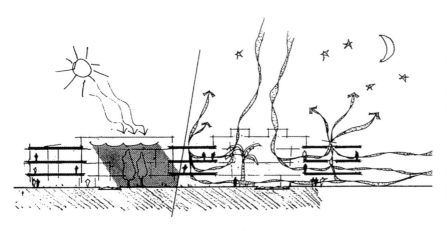

4.179 Schematic competition entry for the IBN-DLO Institute for Forestry and Nature Research in Wageningen, The Netherlands. During the day, heat is absorbed by interior mass; at night that heat is released into cool outdoor air circulated through the space.
BROOK MULLER

The success of this strategy is highly dependent upon the local climate. The diurnal temperature difference must be large (around 20 °F [11 °C]). High daytime temperatures (and/or solar loads and internal heat gains) produce cooling loads. Low nighttime temperatures can provide a heat sink (a source of coolth). The thermal mass connects these two conditions across time.

Key Architectural Issues

Because this strategy relies upon the extensive flow of outdoor air throughout a building, the arrangement of building spaces is critical to its success—especially if natural ventilation will provide the airflow. The use of stack ventilation as the airflow driver is encouraged, since in many climates adequate nighttime cross ventilation may be difficult due to the relatively low wind speeds that tend to prevail on summer nights.

The structural loads associated with mass will affect the spacing and sizing of load-bearing members (of particular concern in a multistory

INTENT
Climate control (cooling), thermal comfort

EFFECT
Passive cooling, natural ventilation, reduced energy consumption

OPTIONS
Location and type of mass, cross ventilation and/or stack ventilation, mechanically assisted ventilation

COORDINATION ISSUES
Building orientation, massing, internal spatial layout, security

RELATED STRATEGIES
Cross Ventilation, Stack Ventilation, Shading Devices, Direct Gain, Indirect Gain

LEED LINKS
Energy & Atmosphere, Indoor Environmental Quality

PREREQUISITES
Reasonable diurnal temperature swing, acceptable nighttime relative humidities, ability to ventilate at night, adequate mass (spread over a large surface area)

ENVELOPE

LIGHTING

HEATING

COOLING

ENERGY PRODUCTION

WATER & WASTE

building). Concrete is often used to provide mass for this strategy, as well as the structural strength to overcome the added loads. Exposed structural systems are a logical means of providing thermal mass. Any material with substantial mass will work as thermal storage, however, including masonry units and water containers.

For this strategy to work effectively, the thermal mass needs to be exposed to the ventilation airflow. The surface area of exposed thermal mass is usually 1 to 3 times that of the conditioned (passively cooled) floor area—which will clearly have a large impact upon the design of a building.

It is critical to reduce thermal loads as much as possible through the use of appropriate microclimate and envelope design techniques before attempting to passively cool a building.

Implementation Considerations

For effective night ventilation, the thermal mass must be washed by a flow of outdoor air. This is a critical implementation issue.

Because the hours of heat gain exceed the hours of cooling potential during the summer, openings need to be large to move a lot of air in a short time period. This strategy relies upon the ability to close the building during the day, and open it up substantially at night. Security, therefore, is an issue. Adequate daytime ventilation will need to be provided to ensure indoor air quality during occupied hours.

Outside air is flushed through the building to provide cooling, allowing anything in the air to be introduced to the building. For this reason, careful consideration to the location of intake openings and ambient air quality is important. This strategy can also easily introduce noise into a building (although this may be less of a concern at night than with daytime ventilation strategies). Attention should be paid to occupancy schedules and nearby noise sources. Openings can be located to minimize the effect of noise on occupied spaces.

Design Procedure

During schematic design, the designer needs to establish the potential of this strategy in a given site/building context, the storage capacity of the mass, and the ventilation strategy to cool the mass. Adapted from guidelines in *Mechanical and Electrical Equipment for Buildings*, 10th ed., this procedure is based upon a "high" mass building—for example, a passive solar-heated, direct gain building with an exposed concrete structure. Buildings with less mass will perform differently and the designer must consider this.

1. Determine the potential of night ventilation of thermal mass for the given location. Climates with a large diurnal swing in temperature are ideal candidates for this strategy. Applicable climate data are available from many sources for populated locales—and can be estimated for more rural/remote sites.

SAMPLE PROBLEM
An 1800 ft^2 [167 m^2] small office in Bozeman, Montana is to be constructed with lightweight, exposed concrete floors and walls with approximately 3800 ft^2 [350 m^2] of exposed surface. A preliminary estimate of average daily cooling load is 170 Btu/ft^2 per day [510 Wh/m^2 day], based upon a 9-hour working day.

1. Climate data suggest that night ventilation of mass is possible during July and August.

ENVELOPE

LIGHTING

HEATING

COOLING

ENERGY PRODUCTION

WATER & WASTE

2. Obtain climate data and calculate the lowest possible indoor air temperature. Find the highest summer design dry bulb air temperature (DBT), the mean daily temperature range for the project site, and calculate the lowest DB temperature.

lowest DBT = (highest DBT − mean daily range)

3. Approximate the lowest mass temperature. This estimate is important because the objective is to cool the mass at night so its temperature is close to the lowest DBT. To approximate the lowest mass temperature for high daily range climates (greater than 30 °F [16.7 °C]), add 1/4 of the mean daily range to the lowest DBT. For low daily range climates (less than 30 °F [16.7 °C]), add 1/5 of the mean daily range to the lowest DBT.

4. Calculate the storage capacity of the thermal mass. From Figure 4.180, use the summer design outdoor dry bulb temperature and the mean daily range of temperatures to determine the thermal mass storage capacity. Coordinated with the operational hours (open or closed mode) of daily heat gain, the thermal mass should have enough capacity to perform satisfactorily with this cooling strategy.

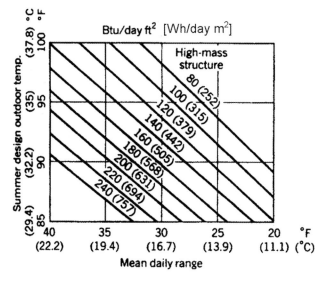

4.180 Estimated storage capacity of high thermal mass buildings. The graph assumes a mass-area to floor-area ratio of 2:1—roughly equivalent to a 3-in. thick [75 mm] concrete slab (or both sides of a 6-in. [150 mm] thick slab or wall) providing thermal storage capacity.
MECHANICAL AND ELECTRICAL EQUIPMENT FOR BUILDINGS, 10TH ED.

5. Determine the percentage of stored heat that can be removed at night. The most heat can be removed from the mass when the Δt, the temperature difference between the mass and the outside air, is the greatest. From Figure 4.181, using the mean daily range and the summer design outdoor temperature, determine the percentage of heat gains that can be removed.

6. Determine the ventilation rate necessary to night cool the thermal mass. If the building is completely passive, refer to the Cross

2. The design summer temperature is 87 °F [30.6 °C], and the mean daily range is 32 °F [18 °C]. The lowest indoor air temperature that can be achieved, then, is (87 − 32) = 55 °F [12.8 °C], which would be very acceptable (at least from a cooling perspective).

3. The lowest mass temperature is estimated as: (1/4)(32 °F) = 8 °F [4.4 °C], where 8 °F + 55 °F = 63 °F [17.2 °C].

4. From Figure 4.180, a building with high mass (with an 87 °F design temperature and 32 °F daily range) will absorb about 210 Btu per ft² per day [630 Wh per m² per day]. The average daily cooling load of 170 Btu/ft² per day [510 Wh/m² day] is less than this capacity.

5. By extrapolation from Figure 4.181 (for the defined design conditions), approximately 12% of the heat stored each day can be removed by night ventilation during the "best" cooling hour. This represents (0.12)(210 Btu/ft² day = 25.2 Btu/ft² day [79.5 Wh/m² day].

6. From Figure 4.182 the maximum hourly difference in temperature is about 15 °F degrees [8.3 °C].

Refer to the Cross Ventilation strategy to determine if it is viable to remove excess heat at night using that strategy, as well as to size the openings. If not, and stack ventilation is also not feasible, consider mechanical circulation of ventilation air.

7. Night ventilation of thermal mass is considered a viable strategy for this situation—assuming that adequate airflow can be provided (either passively or mechanically).

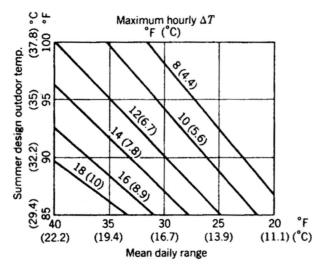

4.181 Percentage of heat gains stored in the thermal mass that can be removed during the "best" hour of night ventilation cooling. *MECHANICAL AND ELECTRICAL EQUIPMENT FOR BUILDINGS,* 10TH ED.

Ventilation or Stack Ventilation strategies to determine if ventilation openings are adequately sized to remove stored heat during the hour of maximum cooling (using the Δt from Figure 4.182). Note that nighttime average wind speeds are often much lower than daytime speeds, hindering the effectiveness of cross ventilation. If forced ventilation is used, the required ventilation rate during the hour of maximum cooling can be estimated from the following equation:

$$Q = q/(1.1)\,(\Delta t)$$

where,

Q = required air flow rate, cfm [L/s]
q = sensible cooling load, Btu/h [W]
F = conversion factor, 1.1 [1.2]
Δt = temperature difference, °F [°C]

4.182 Temperature difference between interior mass and outdoor temperature for the "best" hour of nighttime cooling. *MECHANICAL AND ELECTRICAL EQUIPMENT FOR BUILDINGS,* 10TH ED.

7. Compare ventilation requirements with other design needs. Depending upon the ventilation strategy chosen, the inlet/outlet openings required may or may not work with other building needs. It is critical to double-check that the proposed cooling system is compatible with other building requirements (e.g. security, circulation, indoor air quality, and fire safety).

Examples

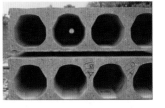

4.183 Cored concrete slabs used as thermal storage and air circulation channels in a night ventilation system. JOHN REYNOLDS

4.184 The Emerald People's Utility District office building in Eugene, Oregon uses mass in the floor, roof/ceiling, and partition walls coupled with cross and mechanical ventilation to cool the building during the overheated season. JOHN REYNOLDS

Further Information

Brown, G.Z. and M. DeKay. 2001. *Sun, Wind & Light: Architectural Design Strategies*, 2nd ed. John Wiley & Sons, New York.

Haglund, B. "Thermal Mass In Passive Solar Buildings," a Vital Signs Resource Package. Available at: arch.ced.berkeley.edu/vitalsigns/res/downloads/rp/thermal_mass/mass-big.pdf

Moore, F. 1993. *Environmental Control Systems: Heating, Cooling, Lighting.* McGraw-Hill, Inc., New York.

Stein, B. et al. 2006. *Mechanical and Electrical Equipment for Buildings*, 10th ed. John Wiley & Sons, Hoboken, NJ.

BEYOND SCHEMATIC DESIGN

If night ventilation of thermal mass proves feasible during schematic design, all design decisions regarding location and quantity of mass and location and size of ventilation openings will be revisited during design development as more accurate information regarding building loads becomes available. Detailing of system elements to ensure that design intents and performance requirements are met is essential.

NOTES

ENVELOPE

LIGHTING

HEATING

COOLING

ENERGY PRODUCTION

WATER & WASTE

EARTH COOLING TUBES (cool tubes) are used to cool a space by bringing outdoor air into an interior space through underground pipes or tubes. The air is cooled (and possibly dehumidified) as it travels. The cooling effect is dependent upon the existence of a reasonable temperature difference between the outdoor air and the soil at the depth of the tube. A cool tube can be used to temper incoming air when the soil temperature is below outdoor air temperature, or to provide actual space cooling effect if soil temperature is below the intended room temperature. A cool tube can also be used to temper outdoor air in the winter, but it will not provide any space heating effect.

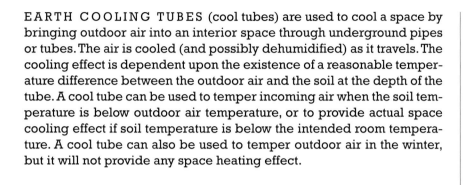

4.186 Schematic diagram showing an open loop cooling tube configuration, assisted by stack effect ventilation. The length of the cooling tube is greatly understated in this sketch. KATE BECKLEY

In an open-loop configuration air exiting a cooling tube is introduced directly into an interior space (usually with the assistance of electric fans). In Figure 4.186 stack ventilation is being used, in addition to a fan, to draw cool air from the earth tube into and through the interior space. In a closed-loop configuration room air is circulated through the tubes and back into the occupied spaces. The use of an electric fan makes the example in Figure 4.186 a hybrid system (as opposed to a fully passive system).

In either open- or closed-loop mode, the cooling effect of the earth tubes is commonly used to reduce overall space cooling load rather than to attempt to cool a space solely with cool tubes. The cooling (or heating) contribution is often focused upon cancelling the outdoor air (ventilation) load. Cooling a building exclusively using earth tubes is rarely cost-effective because of the large quantity of very long tubes required to do the job. Material and installation cost would likely be prohibitive—unless there is a mitigating factor such as easy or cheap excavation.

Key Architectural Issues

Earth cooling tubes need to be constructed from a durable, strong, corrosion-resistant, and cost-effective material such as aluminum or plastic. According to the U.S. Department of Energy (USDOE), the choice of

ENVELOPE

LIGHTING

HEATING

COOLING

ENERGY PRODUCTION

WATER & WASTE

EARTH COOLING TUBES

4.185 Installation of earth cooling tubes for a residential application. TANG LEE

INTENT
Climate control (cooling), tempering of outdoor air

EFFECT
Passive cooling, tempering (cooling/warming) of outdoor air

OPTIONS
Closed-loop or open-loop configuration

COORDINATION ISSUES
Site planning, soil conditions, cooling loads, spatial layout (including partitions), indoor air quality

RELATED STRATEGIES
Stack Ventilation, Cross Ventilation, Night Ventilation of Mass

LEED LINKS
Energy & Atmosphere, Indoor Environmental Quality

PREREQUISITES
Estimated cooling loads, monthly climate data (temperature and relative humidity), basic soils information (type, approximate moisture content)

material has little influence on thermal performance—although thermal conductivity is to be valued and thermal resistance avoided. While PVC or polypropylene tubes have been used, these materials may be more prone to bacterial growth than other materials.

The diameter of earth cooling tubes is typically between 6 and 20 in. [150–500 mm] depending upon tube length. Larger diameter tubes permit a greater airflow, but also place more of the air volume at a distance from the heat exchanging surface of the tube. The length of the tubes is a function of the required cooling capacity, tube diameter, and site factors that influence cooling performance such as:

- local soil conditions
- soil moisture
- tube depth
- other site-specific factors (such as vegetation or evaporative cooling).

To optimize cooling performance tubes should be buried at least 6 ft [1.8 m] deep. When possible the tubes should be placed in shady locations.

According to the USDOE, the temperature of soil typically varies as follows:

- From 20 to 100 ft [6–30 m] deep, about 2–3 °F [1.1–1.7 °C] higher than the mean annual air temperature.
- Less than 10 ft [3 m] deep, soil temperatures are influenced by ambient air temperatures and vary throughout the year.
- Near the surface, soil temperatures closely correspond to air temperatures.

4.187 Non-perforated drainage pipes used as earth cooling tubes. TANG LEE

4.188 Inserting earth cooling tubes through a basement foundation wall. TANG LEE

Implementation Considerations

Earth cooling tubes will not perform well as a source of cooling unless the soil temperature is decidedly lower than the desired room air temperature. Tempering of outdoor air, however, simply requires that the soil temperature surrounding the earth tubes be reasonably lower than the outdoor air temperature. Over the course of the cooling season, the soil surrounding earth tubes will warm up from its normal temperature condition due to the transfer of heat from the tube to the soil. This tends to degrade performance over time during a cooling or warming season.

Although condensation in earth tubes is possible, dehumidification of outdoor air is usually difficult and may require the use of mechanical dehumidifiers or passive desiccant systems.

A major concern with cooling tubes is that the tubes can become a breeding ground for mold, fungi, and/or bacteria. Condensation or

4.189 Three earth cooling tubes enter a building and terminate in a header where an in-duct fan pulls air from the tubes and discharges it into a return air duct. TANG LEE

groundwater seepage can cause water to accumulate in the tubes exacerbating the problem. If the tubes cannot be easily monitored and/or cleaned it might be wise to consider an indirect approach whereby cooling effect is transferred from "tube air" to another independent air stream prior to entry into the building. This will, however, decrease system capacity. Grilles and screens are advisable to keep insects and rodents from entering occupied spaces from the exterior through the tubes.

Design Procedure

1. Determine the summer soil temperature. The summer soil temperature at a depth of 6 ft [1.8 m] is roughly equal to the average monthly dry bulb air temperature of the site. For a rough estimate of the cooling capacity of an earth tube installation calculate the average ambient temperature for the entire cooling season and use this value as an estimate for the ground temperature (T_{GROUND}) at the site.

2. Determine desired tube exiting air temperature. Decide on the desired outflow air temperature from the earth tube ($T_{OUTFLOW}$). This will be the supply air temperature (which must be several degrees lower than room air temperature) if the earth tube installation is handling the entire cooling load (not common or recommended). If the earth tube is precooling air for an air-conditioning system a higher exiting temperature would be acceptable. It is unlikely that exiting air temperature will be lower than 4 °F [2.2 °C] above the temperature of the soil surrounding the tube.

3. Determine the soil moisture characteristics. From on-site testing and observation, establish whether the soil surrounding the earth tube will normally be dry, average, or wet. Figure 4.190 is based upon average soil moisture—the cooling capacity in wet soil conditions would be approximately twice as high as for average soil; for dry soil approximately half as great. Soil conditions play an important role in earth tube performance.

4. Estimate the cooling load for the earth tube installation. Estimate the design cooling load for the building based upon building type and size. This load will be expressed in Btu/h [kW]. For an air tempering installation, the earth tube load will be some reasonable portion of the full cooling load. For outdoor air tempering, simply neutralizing the outdoor air load is the objective.

5. Determine the length of earth tube required. Use Figure 4.190 to estimate the required length of earth tube. The intersection of the $T_{OUTFLOW} - T_{GROUND}$ value (Steps 1 and 2) and the cooling load (Step 4) gives the required tube length. For wet or dry soil conditions use the adjustments noted in Step 3.

SAMPLE PROBLEM
Design an earth tube system to cool ventilation air for a 3000 ft² [279 m²] office building in Michigan. The hourly heat gain is estimated to be 10.2 Btu/h ft² [32.2 W/m²] of which 2.0 Btu/h ft² [6.3 W/m²] is due to required outdoor ventilation air.

1. The average ambient air temperature during the cooling season in Michigan is estimated as 70 °F [21.1 °C], which is considered equal to T_{GROUND}.

2. The desired indoor temperature is 78 °F [25.6 °C]. Assuming that the cooling tube will be sized only to reduce the outdoor air load, set the exiting temperature at 78 °F [25.6 °C], which is equal to $T_{OUTFLOW}$.

3. The soil on the site tests as neither damp nor dry; the "average" soil values of Figure 4.190 are appropriate.

4. The cooling load to be handled by the earth tube is (2.0 Btu/h ft²) (3000 ft²) = 6,000 Btu/h [(6.3)(279) = 1758 W]

5. ($T_{OUTFLOW} - T_{GROUND}$) = (78 − 70 °F) = 8 °F [4.4 °C]. Using Figure 4.190, enter the horizontal axis at 8 and move up to the 6000 line (extrapolating ever so slightly). At this intersection, move horizontally to read the vertical axis value of about 800 ft [244 m] of tube length.

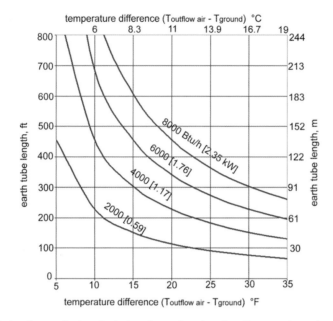

4.190 Estimating required cool tube length as a function of cooling capacity and temperature difference assuming average soil moisture content. The chart is based upon a tube diameter of 12 in. [300 mm] and a reasonably low flow rate. KATHY BEVERS; DERIVED FROM EQUATIONS IN *MECHANICAL AND EQUIPMENT FOR BUILDINGS*, 10TH ED.

Examples

4.191 Air intake (left, under construction) as part of a driveway marker for the house in the distance, Calgary, Alberta, Canada. Air intake (right) designed as a bulletin board and bench. Note the three tubes rising out of the ground; an air filter is located behind the air intake grille. TANG LEE

Further Information

Brown, G.Z. and M. DeKay. 2001. *Sun, Wind & Light: Architectural Design Strategies,* 2nd ed. John Wiley & Sons, New York.

Lee, T.G. 2004. "Preheating Ventilation Air Using Earth Tubes," *Proceedings of the 29th Passive Solar Conference* (Portland, OR). American Solar Energy Society, Boulder, CO.

Solar.org Earth Tubes Exhibit. www.solar.org/solar/earthtubes

Stein, B. et al. 2006. *Mechanical and Electrical Equipment for Buildings,* 10th ed. John Wiley & Sons, Hoboken, NJ.

BEYOND SCHEMATIC DESIGN

During design development the estimated performance of an earth cooling tube system will be verified (although there are, unfortunately, few readily available tools to do so—likely requiring the services of a thermal simulation specialist). Details regarding system components and installation would be finalized. Because of concerns about biological growth in earth tubes it would be wise to develop a User's Manual for the system that describes recommended operation and maintenance procedures.

ENVELOPE

LIGHTING

HEATING

COOLING

ENERGY PRODUCTION

WATER & WASTE

NOTES

ENVELOPE

LIGHTING

HEATING

COOLING

ENERGY PRODUCTION

WATER & WASTE

EARTH
SHELTERING

ENVELOPE

LIGHTING

HEATING

COOLING

ENERGY PRODUCTION

WATER & WASTE

EARTH SHELTERING capitalizes upon the inherent climate control capabilities of the subterranean environment. Earth sheltering is essentially a passive implementation of the principle underlying ground source heat pumps—deep soil provides a warmer environment in the winter and a cooler environment in the summer than the atmospheric environment above ground. Building in this environment can substantially reduce winter heat losses (although not actually heating a building) and reduce summer cooling loads (while perhaps also providing coolth). The magnitude of climate tempering provided by earth sheltering is a function of soil depth. At and beyond 6 ft [1.8 m] below grade, temperatures may vary only a few degrees throughout the course of a year. Near the surface, however, soil temperature is only slightly attenuated from air temperature. In addition to mitigating temperature extremes, soil cover can also produce substantial time lags—shifting the lowest temperatures out of mid winter and into spring and the highest temperatures out of summer and into fall.

4.192 Burying some or all of a building in order to capitalize upon stable subterranean soil temperatures. KATE BECKLEY

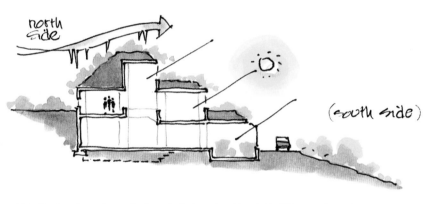

4.193 Section through a typical earth sheltered residential building configuration. MALCOLM WELLS

Earth sheltering improves the performance of building envelope assemblies by reducing the magnitude of conductive and convective heat losses and gains and by reducing infiltration. By providing a very stable exterior environment, building climate control becomes more energy-efficient and cost-effective—and the prospect for passive strategies is improved. Heating and cooling loads and costs may be reduced by 50% or more with effective earth sheltered design. The need for active backup climate control systems may be greatly reduced.

Noise intrusion can be greatly reduced or eliminated by building below grade. Earth shelters are ideally suited for steeply sloped sites and the potential of small sites can be maximized by preservation of exterior space and views. Earth shelters may also reduce insurance premiums due to their ability to withstand fire and high winds.

Key Architectural Issues

Earth sheltering can be implemented under a wide range of site situations. Underground structures may be constructed by building below grade on level sites, by "berming" or banking earth around the perimeter

INTENT
Climate control

EFFECT
Energy efficiency, potential for passive cooling, heat loss reduction

OPTIONS
Earth bermed or fully below-grade wall construction, earth covered or conventional roof

COORDINATION ISSUES
Orientation, ventilation, water runoff and/or catchment, air quality, daylighting, structural loads, soil conditions

RELATED STRATEGIES
Cross Ventilation, Stack Ventilation, Night Ventilation of Mass, Green Roofs, Toplighting, Sidelighting, Direct Gain

LEED LINKS
Sustainable Sites, Indoor Environmental Quality, Energy & Atmosphere, Innovation & Design Process

PREREQUISITES
Site adequately above water table, appropriate soil conditions for excavation or berming

ENVELOPE

LIGHTING

HEATING

COOLING

ENERGY PRODUCTION

WATER & WASTE

of a building, or by excavating into the side of a sloped site. Extensive rock at or near grade will usually restrict excavation. Perpetually moist clays can damage structure and be prone to slides. Depending upon climate control intent and the need for other benefits (such as storm protection), the depth and extent of earth sheltering can be varied. All construction should occur above the water table to reduce the potential for leaks and structural damage via uplift forces. Proper drainage design is integral to the viability of an earth shelter. Appropriate building materials and systems should be used to ensure structural strength and resistance to water damage and leaking. Reinforced concrete and/or masonry are typically utilized.

Orientation is important to the success of an earth sheltered design. With one or more walls covered with earth, daylighting and ventilation become important concerns to be addressed during schematic design. Siting an earth shelter with south-facing glazing will aid in the utilization of solar radiation for passive space heating, especially as adequate thermal mass is usually easily provided. Skylights or light pipes can be used to bring daylight into interior spaces. Natural ventilation can be utilized with an earth shelter if consideration is given to inlet/outlet location. Allowing some portion of the building structure to remain above ground makes cross ventilation more feasible. Courtyards and attached greenhouses can also provide additional ventilation opportunities. Mechanical cooling systems or dehumidifiers are often used to assist with dehumidification in humid climates.

Implementation Considerations

The appropriate use of multiple green design strategies can improve the performance of an earth sheltered building. Each site is different (with varying resources and detriments) and each client has different project requirements. The designer must assess the appropriateness of other strategies outlined in this book in that context. Orientation, glazing ratios, thermal storage, and ventilation strategies must be considered early in the design process.

Two key questions—how much earth shelter is enough and where and how much thermal insulation to use on below-ground or bermed elements—are fundamental decisions that are not terribly amenable to rational analysis, especially in schematic design. Earth covered roofs become "green roofs" and can provide shading to reduce summer cooling loads, thermal mass to shift loads across time, and evaporative cooling potential to also reduce cooling loads.

Design Procedure

The design procedure for an earth sheltered building is as complex as the design process for any other building—but with additional considerations related to structure, waterproofing, earth cover, and insulation design. Several key areas are presented below to guide the designer through schematic design.

SAMPLE PROBLEM
The design of an earth sheltered building involves the design of a complete (if unconventional) building. This many-stepped and complex process cannot be captured in a sample problem.

1. Analyze the site, considering natural drainage patterns, existing vegetation, solar access, wind flow patterns, microclimates, and subsurface conditions. Select a building location that is most amenable to meeting the project's design intents.

2. Select a structural system. Many systems (both conventional and otherwise) can be successfully used with an earth sheltered building. Poured-in-place reinforced concrete is often chosen as it provides appropriate structural capacity and a generally monolithic construction that can enhance waterproofing efforts. This does not preclude other properly engineered structural systems. Load-bearing partitions can be used to reduce structural spans. Partitions, however, can inadvertently divide the floor plan into front (with access to sun and daylight) and rear (darker and cooler) zones (see Figure 4.193).

3. The extent of earth cover (both on the roof and along the walls) is a function of design intent coordinated with site conditions. The minimum viable depth of soil on an earth sheltered roof is in the order of 24 in. [600 mm]. This minimum depth is more for viability of vegetation than thermal effect. See the Green Roofs strategy for further information on roof plantings. In most climates a 2 ft [0.6 m] soil cover will still require the use of thermal insulation at the roof plane. Fire egress must be considered in conjunction with earth covering/berming decisions, such that earth sheltering does not preclude provision of required exit routes.

4. Waterproofing will be addressed during design development, but site decisions (slopes, swales, elevations) should enhance the flow of water away from and around an earth shelter. No element of an earth shelter should act as a dam to water flow.

5. Determine what other green strategies will be included in the building. Passive heating, passive cooling, and daylighting are particularly suitable to an earth sheltered building with inherent thermal mass, reduced thermal loads, and a need for a connection to the outdoor environment.

The schematic plans and sections of an earth sheltered building will show clear provisions for water diversion, adequate egress, an appropriate orientation to support passive heating or cooling strategies, consideration of daylighting, adequate structure (12 in. [300 mm] walls, 12–24 in. [300–600 mm] roof structure depth with reasonable spans), and reasonable soil cover.

ENVELOPE

LIGHTING

HEATING

COOLING

ENERGY PRODUCTION

WATER & WASTE

ENVELOPE

LIGHTING

HEATING

COOLING

ENERGY PRODUCTION

WATER & WASTE

Examples

4.194 Vineyards farmed with sustainable practices surround an earth sheltered building serving as a wine processing and storage facility at the Sokol Blosser Winery in Dundee, Oregon. A green roof is integral with the earth sheltering.

4.195 The earth sheltered Pinot Noir facility of Domaine Carneros Winery in Napa, California, begins to disappear into the soil of the vineyards. The roofscape also features 120 kW of building integrated photovoltaic panels to reduce the winery's annual energy consumption and carbon dioxide emissions. POWERLIGHT, INC.

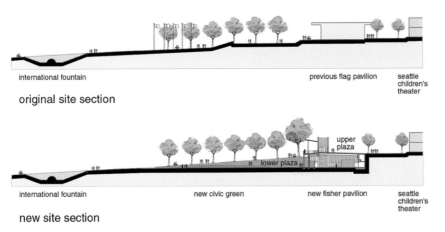

original site section

new site section

4.196 Site section showing the earth sheltered Fisher Pavilion situated within the landscape in Seattle, Washington. MILLER/HULL PARTNERSHIP

4.197 Tower plaza entry (in the foreground) to the Fisher Pavilion during construction shows the grade change to the top of the building via the stairway. MILLER/HULL PARTNERSHIP

ENVELOPE

LIGHTING

HEATING

COOLING

ENERGY PRODUCTION

WATER & WASTE

4.198 Cradle-to-cradle earth-sheltered design. MALCOLM WELLS

Further Information

Baum, G. 1980. *Earth Shelter Handbook*, Technical Data Publications, Peoria, AZ.

Boyer, L. and W. Grondzik. 1987. *Earth Shelter Technology*. Texas A&M University Press, College Station, TX.

Carmody, J. and R. Sterling. 1983. *Underground Building Design: Commercial and Institutional Structures*, Van Nostrand Reinhold, New York.

Sokol Blosser Winery. www.sokolblosser.com/

Sterling, R., W. Farnan and J. Carmody. 1982. *Earth Sheltered Residential Design Manual*, Van Nostrand Reinhold, New York.

Underground Buildings: Architecture & Environment. www.subsurfacebuildings.com/

BEYOND SCHEMATIC DESIGN
Many key design decisions for an earth sheltered building will be made during design development—such as waterproofing details, insulation selection and detailing, structural system sizing, and the integration of mechanical systems. Much of the effort for an earth sheltered design lies beyond schematic design.

ENVELOPE

LIGHTING

HEATING

COOLING

ENERGY PRODUCTION

WATER & WASTE

ABSORPTION CHILLERS, while an active design solution, have a fairly low environmental impact when compared to other refrigeration devices. Absorption chillers produce a refrigeration effect through use of a heat source, as opposed to the more commonly encountered compressor-driven machines that use electric power to generate a cooling effect. Absorption chillers do not consume as much electricity as compressive chillers, and they do not require the use of chlorofluorocarbon (CFC) or hydrochlorofluorocarbon (HCFC) refrigerants. They are best-suited to situations where there is a plentiful, low-cost heat source (such as waste heat or perhaps solar thermal), and mesh nicely with other green design strategies, such as hot water heated by industrial-process waste heat or a fuel cell.

4.199 A single-stage, direct-fired absorption chiller. TRANE

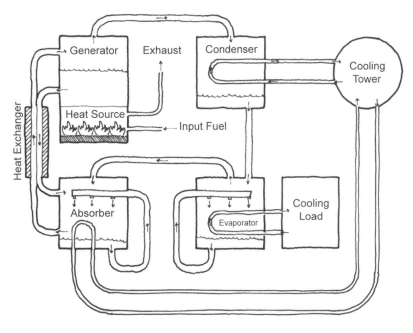

4.200 Schematic diagram of the absorption refrigeration cycle. NICHOLAS RAJKOVICH

There are two general types of absorption chillers. "Indirect-fired" chillers use steam, hot water, or hot gas as energy input. "Direct-fired" chillers utilize a dedicated combustion heat source. Both types work through the absorption cycle, whereby a refrigerant (typically lithium bromide and water) absorbs and discharges heat as it changes state. Water flows through a four-stage process of evaporation, condensation, evaporation, absorption—moving heat as an integral part of the process. The lithium bromide undergoes a two-stage process of dilution and concentration—attracting or releasing water in the loop.

An absorption machine consists of four interconnected chambers. In the generator chamber, heat evaporates water from the lithium bromide/water solution. The concentrated lithium bromide is transferred to the absorber chamber, while the water vapor is condensed in the condenser chamber. The water flows to the evaporator chamber to continue the cycle. In the evaporator chamber, water changing state draws

INTENT
Active cooling, energy cost savings, beneficial use of waste heat

EFFECT
Refrigeration

OPTIONS
Indirect-fired or direct-fired

COORDINATION ISSUES
Active heating and cooling systems, HVAC sizing

RELATED STRATEGIES
Combined Heat and Power Systems, Active Solar Thermal Systems

LEED LINKS
Energy & Atmosphere, Innovation & Design Process

PREREQUISITES
Basic information on utility availability and rates, preliminary floor plans, information on process loads (if applicable)

ENVELOPE

LIGHTING

HEATING

COOLING

ENERGY PRODUCTION

WATER & WASTE

ENVELOPE

LIGHTING

HEATING

COOLING

ENERGY PRODUCTION

WATER & WASTE

heat from chilled water circulating through the chamber. This water vapor passes into the absorber chamber, where it is attracted by the lithium bromide. The vapor pressure is reduced by the absorption of water, and more water vapor can evaporate to continue the process.

With a cheap or free heat source, and with fewer moving parts to maintain, absorption chillers are more cost-effective than mechanical/electrical compressor-driven systems. Their overall coefficient of performance (COP) can be as low as 0.7 (versus 3.0 or higher for a vapor-compression machine), however, and they generate nearly twice as much waste heat as compressive refrigeration machines. This affects overall energy consumption and cooling tower sizing: for each unit of refrigeration, an absorption system must reject around 2.5 units of heat versus approximately 1.3 units for a vapor compression machine.

Key Architectural Issues

Spatial organization relative to required floor area, the structural grid, cooling tower location, and maintenance and access are of key concern when selecting mechanical systems. The separation distance between chiller(s) and cooling tower(s) can be substantial as warranted by site/building conditions.

Absorption chillers can provide between 200 and 1000 tons [703–3517 kW] of cooling capacity. During schematic design, chiller footprint is a primary architectural design consideration. See Figure 4.201 for mechanical (chiller) room sizing information.

The cooling towers used with absorption chillers tend to be larger than those used with comparable capacity vapor-compression systems. External space for the cooling towers must be considered during schematic design. A quality water source, such as a lake or well, can be used instead of a tower as a sink for energy.

Implementation Considerations

Cooling with an absorption chiller should be considered if one or more of the following conditions applies:

- the building or facility uses a combined heat and power (CHP) unit and cannot use all of the heat generated;

- waste heat (from a process of some sort) is available;

- low-cost combustion fuel (typically natural gas) is available;

- low boiler efficiency is projected due to a poor load factor;

- the project site has electrical load limit restrictions;

- the project team has concerns about the use of conventional refrigerants;

- noise and vibration from a vapor-compression chiller are likely to be objectionable.

Depending upon the size of the chiller, a general guideline recommends allowing 40–60 in. [1.0–1.5 m] of space around a chiller for maintenance. Chiller room temperature should not drop below 35 °F [2 °C]. Direct-fired chillers require a supply of combustion air. In general 12 ft^3 [0.4 m^3] of air is needed for every 1000 Btu [0.29 kWh] of heat consumed. It is wise to leave space for additional chillers, which may be required as a building expands or new building loads come online.

Design Procedure

The design procedure for an absorption chiller is complex and beyond the scope of schematic design efforts. Building cooling load, however, can be estimated early in the design process, allowing for a reasonable estimate of space requirements.

1. Establish conditioned (cooled) area of building under design.

2. Estimate cooling load using Table 4.14.

3. Obtain approximate chiller space requirements from Figure 4.201.

4. Integrate this space into development of building floor plans and sections, considering appropriate locations for the mechanical room relative to building loads, access, and adjacent spaces.

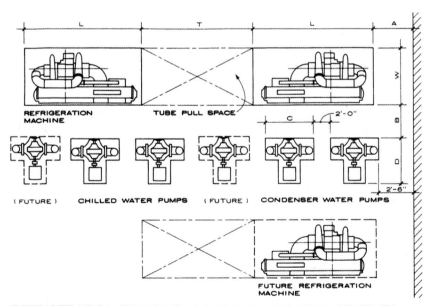

REFRIGERATION EQUIPMENT ROOM SPACE REQUIREMENTS

L = 18 - 30 ft [5.6 - 9 m]	A, B = 3.6 ft [1 m]
T = 18 - 29 ft [5.6 8.9 m]	C = 4.6 7 ft [1.4 - 2 m]
W = 9 - 11 ft [2.7 - 3.4 m]	D = 4 - 6 ft [1.2 - 1.8 m]
Height approx. 14 ft [4.3 m]	Minimum room height: approx. 17 ft [5 m]

4.201 Mechanical (chiller) room sizing requirements. *ARCHITECTURAL GRAPHIC STANDARDS,* 10TH ED. DATA SUMMARIZED BY AUTHORS.

SAMPLE PROBLEM
Estimate the floor area required for absorption chillers to serve a 50,000 ft^2 [4650 m^2] office building in a hot, humid climate.

1. The building area is given as 50,000 ft^2 [4650 m^2]. Conservatively assume all of this area is cooled.

2. The estimated cooling load (assuming this to be a "medium" office and further assuming a load value near the lower end of the range in Table 4.14 due to the climate conditions) is (50,0000 ft^2/ 350 ft^2/ton) = 145 tons [500 kW].

3. From Figure 4.201, a 150 ton absorption chiller (near the lower end of the ranges for this small capacity) requires about 680 ft^2 [63 m^2] of floor area (including access and maintenance space). In addition, space for pumps and accessories must be allocated along with an exterior location for a cooling tower.

4. An appropriate location for the mechanical (chiller) room will be selected.

ENVELOPE

LIGHTING

HEATING

COOLING

ENERGY PRODUCTION

WATER & WASTE

TABLE 4.14 Cooling load estimates by building type. ADAPTED FROM *GUIDELINE: ABSORPTION CHILLERS*, SOUTHERN CALIFORNIA GAS, NEW BUILDINGS INSTITUTE.

BUILDING TYPE	COOLING CAPACITY ft^2 per ton	COOLING CAPACITY m^2 per kW
Medium office	340–490	9–13
Large office	280–390	7–10
Hospital	520–710	14–19
Hotel	350–490	9–13
Outpatient clinic	440–545	12–14
Secondary school	240–555	6–15
Large retail	420–1000	11–26

Examples

4.202 One of six two-stage, direct-fired absorption chillers located in a mechanical room with high bays near the top of Four Times Square in New York, New York. TRANE

ABSORPTION CHILLERS **179**

ENVELOPE

LIGHTING

HEATING

COOLING

ENERGY PRODUCTION

WATER & WASTE

Further Information

Allen, E. and J. Iano. 2001. *The Architect's Studio Companion*, 3rd ed. John Wiley & Sons, New York.

Hoke, J. R. ed. 2000. *Ramsey/Sleeper: Architectural Graphic Standards* 10th ed. John Wiley & Sons, New York.

Southern California Gas Co., New Buildings Institute. 1998. *Guideline: Absorption Chillers.* Available at: www.newbuildings.org/downloads/guidelines/AbsorptionChillerGuideline.pdf

USDOE. 2003. *Energy Matters Newsletter* (Fall 2003). U.S. Department of Energy, Washington, DC. Available at: www.oit.doe.gov/bestpractices/energymatters/fall2003_absorption.shtml

BEYOND SCHEMATIC DESIGN
The selection of a chiller and its integration into an HVAC system requires the expertise of a mechanical engineer. Much of the detailed effort in this regard will occur during design development—but that work will follow upon decisions made during schematic design. Commissioning of refrigeration systems is recommended.

NOTES

ENVELOPE

LIGHTING

HEATING

COOLING

ENERGY PRODUCTION

WATER & WASTE

ENERGY PRODUCTION

Consideration of on-site energy production should begin with a review of energy efficiency strategies. Every effort should first be made to reduce demand. Reducing demand reduces the size of an on-site generation system or permits a system of a given size to offset a greater percentage of building energy load.

Given an efficient building, on-site energy production can further reduce environmental impact. Selecting the best strategy for on-site generation will depend upon factors such as type and location of the project, regional and micro climates, utility rates, and possible tax and financial incentives for clean and/or renewable energy.

Cogeneration, also known as combined heat and power (CHP), is the production of electricity and useful heat in a single process. To be cost-effective, a CHP facility must have a significant heat load. Cogeneration is common in many industrial facilities. At the individual building scale, it is best suited to projects such as restaurants, retirement homes, hotels, large condominium projects, swimming pools, and office buildings with absorption cooling or dehumidification systems.

The cost of electricity generated from wind power has fallen considerably and rivals that of fossil fuel generation. The intermittency of wind resources means that battery storage or a utility grid connection with net metering is needed to assure continuous power at an individual building site.

At the individual building scale, the most common on-site energy production method has been electrical generation using photovoltaics. Photovoltaics may be building integrated—replacing traditional building materials in curtain wall, skylight, or roofing systems. Because photovoltaics generate electricity only during daylight hours, battery storage or a utility grid connection with net metering is needed to assure continuous power. Photovoltaics are attractive at the building scale because they are silent, relatively easily installed, and can be either hidden from view on the roof or prominently featured, depending upon the desires of the building owner and designer.

Fuel cells, while holding considerable promise, are not readily applicable for residential or small commercial buildings at the present time. They are most appropriate for large projects where high quality, uninterruptable power is required.

Whatever type of on-site generation is selected, it will be most effective when integrated with energy efficiency strategies. A dual-focus approach will lead to the greatest reduction in environmental impact. Put simply, it's usually a lot cheaper to save energy than to generate it.

STRATEGIES
Plug Loads
Air-to-Air Heat Exchangers
Energy Recovery Systems
Photovoltaics
Wind Turbines
Microhydro Turbines
Hydrogen Fuel Cells
Combined Heat and Power Systems

ENVELOPE

LIGHTING

HEATING

COOLING

ENERGY PRODUCTION

WATER & WASTE

ENVELOPE

LIGHTING

HEATING

COOLING

ENERGY PRODUCTION

WATER & WASTE

NOTES

PLUG LOADS represent the electrical consumption potential of all the appliances and smaller (not hardwired) equipment in a building. They account for a fair percentage of the total energy needs of many building types (see Figure 4.204). Plug loads are an important green design consideration for several reasons: (1) their inherent impact on building energy consumption, (2) their secondary impact on building cooling loads, and (3) the fact that these loads are amenable to being met by small on-site power generating systems (such as PV, wind, microhydro, or fuel cells).

Because plug loads are by their very nature portable and easily changeable—and also often the result of occupant decisions and preferences (even in non-residential buildings)—they are often determined not by the design team but rather by the building owner (after occupancy commences). Evaluation of projected plug loads, however, is absolutely necessary to size an on-site electrical generation system. In addition, greening of plug loads should be part of the design process for every building.

4.203 Watt meter showing a desktop computer monitor using 32 watts when in active mode.

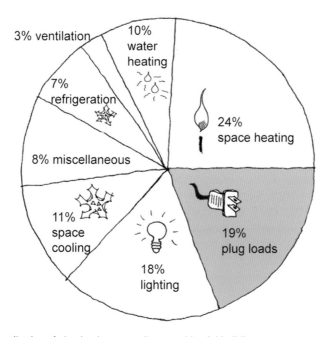

4.204 Contribution of plug loads to overall non-residential building energy usage. KATE BECKLEY; ADAPTED FROM U.S. DEPARTMENT OF ENERGY, *BUILDINGS ENERGY DATABOOK*

Each watt of plug load contributes a watt [3.41 Btu/h] of cooling load that will need to be removed by the active or passive cooling system. In a passively cooled building, plug loads add to what (in many building types and climates) is the already difficult job of matching available natural cooling resources to building cooling demands. In an actively cooled building, plug loads increase system size and energy consumption. Potential plug load is less of a concern than actual plug load (what is being used at any point in time).

INTENT
Energy efficiency

EFFECT
Reduced electricity consumption, reduced electrical demand, reduced cooling loads

OPTIONS
Efficient equipment, alternative equipment, demand control

COORDINATION ISSUES
Building function, client preferences, occupancy schedules

RELATED STRATEGIES
Cooling strategies, energy production strategies, Electric lighting

LEED LINKS
Energy & Atmosphere, Innovation & Design Process

PREREQUISITES
A clear picture of building function and usage

ENVELOPE

LIGHTING

HEATING

COOLING

ENERGY PRODUCTION

WATER & WASTE

ENVELOPE

LIGHTING

HEATING

COOLING

ENERGY PRODUCTION

WATER & WASTE

In most non-residential buildings, plug loads will be a contributor to peak building electrical demands and resulting demand charges. Where demand charges are a major component of the monthly electric bill, aggressive demand control strategies are often undertaken to reduce peak electrical demands and their resulting billings. Such strategies typically involve the automatic shedding of unnecessary loads.

Key Architectural Issues

Plug loads have little direct effect on the architectural design of a building—electrical wiring is easily coordinated and concealed. The energy demands resulting from plug loads, however, will affect building energy efficiency and consumption, the sizing of cooling systems, and the sizing of on-site power generation systems. The greater the plug loads, the larger the supporting electrical system must be.

Implementation Considerations

The design of on-site power and passive and active cooling systems demands that the nature of plug loads be well estimated during schematic design. The direction of design should be toward green (energy-efficient) plug loads.

Incorporating programmable timers into selected equipment/appliance circuits can help shift some electrical load to non-peak hours, likely lowering heat gains and demand charges (a bulk ice maker working at night rather than at noon is an example).

Much electrical equipment such as televisions, stereos, computers, and kitchen appliances have "phantom loads"—such appliances continue to draw a small amount of power even when they are switched off. Phantom loads will increase an appliance's energy consumption by a few watt-hours above what might otherwise be expected.

Design Procedure

The following procedure represents a general approach toward developing green plug loads for a building.

1. Develop a list of equipment/appliances likely to be used in the building and their wattage. The wattage may come from the nameplate of a specific appliance or from a generic table (such as Table 4.15).

2. Estimate the number of hours each unit will be used during the course of a typical day.

3. For those devices that are not in continuous use, estimate the dormant or sleep mode power draw and the number of hours per day that the equipment/appliance would operate in this condition.

SAMPLE PROBLEM
A small writer's retreat cabin in Rice Lake, Wisconsin will be powered solely by on-site generation of electricity.

1. The appliances likely to be in the cabin include: clock radio, coffee maker, clothes washer, clothes dryer, computer and monitor, ink jet printer, fax machine, microwave oven, stereo, refrigerator, and small water heater.

2. Operating hours for each appliance are estimated using

ENVELOPE

LIGHTING

HEATING

COOLING

ENERGY PRODUCTION

WATER & WASTE

4. Estimate the total power consumption of plug loads by multiplying the operating wattage of each item by the number of hours of operation (Step 2). Also include the estimated dormant power consumption (as described in Step 3). For equipment where wattage is not readily available:

   a. Find the voltage (V) and amperage (A) of the equipment. This information can usually be obtained from a manufacturer or from online resources.

   b. Calculate the watts (W) of power draw by:

$$W = V \times A \text{ (for single phase loads)}$$

5. Sort the plug loads in decreasing order of magnitude of daily energy consumption. For the most energy-consuming equipment, investigate energy-efficient options (Energy Star equipment, alternative equipment that provides equivalent service, etc.).

6. Prepare a list of recommended equipment/appliance options for consideration by the client/owner. Include a cost–benefit analysis that demonstrates the effect of inefficient equipment on energy bills, cooling system capacity and cost, and life-cycle costs. Such an analysis can be easily adapted for future projects.

TABLE 4.15 Typical wattages of various appliances. ADAPTED FROM THE U.S. DEPARTMENT OF ENERGY, ENERGY EFFICIENCY AND RENEWABLE ENERGY

APPLIANCE	WATTAGE
Aquarium	50–1210
Clock radio	10
Coffee maker	900–1200
Clothes washer	350–500
Clothes dryer	1800–5000
Computer (personal)	CPU: awake/asleep = 120/30 or less
Computer monitor	30–150
Computer (laptop)	50
Dishwasher	1200–2400
Dehumidifier	785
Drinking fountain	500–800
Fax machine	60
Fans (ceiling)	65–175
Heater (portable)	750–1500
Microwave oven	1000–1800
Photocopiers	200–1800 during photocopying
Printers	10–20
Stereo	70–400
Refrigerator (frost-free, 16 ft³ [0.45 m³])	725
Vending machine refrigerated	3500
Water heater (40 gal [150 L])	4500–5500

best judgment (see Step 4). For some appliances, the operating hours are based upon estimated full-load hours per 24-hour day.

3. Dormant mode use is also estimated (see Step 4).

4. Power consumption is estimated as follows, using Table 4.15:

   Clock: (10 W)(24 h) = 240 Wh
   Coffee maker: (1000 W)(2 h) = 2000 Wh
   Washer: (400 W)(0.5 hr) = 200 Wh
   Dryer: (2200 W)(0.5 h) = 1100 Wh
   Computer: (120 W)(9 h) = 1080 Wh
   Computer: (30 W)(15 h) = 450 Wh
   Monitor: (35 W)(24 h) = 840 Wh
   Printer: (20 W)(9 h) = 180 Wh
   Fax: (60 W)(24 h) = 1440 Wh
   Microwave: (1400 W)(1 h) = 1400 Wh
   Stereo: (100 W)(10 h) = 1000 Wh
   Refrigerator: (725 W)(6 h) = 4350 Wh
   Water heater: (5000 W)(4 h) = 20,000 Wh

5. The three largest power consumers are the water heater, the refrigerator, and the coffee maker.

6. These three appliances will be recommended for upgrade to more energy-efficient devices. The fax machine consumption will be investigated to see if the "sleep" mode load has been overlooked.

ENVELOPE

LIGHTING

HEATING

COOLING

ENERGY PRODUCTION

WATER & WASTE

Examples

4.205 Designers can select from a wide variety of energy-efficient appliances and equipment that use less energy and save money. KATE BECKLEY

Further Information

Oxford Brookes University, Electronic Appliances and Energy Labels. www.brookes.ac.uk/eie/ecolabels.htm#3

Suozzo, M. 2000. *Guide to Energy-Efficient Commercial Equipment*, 2nd ed. American Council for an Energy-Efficient Economy, Washington, DC.

U.S. Department of Energy, 2005. *Buildings Energy Databook*, U.S. Department of Energy, Office of Energy Efficiency and Renewable Energy, Washington, DC.

U.S. Environmental Protection Agency, Energy Star program. www.energystar.gov/

BEYOND SCHEMATIC DESIGN
Implementation of plug load strategies will occur beyond schematic design—during building occupancy in many cases. A means of transferring thinking about plug loads from schematic design to occupancy must be developed by the design team. Educating building operators and occupants about optimizing building and equipment operations is also critical.

AIR-TO-AIR HEAT EXCHANGERS are mechanical devices used to transfer heat from one airflow stream to another. The prototypical application is an air-to-air heat exchanger that transfers heat (or coolth) from exhaust air to incoming outdoor air, preventing significant energy waste in the ventilation process. The resulting increase in system efficiency translates to energy savings and often to reduced heating and cooling equipment capacity since loads are reduced.

In residential and light commercial applications, an air-to-air heat exchanger may be packaged with a fan as a unitary product. For larger applications, there are numerous air-to-air heat exchanger configurations that provide flexibility for HVAC system design efforts and for the locations of building air intake and exhaust.

4.206 Energy recovery ventilator works as an integral part of the total building HVAC system.
NICHOLAS RAJKOVICH

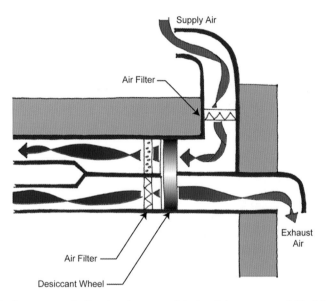

4.207 Typical arrangement of heat exchanger and ductwork for a commercial building.
NICHOLAS RAJKOVICH

Two types of air-to-air heat exchangers designed specifically for residential and small commercial applications are the heat recovery ventilator (HRV) and the energy recovery ventilator (ERV). An HRV exchanges only heat (sensible energy), while an ERV transfers both heat and moisture (sensible and latent energy). An HRV or ERV unit typically includes a fan for air distribution and a filter to remove contaminants from incoming air. Manufacturers offer an array of additional options such as automatic defrosting (a critical feature in moderate and cold climates) and moisture control for HRVs.

Air-to-air heat exchange devices and systems for larger buildings cover a range of types and include packaged devices as well as custom built-up installations of components. The following discussion highlights key points regarding the most common types of air-to-air heat exchangers.

Plate heat exchanger (Figure 4.208): Numerous channels for intake and exhaust air are separated by heat-conducting plates that allow for sensible heat transfer. A plate heat exchanger with a permeable separation medium can transfer moisture as well as heat.

INTENT
Energy efficiency, indoor air quality

EFFECT
Reduced energy use for active ventilation

OPTIONS
Sensible versus sensible and latent exchange, various heat exchanger types and configurations

COORDINATION ISSUES
HVAC system type, exhaust and intake locations, ductwork design

RELATED STRATEGIES
Energy Recovery Systems

LEED LINKS
Energy & Atmosphere, Indoor Environmental Quality, Innovation & Design Process

PREREQUISITES
Preliminary floor plans, a general estimate of minimum required outdoor airflow, preliminary heating/cooling loads

ENVELOPE

LIGHTING

HEATING

COOLING

ENERGY PRODUCTION

WATER & WASTE

Rotary heat exchanger (Figure 4.209): A cylindrical wheel transfers heat from exhaust air to supply air as the wheel turns. This type of heat exchanger is potentially more likely than the other types to permit exhaust air contaminants into the inflow air stream. Latent heat wheels are more common than sensible heat wheels. The heat transfer medium in an energy (latent) wheel allows for the exchange of moisture as well as heat. Some products provide rigorous protection against cross-contamination.

Heat pipe heat exchanger (Figure 4.210): When one end of a heat pipe grows warmer, an enclosed liquid (refrigerant) evaporates. The change in pressure and temperature sends the resulting vapor to the opposite end of the pipe where a cooler temperature causes it to condense on the pipe walls. Heat released by this change of state is transferred through the walls to air flowing outside the pipe; the condensed refrigerant returns to the other end of the pipe via a wick. A typical unit consists of a packaged assembly of multiple heat pipes.

Runaround coil (Figure 4.211): A closed loop connects finned-tube water coils placed in the incoming and outgoing air streams. Heat is exchanged via the heat transfer fluid in this loop, which allows the air streams to be located a good distance apart. Various techniques can be used to protect against freezing of the heat transfer fluid.

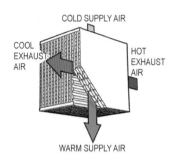

4.208 Plate heat exchanger.
ADAPTED FROM 2004 *ASHRAE HANDBOOK—HVAC SYSTEMS AND EQUIPMENT*

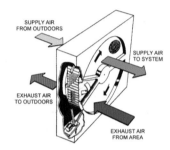

4.209 Rotary heat exchanger.
ADAPTED FROM 2004 *ASHRAE HANDBOOK—HVAC SYSTEMS AND EQUIPMENT*

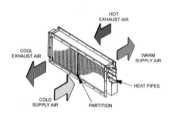

4.210 Heat pipe heat exchanger.
ADAPTED FROM 2004 *ASHRAE HANDBOOK—HVAC SYSTEMS AND EQUIPMENT*

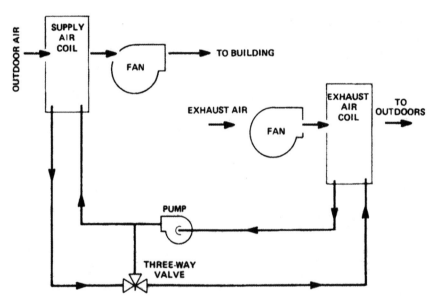

4.211 Runaround coil (or runaround loop). ADAPTED FROM 2004 *ASHRAE HANDBOOK—HVAC SYSTEMS AND EQUIPMENT*

Key Architectural Issues

Location and size are the two most critical architectural design concerns related to use of air-to-air heat exchangers. The fundamental principle in most applications involves running two air streams adjacent to each other such that connections to the heat exchanger are easy to make. Once adjacency of air streams is established, adequate space for the selected device must be provided (along with access for maintenance). Adjacency of exhaust and intake air streams will usually influence the location of intakes (louvers/hoods) and exhausts (louvers/hoods) on the building envelope. Since an air-to-air heat exchanger by definition taps into airflows contained in ductwork, the availability of adequate volume for co-located ducts is important.

Implementation Considerations

Grease and lint, which may be found in some exhaust air streams, are potential fire hazards. Such airflows should not be fed directly to a heat exchanger unless appropriate filters are used. Maintenance is critical to the efficient operation of a heat exchanger. This may involve a filter change several times a year or regular manual cleaning. This is particularly important as a means of lengthening the life of latent heat exchangers. Easy access to the heat exchanger unit will increase the likelihood of proper maintenance and, consequently, have a direct impact on its efficiency. Some types of heat exchangers are designed to handle a high number of air volume exchanges in environments with high contaminant levels—where standard heat wheels or permeable-plate heat exchangers cannot adequately prevent cross-contamination.

To reduce airflow-related noise and increase energy efficiency, ductwork leading to a heat exchanger should be appropriately sized and reasonably routed (not squeezed and contorted).

For residential applications, the choice between an HRV unit and an ERV unit is determined primarily by climate and the resulting economics of cost-effectiveness. In some cold and some hot, humid climates, a heat exchanger may be required by code. If the intended site is in a mild climate where the temperature differential between indoor and outdoor air is minimal, the savings potential of an air-to-air heat exchanger may be too small to make its inclusion cost-effective.

Design Procedure

Residential

1. Estimate the required minimum outdoor airflow to meet local code requirements, good design practice (in the absence of code requirements), or to offset infiltration. This airflow is very much influenced by building location (jurisdiction) and/or building design (air tightness) and is difficult to generalize. It should, however, be relatively easy to estimate this value in the context of a particular project. The airflow rate will be in cfm [L/s].

2. Refer to online product information readily provided by many manufacturers to obtain information on an appropriate capacity unit, unit size, and installation requirements.

3. Provide an appropriate location with adequate space/volume and accessibility for the selected device.

Non-residential

1. There are many variables and equipment types involved with non-residential applications. Nevertheless, it is possible to quickly estimate minimum building outdoor airflow on the basis of prevailing code requirements and obtain rough equipment sizing

4.212 An industrial grade energy recovery wheel designed to handle airflow volumes from 15,000 to 150,000 cfm [7080 to 70,785 L/s] with a total effectiveness of up to 90%. Wheel diameters range from 6 to 20 ft [1.8–6.1 m]. THERMOTECH ENTERPRISES, INC.

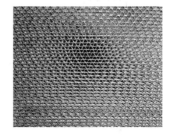

4.213 Close up of energy recovery wheel medium with a 4Å desiccant coating on an aluminum substrate to provide for total enthalpy recovery. The medium has approximately 13 openings per inch [0.5 per mm] and is designed to provide laminar flow. THERMOTECH ENTERPRISES, INC.

SAMPLE PROBLEM
A new, 4-bedroom residence with 3100 ft² [288 m²] of conditioned floor space will be built in International Falls, Minnesota.

1. Per ASHRAE Standard 62.2, this type of building would have a minimum ventilation rate of around 75 cfm [35 L/s]. Using intermittent exhaust, however, an exhaust airflow

and configuration information from manufacturers based upon this flow rate. Several equipment options should be reviewed such that no reasonable approach is precluded by early design decisions.

Examples

4.214 The mechanical closet for the 2005 Cal Poly San Luis Obispo entry for the USDOE Solar Decathlon competition. An energy recovery ventilator is located at the top left corner of the closet. NICHOLAS RAJKOVICH

4.215 Air-to-air heat exchanger (the metal box under the spare air filters) installed in the attic of a day care center.

of 100 cfm [47 L/s] for the kitchen and 50 cfm [24 L/s] for each bathroom would be required, for a total airflow of 200 cfm [94 L/s]. The air-to-air heat exchanger should handle this capacity.

2. From a typical manufacturer's catalog, an estimated ERV size of 31 × 18 × 15 in. [788 × 458 × 380 mm] with 6 in. [150 mm] round ducts appears reasonable.

3. With this size house, using two ERVs may require less extensive ductwork and be easier to coordinate.

ENVELOPE

LIGHTING

HEATING

4.216 These two energy recovery wheels were retrofit into an existing air-handling unit in an Illinois hospital. The system capacity is 30,000 cfm [14,160 L/s]. THERMOTECH ENTERPRISES, INC.

COOLING

Further Information

ASHRAE. 2004. Standard 62.2-2004: "Ventilation and Acceptable Indoor Air Quality in Low-Rise Residential Buildings." American Society of Heating, Refrigerating and Air-Conditioning Engineers, Atlanta, GA.

Dausch, M., D. Pinnix and J. Fischer. "Labs for the 21st Century: Applying 3Å Molecular Sieve Total Energy Recovery Wheels to Laboratory Environments." Available at: www.labs21century.gov/conf/past/2003/abstracts/a3_dausch.htm

Grumman, D.L. ed. 2003. *ASHRAE GreenGuide.* American Society of Heating, Refrigerating and Air-Conditioning Engineers, Atlanta, GA.

State of Oregon. "Demand-Controlled Ventilation: A Design Guide." Oregon Department of Energy. Available at: egov.oregon.gov/ENERGY/CONS/BUS/DCV/docs/DCVGuide.pdf

BEYOND SCHEMATIC DESIGN
Estimates of equipment sizes made during schematic design will be validated during design development. Specific equipment will be selected and connections detailed. Air-to-air heat exchangers should be commissioned (mal-performance is not obvious) and a User's Manual prepared for the owner/operator.

ENERGY PRODUCTION

WATER & WASTE

NOTES

ENVELOPE

LIGHTING

HEATING

COOLING

ENERGY PRODUCTION

WATER & WASTE

ENERGY RECOVERY SYSTEMS are of two basic types: general energy recovery systems and air-to-air heat exchanger systems (see Related Strategies). An energy recovery system transfers sensible heat from one fluid to another fluid through an impermeable wall. In this type of system, the fluids (air and/or water) do not mix. Energy recovery systems have many applications, including industrial and production processes, and can recover heat from fluid streams as diverse as exhaust air ducts, boiler stacks, or waste water piping. An informed designer can often discover applications for harnessing waste heat using heat exchangers that are unique to a particular project.

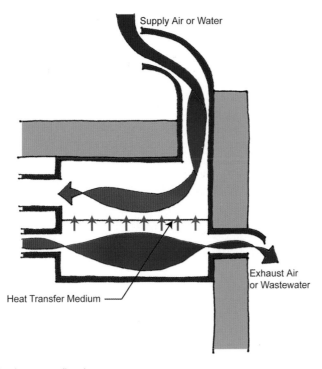

4.218 A simple counter-flow heat recovery system. NICHOLAS RAJKOVICH

An energy recovery system is an integral part of all combined heat and power (CHP) systems, in which "waste" heat from the electricity generation process is recovered for use in another application such as heating domestic hot water, space heating, or space cooling. Other opportunities for heat reclaim exist in most large building projects.

Key Architectural Issues

The heat exchange equipment involved with implementing this strategy requires adequate space/volume. All energy recovery systems include a heat-exchange component, one or more fans or pumps to move the fluids through the heat exchanger, and controls to manage the flow rates. The size of the heat exchanging elements is a function of the capacity and efficiency of the equipment—it is often large.

ENVELOPE

LIGHTING

HEATING

COOLING

ENERGY PRODUCTION

WATER & WASTE

ENERGY RECOVERY SYSTEMS

4.217 Air-to-water heat exchanger (above and to the rear of the oven) transfers heat from a pizza oven exhaust to a hot water supply.

INTENT
Energy efficiency

EFFECT
Reduced consumption of energy resources

OPTIONS
Various fluid streams (usually air or water) and arrangements (parallel-flow, cross-flow, counter-flow)

COORDINATION ISSUES
Active heating and cooling systems, additional space/volume requirements, air/water stream routing, intake/exhaust locations

RELATED STRATEGIES
Air-to-Air Heat Exchangers, Combined Heat and Power

LEED LINKS
Energy & Environment, Indoor Environmental Quality, Innovation & Design Process

PREREQUISITES
Climate data for site, estimated ventilation requirements, estimated hot water requirements, estimated building heating and cooling loads

In addition to providing adequate space for equipment, the designer must consider the location of supply and exhaust ducts and/or piping to and from equipment with recoverable heat potential—the details of which vary depending upon the systems and their configurations.

Energy recovery systems are categorized by how the fluids enter and exit the system. In a parallel-flow arrangement, the fluids enter the system at the same end and travel in parallel with one another until they exit the system. In a cross-flow arrangement, the fluids travel roughly perpendicular to one another. In a counter-flow arrangement, the fluids enter from opposite ends and flow in opposite directions. In general, the counter-flow arrangement is the most efficient (due to beneficial temperature differences throughout the heat exchanger), but often requires the largest area/volume for the heat exchanging equipment and for the navigation of ductwork/piping.

Implementation Considerations

Virtually every building discharges energy into the surrounding environment. The design question is: Can the energy embodied in the various building waste streams be economically recovered? In general, simplicity is the key to cost-effective installation of an energy recovery system. An energy simulation and life-cycle cost analysis can determine if a heat reclaim system will provide a favorable payback on investment for a proposed facility and climate conditions. For most buildings, attempting to recover all of the energy from wastewater or exhaust air will not be worth the incremental cost to get to that level of extraction.

Design Procedure

A review of the following issues during schematic design will help to establish whether an energy recovery system is an appropriate strategy to pursue.

1. Consider demand for hot water and need for outdoor air. Energy recovery systems make economic sense in facilities that require large amounts of hot water and/or outdoor air for control of indoor air quality or process. Such facilities include laundries, restaurants, laboratories, and hospitals.

2. Evaluate available temperature differentials. Heat recovery makes economic sense in applications where there is a large temperature difference (roughly 20 °F [11 °C] or greater) between the supply and exhaust (or waste) streams.

3. Consider cleanliness of the waste/exhaust stream. Systems with relatively clean exhaust air and/or wastewater are the best candidates for an energy recovery system. Contaminants in

SAMPLE PROBLEM
The adjacent design procedure is conceptual. As such, elaboration on this procedure using a sample problem is not necessary.

exhaust air or wastewater can clog or damage heat exchange equipment.

4. Consider the type of heating/cooling system. Generally, it is less expensive to install centralized heat exchange equipment in a facility than numerous smaller, distributed heat exchangers. Large buildings with central heating and cooling plants, such as laboratories and medical facilities, are prime candidates for heat recovery systems.

5. Consider space requirements. Adequate space must be available for the inclusion of an energy recovery system and its equipment. Due to the wide range of potential equipment and systems, it is difficult to generalize these requirements. As a rule, a building with equipment that is not shoehorned into place can probably accommodate a heat recovery system. In most buildings, the routing of fluids (air and water) to the energy recovery equipment will present more of a design challenge than the space requirements for the equipment itself.

Examples

4.219 Heat exchangers are an integral part of the energy-efficient HVAC system at Four Times Square in New York, New York. TRANE

ENVELOPE

LIGHTING

HEATING

COOLING

ENERGY PRODUCTION

WATER & WASTE

4.220 Water-to-water heat recovery system taps into heat in the wastewater from showers at the Goodlife Fitness Club in Toronto, Canada. WATERFILM ENERGY INC.

Further Information

"BetterBricks Case Study: Hot Lips Pizza." Available at: www.betterbricks.com/

Goldstick, R. 1983. *The Waste Heat Recovery Handbook*. Fairmont Press, Atlanta, GA.

Goldstick, R. and A. Thumann. 1986. *Principles of Waste Heat Recovery*. Fairmont Press, Atlanta, GA.

Grumman, D.L. ed. 2003. *ASHRAE GreenGuide*. American Society of Heating, Refrigerating and Air-Conditioning Engineers, Atlanta, GA.

BEYOND SCHEMATIC DESIGN
Design development of an energy recovery system requires the expertise of a mechanical engineer. Energy simulations will typically be undertaken to ensure the selection of optimized equipment and associated control strategies. An energy recovery system should be commissioned to ensure that it performs as intended.

ENVELOPE

LIGHTING

HEATING

COOLING

ENERGY PRODUCTION

WATER & WASTE

PHOTOVOLTAICS are systems that produce electricity through the direct conversion of incident solar radiation. A photovoltaic (PV) cell provides direct current (DC) output. This DC output can be used directly to power DC loads, can be stored in a battery system, or can be converted (inverted) to alternating current (AC) to power AC loads or be fed into an electrical grid. Stand-alone PV systems have no grid interconnection; grid-connected systems typically use the local electrical grid both as a backup electrical supply and a place to "store" excess generation capacity.

4.221 Atrium facade glazing (PV cells laminated within a glass curtain wall) at the Lillis Business School, University of Oregon, Eugene, Oregon. LARA SWIMMER PHOTOGRAPHY

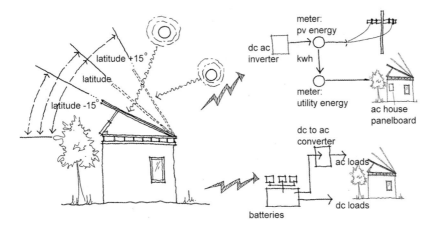

4.222 Schematic diagram of photovoltaic systems; grid-connected (top) and stand-alone (bottom). KATE BECKLEY

There are currently two basic types of PV modules:

1. **Thin-film (amorphous) panels:** these modules appear grainy or crystalline, the PV elements cover the entire panel, and they contain no glass (so are almost unbreakable). Amorphous PV panels have lower efficiencies, are generally cheaper, and lose less power under high temperature conditions—than crystalline panels.

2. **Crystalline (single and multi) panels:** these earliest PV modules look like a series of circles assembled in a frame. They are typically more efficient than amorphous panels—but also more expensive.

Photovoltaic panels are generally available in capacities ranging from 5 W up to 200 W peak output. Lower wattage panels are typically 12-V, while most high-wattage panels are available only in 24-V configurations. As a manufactured product, current information about available PV module options is best found in manufacturers' literature. Manufacturers produce modules, which are assembled on site into arrays. Module output is established by the manufacturer; array output (system capacity) is determined by the building design team. Various module interconnection schemes can be used to vary the output voltage and/or amperage of a PV array.

Key Architectural Issues

Photovoltaic systems can be installed essentially as an add-on system with little integration with other building elements or aesthetics—or as building integrated photovoltaics (BIPV). A BIPV approach involves more consideration of multifunctional uses (such as PV shading devices)

INTENT
On-site generation of electricity

EFFECT
Reduced demand on the electrical grid, use of renewable energy resources

OPTIONS
Angle of exposure, integration with building envelope, stand-alone or grid-connected system

COORDINATION ISSUES
PV orientation and tilt, integration with other architectural elements (shading devices, building enclosure), structural requirements, energy storage (battery system), grid system connection

RELATED STRATEGIES
Wind Turbines, Microhydro Turbines, Hydrogen Fuel Cells, Combined Heat and Power, Shading Devices

LEED LINKS
Energy & Atmosphere, Innovation & Design Process

PREREQUISITES
Clear design intent, a defined budget, local climate data, knowledge of site characteristics and obstructions, information on building electrical loads and usage profiles

ENVELOPE

LIGHTING

HEATING

COOLING

ENERGY PRODUCTION

WATER & WASTE

and/or the complete integration of PV with another technology (such as glazing or roofing products). Intriguing developments (such as flexible PV panels) suggest that greater opportunities for BIPV lie ahead.

As is the case with any alternative energy system (and should be the case with conventional systems as well) maximum implementation of energy-efficiency strategies should precede consideration of a PV system. As PV is rarely cost-effectively used to heat or cool a building, this will usually entail aggressively reducing building plug loads that would be served by the PV system.

A grid-connected system will require less equipment (typically no batteries, saving a fair amount of space), but requires a connection to (and dealings with) the local utility provider. Net metering is a common option with grid-connected systems. Stand-alone systems almost always involve battery storage (requiring more space) and may involve the use of DC equipment and appliances.

The tilt and orientation of PV panels will have a large impact on system efficiency. PV modules should generally be oriented to the south (or nearly so) to maximize daily solar radiation reception. Deviations from south are acceptable (within reason), but will usually incur a penalty on system output—quirky daily patterns of fog or cloudiness may change this general rule. PV panels should be tilted such that the greatest PV output matches periods of greatest load (or so that PV output is optimized). Due to their high first cost, PV modules should be installed in a manner that maximizes their useful output (and increases return on investment).

Depending upon site constraints (and proposed building design intentions), it may be advantageous to locate a PV array on the roof of a building, on the south facade, or on the ground somewhere near the building. PV location will have an impact on landscaping, the appearance of the facade/roof, and perhaps security measures necessary to prevent theft of or vandalism to the array.

PV arrays that track the sun across the sky can increase insolation (accessible solar radiation) by 35–50%, thus increasing power production of the array. The price of this improved output will be the greater expense and maintenance needs of a reasonably complex mounting system. Tracking arrays are most effective at lower latitudes, where the angle of the sun changes significantly throughout the day.

Only 10–20% of the solar radiation striking a PV module is converted to electricity; the majority of the remaining radiation is converted to heat. This heat tends to degrade the performance of a PV module—at the same time, it might have some useful application in a building. Applications where a synergy of electricity and heat production are possible should be considered.

Implementation Considerations

PV systems with meaningful capacities require a substantial initial investment. They will be most cost-effective where there are subsidies (tax credits, utility rebates, etc.) to minimize system first cost. Depending upon competing energy costs, it can take anywhere from 10 to 30 years to reach payback on a typical non-subsidized system. Design intent and client resources may, however, make this consideration moot. Recent

4.223 Installation of lightweight, interlocking photovoltaic panels. POWERLIGHT, INC.

4.224 Monocrystalline silicon roof modules (peak power output of 63 W) are designed to replace composition shingles for residential buildings. POWERLIGHT, INC.

ENVELOPE

LIGHTING

HEATING

COOLING

ENERGY PRODUCTION

WATER & WASTE

studies suggest that the energy payback (about 3–4 years) of a typical PV system is much less than the monetary payback period.

Although PV modules are designed for exposed installations and are electronic (versus mechanical) devices—they do require some maintenance to produce design energy output over the long term. Provision for regular cleaning and access to the panels is advisable.

Design Procedure

A really rough estimate. Assuming a 4% PV module efficiency (pretty low, see below* for adjustments) the required area of PV module necessary to obtain a given output capacity can be estimated as follows:

$$A = C/3.3$$

where,
A = required area of PV module in ft² [divide by 10 for m²]
C = desired PV system output in W
* divide the above-estimated area by 2 for 8% efficiency modules, by 3 for 12% efficiency, or by 4 for 16% efficiency

Sizing a stand-alone PV system. With a stand-alone PV system no power is transferred to or from a utility grid. The PV system generates and stores enough electricity to meet building needs. System size will depend upon electrical loads, peak generation capacity, off-peak generation, storage, and desired safety factor.

1. Estimate average daily building electricity use.

$$ADEU = \Sigma ((P) (U))$$

    where,
    ADEU = average daily energy use (Wh)
    P = average power draw of each load to be supplied by the PV system (W)
    U = average number of hours each load is used per day (h)

    This estimate should consider how loads are served; any AC loads served through an inverter must be adjusted to account for the efficiency of the inverter and associated controls equipment (an overall efficiency of 75% is typically appropriate).

2. Establish required storage capacity. Based upon a sense of how many days without usable solar radiation the system should be able to span or float (a function of climate, design intent, and alternative backup generator capacity—if any) estimate required battery storage capacity as follows:

$$S = (ADEU) (Days)$$

    where,
    S = storage capacity (Wh)
    ADEU = average daily electricity use (Wh)
    Days = desired days of storage

    The number of batteries required can be estimated by converting the storage capacity in Wh to Ampere-hours by dividing by the battery (system) voltage and then dividing that value by the unit storage capacity of the intended battery type.

SAMPLE PROBLEM
Rough estimate: Starting with a general target of providing a 1 kW capacity system for a single family residence, a rough estimate of required array size (assuming 8% efficient modules) gives:

$$(1000\,W/3.3)/2 = 150\,ft^2\,[14\,m^2]$$

Stand-alone system:

1. An 1800 ft² [167 m²] conventional residence on Guam is estimated to use 10,500 kWh/year, while an energy-efficient home of the same floor area would use 8000 kWh/year. (If this type of usage information is available, it is possible to bypass the load-by-load approach to estimating system capacity outlined in the design procedure.) This gives an average daily electricity usage of about 28 kWh (or 22 kWh for the energy-efficient option).

2. The design intent and climate data suggest that 2 days of storage is a reasonable goal. This equates to:

    (28 kWh/day)(2 days) = 56 kWh (44 kWh for the efficient alternative).

    Assume standard 12-V deep-cycle batteries with a capacity of 850 Ah connected in series to provide a 24-V system. Convert kWh to Ah: 56,000 Wh/24 V = 2333 Ah (or, for the more efficient residence, 44,000/24 = 1833 Ah). Thus, 2333/850 = 2.7 (say 4) batteries are needed—in a

3. Estimate required daily PV system output. PV system output must be able to provide for the current day's electricity needs, as well as provide some extra output that can go into storage to recharge batteries. The longer the time allowed for recharge (primarily a function of weather patterns), the smaller the system capacity can be. Note where this discussion leads: in a stand-alone PV system any charging capacity (output in excess of daily needs) will be wasted capacity whenever batteries are fully charged. Note also that "rainy-day" storage capacity is above and beyond the daily storage capacity required to provide electricity during nighttime hours.

The required system size (capacity) can be estimated as:

$$C = ((RDS/RD) + 1) (DL)$$

where,
C = system capacity (kWh)
RDS = required days of storage—which represents the desired system float (see Step 2 above)
RD = recharge days—which represents the number of days over which storage can be charged
DL = daily load—which is the average daily PV-generated electric load

4. Determine required PV array capacity. PV production is primarily a function of available solar insolation—which varies with latitude, climate, module orientation, and module tilt. Rough estimates of annual incremental PV production range from about 2000 kWh/year for very sunny, low latitude climates to 1000 kWh per year for generally cloudy, high latitude climates. This corresponds to a range of 5.5 to 2.7 kWh per day—per kW of system output capacity. These values assume south-facing modules installed at a tilt equal to site latitude. The required array capacity can be estimated as follows:

$$AC = (RADC)/(ADP)$$

where,
AC = array capacity (peak kW)
$RADC$ = required average daily capacity (kWh)
ADP = average daily production (kWh per peak kW)

Estimate size of array required to provide indicated capacity. For schematic design, assume a PV array area of 0.15–0.08 ft^2 [0.0014–0.007 m^2] per W of peak output. The lower values correspond to higher efficiency PV modules.

Sizing a grid-connected array. Sizing a grid-connected system is simpler than a stand-alone system, as there is no need to deal with storage or output capacity required to charge storage. The utility grid provides a place to "store" excess generation capacity and a source of electricity when the on-site PV system cannot provide adequate output.

The sizing method described above (minus the storage elements) can be used to obtain a preliminary estimate of PV system size for a grid-connected system. The limiting constraints are usually budget (how much PV can be afforded) and PV mounting location space availability. As a starting point, an array that provides about 40% of a building's electrical needs (for small to mid-sized buildings) is often reasonable.

parallel/series arrangement—although the efficient building (requiring 2.2 batteries) might be able to make do with just 2 batteries.

3. The required system capacity (assuming that battery recharge can occur over a 4-day period) is:
((2 days of storage/4 days for recharge) + 1) (28 kWh) = 42 kWh—or, for the energy-efficient alternative, 33 kWh.

4. Array capacity is estimated as follows:
(28 kWh per day)/(say 5 kWh per day for a generous climate) = 5.6 kW peak capacity—or 4.4 kW for the efficient alternative.

5. Array size is estimated (using the lower end of the sizing range because the system capacity is fairly large) as:
(5600 W) (0.1 ft^2 per W) = 560 ft^2 [52 m^2].

For the energy-efficient residence, the array size is estimated as:
(4400 W) (0.1) = 440 ft^2 [41 m^2].

The point of looking at an energy-efficient alternative is to note that an investment in reducing electric loads pays off in reduced need for PV capacity. In most cases, the efficiency can be obtained at much lower cost than the PV.

ENVELOPE

LIGHTING

HEATING

COOLING

ENERGY PRODUCTION

WATER & WASTE

A life-cycle cost analysis can be used to determine the most cost-effective PV system size for any given building situation. Although this type of analysis will require computer simulations for any reasonable degree of accuracy, this is a viable schematic design activity. Required input data will include: local climate data, detailed utility tariffs (including information on time of day and demand rates), a reasonable estimate of building electrical loads and usage profiles, equipment costs, and some estimate of system maintenance and repair costs.

Examples

4.225 The Bundy Brown residence in Ketchum, Idaho uses 640 ft^2 [60 m^2] of BIPV (in the form of a photovoltaic laminate product adhered to the standing seam metal roof). The system has an output of 3.52 kW. BRUCE HAGLUND

4.226 The rooftop photovoltaic array on the roof the Martin Luther King Jr. Student Union at the University of California Berkeley in Berkeley, California generates 59 kW of electricity during peak solar conditions. POWERLIGHT, INC.

4.227 Photovoltaic panels incorporated into the roof form of the Ridge Winery, California. POWERLIGHT, INC.

4.228 Photovoltaic panels shade parking areas as well as produce 67 kW of electricity at the Patagonia Headquarters, Ventura, California. MILLER/HULL PARTNERSHIP

Further Information

Florida Solar Energy Center, Photovoltaics. www.fsec.ucf.edu/pvt/

IEA Photovoltaic Power Systems Programme. www.iea-pvps.org/

NREL Solar Radiation Data. redbook/atlas/rredc.nrel.gov/solar/old_data/nsrdb/

U.S. Department of Energy, National Center for Photovoltaics. www.nrel.gov/ncpv/

Whole Building Design Guide: Building Integrated Photovoltaics (BIPV). www.wbdg.org/design/bipv.php

Whole Building Design Guide: Distributed Energy Resources (DER). www.wbdg.org/design/der.php

BEYOND SCHEMATIC DESIGN

The estimated size of a PV system developed for proof-of-concept during schematic design is just that—an estimate. During design development more detailed simulations and analyses will be run to confirm these early estimates and optimize the PV investment in terms of life-cycle costs. Specific PV equipment and associated controls will be selected, detailed, and specified during design development. Without question, a PV system should be commissioned to ensure that it delivers on its potential and a User's Manual should be provided to the client.

ENVELOPE

LIGHTING

HEATING

COOLING

ENERGY PRODUCTION

WATER & WASTE

WIND TURBINES

ENVELOPE

LIGHTING

HEATING

COOLING

ENERGY PRODUCTION

WATER & WASTE

WIND TURBINES produce energy from an ever-renewable resource, the wind. Wind energy is an indirect implementation of solar energy. The sun's radiation warms the earth's surface at different rates in different places and the various surfaces absorb and reflect radiation at different rates. This causes the air above these surfaces to warm differentially. Wind is produced as hot air rises and cooler air is drawn in to replace it. According to the American Wind Energy Association, a large wind project can produce electricity at lower cost than a new power plant using any other fuel source.

Wind turbines change the kinetic energy of the wind into electric energy much the same way that hydroelectric generators do. A wind turbine captures wind with its blades; the rotating blades (called a rotor) turn a drive shaft connected to a generator which converts the rotational movement into electricity. The wind speed determines the amount of energy available for harvest, while the turbine size determines how much of that resource is actually harvested.

A small wind electric system includes: a rotor (the blades), a generator or alternator mounted on a frame, a tail, a tower, wiring, and other system components—called the balance-of-system in photovoltaic systems—controllers, inverters, and/or batteries.

4.229 Large wind turbine in Boone, North Carolina.

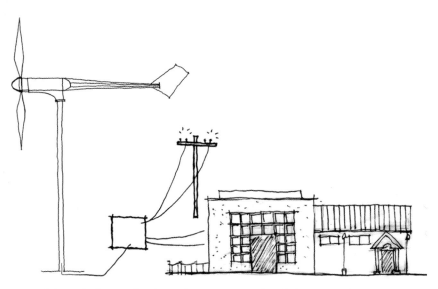

4.230 Schematic diagram showing major components of a wind energy system. KATE BECKLEY

INTENT
On-site electricity production

EFFECT
Reduces use of electricity generated from non-renewable resources

OPTIONS
Various products, capacities ranging from small-scale residential to commercial to large-scale wind farms

COORDINATION ISSUES
Site zoning restrictions, site topography, building electrical loads and profiles, space for balance-of-system components, aesthetics

RELATED STRATEGIES
Plug Loads, Photovoltaics, Hydrogen Fuel Cells

LEED LINKS
Energy & Atmosphere

PREREQUISITES
Site zoning restrictions, site wind data, building electrical load profiles

Horizontal upwind turbines, the most common type of wind machine, have two or three blades. The swept area is the area of the circle created by the turning blades, and determines the quantity of wind intercepted by the turbine. The larger the swept area, the greater the amount of power a turbine can produce. The frame of the turbine holds the rotor and generator and supports the tail, which keeps the turbine facing into the wind.

Wind turbines are sized based upon power output. Small turbines range from 20 W to 100 kW in capacity. The smallest turbines, called "micro" turbines' range from 20 to 500 W and are commonly used to charge batteries for recreational vehicles and sailboats. Turbines of 1 to 10 kW are often used to pump water. Those ranging from 400 W to 100 kW are typically used to generate electricity for residential and small commercial applications.

A residential or farm-sized turbine—with a rotor up to 50 ft [15 m] in diameter and a tower up to 120 ft [35 m] tall—may be used to supply electricity to a home or business. A small wind turbine can be one of the most cost-effective home-based renewable energy systems and may lower a residential electric bill by 50 to 90%.

Key Architectural Issues

The aesthetics of a wind turbine (including the height and profile) should be considered relative to its impact on the overall project. Towers are a necessary part of a wind system because wind speeds increase with height—the higher the tower the more power a turbine can produce.

The power generated by a wind turbine is a function of the cube of the wind speed, so building a higher tower can be economical. For example raising a 10-kW wind turbine from a 60-ft [18 m] tower height to a 100-ft [30 m] tower can produce 29% more power and cost just 10% more to construct.

It might be tempting to mount a turbine on a rooftop but this is not recommended. Vibrations from the turbine can cause structural problems as well as irritate building occupants and users. A rooftop turbine would also be subject to turbulence caused by the building form. The noise produced by early wind turbines was an issue in residential neighborhoods, but newer turbines produce less noise. The ambient noise level of most small turbines is about 52 to 55 decibels (dBA)—no noisier than an average refrigerator.

Implementation Considerations

According to the U.S. Department of Energy's Energy Efficiency and Renewable Energy program, a wind turbine can be reasonably considered in any location where most of the following conditions exist:

- The site has a good-to-acceptable wind resource (an average annual wind speed of at least 9 mph [4 m/s]). Many parts of the world have adequate wind resources to power a small turbine.

- The site is at least 1 acre [0.4 ha] in size.

- Local zoning ordinances allow wind turbines.

- A wind turbine could produce a sizable amount of the electricity used by the building—"sizable" is a function of design intent.

- A wind turbine represents an acceptable life-cycle investment for the client.

- The site is in a remote location that does not have ready access to the electric grid or is served by a very high-cost electric utility.

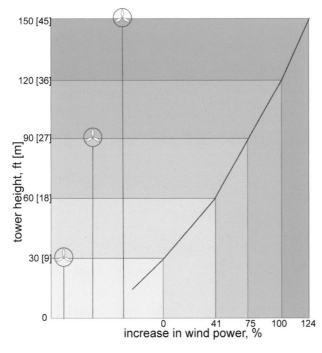

4.231 Wind power increases with height above the ground. KATHY BEVERS; ADAPTED FROM DOE/EERE

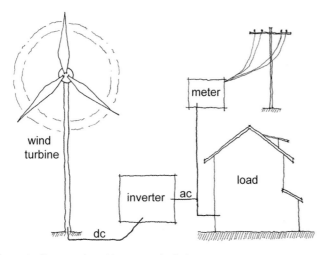

4.232 Schematic diagram of a grid-connected wind power system. KATE BECKLEY

A grid-connected system uses an inverter that converts direct current (DC) generator output to alternating current (AC) to make the system electrically compatible with the utility grid and conventional appliances. This allows power from the wind system to be used in a building or sold to the utility company as most economically appropriate. Batteries are not normally required for a grid-connected system.

A grid-connected system is a good choice when:

* The site has an average annual wind speed of at least 10 mph [4.5 m/s].

* Utility-supplied electricity is relatively expensive.

- Connecting a wind system to the utility grid is not prohibited or overly burdened with bureaucratic roadblocks.

- There are incentives available for the sale of excess electric generation and/or for the purchase of the wind turbine.

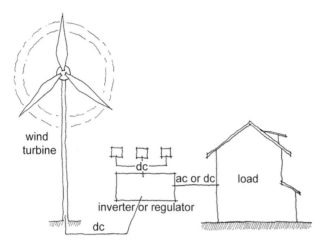

4.233 Schematic diagram of a stand-alone wind power system. KATE BECKLEY

A stand-alone system is not connected to the utility grid. This type of system can provide power in remote locations where access to power lines is difficult or very expensive. With no utility backup, this system configuration requires batteries to store energy that will be used when there is no wind. A charge controller keeps the batteries from overcharging. An inverter is required to convert DC output to alternating current (AC)—unless all loads (including appliances) are DC. DC versions of most residential appliance are readily available.

A hybrid system combines wind and photovoltaic (or other site-based) technologies to produce energy. This can be an optimal combination if wind speed is low in summer when the solar radiation is plentiful for the PVs and wind is stronger in winter when there is less radiation available to the PVs.

A stand-alone or hybrid system is a good choice when:

- The site is in an area with average annual wind speed of at least 9 mph [4.0 m/s].

- A grid connection is either unavailable or prohibitively expensive.

- Independence from purchased energy resources is a key design intent.

- The use of renewable energy resources is a key design intent.

Design Procedure

1. Research land use issues for the proposed site. Determine if a wind turbine would be in compliance with local zoning ordinances. Typical issues addressed by local ordinances include:
    -   minimum parcel size (generally requires 1 acre [0.4 ha]);
    -   maximum allowable tower height;
    -   setback requirements.

2. Evaluate the wind resource. Wind speed and direction are changing all the time; wind speed can change significantly between daytime and nighttime and seasonally. Evaluating the distribution of wind speeds throughout the year is the best way of accurately estimating the energy that a wind turbine will produce on a given site. For preliminary estimates an average wind speed can be used (refer to a wind resource map—such as the *Wind Energy Resource Atlas of United States*). The specific terrain of the site must also be taken into account because local conditions may alter wind speeds. Other methods for evaluating the wind resource for a site include: obtaining wind data from a nearby airport, using portable wind measurement equipment (especially to gauge local effects), and obtaining information from existing wind turbine owners (or wind surfers) in the area.

3. Estimate building energy requirements in kWh per year. Estimates of daily and seasonal distribution of this annual consumption will be useful during design development. According to the U.S. Department of Energy, a typical (not green) U.S. home uses approximately 10,000 kWh of electricity per year. Commercial building electricity consumption can be estimated or correlated from available data sources (typically on a per unit floor area basis).

4. Size the wind turbine. The U.S. Department of Energy (Energy Efficiency and Renewable Energy program) suggests the following formula to obtain a preliminary estimate of the performance of a generic wind turbine.

    $$AEO = 0.01328 \, D^2 V^3$$

    where:
    AEO = annual energy output, kWh/year
    0.01328 = a conversion factor (that also includes an assumed wind system efficiency)
    D = rotor diameter, ft [multiply m by 3.3 to obtain ft]
    V = annual average wind speed, mph [multiply km/h by 0.62 to obtain mph]

    Compare the estimated annual energy output (for a given diameter wind turbine at the site's annual average wind speed) with the energy requirement estimate from the previous step to see how a particular turbine matches needs. The equation can also be rearranged to solve for the rotor diameter required to provide the necessary electrical output.

5. Locate the turbine and establish tower height. The bottom of the rotor blades should be at least 30 ft [9 m] above any obstacle that is within 300 ft [90 m] of the tower. Choose a placement for the turbine that considers prevailing wind direction and obstructions.

SAMPLE PROBLEM

Investigate the feasibility of using a wind turbine to produce electricity for a small, 2-story medical office building on an unobstructed site in the Midwestern United States.

1. A check of local ordinances suggests there are no legal impediments to the installation of a wind turbine on the chosen site.

2. The average wind speed at the site is estimated to be 12 mph [19 km/h]—based upon wind speed maps and the absence of obstructions.

3. The annual electrical energy needs of the office are estimated to be 20,000 kWh.

4. Estimate the required diameter of a wind turbine rotor using the formula:

    $AEO = 0.01328 \, D^2 V^3$,

    and solve for D

    $D = (AEO/(0.01328V^3))^{0.5}$

    Set AEO = 20,000 kWh and

    $V = 12$ mph
    $D = (20,000/(0.01328)(12^3))^{0.5}$
    $D = 29.5$ ft [9 m],

    so a wind turbine with a 30-ft [9-m] diameter rotor could, potentially, produce all of the electricity needed to power the office throughout the year.

5. Because this 2-story office is about 25 ft [7.6 m] tall, a 55-ft [16.8 m] tower would provide reasonable access to winds out of the influence of the building wind shadow.

ENVELOPE

LIGHTING

HEATING

COOLING

ENERGY PRODUCTION

WATER & WASTE

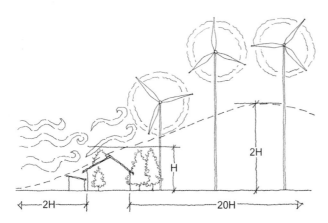

4.234 Turbulent airflow zone (to be avoided) caused by ground level obstructions. KATE BECKLEY

Examples

4.235 Nine Canyon Wind Project in Benton County, Washington was completed in 2002. Each of the 37 wind turbines has a rating of 1300 kW, yielding a project capacity of 48 MW.
ENERGY NORTHWEST, DOE/NREL

Further Information

American Wind Energy Association. "The Wind Energy Fact Sheet." www.awea.org/

U.S. Department of Energy, Energy Efficiency and Renewable Energy. *A Consumer's Guide to Energy Efficiency and Renewable Energy: Sizing Small Wind Turbines.* Available at: www.eere.energy.gov/consumer/your_home/electricity/index.cfm/ mytopic=11010

U.S. Department of Energy. *Wind Energy Resource Atlas of United States.* Available at: www.nrel.gov/wind/

BEYOND SCHEMATIC DESIGN

During design development the preliminary selection of a wind turbine system will be refined. Analyses will be conducted to ensure that system performance is acceptable throughout the year, to size system accessory components (such as a battery bank or inverter), and to develop an estimate of system life-cycle cost. Equipment will be specified. A User's Manual is recommended—as is commissioning of the wind power system.

ENVELOPE

LIGHTING

HEATING

COOLING

ENERGY PRODUCTION

WATER & WASTE

ENVELOPE

LIGHTING

HEATING

COOLING

ENERGY PRODUCTION

WATER & WASTE

MICROHYDRO TURBINES

MICROHYDRO TURBINES generate electricity by tapping into a flow of water. Microhydro electric systems, when thoughtfully designed, can produce low impact, environmentally-friendly power by harnessing the renewable kinetic energy in moving water.

The power available from a microhydro turbine system is derived from a combination of water "head" and "flow." Head is the vertical distance between the water intake and the turbine exhaust. This distance determines the available water pressure. Head distances of less than 3 ft [0.9 m] will usually prove ineffective. A low-head system typically involves 3 to 10 ft [0.9 to 3.1 m] of elevation. Flow is the volume of water that passes through the system per unit of time—usually expressed in gpm [L/s].

4.236 Water inlet to the penstock of a residential microhydro installation. JASON ZOOK

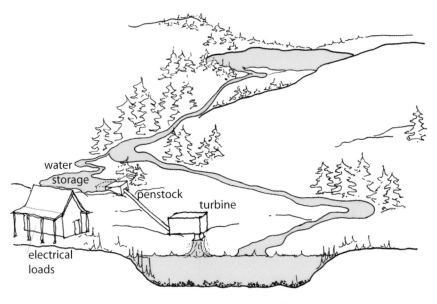

4.237 Components of a microhydro turbine electrical generating system. KATE BECKLEY

Water is delivered from a source (usually a pond or lake that provides storage capacity for the system) to a turbine through a pipe or penstock. The turbine, in turn, powers a generator. A turbine is a rotary engine that derives its power from the force exerted by moving water. Hydroelectric turbines are categorized as impulse, reaction, or propeller types.

The feasibility of a microhydro turbine system is dependent upon governing regulations dealing with water rights and usage, water availability and reliability, the potential power available from that source, and system economics.

Key Architectural Issues

Site selection is essential to the success of a microhydro turbine power system. The site must have a reliable water source that can provide

INTENT
On-site electricity generation

EFFECT
Reduced use of fossil fuel-generated electricity

OPTIONS
Reaction turbines, impulse turbines, propeller turbines

COORDINATION
Site selection, environmental impacts, storage pond location (if applicable), building electrical loads and usage profile

RELATED STRATEGIES
Wind Turbines, Photovoltaics, Hydrogen Fuel Cells, Plug Loads

LEED LINKS
Sustainable Sites, Energy & Atmosphere

PREREQUISITES
Consistently flowing water source, available head of at least 3 ft [0.9 m], regulatory approval

ENVELOPE

LIGHTING

HEATING

COOLING

ENERGY PRODUCTION

WATER & WASTE

adequate water flow. The site must also have adequate slope to provide a minimum of 3 ft [0.9 m] of head for water delivery.

An intake is placed at the highest convenient point of the water source. Water is diverted from a stream, river, or lake into a penstock. The intake penstock may be sited within a dam or diversion pool to increase head (pressure) and create a smooth, air-free inlet to the delivery components. Screens are positioned at the mouth of the penstock to filter debris that could damage the turbine.

A housing of some sort is constructed for the turbine and generator to protect these components from the elements and/or tampering. This "powerhouse" should be located in an area safe from floodwaters. Housing for a battery bank (if used) must also be provided.

A "transmission line" runs from the generator to the point of use. The shortest possible route between generator and point of use should be utilized to minimize voltage losses due to resistance in this line—this is particularly true if DC power is distributed (versus AC from an inverter).

Implementation Considerations

A generator converts the rotational force of the turbine shaft into electricity. Generators produce direct current (DC) that may be used directly by DC appliances, used to charge a battery bank, or run through an inverter to produce AC power (alternating current) to supply conventional plug loads. Typical residential generator units produce 120/240 VAC power that is appropriate for most appliances, lighting, and heating equipment. Generators operate at a frequency determined by the rotational speed of the generator shaft; higher RPM produces a higher frequency.

An emergency system shutdown control can prevent overloading or underloading of the system in the event of a malfunction or accident. If connected to a public grid, an emergency system shutdown will be required.

Impulse turbines operate in an open-air environment in which high velocity jets of water are directed onto "blades" to facilitate shaft rotation. Impulse turbines are best suited for "high" head (and often low-flow) situations. Reaction turbines operate fully immersed in water. The pressure and flow of water to the runner (much like a propeller) facilitates turbine rotation. Reaction turbines are best suited for "low" head (and often high-flow) applications. Propeller turbines are typically used in high-flow, no-head situations (they act much as a boat propeller, but in reverse). Residential microhydro turbine systems may produce up to 100 kW, while larger (but still small-scale) systems can produce up to 15 MW.

MICROHYDRO TURBINES **211**

ENVELOPE

LIGHTING

HEATING

COOLING

ENERGY PRODUCTION

WATER & WASTE

Design Procedure

1. Determine whether it is legally acceptable to divert water from the intended source.

2. Determine the available head. There are a number of ways to do so, including a formal engineering survey or an informal survey using level lines and tape measures. The gross head is the vertical distance from the water surface at the intake point to the exhaust of the turbine. Net (available) head is gross head minus friction loss in the penstock (due to pipe, fittings, and valves). For schematic design purposes, assume that net head will be 80–90% of gross head.

3. Determine flow. If not available from local regulatory agencies, flow rate may be estimated using several simple and approximate methods. There are at least two flows of primary interest—the anticipated lowest flow (required to match loads to output and for design of backup power supplies) and the average flow (which will give a sense of the energy production available from the turbine system).

4. Estimate turbine power output using the equation:

$$P = ((flow)(head))/F$$

where,
    P = power output (W)
 flow = water flow rate (gpm) [L/s]
 head = net head (ft) [m]
    F = 10 [0.192], a conversion factor (that includes a typical efficiency for the turbine)

5. Compare the projected microhydro turbine output with the building's electrical power needs (estimated on the basis of appliances anticipated to be installed in a residential building or unit power density values for larger buildings) to determine whether this strategy can reasonably contribute to the project's electricity needs.

6. If the microhydro turbine is to be located some distance from the building(s) being served, determine the transmission line length and estimate line losses (input from an electrical consultant is advised).

7. Determine where the turbine and associated equipment will be located. Space demands for the turbine/generator are not great (perhaps 100–200 ft² [9–18 m²] depending upon system capacity); space for batteries (if used) will be more substantial. Location of the turbine is an acoustical concern; the equipment can be somewhat noisy.

SAMPLE PROBLEM

A small environmental research station will be built in the foothills of the Rocky Mountains in Canada.

1. Permission to install a microhydro system was readily given considering the pollution and noise generated by an alternative diesel generator power source.

2. Available head on the site (from the mean elevation of a proposed storage pond to the turbine axis) is 45 ft [13.7 m].

3. Average flow is estimated to be 200 gpm [12.6 L/s].

4. Estimated power output is: ((200)(45)/10) = 900 W.

5. The building electrical load is estimated to be 2.5 W/ft² [26.9 W/m²] (including efficient lighting and substantial equipment loads—but excluding heating loads). For the 2000 ft² [186 m²] building this equates to 5000 W—substantially more than the 900 W output. The building will operate 8 hours a day, however, whereas power generation will occur over a 24-hour day. Comparing daily usage to output: (8)(5000) = 40,000 Wh versus (24)(900) = 21,600 Wh.

The proposed microhydro system provides roughly one-half the daily electric needs of the research station—given substantial battery capacity to match output to loads. A wind, PV, or fuel cell system might be considered—or the building loads reduced by a factor of 50% (perhaps through aggressive daylighting).

Examples

4.238 Microhydro turbine at the Ironmacannie Mill in Scotland which operates on 18 ft [5.5 m] of head creating 2.2 kW of power. NAUTILUS WATER TURBINE, INC.

4.239 Looking downstream from two microhydro turbines at the Tanfield Mill in Yorkshire, England. The installation is part of an ongoing development in renewable energy projects focusing upon microhydro applications. NAUTILUS WATER TURBINE, INC.

6. The turbine and generator will be located about 300 ft [91 m] from the research station. The effect of transmission losses across this distance will be addressed in design development.

7. A remote outbuilding will house and protect the turbine, generator, and batteries. Any noise is not an issue at this distance from the occupied building.

4.240 The 400-year old Tanfield Mill now uses one 30-kW Francis turbine and two smaller 3-kW turbines (shown above), with an operating head of 9 ft [2.7 m]. Water flow is 23,760 gpm [1501 L/s] for the large turbine and 2376 gpm [150 L/s] for the smaller units. The turbines are combined with conventional battery storage and inverter technology. NAUTILUS WATER TURBINE, INC.

Further Information

Harvey, A. et al. 1993. *Micro-Hydro Design Manual: A Guide to Small-Scale Water Power Schemes.* ITDG Publishing, Rugby, Warwickshire, UK.

Masters, G. 2004. *Renewable and Efficient Electric Power Systems.* Wiley-IEEE Press, New York.

U.S. Department of Energy, Microhydropower Systems. www.eere.energy.gov/consumer/your_home/electricity/index.cfm/ mytopic=11050

BEYOND SCHEMATIC DESIGN
Assuming that a microhydro turbine system proves feasible during schematic design, the system will be further analyzed, detailed, and integrated during design development. Specific equipment (turbine, batteries, inverter, etc.) will be selected, coordinated, and specified. Commissioning of this type of unconventional system is essential. A User's Manual should be prepared to assist the client/user with training, operations, and maintenance activities.

ENVELOPE

LIGHTING

HEATING

COOLING

ENERGY PRODUCTION

WATER & WASTE

NOTES

ENVELOPE

LIGHTING

HEATING

COOLING

ENERGY PRODUCTION

WATER & WASTE

HYDROGEN FUEL CELLS

HYDROGEN FUEL CELLS produce clean energy through an electrochemical reaction between hydrogen and oxygen. A fuel cell can be seen as three parts, an anode side, a cathode side, and a membrane that divides the two. Hydrogen gas enters the anode side of a fuel cell and reacts with a platinum catalyst, which divides the hydrogen atom into a proton and an electron. Both the proton and electron travel to the cathode side of the fuel cell, but via different routes. The proton passes directly through the membrane to the cathode, while the electron travels through a connecting electrical circuit, providing electrical energy on its journey to the cathode. Once reunited in the cathode, the electron, the proton, and an oxygen atom combine to create potable water and heat. If the heat is utilized (say through cogeneration) the fuel cell can reach overall levels of efficiency that far surpass technologies reliant on the combustion of fossil fuels and other hydrocarbons.

4.241 New York Institute of Technology's 2005 Solar Decathlon entry uses a 5-kW hydrogen fuel cell (next to water tank on top of utility module).

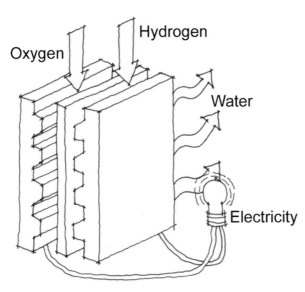

4.242 Diagram of a simple fuel cell. Hydrogen splits and then combines with oxygen to create electricity, heat, and water. AMANDA HILLS

Significant development of fuel cell technology began in the 1970s. Since then much progress has been made, leading to the discovery of numerous fuel cell technologies. These technologies are currently in varying stages of refinement, ranging from preliminary research to commercialization. Today, two types of fuel cells offer promise for providing on-site energy for the built environment; these are proton exchange membrane fuel cells (PEM) and phosphoric acid fuel cells (PAFC).

The *proton exchange membrane* (PEM) fuel cell is currently entering the early stages of commercialization. PEM technology is favorable due to its low core temperature (175 °F [80 °C]), which facilitates quick start-up and shutdown. Another benefit is the PEM fuel cell's high power density, meaning it has a small size to output ratio. According to the U.S. Department of Energy "they are the primary candidates for light-duty vehicles, for buildings, and potentially for much smaller applications such as replacements for rechargeable batteries." In fact, a 3–5 kW system, currently the size of a small refrigerator (see Figure 4.241), would be sufficient to power a typical residence. The largest stumbling block for

INTENT
On-site electricity production, combined heat and power

EFFECT
Reduced use of fossil fuel-generated electricity

OPTIONS
Capacity, fuel cell type, cogeneration strategy

COORDINATION ISSUES
Electrical load profile, emergency/standby/backup power needs, combined heat and power opportunities, product availability, maintenance capabilities

RELATED STRATEGIES
Combined Heat and Power Systems, Energy Recovery Systems, Photovoltaics, Plug Loads

LEED LINKS
Energy & Atmosphere

PREREQUISITES
Acceptance of system cost, an opportunity to make beneficial use of waste heat

PEM technology is its sensitivity to impurities in the hydrogen feedstock. This leads to gradual degradation and eventual failure of the fuel cell. Currently, PEM fuel cell systems can operate for about 5000 hours before vital components require expensive replacement or reconditioning.

Phosphoric acid fuel cells (PAFC) are commercially available and are currently being utilized in over 200 buildings worldwide. Most PAFCs produce between 200 kW and 1 MW. Due to the scale of energy production, PAFCs are usually found in larger buildings such as hospitals, nursing homes, hotels, offices, schools, and airport terminals. The main advantage to using a PAFC is that it can tolerate hydrogen with higher levels of impurities. This is why PAFCs have gained acceptance in the marketplace. On the other hand, disadvantages include high cost, low power density, and large size and weight. Disadvantages aside, PAFCs are the most established fuel cells currently on the market.

Key Architectural Issues

Besides being quiet and generally non-polluting, efficiency is one of the greatest advantages of fuel cells. A fuel cell can produce two times more electricity than a generator set with an internal combustion engine—from an equivalent energy input. A combustion engine has an efficiency of 33–35%. A fuel cell has an efficiency of 40%. This might not seem like a big difference, but when thermal energy produced by the fuel cell is recovered through cogeneration, the efficiency is boosted to about 80%. Designing a building to best utilize energy generated by a fuel cell requires integrating the fuel cell system with other building systems (such as heating and cooling).

Other design issues to consider include the building space required for a fuel cell, including an appropriate location. Fuel cell systems used solely to provide a backup electric supply can sit on a concrete pad outside of a building, much like a generator set used for auxiliary power. If a fuel cell is to be used for continuous generation, however, it is best to integrate it into the mechanical plant room. Direct access to the building's electrical panel as well as HVAC system is essential. It is hard to provide footprint estimates at this point in the development of fuel cell technologies. The following dimensions for some equipment that is commercially available may assist with planning. Fuel cells in other capacities will often be modular assemblies of these units:

- 1 kW unit: 18 in. [450 mm] W × 27 in. [690 mm] D × 20 in. [510 mm] H
- 4 kW unit: 47 in. [120 cm] W × 22 in. [56 cm] D × 55 in. [140 cm] H
- 200 kW unit: 18 ft [5.5 m] W × 10 ft [3 m] D × 10 ft [3 m] H

Implementation Considerations

The designer of a building using alternative energy sources must think in terms of efficiency. Such buildings have to be designed so that both the heat and electricity produced by a fuel cell are used. Domestic water heaters and heat exchangers can be integrated with a fuel cell system. The more synergistic opportunities that are seized, the more cost-effective the fuel cell installation.

ENVELOPE

LIGHTING

HEATING

COOLING

ENERGY PRODUCTION

WATER & WASTE

Design Procedure

When choosing a size and type of fuel cell it is vital to verify what equipment is commercially available. Many fuel cell products are still in the prototype stage of development. Product availability, however, is increasing. The following are general steps for choosing a type and size of fuel cell and deciding where to locate it within a building.

1. Estimate the base energy load and the peak energy load for the building under consideration. The fuel cell must be rated at this peak load if it will be the sole energy provider for the building (a stand-alone installation).

2. The fuel cell rating can be reduced if it is to be used in conjunction with the local energy grid or a bank of batteries that will charge during non-peak hours (a peaking or backup installation).

3. Develop strategies that utilize the heat produced by the fuel cell. In smaller systems such heat might be used in conjunction with a domestic hot water or radiant floor heating system. In larger systems (200 kW and greater) fuel cells are available with prepackaged cogeneration components.

4. Ensure that the fuel cell is located so that it can be easily connected to the building electrical panel, readily integrated with cogeneration opportunities, and vented to the exterior (if installed within the building envelope). In larger buildings the main mechanical room is usually most logical. In smaller buildings or residences a utility-closet-like location may work. Exterior installations are very common.

Examples

SAMPLE PROBLEM
The sample problem for this strategy is embedded in the design procedure—due to the general nature of the procedure.

4.243 Fuel cells do not need to be drab and grey. A colorful 200-kW fuel cell provides electricity for the Los Angeles Zoo in Los Angeles, California. UTC POWER

ENVELOPE

LIGHTING

HEATING

COOLING

ENERGY PRODUCTION

WATER & WASTE

4.244 A 200-kW fuel cell provides electricity and heats domestic hot water at Richard Stockton College, Pomona, New Jersey. UTC POWER

4.245 A 200-kW fuel cell provides electricity and heats domestic hot water for the Ford Premier Automotive Group Headquarters in Irvine, California. UTC POWER

Further Information

Fuel Cells 2000. www.fuelcells.org/

U.S. Department of Energy, Hydrogen Program. www.hydrogen.energy.gov/fuel_cells.html

UTC Power. www.utcfuelcells.com/

Whole Building Design Guide, Fuel Cell Technology. www.wbdg.org/design/fuelcell.php

BEYOND SCHEMATIC DESIGN
Once a decision to use a fuel cell has been made and verified during schematic design, much of the actual design work on the system (including final sizing and equipment selection) will occur during design development. Efforts at that time will include refinement of electrical load estimates, matching of load profiles to fuel cell control and operation strategies, optimization of waste heat usage strategies and equipment, specification of all components, and development of a User's Manual for the fuel cell system.

ENVELOPE

LIGHTING

HEATING

COOLING

ENERGY PRODUCTION

WATER & WASTE

NOTES

ENVELOPE

LIGHTING

HEATING

COOLING

ENERGY PRODUCTION

WATER & WASTE

COMBINED HEAT AND POWER SYSTEMS are on-site (sometimes described as distributed) electricity production systems that are also specifically designed to recover waste heat from the electricity production process for use in heating, cooling, or process applications. The terms "cogeneration" and "total energy systems" also describe combined heat and power (CHP) systems.

4.246 Combined heat and power system using microturbines and a double-effect absorption chiller on the roof of the Ronald Reagan Library in Simi Valley, California. UTC POWER

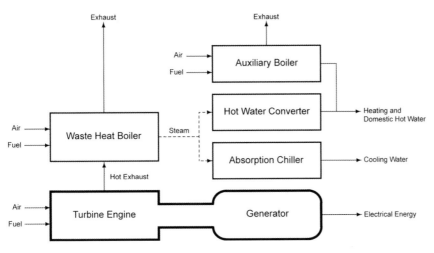

4.247 Schematic diagram of a typical microturbine-based CHP system. NICHOLAS RAJKOVICH

CHP systems are generally more energy efficient than a typical central electric power plant for two reasons:

1. The process of producing electricity at a typical power plant involves the loss of much of the by-product heat to the atmosphere and or cooling ponds.

2. The process of transmitting electricity through the electrical grid to a distant building involves a significant loss of energy due to resistance in power lines and distribution transformers.

A properly designed CHP system can be more than twice as efficient as a typical fossil fuel power plant, converting up to 80% of the energy from input fuel into electricity and useful (as opposed to waste) heat. In addition, because electricity is generated on site, and therefore not subject to grid interruptions and disturbances, CHP technologies are being increasingly used as uninterruptible power supply sources or to provide high-quality (clean) power.

As shown in Figure 4.247, CHP systems are not limited to simply heating and electrifying a building; the by-product heat energy can be directed to an absorption chiller to provide space cooling. In this application, CHP systems are sometimes called cooling, heating, and power systems.

Key Architectural Issues

In addition to adequate space for the CHP equipment, space is required for maintenance and replacement operations. If installed near an

INTENT
On-site electricity production, energy efficiency

EFFECT
Electricity production, active heating and/or active cooling, domestic water heating, process heating

OPTIONS
Various prime movers including: gas turbine, microturbine, steam turbine, reciprocating engine, fuel cell

COORDINATION ISSUES
Active heating and cooling systems, electrical systems, structural systems, noise/vibration control

RELATED STRATEGIES
Energy Recovery Systems, Absorption Chillers

LEED LINKS
Energy & Atmosphere

PREREQUISITES
Utility rate tariffs, building electrical energy loads and profiles, building heating and cooling loads and profiles

ENVELOPE

LIGHTING

HEATING

COOLING

ENERGY PRODUCTION

WATER & WASTE

occupied space, appropriate noise and vibration control strategies must be implemented. Since CHP systems often involve on-site combustion, the location of exhaust stacks and combustion air inlets must be considered. Structural system elements must be sized to accommodate CHP equipment loads.

Implementation Considerations

There are five basic types of combined heat and power systems: gas turbines, microturbines, reciprocating engine-driven generators, steam turbines, and fuel cells.

TABLE 4.16 Advantages, disadvantages, and electrical capacities of typical CHP systems.
ADAPTED FROM U.S. EPA *CATALOGUE OF CHP TECHNOLOGIES*

CHP SYSTEM	ADVANTAGES	DISADVANTAGES	CAPACITY
Gas turbine	High reliability Low emissions High grade heat available No cooling required	Requires high-pressure gas or gas compressor	500 kW–250 MW
Microturbine	Small number of moving parts Compact and lightweight Low emissions No cooling required	High first cost Relatively low efficiency Limited to lower temperature cogeneration applications	30 kW–350 kW
Reciprocating engine	High power efficiency Fast start-up Low first cost	High maintenance costs Limited to low temperature cogeneration applications Cooling required High emissions High noise levels	4–65 MW
Steam turbine	High overall efficiency Multiple fuel options High reliability	Slow start-up Low power to heat ratio	50 kW–250 MW
Fuel cell	Low emissions High efficiency Modular design	High first cost Fuels require special processing unless pure hydrogen is used	200 kW to 250 kW

4.248 A microturbine CHP system provides up to 120 kW of electricity and heat at Floyd Bennett Field in Brooklyn, New York. DENNIS R. LANDSBERG, LANDSBERG ENGINEERING

4.249 The Ritz-Carlton Hotel in San Francisco, California combines four 60-kW microturbines and a double-effect absorption chiller to provide 240 kW of electricity and refrigeration to a 336-room hotel. UTC POWER

Gas turbines use a fuel to turn a high-speed rotor connected to an electrical generator. High temperature exhaust from the combustion process generates steam at conditions as high as 1200 psig [8270 kPa] and 900 °F [480 °C]. Gas turbines are generally available in electrical capacities ranging from 500 kW to 250 MW and can operate on a variety of fuels such as natural gas, synthetic gas, landfill gas, and fuel oils. Large CHP systems that maximize power production for sale to the

COMBINED HEAT AND POWER SYSTEMS **223**

ENVELOPE

LIGHTING

HEATING

COOLING

ENERGY PRODUCTION

WATER & WASTE

electrical grid constitute much of the current gas turbine-based CHP capacity.

Microturbines also burn fuel to turn a high-speed rotor and are similar to gas turbines in construction—but smaller in scale. Microturbines can use a variety of fuels including natural gas, gasoline, kerosene, and diesel fuel/heating oil. In a microturbine CHP application, a heat exchanger transfers heat from the exhaust to a hot water system. This heat is useful for various building applications, including domestic hot water and space heating, to power an absorption chiller, or to recharge desiccant dehumidification equipment. Microturbines have been on the market since 2000 and are generally available in the 30 kW–350 kW range.

A third system type uses a reciprocating engine to drive an electrical generator. Natural gas is the preferred fuel (because of lower emissions); however, propane, gasoline, diesel fuel, and landfill gas can also be used. Reciprocating engines start quickly, are able to throttle up or down to follow changing electrical loads, have good part-load efficiencies, and are generally highly reliable. Reciprocating engines are well suited for applications that require a quick start-up and hot water or low-pressure steam as the thermal output.

TABLE 4.17 A Comparison of Common CHP Systems. ADAPTED FROM THE U.S. EPA *CATALOGUE OF CHP TECHNOLOGIES*

CHP SYSTEM TYPE	INSTAL- LATION COST (PER KW)	GREEN- HOUSE GAS EMISSIONS	POWER EFFICIENCY	OVERALL EFFICIENCY	RELATIVE NOISE
Gas turbine	Low	Moderate	22–36%	70–75%	Moderate
Microturbine	Moderate	Moderate	18–27%	65–75%	Moderate
Engine-driven generator	Moderate	High	22–45%	70–80%	High
Steam turbine	Low	Moderate	15–38%	80%	High
Fuel cell	High	Low	30–63%	65–80%	Low

Steam turbines generate electricity as high-pressure steam from a boiler rotates a turbine and generator. Steam turbines can utilize a variety of fuels including natural gas, solid waste, coal, wood, wood waste, and agricultural by-products. The capacity of commercially available steam turbines typically ranges from 50 kW to over 250 MW. Ideal applications of steam turbine-based CHP systems include medium- and large-scale industrial or institutional facilities with high thermal loads and/or where solid or waste fuels are readily available for use in the steam boiler.

The fifth system type, fuel cells, is an emerging technology that has the potential to meet power and thermal needs with little or no greenhouse gas emissions. Fuel cells use an electrochemical process to convert the chemical energy of hydrogen into water and electricity. Heat in CHP applications is generally recovered in the form of hot water or low-pressure steam. Fuel cells use hydrogen, processed from natural gas, coal gas, methanol, or other hydrocarbon fuels.

Design Procedure

Review the following steps to determine if a CHP system is appropriate for the intended building/facility context. Specifying and designing a CHP system will require the expertise of a qualified electrical/mechanical engineer, and will usually involve a detailed energy simulation to establish peak (and partial) electrical and thermal loads for the facility.

1. Consider electrical and thermal loads: As the smallest CHP capacity is around 30 kW, facilities with relatively high electrical loads—with coincident (and substantial) thermal loads—are best suited for CHP applications.

2. Consider load schedules: Most successful applications of CHP systems involve facilities where demands for electricity and heat are generally in sync (avoiding a need for thermal storage or substantial operations of an independent heating boiler). Continuous use facilities often fit this condition.

3. Consider infrastructure: Facilities with central heating and cooling capabilities, such as a college campus, provide a good match for CHP systems because an infrastructure for distributing heating and cooling already exists, and there is generally a continuous or large demand for electricity and heat.

4. Consider power quality and required reliability: A facility requiring high quality or uninterruptible power, such as a data center or hospital, typically requires standby electrical generation equipment. As a significant part of the cost of a CHP system resides in the purchase, installation, and interconnection of the electrical generation system to the grid, if a generator is required, it is often easier to justify the first cost of a CHP system.

5. Consider electrical demand charges: CHP systems are often financially viable when the peak electrical and thermal loads of a facility coincide with times of high utility rates or cause high demand charges. A CHP system can help to "shave" energy usage during peak demand hours.

6. Consider fuel availability: Fuel (such as natural gas, diesel, or biofuel) used to power a CHP system must be readily available at the project site. Depending upon the type of system selected, auxiliary equipment such as compressors or storage tanks may be required. Such accessories require space and affect the economic viability of a CHP system.

7. Consider space requirements: Adequate space must be provided for CHP system components. It is hard to generalize about these requirements. In many cases, CHP system elements (boilers, chillers, perhaps even a generator) would be required even without the CHP system. The designer must deal with system aesthetics, as well as spatial integration.

If, after reviewing the above issues, a facility appears to be a good match for a CHP system, planning for such a system should be included in schematic design decisions.

Examples

4.250 Four 60-kW gas microturbines at the University of Toronto, Canada are integrated with a 110-ton, double-effect absorption chiller. In the winter, waste heat from the microturbines helps to heat the campus. In the summer, waste heat drives the absorption chiller, reducing both the peak cooling and electrical loads for the campus. UTC POWER

4.251 The A&P Fresh Market in Mount Kisco, New York uses four 60-kW microturbines with a double-effect absorption chiller to provide electricity, summertime cooling, winter heating, sub-cooling for the process refrigeration system, and desiccant regeneration. UTC POWER

ENVELOPE

LIGHTING

HEATING

COOLING

ENERGY PRODUCTION

WATER & WASTE

Further Information

Case study profiles on CHP systems from UTC Power. www.utcpower.com/

Grumman, D.L. ed. 2003. *ASHRAE GreenGuide.* American Society of Heating, Refrigerating and Air-Conditioning Engineers, Atlanta, GA.

U.S. Combined Heat and Power Association. uschpa.admgt.com/

U.S. Environmental Protection Agency, Combined Heat and Power Partnership. www.epa.gov/chp/

U.S. Environmental Protection Agency. 2002. *Catalogue of CHP Technologies.* United States Environmental Protection Agency, Combined Heat and Power Partnership, Washington, DC. Available at: www.epa.gov/chp/project_resources/catalogue.htm

BEYOND SCHEMATIC DESIGN
The design of a CHP system is highly technical and requires the early input of mechanical and electrical engineering consultants, and simulations of load patterns and coincidences (which are the basis for a successful system). Some of this detailed analysis will occur during schematic design. During design development, system components, interconnections, and controls are selected and detailed. A CHP system should be commissioned and the client provided with a User's Manual to assist with operator training for ongoing operations and maintenance requirements.

WATER AND WASTE

Reduction of water use requires the implementation of strategies at both the building and site scales. Many water-efficiency strategies, such as low-flow fixtures and automatic controls, involve little or no additional first cost and/or very short payback periods. Other measures—such as greywater recycling or rainwater harvesting at the building scale, and constructed wetlands or bioremediation at the site scale—have significant cost impacts.

Low-flow plumbing fixtures have been the norm for more than a decade. To move beyond these now common standards, consider ultra-low-flow toilets, dual-flush toilets, waterless urinals, composting toilets, and automatic lavatory controls. Further reductions in building water use can be achieved by separately plumbing potable and greywater systems. Waterless urinals, composting toilets, and greywater recycling are not acceptable in all jurisdictions. Confirm local requirements before proceeding with these systems. In a small number of projects, on-site water treatment (such as a Living Machine) may be appropriate.

At the site scale, reductions in water use can be achieved by using greywater or harvested rainwater for landscape irrigation. Reduced water runoff and increased groundwater recharge can be achieved through reductions in paved site areas, the use of pervious materials where paving is required, bioswales, water retention areas, and constructed wetlands.

Green features such as waterless urinals and composting toilets may require special training or instructions for building occupants. These features, and others such as pervious pavement and bioswales, also require revised maintenance procedures. Designers and building owners should educate operations personnel about the environmental intent, as well as the operation and maintenance requirements, of these systems.

WATER AND WASTE

ENVELOPE

LIGHTING

HEATING

COOLING

ENERGY PRODUCTION

WATER & WASTE

STRATEGIES
Composting Toilets
Water Reuse/Recycling
Living Machines
Water Catchment Systems
Pervious Surfaces
Bioswales
Retention Ponds

NOTES

ENVELOPE

LIGHTING

HEATING

COOLING

ENERGY PRODUCTION

WATER & WASTE

ENVELOPE

LIGHTING

HEATING

COOLING

ENERGY PRODUCTION

WATER & WASTE

COMPOSTING TOILETS

COMPOSTING TOILETS (sometimes called biological toilets, dry toilets, or waterless toilets) manage the chemical breakdown of human excrement, paper products, food wastes, and other carbon-based materials. Oxygenated waste is converted into "humus," a soil-like product that can be used as a fertilizer for non-edible agricultural crops.

The benefits of composting toilets include reduced potable water usage (especially for a low-grade task such as waste removal) and reduced loads on central sewer or local septic systems. Composting toilets have been used with success in both residential and commercial/institutional buildings. Waterless urinals are often used in conjunction with composting toilets in commercial/institutional buildings.

4.252 A typical self-contained composting toilet.

4.253 Schematic diagram of a composting toilet system—with input, digestion, and disposal components. KATE BECKLEY

Composting toilets rely upon aerobic bacteria and fungi to break down wastes—just as occurs in yard waste composting. Proper sizing and aeration enable the waste to be broken down to 10–30% of its original volume. Some composting toilet systems require "turning" the pile or raking to allow surface areas to receive regular oxygen exposure. Other systems allow for adequate air spaces and facilitate oxygenation through the introduction of high-carbon materials like sawdust, straw, or bark.

Composting toilet systems may utilize self-contained (local) water closets (toilets) or centralized units with a "destination" catchment area. Self-contained units are more labor intensive, utilizing relatively small pans or trays for removal of the humus. Centralized systems reduce the need for operator/user attention and are available in both batch and continuous systems. A batch unit uses a compost receptacle that is replaced as the container reaches capacity. Continuous systems rely on "raking" and removal of finished humus to assist the composting process. Both systems need only infrequent attention, often as little as once or twice per year. Some regular maintenance will be necessary with any composting toilet system.

INTENT
Reduce the use of potable water

EFFECT
Water conservation, reduced load on central or local sewage disposal systems

OPTIONS
Self-contained equipment, remote composting equipment—in batch or continuous operation configurations

COORDINATION ISSUES
Local plumbing regulations, spatial organization, humus disposal area

RELATED STRATEGIES
Water Reuse/Recycling

LEED LINKS
Water Efficiency

PREREQUISITES
Local plumbing regulations, building occupancy information, information on client maintenance practices

Key Architectural Issues

Ventilation of catchment spaces, as well as direct system ventilation, is necessary. Ventilation systems should exhaust a minimum of 2 ft [0.6 m] above the building roof peak—typically using 4 in. [100 mm] PVC or other code-approved pipe. Effective composting requires a minimum ambient temperature of 65 °F [18 °C]; lower temperatures slow the composting process.

Water closets must be placed vertically above a catchment tank to permit proper transport of solid waste materials. (Low water-flow models are available that permit offset installations—if absolutely required by design constraints.) Pipes or chutes that connect fixtures to tanks generally have a diameter of 14 in. [355 mm] and must connect to the highest point at the rear of the tank to ensure that the composting process is continuous. A maximum of two water closets per catchment tank is generally advised.

Catchment tanks require a minimum of 1 ft [0.3 m] of overhead clearance for pipe connections and 4 ft [1.2 m] of clearance in front of tanks for removal of composted material. Direct access to the exterior of the building from the catchment tank area is suggested. The area housing the catchment tank should be properly drained and free of flood risk.

Sizing of composting toilet units or systems is dependent upon building occupancy and anticipated usage. Tank sizes vary from manufacturer to manufacturer. Table 4.18 provides a sense of the dimensions of common equipment. Multiple tanks are common in higher-use (commercial/institutional) situations to obtain the required capacity. Composting toilet (water closet) units are similar in footprint to conventional water closets, but generally appear a bit "clunkier" or "chubbier."

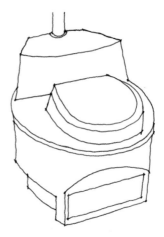

4.254 Self-contained residential composting toilet. AMANDA HILLS

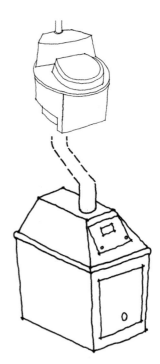

4.255 Composting toilet with remote, continuous composting tank. AMANDA HILLS

TABLE 4.18 Typical composting toilet dimensions

TYPE	USES/DAY	LENGTH in. [cm]	WIDTH in. [cm]	HEIGHT in. [cm]
Self-contained	6	25 [64]	33 [84]	25 [64]
Remote tank	9	44 [112]	26 [66]	27 [68]
Remote tank	12	69 [175]	26 [66]	30 [76]
Remote tank	80	115 [292]	62 [158]	64 [162]
Remote tank	100	115 [292]	62 [158]	89 [226]

Dimensions for remote tank units include the catchment tank, but not the toilet (which is a separate component).

Implementation Considerations

Disposal of humus should be considered during schematic design. Adequate garden or other planted area should be available if humus is to be used as fertilizer (the most logical and ecological means of disposal). For planning purposes, assume that every 25 uses will produce

ENVELOPE

LIGHTING

HEATING

COOLING

ENERGY PRODUCTION

WATER & WASTE

1 gal [3.8 L] of humus. Humus/fertilizer should not be used near water wells or edible crops. Local codes also need to be checked for specific requirements.

Maintenance of adequate temperatures in catchment areas is a design concern to be addressed early on—and is a good application for a passive solar heating system.

Design Procedure

1. Estimate the daily composting toilet usage by establishing a building occupancy count and assuming 3 uses per person per 8-hour stay.

2. Choose a self-contained or central system on the basis of required capacity, design intent, and a sense of how the building will be operated and maintained. A central system will make more sense in most public, high-use facilities.

3. Allocate space for a remote tank(s) as required by selected system type and required capacity.

4. Allocate space for access and maintenance around the remote tank(s). Ensure that plan layout and building structure will permit connection of the water closet to the remote tank (if that option is selected).

Examples

SAMPLE PROBLEM
A small research lab with a daily occupancy of a dozen people will be equipped with composting toilets.

1. The toilet capacity is estimated as: (12 occupants) (3 uses per day) = 36 daily uses.

2. A remote tank system is considered appropriate for this commercial application.

3. From Table 4.18, an 80-use per day system is selected with a tank footprint of roughly 10 ft [3 m] by 5 ft [1.5 m].

4. An additional 100% of this footprint will be allocated for access and maintenance.

4.256 Composting toilet (left) in the classroom building of IslandWood Campus, Bainbridge Island, Washington. Composting toilet (right) in the Chesapeake Bay Foundation offices, Annapolis, Maryland—with a bucket of sawdust for users to sprinkle in after use.

ENVELOPE

LIGHTING

HEATING

COOLING

ENERGY PRODUCTION

WATER & WASTE

4.257 Remote, continuous composter tanks receive waste from toilets located on the floor directly above.

Further Information

Del Porto, D. and C. Steinfield. 2000. *Composting Toilet System Book: A Practical Guide to Choosing, Planning and Maintaining Composting Toilet Systems.* The Center for Ecological Pollution Prevention, Concord, MA.

Jenkins, J. 1999. *The Humanure Handbook: A Guide to Composting Human Manure.* Jenkins Publishing, Grove City, PA.

Oikos, Green Building Source, "What is a Composting Toilet System and How Does it Compost?" oikos.com/library/compostingtoilet/

Reed, R., J. Pickford and R. Franceys. 1992. *A Guide to the Development of On-Site Sanitation.* World Health Organization, Geneva.

BEYOND SCHEMATIC DESIGN

Decisions regarding system capacity and toilet type made during schematic design will be validated during design development using more detailed information. Specific equipment will be sized, selected, detailed, and specified. Commissioning of the system might be prudent—but it is absolutely critical that a User's Manual be provided to the client. Signage informing users of composting toilet etiquette are commonly employed to educate occasional users.

WATER REUSE/RECYCLING conserves water by using a given volume of water more than once on the same building site. Water reuse is the reutilization of water for any application other than the original use—greywater systems are perhaps the most well-known example of this approach. Water recycling is the reutilization of water in the same application for which it was originally used. These two terms, however, are often used loosely and interchangeably.

Successful application of a water reuse strategy requires evaluating the degree of potability required for each water use. For example, the flushing of water closets and urinals can be accomplished using non-potable water, whereas cooking can only be done using potable water. Design for water reuse involves the integration of "effluent" from one system into the supply stream for another system. Success involves balancing the entering water quality needs for one usage with the quality of water leaving another usage. Intermediate treatment may be necessary for some reuses.

4.258 Quayside Village courtyard uses recycled water in North Vancouver, British Columbia, Canada. COHOUSING DEVELOPMENT CENTER

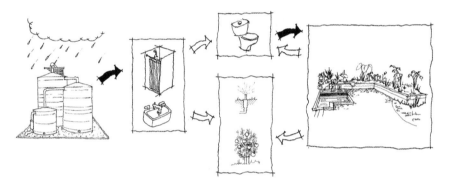

4.259 Schematic diagram of a greywater system, showing greywater sources, storage and treatment, and usage components. JONATHAN MEENDERING

Greywater consists of wastewater (from lavatories, showers, washing machines, and other plumbing fixtures) that does not include food wastes or human waste. Wastewater containing food and human wastes is termed "blackwater." Greywater is relatively easy to reuse, whereas blackwater is not. Greywater contains less nitrogen and fewer pathogens, and thus decomposes faster than blackwater. Reusing greywater can be an economical and efficient strategy to reduce a building's overall water consumption by directing appropriate wastewater not to the sewage system, but instead to other uses (such as irrigation and heat recovery). Reusing greywater in a building can reduce the load on a building's sewage system, lower a building's overall energy and chemical usage, and create new landscaping opportunities. The extent of potential greywater reusage depends upon a building's potable water usage, distributions of that water usage across time, and the ability to conveniently collect and use greywater on site.

Key Architectural Issues

Water reuse strategies can have as much (or as little) effect on the feel and aesthetics of a building as a designer wishes. Water reuse can be

INTENT
Water conservation

EFFECT
Reduced demand on potable water supplies, reduced energy use for water treatment and distribution

OPTIONS
Scale, applications (sources and uses), treatment levels, heat recovery

COORDINATION ISSUES
Landscaping and irrigation, sewage treatment and disposal system, HVAC and plumbing systems (for heat reclaim), space for storage, local codes

RELATED STRATEGIES
Living Machines, Water Catchment Systems, Retention Ponds, Bioswales

LEED LINKS
Water Efficiency

PREREQUISITES
Site information, inventory of water uses/consumptions, local regulatory requirements

ENVELOPE

LIGHTING

HEATING

COOLING

ENERGY PRODUCTION

WATER & WASTE

ENVELOPE

LIGHTING

HEATING

COOLING

ENERGY PRODUCTION

WATER & WASTE

celebrated as a visual learning tool, or treated as just another background building support system. Water storage and treatment systems can serve as beautiful organizing elements (wetlands or cisterns) in a design—but require space.

See Figure 4.260 for examples of water treatment levels for potential water reuses. Rain catchment water, in most areas of the United States, needs to be treated at a tertiary level before being used in water closets/urinals (see, for example, U.S. Environmental Protection Agency Region 9 water reuse guidelines). The perceptions of building occupants must be considered when employing any water reuse/recycling strategy.

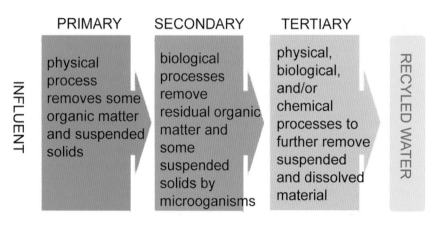

4.260 Treatment levels for recycled water. Disinfection to kill pathogens after secondary and tertiary treatment allows controlled uses of effluent. ADAPTED FROM *GRAYWATER GUIDE: USING GRAYWATER IN YOUR HOME LANDSCAPE,* STATE OF CALIFORNIA, OFFICE OF WATER USE RESOURCES

Implementation Considerations

Perhaps more than any other green building strategy, water reuse and recycling strategies are likely to incur close supervision from local code authorities as a result of health and safety concerns. Be prepared to address any such concerns directly and early in the design process. Do the necessary research to understand potential concerns and be able to provide support for proposed strategies (in other building codes or via case studies of successful applications).

Implementing a workable greywater reuse strategy requires a building with sufficient potable water usage demands to generate adequate greywater and appropriate uses for the greywater that is generated. The building must also have space available to accommodate the infrastructure of a greywater system: additional piping to carry greywater (with a separate blackwater system) along with storage and treatment tanks to prepare the greywater for reuse. The ideal building for greywater reuse is a high-occupancy residential building (or a similar occupancy) that generates significant greywater. For a greywater system to be technically viable and economically feasible, a building must produce significantly more greywater than blackwater.

Design Procedure—Greywater

1. Conduct a water-use inventory for the proposed building. The inventory includes an estimate of the types of water usage and their respective amounts for a typical time frame. Table 4.19 can be used as a starting point for such an estimate for residential applications.

TABLE 4.19 Estimating greywater resources in residential occupancies. ADAPTED FROM WWW.GREYWATER.COM/PLANNING.HTM AND *MECHANICAL AND ELECTRICAL EQUIPMENT FOR BUILDINGS*, 10TH ED.

WATER USAGE	WATER OUTFLOW	OUTFLOW QUALITY

Clothes washing machine	Top loader:
	   30–50 gal [115–190 L]/load
	Front loader:
	   10 gal [38 L]/load
	   @ 1.5 loads/week/adult
	   @ 2.5 loads/week/child
		Greywater

Dishwasher	5–10 gal [19–38 L]/load	Greywater

Shower	Low-flow:
	   20 gal [75 L]/day/person
	High-flow:
	   40 gal [150 L]/day/person
		Greywater

Kitchen sink	5–15 gal [19–56 L]/day/person	Greywater

2. Establish appropriate applications for greywater usage and estimate the greywater quantity needed. Estimating techniques will vary depending upon the anticipated usage—an inquiry to a local agricultural extension agent or landscape professional is suggested for many potential greywater uses.

3. Decide if greywater reuse is appropriate based upon the available greywater capacity, architectural and site considerations, and the quantity of water that could be utilized by potential greywater applications.

4. Decide if treatment/storage or immediate reuse should be employed based upon design considerations and the relationship between greywater production and consumption over a representative period of time.

5. Determine whether filtration will be employed based upon the nature of the reuse application and storage needs.

6. Incorporate the greywater collection/storage elements into the project design.

SAMPLE PROBLEM

A 10-unit apartment complex in Las Vegas, Nevada will use greywater for landscape irrigation. Estimate the weekly quantity of greywater produced.

1. Each apartment unit will be occupied by 4 people and will contain 1 kitchen sink, 2 lavatories, 2 water closets, 2 showers, 1 dishwasher, and 1 washing machine. Weekly greywater production is estimated as follows (making assumptions regarding flows and usage from Tables 4.19 and 4.21):

   Showers:
   (2 units)(30 gal)(2 users) = (120 gal/day)(7 days/week) = 840 gal [3180 L] / week

   Kitchen sink (included as a greywater resource since food waste management is addressed in green tenant guidelines):
   (1 unit) (10 gal) (4 users) = (40 gal/day) (7 days/week) = 280 gal [1060 L] / week

   Dishwasher:
   (1 unit) (10 gal) (0.5 load/day) = (5 gal/day) (7 days/week) = 35 gal [135 L] / week

   Washing machine:
   (1 unit) (40 gal) (6 loads/week) = 240 gal [910 L] / week

   Total weekly greywater production = 1395 gal [5280 L]

   The effluent from water closets and lavatories is not included as it is considered blackwater.

2. The estimated irrigation water requirements for 4000 ft^2 [372 m^2] of mixed use garden in Las Vegas are as follows

ENVELOPE

LIGHTING

HEATING

COOLING

ENERGY PRODUCTION

WATER & WASTE

ENVELOPE

LIGHTING

HEATING

COOLING

ENERGY PRODUCTION

WATER & WASTE

Examples

4.261 Quayside Village Cohousing Community in North Vancouver, British Columbia, Canada, a mixed use community with 19 residential units, uses a greywater recycling system to irrigate the community's compact, highly productive gardens. COHOUSING DEVELOPMENT CENTER

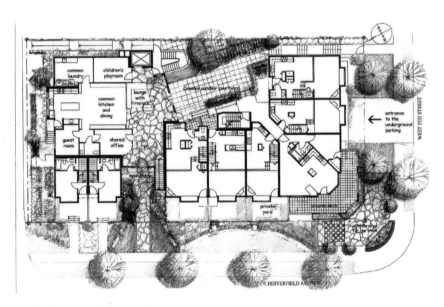

4.262 Site plan of Quayside Village showing community garden areas. COHOUSING DEVELOPMENT CENTER

(assuming a 1 in. [25 mm] weekly watering requirement: $(4000\,ft^2)(1$ in. water /wk) = $(4000)(1/12) = 333\,ft^3/wk$ $333\,ft^3 = 2490$ gal [9,425 L]

Thus, the greywater system should be able to provide for roughly $1395/2490 = 55\%$ of the garden's water needs.

3. This application of greywater is considered appropriate (even though it only partially meets the needs) because of its water conservation potential.

4. A continuous irrigation system will be used to mitigate the need for greywater storage.

5. Sand filtration will be used to improve water quality for this public use and to minimize the deposition and collection of sediments over time.

6. No storage elements are required for this application.

4.263 Courtyard at Quayside Village showing healthy, flowering vines and garden plots irrigated with recycled greywater. MJB/QUAYSIDE VILLAGE

Further Information

State of California, Department of Water Resources. 1995. "Graywater Guide: Using Graywater in Your Home Landscape." Available at: www.owue.water.ca.gov/docs/graywater_guide_book.pdf

The Chartered Institution of Water and Environmental Management. Water Reuse. www.ciwem.org/resources/water/

State of Florida, Department of Environmental Protection. 2003. "Water Reuse for Florida: Strategies for Effective Use of Reclaimed Water." Available at: www.dep.state.fl.us/water/reuse/techdocs.htm

"Greywater: What it is … how to treat it … how to use it." www.greywater.com/

Ludwig, A. 2000. *Create an Oasis with Greywater*, 4th ed. Oasis Design, Santa Barbara, CA.

Oasis Design. Greywater Central. www.greywater.net/

Quayside Village Cohousing Community. www.cohousingconsulting.ca/subpages/projects_quay.html

U.S. Environmental Protection Agency (Region 9). "Water Recycling and Reuse: The Environmental Benefits." Available at: www.epa.gov/region9/water/recycling/

BEYOND SCHEMATIC DESIGN

The nuts and bolts of water reuse and recycling will be worked out during the design development phase as treatment equipment, storage facilities, and piping interconnections are selected and/or designed. The success of this strategy, however, will lie in the schematic design analysis of feasibility and connections between effluent and influent. Commissioning of these systems is imperative—as is development of a User's Manual.

ENVELOPE

LIGHTING

HEATING

COOLING

ENERGY PRODUCTION

WATER & WASTE

ENVELOPE

LIGHTING

HEATING

COOLING

ENERGY PRODUCTION

WATER & WASTE

NOTES

LIVING MACHINES are a proprietary, engineered waste treatment system designed to process a building's sanitary drainage on site. The treatment is accomplished via a series of anaerobic and aerobic tanks that house key bacteria that consume pathogens, carbon, and other nutrients in the wastewater thereby making it clean and safe for reuse/recycling (for selected applications) or reintroduction into the local landscape.

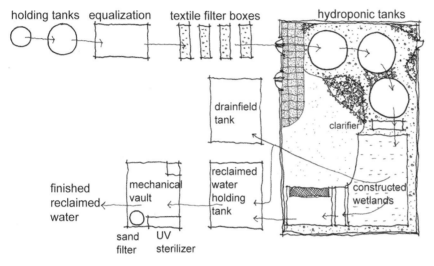

4.265 Diagram showing the typical components and sequence of flows in a Living Machine.
KATE BECKLEY

4.264 One of three hydroponic reactors that treat and recycle wastewater at IslandWood Campus, Bainbridge Island, Washington.

The most common type of Living Machine is the hydroponic system that relies on bacteria, plants, and an overflow wetland to clean wastewater. More specifically, it consists of two anaerobic tanks, a closed aerobic tank, three open aerobic (hydroponic) tanks, a clarifier, an artificial wetland, and a UV filter.

Water is a precious resource that is essential for life, yet human impacts on freshwater reserves—salinization, acidification, and pollution, to name a few—jeopardize its availability for many. Institutional buildings typically use 75–125 gallons [285–475 L] per person per day. Most of this consumption then becomes wastewater that flows, usually many miles, to a treatment center where it is cleaned and dumped into a river, lake, ocean, or perhaps aquifer. A Living Machine can provide an alternative to this centralized disposal paradigm or to less-effective or less-desirable on-site sewage disposal methods. In either case, water is retained on site, which can be ecologically desirable.

Key Architectural Issues

Living Machines are large objects with a substantial footprint—accommodating these spatial and volumetric demands will be a key architectural design concern.

Living Machines require ongoing care for proper operation. This maintenance must be within the capabilities of the client and be addressed during design.

INTENT
On-site wastewater treatment

EFFECT
Treats sanitary drainage for recycling/reuse or on-site disposal

OPTIONS
Approach to housing the aerobic digesters, water "disposal" approach (constructed wetland or other technique)

COORDINATION ISSUES
Building wastewater loads, local jurisdiction approval, location on site, footprint

RELATED STRATEGIES
Water Reuse/Recycling, Water Catchment Systems, Composting Toilets, Bioswales

LEED LINKS
Water Efficiency, Innovation & Design Process

PREREQUISITES
Sufficient area on site, amenable client and design intent, local jurisdiction approval, estimated wastewater loadings

ENVELOPE

LIGHTING

HEATING

COOLING

ENERGY PRODUCTION

WATER & WASTE

ENVELOPE

LIGHTING

HEATING

COOLING

ENERGY PRODUCTION

WATER & WASTE

Living Machines produce liquid output generally equal in volume to the potable water intake of the building. This water discharge must be accommodated on site. A fair amount of vegetation is also produced and should be beneficially used on site upon harvesting.

There are landscape design implications for an on-site wetland and aesthetic possibilities for the various processing tanks and their enclosure.

Implementation Considerations

Living Machines require exterior space, preferably adjacent to the building being served, where the closed aerobic tanks can be buried. These tanks should be located where they are accessible to maintenance workers and machinery.

The Living Machine treatment cycle relies upon metabolic processes that occur best within a specific range of temperatures. Nitrification, which occurs in the open aerobic tanks, has an optimal temperature range of 67–86 °F [19–30 °C]. Therefore, these particular tanks must be housed within a temperature-controlled facility for optimal performance. A solar greenhouse (or sunspace) has worked well in some climates and can reduce the use of purchased energy to support wastewater treatment.

Living Machines are functioning wastewater treatment systems and should be treated as such. Separation of the Living Machine (at least from the thermal, airflow, and occupant circulation perspectives) from the building being served by the system is recommended. This does not preclude tours through the system.

Design Procedure

As a proprietary technology, there is no general guideline available for the sizing of a Living Machine. Living Machine design for a specific project will involve consulting with a system design specialist. For schematic design purposes the following information should permit allocation of appropriate spaces. The values are based upon information from several existing Living Machine installations.

1. Determine the building wastewater load in gallons per day (gpd) [L/d]. Building design handbooks can provide values in support of this estimation.

2. Estimate the approximate sizes of aerobic tank and clarifier from Table 4.20. If an on-site wetland will be used to facilitate the flow of processed water back into the ecosystem, estimate its size (also from Table 4.20).

3. Lay out a conditioned space for the aerobic digesters so that there is enough space for maintenance workers to walk around the tanks, prune plants, and conduct water quality tests. Allow space (10% more is suggested) for additional equipment including pumps, meters, piping, and a UV filter. If Living Machine tours are anticipated as part of the project design intent, provide for adequate circulation and "stop and look" spaces.

4.266 Healthy and flourishing plants in a Living Machine hydroponic reactor.

SAMPLE PROBLEM
A proposed renewable energy museum in Boulder, Colorado will include two bathrooms, a small kitchen space, and a small classroom/lab with several sinks. Approximately 100 people visit and work at the museum each day.

1. An institutional building of this type is estimated to produce 87 gal [330 L] per person/day of wastewater. (100 visitors) (87 gdp) = 8700 gdp [32,930 L/d]

2. From Table 4.20, a Living Machine for this "medium" load would require 3 at 8 ft [2.4 m] diameter aerobic tanks, a clarifier tank with the same dimensions, and a wetland that is about 20 × 20 ft [6.1 × 6.1 m]. Due

4. Provide space nearby for a supplemental equipment room: 6 × 10 ft [1.8 × 3 m] should suffice for a medium capacity system.

5. The exterior space required for the anaerobic tanks is roughly equal to the space needed for the aerobic tanks.

TABLE 4.20   Approximate dimensions of Living Machine components for three system sizes (capacities)

SYSTEM CAPACITY	AEROBIC TANK DIMENSIONS	CLARIFIER DIMENSIONS	WETLAND DIMENSIONS
Small: 2500 gpd [9460 L/d], use 3 aerobic tanks			
	diameter 6 ft [1.8 m]	diameter 8 ft [2.4 m]	15 × 30 ft [4.6 × 9.1 m]
	height 3 ft [0.9 m]	height 3 ft [0.9 m]	depth 3 ft [0.9 m]
	1500 gal [5680 L]	700 gal [2650 L]	
Medium: 10,000 gpd [37,850 L/d], use 6 aerobic tanks			
	diameter 8 ft [2.4 m]	diameter 8 ft [2.4 m]	20 × 20 ft [6.1 × 6.1 m]
	height 4 ft [1.2 m]	height 4 ft [1.2 m]	depth 4 ft [1.2 m]
	depth 8 ft [2.4 m]	depth 8 ft [2.4 m]	
	3000 gal [11,360 L]	3000 gal [11,360 L]	
Large: 35,000 gpd [132,475 L/d], use 4 aerobic tanks			
	diameter 14 ft [4.3 m]	diameter 14 ft [4.3 m]	custom sizing required
	height 3 ft [0.9 m]	height 3 ft [0.9 m]	
	depth 10 ft [3 m]	depth 10 ft [3 m]	
	10,000 gal [37,850 L]	10,000 gal [37,850 L]	

to Boulder's cold winter climate the aerobic tanks should be housed in a heated enclosure (a solar greenhouse is suggested).

3. An 800 ft² [75 m²] greenhouse space is proposed to house the aerobic tanks, supplemental equipment, and access for a limited number of visitors.

4. Space for a 100 ft² [9 m²] equipment room will be allocated.

5. About 400 ft² [37 m²] of exterior space adjacent to the greenhouse and wetlands will be required for the anaerobic tanks.

Examples

4.267 The Living Machine system at IslandWood Campus on Bainbridge Island, Washington is designed to treat and recycle an average flow of 3000 gallons per day [11,360 L/d], approximately 70–80% of potable drinking water flow.

ENVELOPE

LIGHTING

HEATING

COOLING

ENERGY PRODUCTION

4.268 The Living Machine (foreground enclosure) at the Adam J. Lewis Center for Environmental Studies, Oberlin College, Oberlin, Ohio. System performance may be viewed online (see Further Information).

Further Information

Corkskrew Swamp Sanctuary Living Machine. www.audubon.org/local/sanctuary/corkscrew/Information/ LivingMachine.html

Living Designs Group (Living Machines). www.livingmachines.com/

Oberlin College, Adam Joseph Lewis Center, Living Machine. www.oberlin.edu/ajlc/systems_lm_1.html

Todd, J. and B. Josephson. 1994. "Living Machines: Theoretical Foundations and Design Precepts." *Annals of Earth*, Vol. 12, No. 1, pp. 16–24.

Todd, N.J. and J. Todd. 1994. *From Eco-Cities to Living Machines: Principles of Ecological Design.* North Atlantic Books, Berkeley, CA.

USEPA. 2001. *The "Living Machine" Wastewater Treatment Technology: An Evaluation of Performance and System Cost.* EPA 832-R-01-004. U.S. Environmental Protection Agency, Washington, DC.

USEPA. 2002 *Wastewater Technology Fact Sheet: The Living Machine®.* U.S. Environmental Protection Agency, Washington, DC.

BEYOND SCHEMATIC DESIGN

As a proprietary technology, a Living Machine will be designed by the manufacturer to suit the needs of a given facility. Detailed information regarding building usage and operation will be provided to the manufacturer as soon as possible to ensure that actual system requirements match those estimated during schematic design. Living Machines often require special certification and testing from local code authorities. Commissioning and development of a detailed User's Manual are strongly recommended.

WATER CATCHMENT SYSTEMS have historically been used to collect water for potable uses, irrigation, laundry, and passive cooling. Also known as rainwater harvesting, this is a simple technique with numerous benefits.

Wise use of water resources should be an inherent element of green building design. This strategy can be used to reduce the consumption of potable water from other sources or to supplement such sources to permit an application (such as gardening) that might otherwise be resource expensive. Rainwater stored in cisterns can provide a standby water source in times of emergency, or a supplemental source in times of increased need or reduced resources. Collecting and storing rainwater that runs off roofs and other impervious surfaces helps reduce stormwater flows and possible downstream flooding. Economically, water catchment can result in lower water supply costs.

4.269 A concrete cistern fed by a large gutter at IslandWood Campus on Bainbridge Island, Washington.

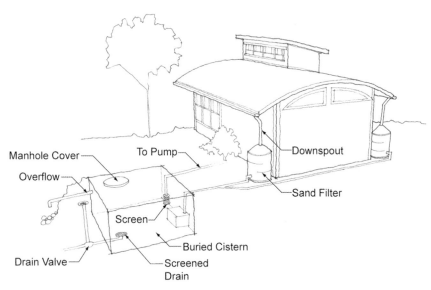

4.270 Schematic layout of a rainwater catchment and storage system for a residential building. JONATHAN MEENDERING

There are two commonly used scales of rainwater harvesting systems:

* smaller systems that collect roof runoff for domestic uses, and

* larger systems that use land forms as catchment areas to provide supplemental irrigation for agriculture.

The scale of a domestic system can be increased to encompass larger projects. On a building site scale, water catchment systems can incorporate bioswales and retention ponds. In general, components in a rainwater collection system serve one of the following functions: catchment, conveyance, purification, storage, and distribution.

Key Architectural Issues

A design approach based upon water conservation reserves high quality water for high-grade (potable) tasks and lower-quality water for

INTENT
Water conservation

EFFECT
Reduced use of purchased water supplies, increased availability of water resources

OPTIONS
Collector location and surface (roof, field, etc.); type, location, and capacity of storage

COORDINATION ISSUES
Site coordination, roof planes and materials, storage location, plumbing systems, landscaping design

RELATED STRATEGIES
Water Reuse/Recycling, Bioswales, Retention Ponds, Green Roofs, Pervious Surfaces

LEED LINKS
Water Efficiency, Sustainable Sites, Materials & Resources, Innovation & Design Process

PREREQUISITES
Local code requirements, information on water demands, local rainfall data

ENVELOPE

LIGHTING

HEATING

COOLING

ENERGY PRODUCTION

WATER & WASTE

lower-grade (non-potable) tasks. Such an approach emphasizes water recycling as a means of reducing the use of potable water resources, as well as reducing overall water usage. Water storage will require a substantial volume that can either be concealed or celebrated as a visible aspect of the project design. In either approach, the storage volume must be squarely addressed during schematic design.

Implementation Considerations

For most residential/commercial scale systems, roof design is the key consideration relative to catchment. The design process must address roofing materials as their selection will affect water quality. Factory-enameled (baked) galvanized steel or uncoated stainless steel are good roofing choices. Metal finishes must be lead- and heavy-metal-free. Asphalt shingles, wood shakes, and concrete/clay tiles are more likely to support the growth of mold, algae, and moss than are metal surfaces. Treated wood shingles may leach preservatives; asphalt shingles may leach petroleum compounds. A rough or porous roofing material will retain some water that might otherwise run off and be collected. Water purification is primarily a design development consideration, but must be considered if the collected water is to be used for potable purposes.

Water storage typically involves a cistern. Cistern materials include cast-in-place reinforced concrete, sealed concrete masonry units, brick or stone set with mortar and plastered with cement on the inside, ready-made steel tanks, precast concrete tanks, redwood tanks, and fiberglass tanks. Cisterns must be upslope of on-site sewage facilities. Avoid low places where flooding may occur. Cisterns can be incorporated into building structure, in basements, or under porches. An underground system can prevent freezing of stored water and keep water cool in the summer.

TABLE 4.21   Estimated daily per capita water needs (residential)

	GALLONS PER CAPITA DAY	LITERS PER CAPITA DAY
Recommended sustainable minimum	13	50
Developing countries	13–26	50–100
European countries	65–92	250–350
Australia (50% for exterior uses; 25% for toilets)	92	350
United Kingdom	89	335
United States (75% for interior uses; 25% for toilets)	106–145	400–550

Notes: Consumption estimates vary greatly from source to source (the above represents the consensus of several public sources); daily consumption is substantially affected by the use of water-efficient fixtures (the above values are based upon conventional fixtures).

ENVELOPE

LIGHTING

HEATING

COOLING

ENERGY PRODUCTION

WATER & WASTE

Design Procedure

This procedure provides representative values for preliminary estimation purposes for domestic water use systems. Actual water quantities may vary widely from project to project and are highly climate dependent.

1. Plan for the use of low-flow plumbing devices. It makes no sense to embark on a water collection strategy without first reducing demand through appropriate selection of fixtures. Reduced flow fixtures can cut water demand by 25–50% (compared to conventional fixtures).

2. Estimate the water needs of the building. Interior water needs typically include: water closets/urinals, showers, dishwashing, laundry, and drinking/cooking water. Water consumption is expressed in gpd [L/d] (gallons [liters] per day); a per capita consumption would be multiplied by building occupancy. Annual water needs can be estimated by multiplying gpd [L/d] by 365 days. For typical daily water needs see Table 4.21.

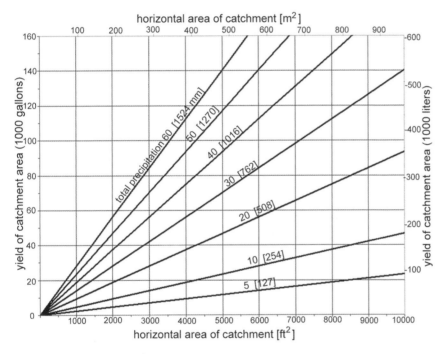

4.271 Sizing rainwater catchment areas. KATHY BEVERS; ADAPTED FROM U.S. EPA OFFICE OF WASTE WATER MANAGEMENT

3. Determine available rainfall for the building site. Data are often available from government-source annual summaries. For rainfall collection purposes, assume that a "dry" year will produce 2/3 the precipitation of an average year. Therefore, (design precipitation) = (2/3) (average annual precipitation).

4. Determine required catchment area. From Figure 4.271, determine the catchment area required to provide for the annual water needs

SAMPLE PROBLEM

A 5000 ft^2 [465 m^2] single-story addition to an existing library in Allegheny River Valley, Pennsylvania will provide rainwater for flushing water closets in the existing building.

1. Conventional water closets are used in the existing building.

2. Water usage is estimated to be 72 gpd [273 L/d] as follows: (1.6 gal/flush [10.6 L] × 3 flushes/day × 15 employees).

3. The design precipitation is (2/3) (41 in.) = 27.3 in. [(2/3) (1041 mm) = 694 mm].

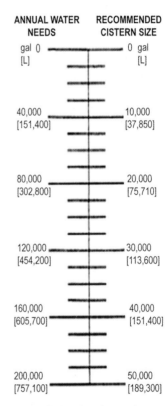

ANNUAL WATER NEEDS	RECOMMENDED CISTERN SIZE
gal 0 [L]	0 gal [L]
40,000 [151,400]	10,000 [37,850]
80,000 [302,800]	20,000 [75,710]
120,000 [454,200]	30,000 [113,600]
160,000 [605,700]	40,000 [151,400]
200,000 [757,100]	50,000 [189,300]

4.272 Estimating cistern size based upon storage capacity equal to 1/4 of annual water needs. ADAPTED FROM *PRIVATE WATER SYSTEMS HANDBOOK*, 4TH ED. MIDWEST PLAN SERVICE

of the project (considering design annual rainfall). The area of a roof used for catchment should be the projected horizontal area of the roof—not the actual surface area. In general, only 75% of average annual rainfall is actually going to be available for cistern storage (due to unavoidable losses such as evaporation, snow, ice, and roof-washing cycles).

5. Calculate cistern volume. The estimated capacity should be based upon the length of the most extensive rainless period obtained from local climatological data. Cistern capacity = (gpd [L/d] of usage) (days in rainless period). The volume can be calculated as follows: $1 \, ft^3 = 7.48$ gal of water [$1 \, m^3 = 1000 \, L$]. Alternatively, a rough estimate of cistern size can be found using Figure 4.272.

6. Establish cistern location. A cistern placed close to water usage locations is most logical and can reduce required pump capacity. An underground location can reduce visual impact and provide stability of water temperature. An above-ground location can provide an opportunity for visual impact.

7. Select or design cistern. This will be based upon the required volume, desired material, maintenance, and site considerations.

Examples

4. Calculating annual water needs:

72 gpd [273 L/d] × 365 days = 26,280 gal [99,645 L].

From Figure 4.271, the catchment area needed for 26,280 gal [99,645 L] of water with 27 in. [694 mm] of design precipitation is approximately $2600 \, ft^2$ [$242 \, m^2$].

This is about 50% of the library addition's roof area—which is quite feasible.

5. From climate data, the dry period for this area is estimated to be 90 days.

Cistern capacity = 72 gpd [273 L/d] × 90 days = 6480 gal [24,525 L]. A quick check of Figure 4.272 shows that this estimation is reasonable.

Cistern volume = 6480 gal/ $7.48 \, gal/ft^3 = 866 \, ft^3$ [$25 \, m^3$].

4.273 Observation tower and 5000 gal [18,930 L] cistern collect rainwater from the visitor's gallery and administration buildings at Lady Bird Johnson Wildflower Center in Austin, Texas.

4.274 A large cistern at the entry to the Lady Bird Johnson Wildflower Center in Austin, Texas is constructed with native rock and is part of the extensive rainwater harvesting system at the Center.

4.275 Cisterns assembled from recycled pickle barrels from a nearby factory are part of the highly-visible rainwater catchment system at the Chesapeake Bay Foundation in Annapolis, Maryland.

ENVELOPE

LIGHTING

HEATING

COOLING

ENERGY PRODUCTION

WATER & WASTE

Further Information

Iowa State University. 1979. *Private Water Systems Handbook*, 4th ed. Midwest Plan Service, Ames, IA. www.mwpshq.org/

Montana State University Extension Service, Rainwater Harvesting Systems for Montana. www.montana.edu/wwwpb/pubs/mt9707.html

Stein, B. et al. 2006. *Mechanical and Electrical Equipment for Buildings*, 10th ed. John Wiley & Sons, Hoboken, NJ.

USEPA. 1991. *Manual of Individual and Non-Public Water Supply Systems* (570991004). U.S. Environmental Protection Agency, Washington, DC.

WaterAid International, Rainwater Harvesting. www.wateraid.org/international/what_we_do/how_we_work/sustainable_technologies/technology_notes/2055.asp

Young. E. 1989. "Rainwater Cisterns: Design, Construction and Water Treatment" (Circular 277). Pennsylvania State University, Agriculture Cooperative Extension, University Park, PA.

BEYOND SCHEMATIC DESIGN

The feasibility and rough sizing of a water catchment system will be established during schematic design. Further analysis during design development will optimize these early estimates. System equipment and components will be sized, selected, and detailed. Non-residential water catchment systems should be commissioned; design of any scale of system should include development of a User's Manual that outlines the designer's assumptions, expectations, and provides maintenance and operations information.

ENVELOPE

LIGHTING

HEATING

COOLING

ENERGY PRODUCTION

WATER & WASTE

PERVIOUS SURFACES are ground covers that allow rainwater to infiltrate and flow through to subsurface layers. Pavings of pervious surface materials are of particular interest to green building design as a means of preventing urban stormwater runoff and reducing the flow of pollutants off site. Pervious surfaces can be used at a variety of scales (from patios to parking lots) and vary in composition and construction. The effectiveness of this strategy depends upon the type of pervious surface selected and its intended use (i.e. parking, roadway, walkway, etc.). Pervious surfaces are amenable to use in most climates.

4.276 Pervious surfaces can play a significant role in the development of green sites.

4.277 Cross section through a typical porous pavement installation. The components include: a porous asphalt top course, a filter course of fine aggregate; a reservoir course of rough stone; and the subsurface ground layer. KATE BECKLEY

Pervious surface options include plastic grid systems, porous asphalt pavements, porous block pavement systems, porous Portland cement concrete, and a range of granular materials (such as gravel or bark mulch)—as well as many types of vegetation. Vehicle or pedestrian circulation requirements and loads will dictate surface appropriateness.

Plastic grid systems are designed to support pedestrian or light traffic loads. These prefabricated pavement elements consist of a plastic lattice structure that can be filled with rock aggregate, soil and grass, or ground cover. The lattice structure retains the fill material while the fill material reinforces the rigidity of the lattice structure.

Porous (or open-graded) **asphalt pavement** contains no small aggregate particles, which results in a pavement structure with substantial voids. This allows water to enter—and subsequently drain through—the pavement layer. Porous asphalt pavement is appropriate for roads and parking lots.

INTENT
Reduce stormwater runoff

EFFECT
Increases on-site percolation of stormwater, decreases off-site runoff

OPTIONS
Several manufactured products and generic materials are available

COORDINATION ISSUES
Site coordination, landscaping design and soil grading, accessibility

RELATED STRATEGIES
Water Catchment Systems, Water Reuse/Recycling, Bioswales, Retention Ponds

LEED LINKS
Sustainable Sites, Water Efficiency, Materials & Resources

PREREQUISITES
Rainfall data for site, information regarding surface/subsurface drainage conditions, local code requirements

Porous block pavement systems are constructed from interlocking brick, stone, or concrete elements; a modular assembly that provides channels through which water can flow to the underlying substrate. Block pavements come in a range of patterns and colors. They are usually installed over a conventional aggregate base with sand bedding. Porous block systems can be used for high load conditions (as well as low-traffic applications such as sidewalks and driveways).

Porous Portland cement concrete differs from non-porous concrete in that fine particles such as sand and small aggregates are left out of the mix. This leaves voids between the large aggregate components and allows water to drain through the concrete. Porous concrete is appropriate for many paving applications, including parking lots and streets.

Key Architectural Issues

Pervious surfaces can be used for a variety of vehicular and foot traffic loadings. It is important, however, to ensure a match of material to anticipated loading. Suitability for foot traffic (providing an even walking surface) may hinge more upon quality installation and stability over time than on the paving material selected.

The consideration of pervious surfaces opens the door to a comprehensive look at site landscaping. Some pervious surface materials will require the selection of an infill material (which might be organic); all pervious materials will be bounded by building or landscape surfaces with inherent opportunities for integration of hard and softscapes.

Paved surface temperatures can be mitigated by using pervious paving. The voids in the material trap moisture which, due to the high specific heat of water, reduces the temperature increase that accompanies the absorption of solar radiation. The soil captured by plastic grid pavers also tends to reduce surface temperatures (relative to other forms of paving). Providing a more reflective surface will also help to reduce paving temperatures and improve the microclimate (at least during the summer). Evapotranspiration from vegetation housed in plastic grid pavers can also act to reduce surface temperatures.

Implementation Considerations

The two most critical implementation considerations related to pervious paving are suitability to task and appearance. In general, the appearance of most pervious paving systems is identical to (or an improvement upon) comparable impervious paving materials. Pervious paving systems with infill vegetation, however, can look "ragged" and this should be addressed if believed to be important. Manufacturers/suppliers can provide detailed information regarding load capabilities. Design judgment should be exercised regarding the suitability of foot traffic on pervious paving products.

4.278 Pervious paving of 100% recycled plastic provides adequate strength for parking and driveways while protecting plant roots. INVISIBLE STRUCTURES, INC.

4.279 Porous geotextile fabric sits atop an engineered porous base course, is anchored with galvanized anchors and filled with gravel, and supports substantial loads. INVISIBLE STRUCTURES, INC.

4.280 This product is a three-dimensional reinforcement and stabilization matrix for steep vegetated slopes, channel banks, and vegetated swales. The system can withstand intense rainfall or water flow. INVISIBLE STRUCTURES, INC.

ENVELOPE

LIGHTING

HEATING

COOLING

ENERGY PRODUCTION

WATER & WASTE

Design Procedure

The following procedure has been adapted from USEPA Document EPA 832-F-99-023 (Storm Water Technology Fact Sheet: Porous Pavement).

1. **Evaluate site conditions**

   a) Verify soil permeability and porosity, depth of the water table at its highest point (during the wet season), and depth to bedrock. This is usually done by on-site testing, and is often part of the site selection/analysis process.

   b) Check the slopes on the site. Most pervious surfaces are not recommended for slopes greater than 5%.

   c) Verify soil drainage rates by on-site testing. Pervious paving requires a minimum infiltration rate of 0.5 in. [13 mm] per hour for at least 3 ft [0.9 m] below the bottom of the installed pervious layers.

   d) Verify soil depth. A minimum depth of 4 ft [1.2 m] to bedrock and/or the highest water table is recommended.

   e) Verify site conditions. A minimum setback from water supply wells of 100 ft [30 m] is recommended—to be confirmed with local code authorities. A minimum setback from building foundations of 10 ft [3 m] down gradient and 100 ft [30 m] up gradient is suggested (unless provision is made for appropriate foundation drainage).

   f) Consider the potential for clogging of pavement voids. Pervious asphalt and concrete are not recommended for use in areas where significant amounts of windblown (or vehicle-borne) sediment is expected.

2. **Evaluate traffic conditions**

   a) Evaluate vehicle loadings. Pervious pavements are most successfully used for low-volume automobile parking areas and lightly used access roads. High traffic areas and significant truck traffic require detailed analysis of loads versus material capabilities.

   b) Consider seasonal conditions. Avoid use in areas requiring snow plow operations; avoid the use of sand, salt, and deicing chemicals. Consider the ramifications of wind- or water-deposited sand in coastal areas.

3. **Design-storm storage volume**

   a) Most jurisdictions do not require pervious surfaces to provide for mitigation of a design-storm storage volume unless they entirely replace conventional storm runoff solutions. Consult local code authorities for specifics.

SAMPLE PROBLEM

The adjacent design procedure is conceptual and involves no calculations that would be further illustrated by a sample problem.

ENVELOPE

LIGHTING

HEATING

COOLING

ENERGY PRODUCTION

WATER & WASTE

ENVELOPE

LIGHTING

HEATING

COOLING

ENERGY PRODUCTION

WATER & WASTE

Examples

4.281 Garden pavers and grass (left) provide a permeable, green courtyard at the Chinese wing of the Honolulu Academy of Arts in Honolulu, Hawaii. A hierarchy of stone sizes and landscaping (right) provides a pervious entry path to a private house in Kanazawa, Japan.

4.282 A porous paving system at an apartment complex in Virginia. INVISIBLE STRUCTURES, INC.

4.283 Installation of a pervious slope and erosion control system along a park path (left) and a porous grass pavement system (right) at the Sabre Holdings Headquarters in Southlake, Texas. INVISIBLE STRUCTURES, INC.

4.284 Pavers and tile artwork create a pervious patio near the dining hall of the IslandWood Campus on Bainbridge Island, Washington.

ENVELOPE

LIGHTING

HEATING

COOLING

ENERGY PRODUCTION

WATER & WASTE

Further Information

Partnership for Advancing Technology in Housing, Toolbase, Permeable Pavement. www.toolbase.org/techinv/techDetails.aspx?technologyID=98

Sustainable Sources. 2004. Pervious Paving Materials. www.greenbuilder.com/sourcebook/PerviousMaterials.html

USEPA. 1980. Porous Pavement Phase I Design and Operational Criteria (EPA 600-2-80-135). United States Environmental Protection Agency, Urban Watershed Management Research, Washington, DC.

USEPA. 1999. Storm Water Technology Fact Sheet: Porous Pavement (EPA 832-F-99-023). United States Environmental Protection Agency, Office of Water, Washington, DC.

BEYOND SCHEMATIC DESIGN

The schematic design aspects of pervious surfaces are primarily related to proof of concept. Selection, design, detailing, and specification of a particular paving approach will occur during design development. This will include verification of traffic loading capabilities—as necessary and appropriate.

BIOSWALES are densely vegetated open channels designed to attenuate and treat stormwater runoff. These drainage ways have gentle slopes to allow runoff to be filtered by vegetation planted on the bottom and sides of the swale. A bioswale is not designed to hold water for an extended period of time. Swales are shallow and standing water exposed to solar radiation heats up; such warming is detrimental to some ecosystems.

Stormwater runoff has historically been dealt with through the use of drainage ditches that quickly routed stormwater to storm sewers. The stormwater problem was simply passed along to someone downstream. More ecologically-minded (and site-focused) stormwater management systems include bioswales and/or retention/detention ponds to cleanse stormwater before returning it to the local ecosystem.

4.285 Bioswale used in conjunction with expressive roof downspouts at the Water Pollution Control Laboratory in Portland, Oregon.

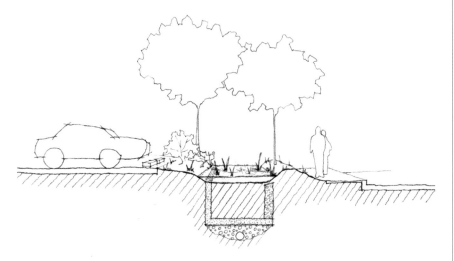

4.286 Section showing the general configuration of a bioswale at a parking lot. JONATHAN MEENDERING

After stormwater traverses a bioswale, the filtered runoff can be managed in one of the following ways:

- infiltration into the soil;
- flow into a bioretention area or retention/detention pond;
- discharged to a storm sewer system;
- directed to receiving waters.

There are several different kinds of swales—with varying arrangements and filtration mechanisms. Several common configurations are discussed below.

Grass channels are similar to conventional drainage ditches but with wide, flattened sides, providing greater surface area to slow down runoff. Such a channel provides preliminary treatment of stormwater as it flows to another stormwater management component such as a bioretention area.

INTENT
Stormwater management

EFFECT
Cleanses (via phytoremediation) and directs stormwater

OPTIONS
Wet, dry, and/or grassed swale

COORDINATION ISSUES
Site grading, placement of swales relative to drainage surfaces, integration of additional bioremediation features

RELATED STRATEGIES
Retention Ponds, Water Catchment Systems, Water Reuse/Recycling

LEED LINKS
Sustainable Sites, Water Efficiency

PREREQUISITES
Site plan, information on soil conditions, rainfall patterns, and storm sewer locations

ENVELOPE

LIGHTING

HEATING

COOLING

ENERGY PRODUCTION

WATER & WASTE

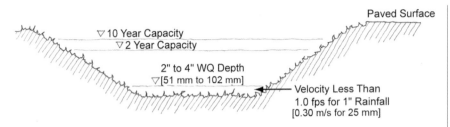

4.287 Section through grass channel bioswale, which slows stormwater runoff and passes it through grass. JONATHAN MEENDERING; ADAPTED FROM *DESIGN OF STORMWATER FILTERING SYSTEMS,* CENTER FOR WATERSHED PROTECTION

Dry swales are similar in concept to a detention pond in that they have water-holding capacity and permit water to flow through the bottom of the swale—but are designed to leave the grassy top relatively dry. Dry swales include a large layer of soil fill inside a filter-fabric-lined channel with a perforated pipe system at the bottom of the swale—similar to a foundation perimeter drain. The underdrain perforated pipe usually directs treated stormwater to a storm drain system. Dry swales are a good strategy in residential areas (from a safety/usage perspective) and can be easily located along a roadway or at the edge of a property.

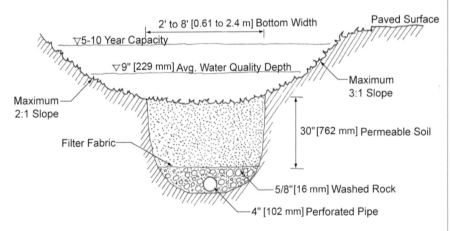

4.288 Section through a parabolic-shaped dry swale showing the various layers and their arrangement. JONATHAN MEENDERING; ADAPTED FROM *DESIGN OF STORMWATER FILTERING SYSTEMS,* CENTER FOR WATERSHED PROTECTION

Wet swales are essentially long, linear wetlands, designed to temporarily store water in a shallow pool. Because it does not have a filtering bed of soil, a wet swale treats stormwater (similar to wetlands) by the slow settling of particles, infiltration of water, and bioremediation of pollutants. Vegetation can be purpose-planted or the swale can be allowed to naturally populate with emergent wetland plant species.

ENVELOPE

LIGHTING

HEATING

COOLING

ENERGY PRODUCTION

WATER & WASTE

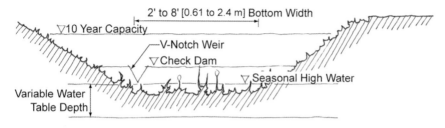

4.289 Section through a trapezoidal wet swale. Generally the bottom width is between 2 and 8 ft [0.6 and 2.4 m]. JONATHAN MEENDERING; ADAPTED FROM *DESIGN OF STORMWATER FILTERING SYSTEMS*, CENTER FOR WATERSHED PROTECTION

Key Architectural Issues

The physical integration of swales relative to the locations of buildings, parking lots, and other water-shedding surfaces is a key consideration. The visual integration of swales into a site (including landscaping) is another concern.

Implementation Considerations

National and local stormwater management requirements should be verified. There are some restrictions on the use of grassed bioswales. In some locations, soil conditions such as underlying bedrock or high water table would prevent the cost-effective or technically-effective use of this strategy. As a spatially extensive strategy, the availability of adequate site area and early integration into site planning is critical to the implementation of effective bioswale remediation strategies. The suitability and extent of bioswales for a given site will depend upon land use, size of the drainage areas, soil type, and slope. Many local jurisdictions have developed guidelines for the design of dry and wet swales; such guidelines should be consulted when available.

Design Procedure

The design process presented herein (extracted from *Design of Stormwater Filtering Systems*) is simplified for the schematic design process. While other stormwater treatment practices are sized on the basis of volume of runoff water, bioswales are designed based upon flow rate and volume of water for surface storage. Dry swales are generally used in moderate to large lot residential settings. Wet swales are mainly used in high volume situations, such as to control runoff from highways, parking lots, rooftops, and other impervious surfaces. The dry and wet swale design procedure follows.

1. Determine water quality treatment volume (WQV) for the site.
    *   Establish the runoff coefficient (R_v). For schematic design this is equal to the percentage of the site that is impervious (essentially the percentage of the site that is hard surfaced). This estimate can be finessed to include semi-pervious materials by using weighted average areas.

ENVELOPE

LIGHTING

HEATING

COOLING

ENERGY PRODUCTION

WATER & WASTE

- Use the following equation to estimate the required water "storage" volume (volume of swale):

$$WQV = (P) (R_v)$$

where,

P = design 24-hr rainfall (this value should be selected to allow the on-site detention of most common precipitation events; 1 in. [25 mm] is recommended for the mid-Atlantic United States, while 2 in. [50 mm] may be more appropriate for areas with more intense downpours)

R_v = the site runoff coefficient

- Convert WQV to swale volume as follows:
  swale volume in ft^3: (WQV) (site area in acres) (3629)
  swale volume in m^3: (WQV) (site area in hectares) (10)

2. Select the preferred shape of swale. Swales are generally trapezoidal or parabolic. In a trapezoidal section, 2–6 in. [50–150 mm] of soil/sand mix will be installed over approximately 5 in. [125 mm] of soil/gravel mix, which is placed over a perforated underdrain system. A parabolic section (see Figure 4.288) will have approximately 30 in. [760 mm] of permeable soil over 5 in. [125 mm] of gravel that surrounds a perforated underdrain pipe.

3. Establish bioswale dimensions. The dimensions should accommodate the swale volume calculated in Step 1.
   - Bottom width: typically 2–8 ft [0.6–2.4 m]
   - Side slopes: 2:1 maximum, with 3:1 or flatter preferred; the longitudinal slope is usually 1–2%
   - Length: as required to obtain necessary swale volume
   - Depth: A rough guideline is to use an average 12 in. [300 mm] depth for effective water treatment and another 6 in. [150 mm] to provide adequate capacity for a 10-year storm event
   - Underlying soil bed: below a dry swale, the soil bed should consist of moderately permeable soil, 30 in. [760 mm] deep, with a gravel/pipe underdrain system. Below a wet swale the soil bed may be wet for a long period of time and should consist of non-compacted (undisturbed) soils

4. Verify slope and groundwater clearance. Stormwater moving too fast can cause erosion and may not be properly filtered by the vegetation in the swale. This is controlled by limiting the slope of the swale in the direction of flow. The bottom of a bioswale should be at least 2 ft [0.6 m] above the water table to prevent groundwater contamination via short-circuiting.

5. Select vegetation. The plant species in the swale should withstand flooding during runoff events and withstand drying between runoff events. Recommended plant species for bioretention are region-specific.

For a 1 in. [25 mm] rainfall,
WQV = (P) (R$_v$)
= (1) (0.0039)
= 0.0039
[(25) (0.0039) = 0.0967]

Swale volume in ft^3
= (0.0039) (90.45) (3629)
= 1280 ft^3

Swale volume in m^3
= (0.0967) (36.18) (10)
= 35 m^3

2. A trapezoidal swale is selected.

3. A swale with a 6 ft [1.8 m] bottom width and a 9 in. [230 mm] depth is proposed. The area of this swale is: (6 ft) (0.75 ft) = 4.5 ft^2 [0.4 m^2]

Swale volume at 300 ft [91 m] length = (300 ft) (4.5 ft^2) = 1350 ft^3 [(91 m) (0.4 m^2) = 36 m^3]

Adequate swale volume to handle the projected runoff is available (1350 > 1280 [36 > 35]).

4. Swale slope is checked and found acceptable. The water table (during the wet season) is 4 ft [1.2 m] below the bottom of the swale.

5. Native grasses and herbaceous plant species are selected that are in keeping with the region.

Examples

4.290 A swale planted with native California grasses and shrubs, next to a pervious surface parking lot at the Hewlett Foundation in Menlo Park, California.

4.291 A porous paved parking lot is surrounded by vegetated bioswales at the Jean Vollum Natural Capital Center (Ecotrust Building) in Portland, Oregon.

ENVELOPE

LIGHTING

HEATING

COOLING

ENERGY PRODUCTION

WATER & WASTE

4.292 In Portland, Oregon, vegetated bioswales at the Jean Vollum Natural Capital Center (left) and the Water Pollution Control Laboratory (right) take rainwater runoff from the adjacent building and parking lot.

Further Information

California Stormwater Quality Association. 2003. "Vegetated Swale," in California Stormwater BMP Handbook. Available at: www.cabmphandbooks.org/Development.asp

Center for Watershed Protection. 1996. *Design of Stormwater Filtering Systems*. Ellicott City, MD.

USEPA. 2004. "Stormwater Best Management Practice Design Guide, Vol. 2, Vegetative Biofilters." U.S. Environmental Protection Agency, Washington, DC. Available at: www.epa.gov/ORD/NRMRL/pubs/600r04121/600r04121asect6.pdf

BEYOND SCHEMATIC DESIGN

Prior to construction, the area where swales will be located should be protected from car and truck traffic to prevent compaction of the soil (which will reduce infiltration). During construction, equipment and tools should be cleaned off site to prevent polluting materials from contaminating the swales.

After construction is complete, optimum performance of a bioswale requires scheduled maintenance. Maintenance includes regular inspection twice a year, seasonal mowing and lawn care, removal of debris and litter, removal of sediment, grass reseeding, mulching, and the replacement or tilling of a new layer of topsoil into the existing surface. This information needs to be conveyed to the owner via a User's Manual.

ENVELOPE

LIGHTING

HEATING

COOLING

ENERGY PRODUCTION

WATER & WASTE

ENVELOPE

LIGHTING

HEATING

COOLING

ENERGY PRODUCTION

WATER & WASTE

RETENTION PONDS

RETENTION PONDS (also called detention ponds) are designed to control stormwater runoff on a site—and, in some cases, to remove pollutants from the retained water. Stormwater control strategies include ditches, swales, ponds, tanks, and vaults. These generally function by capturing, storing, treating, and slowly releasing stormwater downstream or allowing infiltration into the ground. A retention (or infiltration) pond collects water as a final storage destination, where water is held until it either evaporates or infiltrates the soil. Detention ponds are designed to temporarily store accumulated water before it slowly drains off downstream. Since the primary purpose of both pond types is the same, the discussion here will focus on retention ponds.

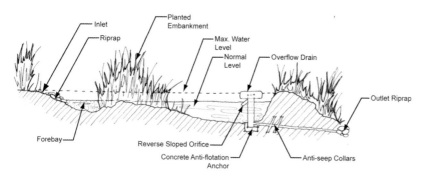

4.294 Section diagram of a retention pond. JONATHAN MEENDERING

Retention ponds are related to bioswales (see the Bioswale strategy). Bioswales, however, primarily direct the flow of moving water. Ponds are a destination for a quantity of water, which is held until it evaporates or infiltrates the soil. If water treatment is required, bioremediation methods can be included (thus the term bioretention pond). These methods involve the use of soil bacteria, fungi, and plants to remove pollutants. These organisms can rapidly break down the organic pollutants (e.g. oil) in stormwater. Bioretention areas are most beneficially employed near large impervious surfaces, such as adjacent to parking lots, in street medians, and in the zones between buildings.

Key Architectural Issues

Principal areas of architectural concern with retention ponds are scale, site placement, and landscaping. Retention ponds can take up a fair amount of land, depending upon the amount of stormwater to be handled. The relationship between retention pond and buildings or other site structures (such as parking lots, driveways, outdoor areas) can be creatively addressed during the design process so that the pond functions well and integrates into a given site.

Implementation Considerations

Retention ponds are best suited to sites that will be graded or excavated, so the pond can be incorporated into the site plan without otherwise unnecessary environmental impact. They are generally ineffective

4.293 Stormwater retention pond at the Water Pollution Control Laboratory in Portland, Oregon. TROY NOLAN PETERS

INTENT
Bioremediation, water recycling, reduced off-site stormwater flow

EFFECT
Reduces site runoff, cleanses and returns water to ecosystem

OPTIONS
Retention/detention or bioretention

COORDINATION ISSUES
Pond footprint relative to site, local code requirements, site grading

RELATED STRATEGIES
Bioswales, Pervious Surfaces, Water Catchment Systems, Water Reuse/Recycling

LEED LINKS
Sustainable Sites

PREREQUISITES
Information on soil conditions, average monthly rainfall on site, surface characteristics of the developed site

in areas where the water table is within 6 ft [1.8 m] of the ground surface, where the soil is unstable, or where the slope of the adjacent areas is greater than 20% (which could lead to erosion). Sites with unstable soil conditions or poor permeability (more than 25% clay content) would not be appropriate for bioretention. The U.S. Environmental Protection Agency (USEPA) recommends an infiltration rate of 0.5 in. [12 mm] per hour and soil pH between 5.5 and 6.5. Ideally, the soil should have a 1.5% to 3% organic content and a maximum 500-ppm concentration of soluble salts for good bioremediation of pollutants.

For high performance, the soil surface (bottom of the retention pond) and pollutants must be in contact for adequate periods of time. The infiltration rate of water through the soil must not exceed the rate specified above. Metals, phosphorus, and some hydrocarbons can be removed via adsorption. Further filtration occurs as runoff passes through the sand bed and vegetation surrounding the area. The filtering effectiveness of a retention area can decrease over time, unless maintained by removing debris and repairing the active components.

Design Procedure

There are a number of design methods for stormwater runoff—ranging from simple, intuitively-designed systems of swales and ponds (without many calculations) to software programs that define and calculate drainage areas. The following procedure is adapted from the USEPA's "Factsheet on Bioretention." The size of the bioretention area is a function of the volume of rainfall and the drainage area of the site. The calculation of runoff is complex, so for preliminary sizing during schematic design the following procedure provides very rough guidelines.

1. Develop a preliminary site plan. This plan will show the relative areas of various surface types and the potential location(s) for a retention/detention pond.

2. Calculate the size of the drainage areas. Estimate the areas of pavement, grass, and other surfaces from which runoff will occur.

3. Determine the runoff coefficients "c" for the site elements. The rational method runoff coefficient is a unitless number that accounts for soil type and drainage basin slope. Coefficients for various exterior surfaces are shown in Table 4.23.

4. Calculate the bioretention area. Multiply the rational method runoff coefficient "c" by the drainage area for each surface type and sum the results. To estimate the required retention pond area, multiply the sum by 5% if a sand bed is used or by 7% without a sand bed. The USEPA recommends minimum dimensions of 15 ft [4.6 m] by 40 ft [12.2 m] to allow for a dense distribution of trees and shrubs. A rough guideline is to use a 25-ft [7.6 m] width, with a length at least twice the width. The recommended depth of the retention area is 6 in. [150 mm] to provide adequate water storage area, while avoiding a long-lasting pool of sitting water.

TABLE 4.22 Typical performance of bioretention areas. U.S. EPA OFFICE OF WASTE WATER MANAGEMENT

POLLUTANT	REMOVAL RATES
Phosphorus	70–83%
Metals (Cu, Zn, Pb)	93–98%
TKN*	68–80%
Suspended solids	90%
Organics	90%
Bacteria	90%

*Total Kjeldahl Nitrogen

SAMPLE PROBLEM

A new elementary school in Chicago, Illinois will include a small parking lot. The architects want to provide a bioretention pond adjacent to and on the downhill side of the parking lot.

1. A rough plan of the site shows an asphalt parking lot with interspersed grassy areas.

2. Drainage areas are estimated as: asphalt = 15,000 ft^2 [1394 m^2] and grass = 3000 ft^2 [279 m^2].

3. The "c" factors for these surfaces are assumed as asphalt: 0.9, and grass: 0.25.

4. Find the drainage area for each type of surface using the relationship (surface area)("c"). For asphalt this is (15,000 ft^2 [1394 m^2]) (0.9) = 13,500 ft^2 [1255 m^2]

   For grass this is (3000 ft^2 [279 m^2]) (0.25) = 750 ft^2 [70 m^2]

   Required retention pond area (with a sand bed): = (0.05) (13,500 ft^2 + 750 ft^2) = 712 ft^2 [66 m^2]

   Required retention pond area (without a sand bed): = (0.07)

TABLE 4.23 Rational method runoff coefficients. LMNO ENGINEERING, RESEARCH AND SOFTWARE, LTD

	RUNOFF COEFFICIENT, c
Asphalt pavement	0.7–0.95
Brick pavement	0.7–0.85
Concrete pavement	0.7–0.95
Cultivated land	0.08–0.41
Forest	0.05–0.25
Lawns	0.05–0.35
Meadow	0.1–0.5
Parks, cemeteries	0.1–0.25
Pasture	0.12–0.62
Roofs	0.75–0.95
Business areas	0.5–0.95
Industrial areas	0.5–0.9
Residential areas	0.3–0.75
Unimproved areas	0.1–0.3

5. Develop a rough layout of the retention pond system. On a project site plan, develop a schematic layout showing approximate location and size of the drainage and bioretention areas. This should be done with consideration to site parameters such as utilities, soil conditions, topography, existing vegetation, and drainage.

$(13{,}500 \text{ ft}^2 + 750 \text{ ft}^2) = 998 \text{ ft}^2$ [93 m²].

5. The required area of retention pond is included in a schematic layout of the site in a logical location that permits gravity drainage into the pond.

Examples

4.295 Native plants, shrubs, and grasses in the retention pond at the Water Pollution Control Laboratory in Portland, Oregon. TROY NOLAN PETERS

ENVELOPE

LIGHTING

HEATING

COOLING

ENERGY PRODUCTION

WATER & WASTE

4.296 Wetland retention pond adjacent to a pervious surface parking lot at the Chesapeake Bay Foundation in Annapolis, Maryland. The raised overflow component allows for the infiltration of water during most storm events before returning any site runoff directly to the Bay.

Further Information

Center for Watershed Protection. 1996. *Design of Stormwater Filtering Systems*. Ellicott City, MD.

LMNO Engineering, Research, and Software, Ltd. Rational Equation Calculator (an online tool to calculate drainage basin peak discharge rate). www.lmnoeng.com/Hydrology/rational.htm

USEPA. 1999. *Storm Water Technology Fact Sheet: Bioretention* (EPA 832-F-99-012). U.S. Environmental Protection Agency, Washington, DC.

BEYOND SCHEMATIC DESIGN

The estimated sizes of retention ponds or bioretention areas established during schematic design will be verified during design development as more complete information about the site design is available and more detailed methods of analysis become appropriate.

Design details will be finalized during design development—including site landscaping, water collection elements, and the pond itself. A User's Manual should be developed to assist the owner with proper care and maintenance of the pond/bioremediation area.

CHAPTER 5

The case studies presented in this chapter include a range of buildings selected to provide a diversity of geographic locations, climates, building types, and strategies. The design teams for these projects have made strong statements about green design intentions and have provided fertile ground for designers to learn from their projects. Each case study is organized as follows:

- a general description of the project;

- a sidebar "scorecard" with building, climate, client, and design team information;

- a statement of design intent and related design criteria;

- design validation methods used (modeling, simulation, hand calculations, etc.);

- a description of the green strategies used;

- post-occupancy validation results (if available).

Each case study describes an outstanding project that integrated green strategies via an informed design process—and that offers informative lessons for future projects.

NOTES

Background and Context

A suburban site in the new Blythe Valley Research Park, on the Coventry side of Birmingham was chosen for the Arup Campus Solihull. It is easily accessible via motorway and is close to the Birmingham international airport, but has restricted transit access. Nevertheless, only 200 parking spaces were allocated to this building designed for 350 employees. In Phase 2, an expansion planned to add 250 more people, 135 additional parking spaces will be provided.

The intent of this Midlands headquarters building, conceived to consolidate offices in Birmingham and Coventry, was to set an example of sustainability. The meta-goals for the building were to minimize carbon emissions and to maximize worker productivity. Design strategies focused on providing natural ventilation and daylighting. Arup opted to design the £7 million building for the park owner, BVP Developments, and to lease it for 20 years. The jointly developed project brief (program) called for a well-equipped, socially cohesive, and productive environment that would also be cost-effective, flexible, and commercially viable.

5.2 The Arup Campus, viewed from the south, fits the site contours. ARUP ASSOCIATES

Arup Associates, an integrated architectural practice within the Arup corporate community, was chosen to design the facility. Formally established as a practice in 1963, Arup Associates has earned a reputation for innovation and concern for the social impact of design. Ove Arup described it at the time of its founding as "a laboratory inside our organization in which we hope to develop new ideas."

Arup Associates' multidisciplinary design approach addressed green issues in the building, including natural ventilation of deep-plan offices, low-energy design to avoid the use of CFCs and HCFCs while reducing CO_2 emissions, use of life-cycle and environmental analyses for design decision making, use of recycled and non-processed materials, implementation of an environmental management system, and a green travel plan.

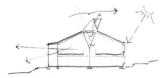

5.1 Conceptual sketch of upper pavilion with solar control and ventilation through roof monitor.
ARUP ASSOCIATES

LOCATION
Blythe Valley Park, Solihull, UK
Latitude 52 °N
Longitude 2 °W

HEATING DEGREE DAYS
6248 base 65 °F
[3471 base 18 °C]

COOLING DEGREE DAYS
1200 base 50 °F
[667 base 10 °C]

SOLAR RADIATION
Jan 238 Btu/ft²/day
[0.75 kWh/m²/day]
Jul 1518 Btu/ft²/day
[4.79 kWh/m²/day]

ANNUAL PRECIPITATION
26 in. [660 mm]

BUILDING TYPE
Office

AREA
~50,000 ft² [~5000 m²]
2 stories

CLIENT
Arup

DESIGN TEAM
Arup Associates

COMPLETION
2001

5.3 Site section shows how the floors are spaced at half level intervals and how the edge voids of the upper floors face each other. ARUP ASSOCIATES

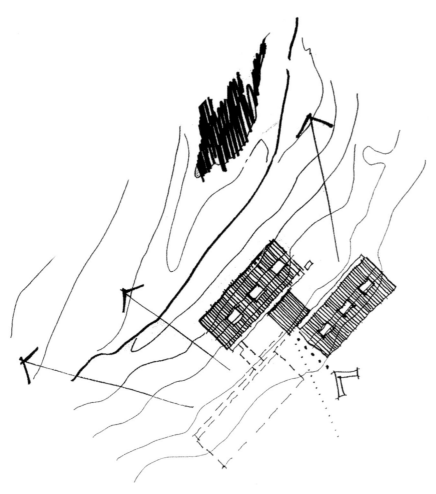

5.4 Conceptual site plan sketch showing contours of the northwest-facing slope and future location of a third pavilion. ARUP ASSOCIATES

Design Intent and Validation

Arup Associates' goals for the campus included:

*   Provide natural ventilation and adequate daylighting, with direct occupant control of the internal environmental conditions.

*   Help shape a coherent social organization to reflect Arup's teamwork ethic.

*   Explore the vernacular in relation to the landscape.

*   Express the notion of sustainability by optimizing environmental, economic, and social dimensions.

The design concept involved three (two constructed, one planned) well-lit and ventilated office pavilions sitting lightly on the land, with their long axes running southwest to northeast following the site contours. In siting the buildings, cut and fill quantities were equalized, resulting in no import or export of soil. The two-story, 79 ft [24 m] deep pavilions are joined by an entry/reception module that mediates the slope of the site by connecting the lower floor of the southern pavilion with the upper floor of the northern pavilion. The floors are eroded by voids cut into the center of the slabs for connecting staircases and along one edge of each pavilion. These voids allow for strong visual contact among the four floors of the two buildings and the connecting reception. The daylight and natural ventilation strategies are visually expressed by six prominent roof pods that combine light scoops and ventilating chimneys.

During design, extensive computational fluid dynamics (CFD) testing and physical modeling were performed to perfect the ventilation and lighting schemes. The roof pods serve as stack and cross ventilators as well as the smoke vents in case of fire, functions refined through CFD testing. A daylighting model was tested under the artificial sky at the Bartlett School of Architecture in London. "This showed that we are attaining three or four times the recommended levels of light in offices," said Daniel Wong, the lead designer. Using LBL's *Radiance* software, Arup Associates was able to demonstrate that this brightness would leave computer users unaffected by glare.

Strategies

Several well-integrated strategies were used to attain the designers' intent and goals. Especially notable are the roof pods and perforated floor plates that integrate the daylighting and natural ventilation schemes.

Natural ventilation. The roof-mounted light scoop/chimneys, designed to enhance stack effect, are coupled with motorized trickle vents for each facade zone. The Building Management System (BMS) controls the trickle vents and the modulating vents located in the light scoop chimneys to provide natural ventilation. Occupants have control of the operable windows in the office spaces.

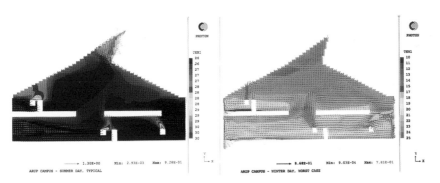

5.5 Computational fluid dynamics (CFD) modeling shows ventilation performance characteristics in summer (left) and winter (right). ARUP ASSOCIATES

5.6 Three-image sequence shows exterior shades on the southeast facade of the lower pavilion controlled by the BMS, but with user override. TISHA EGASHIRA

Thermal mass. Exposed precast floor and ceiling panels provide sufficient thermal mass for a low-energy ventilation strategy.

Exterior shading. The building's orientation, 45° off a true east-west axis, makes effective shading to control solar heat gains and glare both difficult and necessary. Consequently, the few windows on the southwest and northeast facades are protected by fixed, external horizontal louvers. The windows on the longer southeast facade of the upper pavilion are shaded by casement-hinged exterior shutters with horizontal louvers. These shutters can be adjusted manually by the occupants. On the northeast facades of both pavilions external horizontal louvers are used. All of these external devices are complemented by interior miniblinds. The southeast facade of the lower pavilion, which abuts the edge void of the second floor, has operable, roll-down horizontal louvers that are controlled by the BMS, but with occupant override. Occupant control over shading is important in achieving satisfaction. The facade also becomes punctuated by the users' shading choices, providing a level of detail and interest not present in monolithic glass buildings operated solely by a BMS.

Daylighting. The wide floor plates are illuminated by sidelighting, primarily from the southeast and northwest facades, and by toplighting from the roof pods. The northwest-facing roof lights have fixed louvers in the glazed cavity to reduce glare and solar gain from the setting sun in summer. The second floor slab has voids along one edge and in the center to help distribute the toplight to the lower floors. These voids also make the stack and cross ventilation schemes effective. Higher than usual ceilings (10.2 ft [3.1 m]) also make the daylighting strategy more effective. In summer electric lighting is rarely needed.

5.7 External wood shutters with horizontal louvers protect operable windows on the southeastern facade of the upper pavilion. TISHA EGASHIRA

5.8 Roof pods provide daylight to both upper and lower floors.
TISHA EGASHIRA

5.9 Arup lighting designer Haico Shepers poses with a daylighting model of an Arup Solihull building in the artificial sky at the Bartlett School of Architecture. ARUP ASSOCIATES

5.10 Daylight distribution to lower floors is facilitated by voids in the center and at one edge of the upper floor plate. TISHA EGASHIRA

5.11 The lower floor receives daylight from the side and from above. Specially designed lighting fixtures provide direct and indirect illumination and sound absorption. TISHA EGASHIRA

Electric lighting. Specially constructed luminaires provide even direct-indirect illumination and needed acoustic softness to absorb sound (because the exposed concrete ceilings do not).

Stormwater management. Stormwater from roofs and parking areas is directed to an on-site retention pond from which it is evaporated into the air or percolated into the earth.

5.12 A retention pond below the buildings holds stormwater for ultimate evaporation or percolation. TISHA EGASHIRA

5.13 Water feature next to entry path to the reception cube along the southwest facade of the upper pavilion. TISHA EGASHIRA

Green transportation. The project site between Birmingham and Coventry was chosen to minimize overall car journeys by occupants of the merged office. Only 200 parking spaces were provided in Phase 1 for the 350+ employees, thus encouraging car-pooling, bicycle riding, and transit use. The original bicycle parking accommodation proved too small and has been doubled. Bicycle parking will again be doubled in Phase 2.

Recycling. The building structure has been designed for deconstruction and reuse of its components. Structural steel work features site-bolted connections. The precast hollow-core floor and ceiling panels are installed without an in-situ structural concrete topping. These two systems facilitate deconstruction. The building is potentially 100% recyclable at the end of its lifetime. Recycled and non-processed materials were also used in the building.

How Is It Working?

Arup Campus occupants were surveyed in 2003 under auspices of the Building Use Survey (BUS). The Solihull Campus achieved an overall building rating score of 95 out of 100 and is classed as a very good building.

Barry Austin of Arup R&D reports that the Solihull Campus has performed well compared to the UK national benchmarks established from the BUS UK 2003 dataset. For the Summary and Comfort indices, the Solihull Campus was found to be in the top 20%. For the Satisfaction index, the Campus was found to be in the top 10% of the buildings in the dataset.

Austin points out that the Campus works particularly well in the following areas:

- The occupants' perceived health when in the buildings was high: within the top 5% of the BUS 2003 dataset.

- The occupants reported an increase in productivity due to the environmental conditions of the building, which places the Campus within the top 17% of the buildings in the BUS dataset. The occupants' perceived increase in their productivity since moving to the campus was also good. This second rating includes the influence of not only the environmental conditions but the location, building facilities, the work area, and the management and organizational structure.

- The conditions in the summer were highly rated and placed the Campus within the top 5% for the overall summer conditions. This is a very good score for an advanced naturally ventilated building.

There were a significant number of extremely positive comments, rare for UK buildings. Yet a number of problems were identified, including:

- The winter conditions overall were rated the same as the UK benchmark. Anecdotal evidence suggests that this anomaly could be partly due to problems with boiler lock outs, particularly on Monday mornings.

- Comments from the occupants indicated that there is significant variation in internal temperature conditions throughout the Campus. There appears to be a certain degree of acceptance of this fluctuation.

Further Information

Arup Associates: www.arupassociates.com/

Austin, B. et al. 2003. "Design for Workplace Performance—Fact or Fiction—Sustainability and Profit." www.cibse.org/pdfs/7caustin.pdf

Haddlesey, P. 2001. "Shedding the Light," *Light and Lighting* 23: 8–10.

Hawkes, D. and W. Forster. 2002. "Arup Campus," *Architecture, Engineering, and Environment,* Lawrence King Publishing Ltd, London.

Long, K. 2000. "Health Resort," *Building Design* 1453: 15–17.

Long, K. 2001. "A Job Well Done," *Surface:* 26–27, 29–30.

Powell, K. 2001. "Candid Campus," *Architects Journal* 215/7: 24–35.

Wong, D. J. and C. Perkins. 2002. "The Integrated Arup Campus," *New Steel Construction* 10/1: 21–23.

NOTES

Background and Context

The driving concept behind BedZED (Beddington Zero Energy Development) is to provide housing that makes it possible for a UK citizen to live within a 4.7 acre [1.9 ha] ecological footprint—currently the global equivalent of one "Earth's" worth of resources. The ideal BedZED lifestyle will accomplish this goal, while a resident living a conventional UK lifestyle will need 10.8 acres [4.36 ha] or 2.3 earths, and the average UK resident requires 15.3 [6.19 ha] equivalent to 3.3 earths.

BedZED's developer, Peabody Trust, appointed Bill Dunster Architects and Arup to the design team in early 1999. The trust is a long-established, forward-thinking social housing provider that manages about 20,000 homes in the UK. The design team was charged with answering the challenges inherent in providing ecologically-sound urban housing.

During Dunster's time with Michael Hopkins & Partners he worked with Arup on several significant environmentally-responsive buildings including Inland Revenue Centre Nottingham, Portcullis House, and Nottingham University Jubilee Campus. Dunster also served as a unit leader in environmental design at the Architectural Association school in London where he explored fully harnessing renewable natural resources, achieving closed-loop material use, gaining site resource autonomy, stimulating social involvement, and how all these issues could be addressed while responding to ever-increasing lifestyle expectations.

The other key player at BedZED was BioRegional Development, a charity dedicated to bringing sustainable business to the commercial market. They secured concept marketing funding from the World Wildlife Fund, located a site in southwest London, and introduced the Peabody Trust as funder/developer.

5.15 BedZED as viewed from the London Road. BRUCE HAGLUND

5.14 Southern facade of a residential unit at BedZED showing sunspaces and wind cowls. BRUCE HAGLUND

LOCATION
Wallington, Surrey, UK
Latitude 51 °N
Longitude 8 °W

HEATING DEGREE DAYS
5960 base 65 °F
[3311 base 18 °C]

COOLING DEGREE DAYS
1411 base 50 °F
[784 base 10 °C]

SOLAR RADIATION
Jan 231 Btu/ft²/day
[0.73 kWh/m²/day]
Jun 1531 Btu/ft²/day
[4.83 kWh/m²/day]

ANNUAL PRECIPITATION
23 in. [580 mm]

BUILDING TYPE
Multifamily residential/mixed use

CLIENT
Peabody Trust

DESIGN TEAM
Bill Dunster Architects/
ZEDfactory and Ove Arup &
Partners

COMPLETION
2002

Design Intent and Validation

Apart from producing no net carbon dioxide (CO_2) emissions from energy use, BedZED aims at performance targets across a range of environmental, social, and economic concerns:

- **environmental**—low-energy and renewable energy resources, including solar heating, natural ventilation, biomass combined heat and power (CHP), and photovoltaics (PVs); zero net carbon emissions; water saving; reclaimed materials; Green Travel Plan; biodiversity measures; and private gardens for most units;

- **social**—mixed tenure, two-thirds affordable or social housing; lower fuel costs; healthy living centre; community facilities; sports pitch and "village square;" crèche; and café;

- **economic**—locally sourced materials; workspace for local employment and enterprise; locally available renewable energy sources.

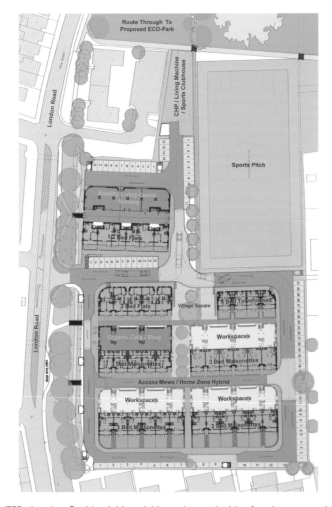

5.16 BedZED site plan. Residential (purple) is on the south side of each terrace, with workplaces (yellow and orange) to the north. BILL DUNSTER ARCHITECTS/ZEDFACTORY.COM

A brownfield site (a former sewage works) was chosen for BedZED to demonstrate that the UK's projected new housing needs can be entirely accommodated at high density on existing brownfield sites—while still allowing for passive solar and daylighting access. The site is 3.5 acres [1.7 ha] and supports 82 housing units and over 26,900 ft² [2500 m²] of space for offices, studios, shops, and community facilities. The housing is a mix of one- and two-bedroom flats, maisonettes, and townhouses for rent and for sale as subsidized and market-rate housing. The workspace provides jobs in a suburban area close to public transit and gives residents an opportunity to work on-site and avoid transit and car use. The housing and work spaces are organized in seven terrace blocks with elongated east-west axes that are spaced far enough apart to avoid shading neighboring buildings during prime solar gain hours in winter.

5.17 Each residential unit has a garden, most of which are roof gardens. TISHA EGASHIRA

5.18 Some rooftop gardens are accessible by bridges over the pedestrian ways. BRUCE HAGLUND

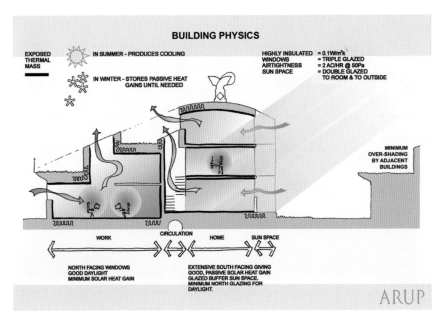

BUILDING PHYSICS

EXPOSED THERMAL MASS

IN SUMMER - PRODUCES COOLING

IN WINTER - STORES PASSIVE HEAT GAINS UNTIL NEEDED

HIGHLY INSULATED = 0.1W/m²k
WINDOWS = TRIPLE GLAZED
AIRTIGHTNESS = 2 AC/HR @ 50Pa
SUN SPACE = DOUBLE GLAZED TO ROOM & TO OUTSIDE

MINIMUM OVER-SHADING BY ADJACENT BUILDINGS

WORK   CIRCULATION   HOME   SUN SPACE

NORTH FACING WINDOWS
GOOD DAYLIGHT
MINIMUM SOLAR HEAT GAIN

EXTENSIVE SOUTH FACING GIVING
GOOD, PASSIVE SOLAR HEAT GAIN
GLAZED BUFFER SUN SPACE.
MINIMUM NORTH GLAZING FOR
DAYLIGHT.

ARUP

5.19 North–south section through a typical terrace illustrates thermal zoning, cross and stack ventilation, and building spacing. ARUP

Because the design intent was to omit conventional active climate control systems (achieved through the use of enhanced passive systems), advanced analytical techniques were used to assist with the design of the building enclosure, passive heating, and natural ventilation systems—to permit them to act as primary thermal systems. Dynamic thermal analysis tools, using real weather data sequences, were employed to establish the required enclosure performance (superinsulation) and massing (exposed thermal mass) for zero-heating homes. Testing for extreme conditions (both clear, cold days and long periods of cloudiness) and unoccupied holidays verified that solar energy and internal gains are usually sufficient for space heating and that only minor backup heating was needed. Because no individual heating or cooling systems were required, the resultant saved costs were used to finance a central biofueled combined heat and power system (CHP) that provides electricity, hot water, and backup heating.

Post-occupancy monitoring of BedZED is an ongoing project being conducted under the supervision of BioRegional and the Peabody Trust.

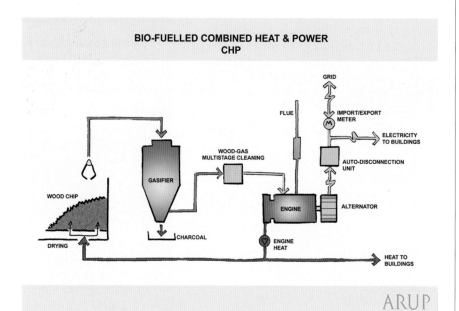

5.20 The combined heat and power (CHP) system burns biofuel to provide electricity, hot water, and backup heat to the complex. ARUP

Strategies

BedZED uses a plethora of strategies from site to component scale.

Solar access. Each housing terrace has an elongated east-west axis and is spaced so that the next terrace southward does not block winter sun access.

Thermal zoning. Within each terrace, the skin-load-dominated housing units are south-facing to allow passive solar heating and the internal-load-dominated live-work and commercial spaces are north-facing to ease passive cooling.

Passive solar heating. Each residential unit has a south-facing sunspace that can be opened to the residence or isolated from it. High values of thermal insulation and adequate thermal mass combine with the solar gain to make the sunspace the primary heating strategy. Double-pane glazing is used.

Exposed thermal mass. Both residential and work units have exposed thermal mass in plastered concrete block walls and precast concrete floors and ceilings—ample enough to dampen temperature swings and to provide summer cooling in conjunction with night ventilation.

5.21 North-facing operable skylights provide daylight and ventilation to the north zone workplaces. TISHA EGASHIRA

5.22 Sunspaces in the residential units provide solar gain and extended living space when the weather allows. GRAHAMGAUNT.COM

5.23 Construction features recycled steel framing and precast concrete floor planks. GRAHAMGAUNT.COM

5.24 Exterior wall section shows concrete thermal mass on the interior, 12 in. [300 mm] of rock fiber insulation, and a brick veneer rainscreen. GRAHAMGAUNT.COM

Natural ventilation. Besides operable windows that allow cross ventilation and operable skylights that allow stack ventilation, each unit is equipped with a wind cowl. These cowls are wind-powered air-to-air heat exchangers that allow for preheating of winter ventilation air and precooling of summer ventilation air. They're connected to each conditioned living space via ductwork. Residents have control over the supply registers. Exhaust air is extracted from bathrooms and kitchens.

High performance windows. Triple-glazed, argon-gas-filled, thermally broken windows and doors are used on east, west, and north facades throughout. The glazing is clear to maximize daylighting and employs a low-ε film to improve thermal performance. Even these windows lose ten times the heat of an equivalent wall area, so the balance between window size relative to heat loss and the need for daylight and view was carefully considered.

Daylighting. The residences are mainly daylit through the south facade. Centrally located stairwells and north-facing work spaces use operable skylights for daylighting.

Photovoltaics. A dispersed 107 kW array of PVs has been integrated into the roofs and south facades of the units and the CHP plant roof. Supported with EU/UK grants that paid for half of the capital costs, the payback time is calculated to be 6.5 years. Since the CHP provides sufficient electricity for the entire complex, the PVs are provided to operate 40 electric cars. Charging stations have been installed and residents can have free parking and charging if they own electric vehicles. Excess electricity is fed to the national grid.

5.25 BedZED roofscape features windcowls, sedum, and photovoltaics. BILL DUNSTER ARCHITECTS/ZEDFACTORY.COM

5.26 The CHP plant and its BIPV (building integrated photovoltaics) roof. TISHA EGASHIRA

5.27 The ecological wastewater treatment facility occupies a greenhouse. TISHA EGASHIRA

5.28 Forest Stewardship Council (FSC) certified wood was used for sheathing. GRAHAMGAUNT.COM

On-site energy generation. As well as the solar heating and photovoltaics, a 130 kW combined heat and power (CHP) generation plant that burns regionally produced carbon-neutral biofuel has been constructed. The CHP plant provides hot water, backup heating, and electric power to the development.

Superinsulation. Walls, roofs, and foundations are insulated with 12 in. [300 mm] of mineral fiber. The insulation is installed full cavity so there are no thermal bridges. It is placed exterior to the concrete block walls and precast concrete roof and floor planks to improve the effectiveness of the thermal mass. It is protected by the roofing and vertical rain screens of brick or board.

Green roofs. Sedum roofs are used where roof access is not expected. In accessible locations sod roofs are used to provide occupants with private garden spaces. Both types of green roof increase the site's ecological value and carbon absorbing ability as well as manage storm water. Runoff from these roofs is collected and stored underground for irrigation and toilet flushing.

Water conservation. Various measures have been incorporated, including fixture restrictors to prevent excessive flow, banning of power showers, EU grade-A water consuming appliances, and low-flow dual-flush toilets. The toilets use mostly site-harvested or recycled water. Mains water (city water) is rarely used for toilet flushing.

On-site blackwater treatment. An ecological system (similar to a Living Machine), operated by the local water authority, treats all the wastewater to a high enough standard to feed recycled "green" water to the rainwater storage tanks for use in irrigation and toilet flushing. Excess water from this system is fed to a leaching field beneath the on-site football pitch (soccer field) where it seeps into the water table.

Materials. Three criteria were used in selecting materials—local production (within a 35 mile [55 km] radius), recycled content, and ecologically benign character. Most of the heavier building materials were manufactured within the 35 mile [55 km] radius. Reused structural steel was used for the workspace framing; reclaimed timber for the interior partition walls; Forest Stewardship Council (FSC) certified wood was used extensively; and kitchen units used local plywood rather than particle board.

Recycling. Construction wastes were recycled. Segregation bins are provided in each kitchen and around the site to facilitate collection of recyclables by the local authority. The goal is to reduce landfill contributions by 60%.

Green travel plan. BedZED aims to reduce automobile use in several ways. As a mixed-use development, it provides residents the opportunity to work on site. Shops, a café, and community facilities are located on site to reduce off-site travel for these services. All dwellings have bicycle storage space and bike parking frames are available for workers and visitors. Workspace showers are available and the site has easy access to Sutton's existing cycle network. Buses, tramlines, and railways all stop within 0.7 miles [1.2 km] of BedZED. The ZEDcars carpool is designed to provide "mobility insurance" without the necessity of owning a car. The photovoltaic-powered electric vehicle stations provide encouragement to residents to purchase these alternative vehicles.

5.29 Free electric vehicle charging stations powered by photovoltaics. TISHA EGASHIRA

How Is It Working?

Bioregional and the Peabody Trust are monitoring the resource use and financial implications for BedZED. The first monitoring results (as shown in Tables 5.1–5.3 below) were reported at the end of October 2003. Ongoing results will be made available on the Bioregional website. Additionally, each unit is equipped with energy and water use meters mounted in glass-doored cabinets so residents can monitor their own usage. This feedback mechanism encourages conservation.

Resource use. First year results show that BedZED has exceeded expectations in several areas while rarely falling very short in others.

5.30 Water and electricity usage meters in each unit (seen through glass cover) provide continuous feedback to residents. TISHA EGASHIRA

TABLE 5.1 Comparisons with the national average for space heating and hot water, with new homes built to year 2000. BIOREGIONAL DEVELOPMENT GROUP

	MONITORED REDUCTION	TARGET REDUCTION
Space heating	88% (73%)	90%
Hot water	57% (44%)	33%
Electricity	25%	33%
Mains water	50%	33%
Fossil fuel car mileage	65%	50%

Building regulations in parentheses.

Costs and savings. Table 5.2 shows costs and savings for a BedZED terrace that combines six 3-bedroom maisonettes, six 1-bedroom flats, and six live/work units, as compared to a conventional development with a similar floor area. These figures include 100% renewable electricity supply, 100% wastewater recycling, and a full green transport plan.

TABLE 5.2 Costs and savings for various residential units. BIOREGIONAL DEVELOPMENT GROUP

Developer	• Added building costs	£521,208
	• Potential added revenue	£668,000
Occupants	• Reduced bills	£3847/yr
	• Added value	qualitative
The Planet	• CO_2 savings	147.1 tonnes/yr
	• Water savings	1025 m^3/yr

Predicted sales premiums for future ZED developments. The market for exceptionally green housing has been clearly demonstrated at BedZED. An assessment by FPD Savills has shown that buyers are willing to pay up to a 20% premium for innovative design and "green" features such as those at BedZED.

TABLE 5.3 Premium that buyers are willing to pay for green features. BIOREGIONAL DEVELOPMENT GROUP

UNIT TYPE	AVERAGE CURRENT SALES (AUGUST 2003)		DIFFERENCE %
	LOCAL, MARKET	BEDZED, ESTIMATED	
1 bed flat	£ 125,000	£ 150,000	20%
2 bed flat	£ 175,000	£ 190,000	8.57%
3 bed flats/terrace house	£ 225,000	£ 265,000	17.78%
4 bed semi	£ 300,000	£ 350,000	17.78%
Average	£ 206,250	£ 238,750	15.75%

Further Information

Bioregional Development Group. www.bioregional.co.uk/

BRE. 2001. Case Study: "BedZED–Beddington Zero Energy Development, Sutton" (General Information Report 89). Building Research Establishment, Ltd, Garston, Watford, UK.

Bill Dunster Architects/ZEDfactory. www.zedfactory.com/

Dunster, B. 2003. *From A to ZED: Realising Zero (fossil) Energy Developments*, Bill Dunster Architects/ZEDfactory Ltd, Wallington, Surrey, UK.

Hawkes, D. and W. Forster. 2002. "BedZED Sustainable Development," in *Architecture, Engineering, and Environment*, Lawrence King Publishing Ltd, London.

Ove Arup & Partners. www.arup.com/

Smith, P.F. 2001. *Architecture in a Climate of Change: A Guide to Sustainable Design*, Architectural Press, Oxford.

Twinn, C. 2003 "BedZED," *The Arup Journal*, 1/2003.

Background and Context

The Solar Decathlon competition is sponsored by the U.S. Department of Energy, the National Renewable Energy Laboratory, and several international, private-sector corporations. The competition challenges student and faculty teams from colleges and universities to design and construct a house that runs only on solar energy.

In order to participate in the competition, teams must design and build their solar houses within the constraints of the Solar Decathlon rules and regulations, and transport them from their home institution to the competition site on the National Mall in Washington, DC for a week of public tours and evaluated contests. Two to three years of research and planning go into the creation of each of the houses.

In the fall of 2002, 14 teams from across the United States and Puerto Rico came together to participate in the first Solar Decathlon competition. In October 2005, 18 teams from the United States, Puerto Rico, Canada, and Spain competed in the second competition, with Cornell University's house placing second to the University of Colorado.

5.31 Concept rendering of Cornell University's 2005 entry for the Solar Decathlon. CORNELL UNIVERSITY SOLAR DECATHLON

LOCATION
Ithaca, NY, USA
Latitude 42.27 °N
Longitude 76.27 °W

HEATING DEGREE DAYS
6785 base 65 °F
[3768 base 18 °C]

COOLING DEGREE DAYS
2488 base 50 °F
[1382 base 10 °C]

SOLAR RADIATION
Jan 550 Btu/ft^2/day
[1.74 kWh/m^2/day]
Jul 1840 Btu/ft^2/day
[5.80 kWh/m^2/day]
(Binghampton, NY data)

ANNUAL PRECIPITATION
39 in. [990 mm]

BUILDING TYPE
Residential demonstration project

AREA
640 ft^2 [60 m^2]

CLIENT
U.S. Department of Energy, National Renewable Energy Laboratory

DESIGN TEAM
Student-led, faculty-advised design team from the College of Engineering; the College of Architecture, Art and Planning; the College of Agriculture and Life Sciences; and the School of Business at Cornell University

COMPLETION
October 2005

5.32 The Cornell Solar Decathlon House sited on the National Mall in Washington, DC.
NICHOLAS RAJKOVICH

The 2005 entry was the first house Cornell University had constructed for the Solar Decathlon competition. The house was built on Cornell University's campus in Ithaca, New York, and shipped to Washington, DC by truck in October of 2005 for the Solar Decathlon competition. Following the competition, the house was returned to the campus in Ithaca, New York, but may be moved to an alternative site in New York State for demonstration or research purposes.

Design Intent and Validation

The Cornell House responds to critical issues facing the United States (and the world in general): energy consumption, home ownership, and personal finance. As the next generation of architects, engineers, and businesspeople, the Cornell student Decathlon leaders felt that the challenge of the competition was not to technologically integrate solar panels into a spectacular, high-tech demonstration home, but to integrate renewable energy into the culture of suburban America.

To this end, the Cornell House was based upon a modular system that would allow home buyers to customize their home by choosing environmentally-responsible components that suit their particular lifestyles and preferences. The modular system also allows homeowners to make incremental investments in their homes by adding modules to an existing structure. Such flexibility would enable home buyers to purchase a more affordable, smaller-scale home earlier in life, and add to the house as the family grows.

5.33 Computer rendering of the interior of the Cornell House.
CORNELL UNIVERSITY SOLAR DECATHLON

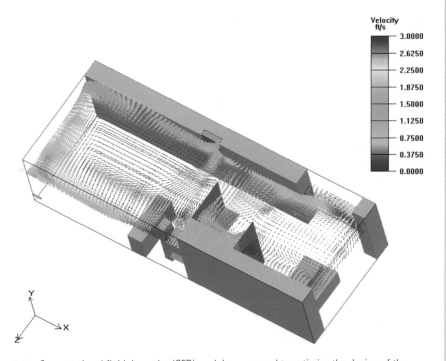

5.34 Computational fluid dynamics (CFD) models were used to optimize the design of the active heating and cooling systems. CORNELL UNIVERSITY SOLAR DECATHLON

During the course of the competition in October 2005, the house was tested by researchers from the National Renewable Energy Laboratory involving a series of ten contests totaling 1100 points. The ten contests for the 2005 competition were:

1. Architecture (200 points)—Evaluated the architectural design of the house on both an aesthetic and functional level.

2. Dwelling (100 points)—Evaluated the "livability" of the house: that is, how well the house design was aligned with the habits of everyday living.

3. Documentation (100 points)—Evaluated record keeping regarding the design and evolution of the house from beginning to completion, including construction documents.

4. Communications (100 points)—Evaluated how effectively the team was able to relay information about its house and related research to the public.

5. Comfort Zone (100 points)—Evaluated the house's ability to maintain appropriate humidity and a steady temperature over a given time interval.

6. Appliances (100 points)—Evaluated the efficiency and effectiveness of the appliances in the house through a set of tasks. These tasks included being able to cook meals, clean dishes in the dishwasher, wash and dry clothing, leave the television on for 6 hours, and leave the computer on for 8 hours.

7. Hot Water (100 points)—Evaluated the house's ability to deliver 15 gal [57 L] of hot water in 10 minutes or less and demonstrate original improvements relative to traditional hot water systems.

8. Lighting (100 points)—Evaluated the lighting levels inside the house (from both electric and daylighting sources) against the energy it took to maintain these lighting levels.

9. Energy Balance (100 points)—Evaluated the house's energy production and consumption, ensuring that the house produced at least as much as it consumed.

10. Getting Around (100 points)—Evaluated the team's ability to power an electric vehicle with surplus energy from the house. Points were based on the number of miles accumulated on the vehicle.

5.35 Shipping constraints drove much of the design and the ultimate form of the Cornell House. NICHOLAS RAJKOVICH

To ensure that the team did well in the competition, and that the house would perform as designed, sophisticated computer models were created to test interior lighting conditions, energy use, airflow, temperature, humidity, and to control construction costs.

Because the house needed to be shipped by truck from Ithaca, New York to Washington, DC, the overall size and form of the house were dictated by local and national laws regarding over-road shipping dimensions.

Strategies

Many energy efficiency and active solar strategies were considered during the design process and are incorporated in the Cornell University House. Each of the strategies was designed to operate well in Washington, DC during the competition, and also to operate well over the long term when the house was returned to a permanent foundation in Ithaca, New York.

Active heating and cooling. The active heating and cooling system uses a high efficiency air-to-air heat pump connected to a variable speed air handler to provide the majority of the heating and cooling for the house. The heating and cooling system is controlled by a centrally located thermostat/hygrometer that is tied into the building management system for the house, allowing for tight control of the building's interior temperature and humidity.

Energy recovery ventilator. To reduce energy losses when the house is being mechanically ventilated, the air handler is connected to an energy recovery ventilator, or ERV. Most ERV systems utilize lithium bromide as the primary desiccant, but to reduce the environmental impact of using an ERV, the Cornell team specially designed and fabricated an ERV that used silica gel, an environmentally benign material often used in the packaging of consumer products (such as tennis shoes).

Cross ventilation. Large openings on the northern and southern exposures of the house allow for cross ventilation. Casement windows and special casement sliding glass doors were selected to assist with directing airflow through the house.

Photovoltaics. Fifty-six 110-watt solar panels are installed on an adjustable steel frame over the flat roof of the house. The steel frame is adjustable—a necessity so that the PV system could achieve the greatest power yield during the competition in Washington, DC, and also when the house returned to Ithaca, NY after the competition. In New York the panels are tilted at 42° above the horizontal, the optimum angle for this type of solar collection for Ithaca.

The fifty-six panels provide up to 6.16 kW of power, which is estimated to be three times the amount needed to actually support "normal living" in such a house. The additional solar panel capacity was installed to support a rechargeable electric car for the Solar Decathlon competition. Excess power not used by the house is diverted to a battery bank for storage. When the house is sited on its final, permanent foundation, the photovoltaic panels will be tied into the electrical grid, and the battery bank will be removed and reused in future Solar Decathlon homes.

5.36 The Cornell University Solar Decathlon House utilized photovoltaics and evacuated tube solar collectors to provide for all of the energy needs during the competition. NICHOLAS RAJKOVICH

5.37 Light-colored materials were used throughout the interior to promote good daylight distribution. NICHOLAS RAJKOVICH

Solar thermal collectors. Evacuated tube solar thermal collectors were specified for the Cornell House to supply all of the domestic hot water needs, and part of the heating load for the house in the winter. Evacuated tubes were a good choice for the Cornell House because they work efficiently, and have high absorber temperatures under low solar radiation (such as on overcast days in Ithaca).

Glazing selection. Triple-glazed, low-ε, argon-filled windows were used throughout the house to reduce wintertime heat losses, and to reduce summer heat gains.

Shading devices. Aluminum sunshades were designed to provide maximum protection from the sun during the summertime, while allowing partial penetration of the sun during the shoulder seasons. In the winter, the sun readily penetrates into the living area of the house.

Structural insulated panels. Structural insulated panels (SIPs) were used as both structure and insulation for the walls and roof of the house. The panels have oriented strand board (OSB) on the interior and exterior surface of the panel, and the insulation material is a urethane-based foam. The panels have a minimum R-value of R-38 [RSI-6.7].

Insulation materials. The floor was conventionally framed with wood I-joists and the space between the joists was filled with a batt insulation fabricated from recycled denim blue jeans. The R-value of the insulation is comparable to glass fiber batt insulation, but the material is non-toxic, contains no harmful chemicals, and does not require any personal protective devices to install.

Appliances. All of the appliances in the house were specified to be extremely energy and water efficient. All appliances were Energy Star rated.

Building management system. A building management system controls interior lighting levels, humidity, and temperature from a touch screen pad located in the office area of the house.

5.38 External shading on the south facade. NICHOLAS RAJKOVICH

5.39 Electric lighting in the house is automatically dimmed by the building management system, depending upon outdoor light levels, to conserve electrical energy. NICHOLAS RAJKOVICH

Daylighting. Windows were located adjacent to areas with critical visual tasks, such as the kitchen counter, the desk in the office, and the bathroom, and were sized to provide ample daylight. Light-colored materials were used throughout the house to promote the widespread and even distribution of daylight and electric light.

Electric lighting. The lighting system uses T5 high-output fluorescent lamps to provide general ambient lighting, and halogen lamps where color rendering is critical (such as the bathroom, over the dining room table, and in the bedroom) to provide warmth and "sparkle." The ambient light levels adjust according to the outdoor daylight conditions; to do this a daylight sensor was mounted on the ceiling and tied into the building management system.

Water conservation. Low-flow fixtures were used throughout the house, including the dishwasher, washer/dryer, and for the shower. A dual-flush toilet was installed in the bathroom to reduce water consumption. A greywater recycling system was installed on the washer/dryer, bathroom sink, and shower, and water from these fixtures was used to irrigate the landscape plantings.

Landscaping. An organic, edible, modular, and portable landscape was designed by students in the Cornell University Landscape Architecture department. Plants were selected that would provide adequate nutrition to people living in the house and require little to no irrigation. No pesticides were used in the production of the landscape. Reclaimed greywater from the house, and rainwater harvested from the roof, are used to irrigate the landscape.

Appropriate materials. Materials for the interior of the house were selected to promote good indoor air quality and for ease of maintenance. All wood used in the house was from sustainable, rapidly-renewable sources, including a Brazilian redwood for the exterior and bamboo for the flooring and cabinetry in the house. Wherever possible, the team selected recycled or recyclable materials, and attempted to avoid the use of vinyl due to its significant environmental impact.

How Is It Working?

During the course of the Solar Decathlon competition (from 6–14 October 2005) the house was tested and evaluated by researchers from the National Renewable Energy Laboratory over a series of ten contests totaling 1100 points. The results from the ten contests are as follows (scores are rounded off):

1. Architecture (188/200 points, 3rd place)—Judges commended the quality of the interior finishes and the integration of the landscape into the overall design.

2. Dwelling (85/100 points, 5th place)—Judges commended the layout of the space, but felt there was inadequate storage space and privacy in the large, single room layout of the house.

3. Documentation (76/100 points, 9th place).

4. Communications (70/100 points, 14th place).

5. Comfort Zone (84/100 points, 1st place)—The energy recovery ventilator and heat pump system was able to keep the house within the specified temperature and humidity range throughout testing.

6. Appliances (74/100 points, 2nd place)—The appliances performed well, allowing the team to wash and dry dishes and towels per the competition requirements.

7. Hot Water (97/100 points, 1st place)—The evacuated tube solar collectors performed extremely well, providing adequate hot water even though the weather was overcast and rainy for the entire week of testing.

8. Lighting (91/100 points, 2nd place)—The lighting demonstrated good distribution and low energy use throughout the week of testing.

9. Energy Balance (0/100 points, 6th place)—A lack of sunny weather (solar resource) prevented the Cornell House from replenishing the energy used from the battery banks, a common problem for many of the teams during the exceptionally rainy week of the competition.

10. Getting Around (61/100 points, 2nd place)—The Cornell team utilized its deep battery bank to run the electric car as much as possible during the week of the competition.

The Cornell House placed second behind the University of Colorado (Denver and Boulder), the defending champions of the 2002 Solar Decathlon competition. After the competition, the house was transported by truck to Ithaca, New York, where it was reassembled on campus as a demonstration unit. Current plans are to put the house up for sale and then to conduct a post-occupancy evaluation of the house.

Further Information

Bonaventura-Sparagna, J., E. Chin-Dickey and N. Rajkovich. 2005. "The Cornell University Solar Decathlon Team: Learning Through Practice." *Proceedings of the ASES/ISES 2005 Solar World Congress* (Orlando, FL). American Solar Energy Society, Boulder, CO.

Cornell University Solar Decathlon. www.cusd.cornell.edu/

Northeast Regional Climate Center. www.nrcc.cornell.edu/

PVWatts: A Performance Calculator for Grid-Connected PV Systems. rredc.nrel.gov/solar/codes_algs/PVWATTS/

U.S. Department of Energy, Solar Decathlon. www.eere.energy.gov/solar_decathlon/

NOTES

Background and Context

This long-term school project began in 1997 when the Drukpa Trust (under the patronage of the Dalai Lama) initiated a master planning effort with Arup Associates. From this planning, detailed designs for several phases of development were prepared. The school will serve 750 elementary and high school students when all phases are completed. In addition to providing for typical school functions, students from distant towns and villages (and their house parents) will reside in on-site dormitories.

Arup has provided a leave-of-absence for an architect or engineer from the design team so they might reside at the school during the summer months to assist local builders with the project. The building team is a diverse group, which includes London-based design professionals, Punjabi carpenters, and Nepalese masons and laborers. The construction of the first building proved to be a learning experience about design appropriateness, materials supply, local construction techniques, and project management.

5.40 The Druk White Lotus School site is in a high desert valley bounded on the north by mountains. CAROLINE SOHIE, ARUP + ARUP ASSOCIATES

5.41 A series of outdoor classrooms comprise the Infant School courtyard of the Druk White Lotus School—one of several such courtyards. The planter boxes shown in this photo have been planted with willows. CAROLINE SOHIE, ARUP + ARUP ASSOCIATES

LOCATION
Shey, Ladakh, India
Latitude 34 °N
Longitude 77.40 °E

HEATING DEGREE DAYS
14,785 base 65 °F
[8214 base 18 °C]

COOLING DEGREE DAYS
0 base 50 °F
[0 base 10 °C]

SOLAR RADIATION
Jan 640 Btu/ft^2/day
[2.02 kWh/m^2/day]
Jun 1886 Btu/ft^2/day
[5.95 kWh/m^2/day]

ANNUAL PRECIPITATION
2 in. [50 mm]

BUILDING TYPE
School

CLIENT
Drukpa Trust

DESIGN TEAM
Arup Associates and Ove Arup & Partners

COMPLETION
Phase 1: 2001
Phase 2: 2004
All phases by 2009

The overriding design goal for the school was to provide flexible, high-quality teaching spaces in a sustainable building. The design and construction were to respect local building materials and appropriate building technologies (both traditional and modern). The school should be a model of appropriate and sustainable modernization for Ladakh. Underlying this intent was an imperative to use no imported energy, to maximize the potential of solar radiation in a high desert climate, and to provide potable water and treat wastewater on site.

As a result of successful preconstruction planning and design efforts, the first phase of the school was completed under budget and also within acceptable local cost constraints—around 15% of the cost of a similar school in the UK. The design team intends to inform ongoing design and construction decisions by tapping into experiences from Phase 1. An effort will also be made to optimize expenditures, given the limited resources of the client and the balancing of value between capital investments and financially sustainable operations.

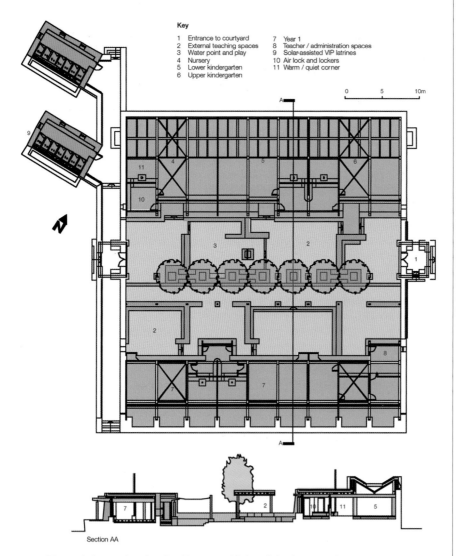

Key

1	Entrance to courtyard	7	Year 1
2	External teaching spaces	8	Teacher / administration spaces
3	Water point and play	9	Solar-assisted VIP latrines
4	Nursery	10	Air lock and lockers
5	Lower kindergarten	11	Warm / quiet corner
6	Upper kindergarten		

Section AA

5.42 Plan and site section showing Nursery and Infant School courtyard. ARUP + ARUP ASSOCIATES

Design Intent and Validation

This ambitious project was intended to become a model sustainable school—a vision presented at the September 2002 Johannesburg Earth

Summit. The Druk White Lotus School addressed the realities of construction, energy, site infrastructure, buildings, material resource use, and project management in a challenging site context. The project also serves to demonstrate a new approach to teaching in a distinct rural community. This demonstration should contribute to the development of appropriate building technologies and methodologies in remote locations worldwide.

Arup developed and used software tools to analyze the performance of the ventilated Trombe walls, the feasibility of using various thermal insulations, the desirability of double glazing, and the use of daylighting. The design team also had access to the firm's broad seismic engineering experience. Many in Arup have experience examining the effects of earthquakes, often in developing countries. Lessons learned from these experiences were applied on the Druk White Lotus project. The resulting design balances economic and environmental factors while meeting the needs of the school's students and teachers.

5.43 Arup designed the project to work with local construction crews. CAROLINE SOHIE, ARUP + ARUP ASSOCIATES

5.44 The Druk White Lotus School classrooms appear to emerge from the landscape. Their orientation takes advantage of early morning sunshine. CAROLINE SOHIE, ARUP + ARUP ASSOCIATES

As reported in the *Arup Journal*, Arup Project Director Rory McGowan said: "We had great ambitions when we began this project believing that high-powered engineering software and the latest thinking in design could be applied just as easily to Ladakh as to a London office block." Arup realized that this approach wouldn't work when it became clear that the cost and difficulty of importing materials to the remote site would make the use of mud brick, granite, and wood preferable to steel. Site manager Sonam Angdus, who was raised in the nearby village of Shey, said: "Everyone agreed on granite walls with a mud core. These are stable and well insulated and they blend in naturally with the surroundings. They are also available locally."

5.45 School rooms feature southeast-facing direct gain windows that ensure early morning warm-up in Shey's sunny climate. CAROLINE SOHIE, ARUP + ARUP ASSOCIATES

Strategies

The Druk White Lotus School employs a range of green design strategies appropriate to its remote high desert climate.

Passive solar heating. The classroom buildings are oriented 30° east of true south with an elongated east-west axis to assure early morning warm-up. There is abundant sunshine all year long in the high desert climate—even during the winter when temperatures can fall to −22 °F [−30 °C]. Indirect gain Trombe walls (made of ventilated mud brick) and granite cavity walls with double glazing provide evening heating in the dormitories. Provisions have been made for small wood stoves to supply backup heating (not yet used). All residential buildings are oriented on a true north-south axis to maximize daily solar gains. The solar-assisted latrines have a solar wall (Figure 5.50) facing directly south for the same reason.

Insulation. The roofs are generally constructed of mud on talu lath resting on local poplar rafters supported by timber framing. In the Infant School a butterfly roof structure uses a felt weather skin, rock wool insulation, and timber framing.

Air locks. Air locks are provided at the entries to the classroom buildings; these act as a buffer between the cold exterior and the warm interior in the winter.

Daylighting. The classrooms are designed to optimize the use of daylight. In the wider Nursery and Kindergarten Building, light admitted by the direct gain windows is balanced by toplighting provided by north- and south-facing clerestories diffused by a splayed ceiling. No electric lighting is typically used in the classrooms, although a minimal electric lighting system is installed in all buildings.

Natural ventilation. All the rooms have well-shaded openable windows that allow cross-ventilation that provides a cool, glare-free, teaching environment.

Migration. Migration involves moving from one environment to a more comfortable or interesting environment. The courtyards between the classroom buildings are subdivided into smaller spaces where classes may be held on mild, sunny days. The school buildings and courtyard trees provide shade and wind protection for these spaces.

Water use. The Druk White Lotus School is located in a desert, so water is precious. Groundwater extracted from a 105-ft [32-m] deep well is pumped by PV power to a 16,000-gallon [60,560 L] storage tank located on ground higher than the buildings. A new well is planned for a location above the storage tank in order to reduce pumping demands. When not needed for pumping, the PV system charges batteries that provide power to the school's computers. Waterless "ventilated improved pit" (VIP) toilets (latrines) use solar-assisted stack ventilators to help process waste into odorless compost—an excellent fertilizer.

5.46 Clerestory and view windows provide balanced daylight for the classrooms.
CAROLINE SOHIE, ARUP + ARUP ASSOCIATES

5.47 The splayed roof in the classroom acts as an indirect daylight source. Note the lack of operating electric luminaires.
CAROLINE SOHIE, ARUP + ARUP ASSOCIATES

Light enters solar flue
through fly screen and attracts flies

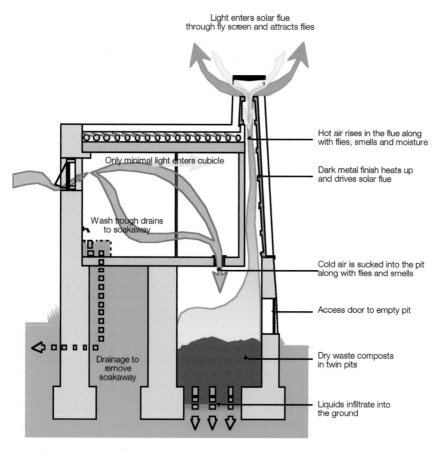

Hot air rises in the flue along
with flies, smells and moisture

Only minimal light enters cubicle

Dark metal finish heats up
and drives solar flue

Wash trough drains
to soakaway

Cold air is sucked into the pit
along with flies and smells

Access door to empty pit

Drainage to
remove
soakaway

Dry waste composts
in twin pits

Liquids infiltrate into
the ground

5.48 The composting "VIP" latrine uses solar assisted stack ventilation for drying and odor control. ARUP + ARUP ASSOCIATES

5.49 Granite block facing is stable and also locally obtained.

CAROLINE SOHIE, ARUP + ARUP ASSOCIATES

5.50 The latrine building with solar collector. CAROLINE SOHIE, ARUP + ARUP ASSOCIATES

Materials. Design emphasis was placed on the use of local materials. Soil from the site was used in roof construction and the mud bricks for the inner walls were hand-made in Shey. The granite blocks of the exterior wall are formed and finished from stone found on the site or gathered from the surrounding boulder field. Nearby monastery plantations grew the willow used in the roof construction.

How Is It Working?

Arup has been monitoring building performance and site comments to provide feedback for its practice. Construction on the school will span up to eight years (2001–2009). A senior design team member visits the site in April at the beginning of each year's building season, followed by an Arup resident who typically remains on site for around four months starting in June. Building performance feedback was already being collected at the time the Nursery and Infant School and Junior School were completed and brought into use.

The design team and the Drukpa Trust both anticipate a continuous learning process regarding the school's performance as it is used and evolves over the next few years. Lessons learned from this experience will inform the remaining design and construction work.

Sustainable design for this project means that the buildings must be constructed within local cost parameters as well as employ natural and local resources. The Druk White Lotus School has garnered positive feedback from the architectural community. It won World Architecture Awards in 2002 as Best Education Building of the Year, Best Green Building of the Year (joint winner), and Regional Winner—Asia.

5.51 A typical classroom interior. CAROLINE SOHIE, ARUP + ARUP ASSOCIATES

Further Information

Arup Associates. www.arupassociates.com/

Barker, D. 2002. "Building a School in India," *Architecture Week*, 31 July.

Druk White Lotus School. www.dwls.org/

Fleming, J. et al. 2002. "Druk White Lotus School, Ladakh, Northern India," *The Arup Journal*, 2/2002.

NOTES

Background and Context

The Habitat Research and Development Centre (HRDC) is located in Namibia, in southwestern Africa. The HRDC is a joint project of the Namibian Ministry of Regional and Local Government Housing (MRLGH), the National Housing Enterprise (NHE), and the Municipality of Windhoek (CoW).

The HRDC mission reads: *"The mission of the HRDC is to promote the use of local, indigenous building materials and designs, engage multidisciplinary teams in basic research, the adaptation of existing knowledge, and applied research to achieve a holistic approach to problem solving in the field of housing and its related issues."* The HRDC offers services to the community such as monitoring and evaluation of housing projects and housing programs, and evaluating national building standards, as well as community education and outreach programs.

5.53 The administration building of the Habitat Research and Development Centre in Namibia, Africa. HEIDI SPALY

The Centre is essentially focused upon the housing needs of the Namibian community. Housing is a pressing need in the country due to rapid urbanization and the poverty level of the majority of the population. The Centre's main goal is to become a talking point for sustainable housing options and building alternatives—with a focus upon environmental appropriateness through implementation and research. The Centre is located in Katutura, a former black township on the outskirts of the capital city of Windhoek. The building is surrounded by a residential area making it highly visible and accessible, and is a landmark in the community.

The construction of the Centre is scheduled in three phases. Phase 1 (Figure 5.53) was completed in April 2004. Phase 1 consists of an administrative wing with reception, director's office, open-plan office

HABITAT RESEARCH AND DEVELOPMENT CENTRE

5.52 Conceptual drawing of the HRDC foyer. NINA MARITZ

LOCATION
Windhoek, Namibia, Africa
Latitude: 22.6 °S
Longitude: 17.1 °E

HEATING DEGREE DAYS
724 65 °F base
[402 18 °C base]

COOLING DEGREE DAYS
6561 50°F base
[3645 10°C base]

SOLAR RADIATION
Dec 2273 Btu/ft^2/day
[7.17 kWh/m^2/day]
Jun 1385 Btu/ft^2/day
[4.37 kWh/m^2/day]

ANNUAL PRECIPITATION
12–14 in. [300–350 mm]

BUILDING TYPE
Institutional

AREA
Phase 1: 23,640 ft^2 [2196 m^2];
Phase 2: 21,600 ft^2 [2007 m^2]

CLIENT
Ministry of Regional and Local Government Housing, National Housing Enterprise, and Municipality of Windhoek

DESIGN TEAM
Nina Maritz, Architect; C.P. de Leeuw, Quality Surveyors; Buhrmann and Partners, Civil and Structural Engineers; G. S. Fainsinger, Electrical and Mechanical Engineers; Emcon Solar Engineers; Groenewald Construction, Contractor

COMPLETION
Phase 1: April 2004
Phases 2 and 3: September 2006

module for 24 staff and archive storage, and a public wing consisting of an open foyer, library, exhibition hall, and services.

Housing in Namibia currently consists of 37% conventional (brick and mortar), 14% "other" (including waste timber and corrugated iron shacks), and 50% "traditional" (thatched wattle and daub). As thatch and timber become more difficult to source due to the high rate of deforestation in Namibia, and as social and cultural mores change, people's housing desires are moving toward "western" or "modern" houses for reasons of perceived status and lower maintenance. Conventional "modern" housing is generally constructed from single-skin load-bearing cement brickwork on concrete strip footings—with South African pine roof-trusses and metal sheeting roofs. Thermally, this type of construction is extremely unpleasant. In addition, the necessary manufactured, imported, and commercially available materials are often too expensive for the poor sectors of the community.

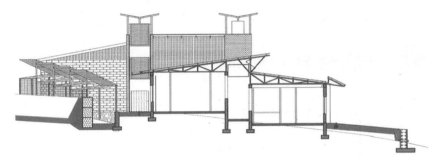

5.54 Section through evaporative cool towers and offices at HRDC. NINA MARITZ

Design Intent and Validation

Windhoek is located in the southern hemisphere; the sun moves through the northern sky and all northern hemisphere rules regarding orientation are reversed. The main concern in the design of the Centre, and of building design in Namibia in general, is cooling during the summer when the average maximum temperature reaches 90–93 °F [32–34 °C]. Cooling is the main comfort concern; few buildings are heated, as winter days are sunny and warm and the heating season is short. Nevertheless, comfort during the winter still needs to be taken into consideration.

The design intent and process that shaped the HRDC included a focus upon hybrid building—seeing the element of compromise (for all involved in the design and construction) as a virtue and an element to work with creatively. The aesthetic collage character of the building, through its flexibility and its ability to allow for change, was an outcome of the design goals. With the collaborative involvement of the client, contractor, and architect, the design team worked to generate creative responses to goals, including philosophical goals (not just to design a practical, functional building), and attempted to maintain a clear expression of sustainability principles. Embodied energy was a design focus, leading to the use of local or Namibian materials as much as possible, recycled or waste materials, materials that could be used unaltered or close to their natural state, and labor-intensive methods of construction rather than full factory prefabrication.

Strategies

Orientation. Fundamental passive solar design principles were considered during the design of the HRDC. The layout of the plan is an overall north-facing orientation pointing toward the equator. The office block is rotated 25° to the east, which is optimal for daytime use as this allows the morning winter sun to warm the building interior.

Shading. The east-west facades are solid and openings in these walls are limited to narrow shaded vertical slits. The building form provides for service areas that are used as thermal buffers. Roof overhangs are generous throughout the building and are extended where necessary with thin timber laths. This combination creates large overhangs that accept winter sun and exclude summer sun. Additional overhangs incorporate solar panels (or are designed for the future installment of solar panels).

Earth berm. The southwest side of the site includes an earth berm to protect against southwest summer sun. Walls on the south side of the complex are built of a solid wall fabric using soil-cement bricks and stone with high thermal capacity. The courtyard is planted with indigenous vegetation that provides cooling through evapotranspiration. These plants also require very little water.

Thermal mass. Interior strategies include high thermal mass floors of floated polished concrete, which are left uncovered to allow for radiant cooling. Natural ventilation is encouraged by the use of operable windows and high ceilings. Window openings are placed directly across from each other to maximize airflow (especially at low wind speeds). In addition, the windows at work stations are operable and allow control of air movement to meet personal comfort expectations. Clerestory windows are operable and located at the central apex of the up-sloping ceiling. High ceilings are incorporated into the design allowing rising hot air to accumulate above head height.

Daylighting. Daylighting is provided by combinations of side windows and central clerestory windows (Figure 5.55), distributing light evenly through the space. Curtains on the windows are made from translucent calico which lets in light, but helps to reduce the potential for glare at computers in the work spaces. "Fake" light shelves function as a fanlight above the curtains and allow more light into the space while the curtains are drawn. Task-lighting with individual switching is installed to give the occupants control of personal lighting needs and reduce the need for general overhead lighting. Electric lighting needs are met using low-energy fluorescent or compact fluorescent lamps.

Evaporative cooling. Cooling systems implemented at HRDC include low-energy evaporative cooling and passive downdraft evaporative cooling (PDEC) systems. The south tower functions as an evaporative cooler. Rainwater is collected in tanks in the south tower and the collected water supplies the evaporative cooler located in the top of the tower.

5.55 View of ceiling showing clerestory windows and wool and reed ceiling materials. NINA MARITZ

The north tower (shown in Figure 5.57) functions as a passive downdraft cooler. Wind passes through screens at the top of the tower and is cooled by a sprinkler grid inside the tower. As the air cools, it drops to a catch pond below which collects the water from the sprinklers; the cooled air continues to drop and enters the building through outlets placed high in the walls.

5.56 Bathroom tiling made of secondhand and broken tiles. HEIDI SPALY

5.57 Evaporative cool tower with prosopis (mesquite) branches used to shade the storage tanks. NINA MARITZ

Water conservation. Many water-saving techniques are employed in the HRDC. Several different patented, dry, self-composting toilets are installed for demonstration and testing. These include the "Enviroloo," the "Eco-san," a Namibian produced "cool-drawer" design, and an additional type designed specifically for the HRDC. Waterless urinals are used in conjunction with the dry toilets. The dry toilets typically work through a design in which solids fall into a basket and liquids drain through. The liquids evaporate through an attached chimney, while the solids dry out and break down biologically. They are removed and used as compost. Additional water-saving measures in the toilet rooms include: aeration devices on existing faucet fittings and demand taps.

The building's greywater is filtered through home-made filters and used for the irrigation of indigenous vegetation on site. Rainwater from the roof is stored in stacked rainwater tanks and used for evaporative cooling and irrigation. These plastic tanks (shown in Figure 5.58) are located in the towers and elevated to create gravity water pressure; they are shaded by timber pole screens.

The reuse of as much construction "waste" material as possible in the construction of the building reduced the amount of waste going into local landfills—reducing the effect on the city's main underground water source.

Photovoltaics. The building receives energy from a grid-connected photovoltaic system. This was the first use of an urban grid-tied PV system in Namibia. The spatial benefits of a grid-tied system include no need to allot space for batteries or a battery room. The solar panels are located on the roof of the lecture room and comprise a 4.5 kW peak array. A limited (due to limited funding) array is also installed along walkways (see Figure 5.59) with additional space designed for future additions leading to a total of six arrays of between 4 and 6 kW peak each.

Factors limiting the use of solar in Namibia include the cost of the technology, high import duties, little demand in Namibia, and a lack of current government support and subsidies. Through its solar installation the HRDC hopes to increase interest in solar through education and growing consumer awareness, in the context of a consistent increase in electricity prices and donor funding that favors the support of renewable energy sources.

Appropriate materials. The HRDC's use of appropriate building materials is apparent in many aspects of the building. The wall materials are mostly load bearing based upon material availability and thermal potential. Timber is scarce in Namibia as there is a high rate of deforestation and there are no managed forests in the country. Many of the materials used in the HRDC help to reduce the need for timber in the building. Charcoal-fired clay bricks were used in the multistory section of the building and were left unplastered, an unusual practice in Namibia. The bricks are manufactured by two Namibian companies that use charcoal made from invasive plants.

5.58 Roof water storage tank and cooling access area. HEIDI SPALY

5.59 Photovoltaics as shading devices along walkway. NINA MARITZ

5.60 A sample wall at HRDC demonstrates the use of a variety of appropriate materials and construction techniques. HEIDI SPALY

To further the Centre's objectives in construction education, a wall and paving sample (shown in Figures 5.60 and 5.61) was built in the main entry foyer for testing and demonstration purposes. Construction techniques demonstrated in the sample wall include sandbags, cob, adobe bricks, limestone, glass bottles, mortar and rubble, and patented polystyrene blocks. The sample wall will remain in place and be used in conjunction with pilot housing projects as the techniques prove successful.

The adobe or sun-dried clay bricks used in building the public toilets spaces were made by the Namibia Clay House Project. Reclaimed cement bricks and pavers were obtained from building demolition rubble dumped by the municipality. Unskilled labor was used to clean the bricks and pavers. Compressed soil-cement blocks created using the Namibian invented Hydraform system, which uses an on-site mixer and hydraulic compressor to make the blocks, are also used in the HRDC. The blocks are profiled and interlock so that they can be dry-stacked without the need for mortar. The soil was supplied from a stockpile 2.5 miles [4 km] from the site.

5.61 Concrete block and paver demonstration. HEIDI SPALY

5.62 The exhibition hall, constructed of rammed earth (compacted by hand) and with reusable steel shutters. The load-bearing walls have a 4% cement mix and walls with 0–2% mixes alternate as infill panels. HEIDI SPALY

The archive storerooms were built with tire walls and tires are also used in retaining walls on the site. The "earthship" technique of filling the tires with compacted soil was used and the walls are unplastered to display the building technique. Interior walls are painted white to enhance the reflection of light.

Outdoor balustrade walls are constructed using local mica stone obtained from a nearby construction site. Rubble filled wire gabions are used for an exterior retaining and shading wall for the offices (Figure 5.63); the wall materials are imported from South Africa and used for civil engineering projects in Namibia.

Appropriate building materials in the roof structures and coverings include an invasive timber, prosopis (mesquite), for poles that were cut by unskilled workers and soaked in used motor oil (which serves as an insecticide and waterproofing). These poles were used in a pin-jointed space frame and a short-span purlin-only system, in exterior shading screens for walkways and water tanks, and for security.

Corrugated iron is preferred as a roofing material (compared to clay tiles, concrete tiles, or thatch) because of its longer life span, lower initial cost, potential reuse, light weight, low fire risk (brush fires caused by lightning strikes are common in Windhoek), lower transport costs, and the availability of locals who are skilled at working with the material (thereby increasing local employment opportunities). Corrugated iron is used in shacks in the local township, making it readily available. Its ability to be used in rainwater runoff collection is also an advantage.

Exterior floor finishes include a waste mica stone with a clay bedding layer, round boulders, and concrete cubes. Narrow gravel strips separate the mica strips permitting rainwater penetration from the flooring surface. The round boulders were recovered from recent floods and placed around the building edges to reduce runoff splashing. The ramped roadways in the parking areas are composed of concrete cubes, with natural gravel covering the flatter parking areas.

Interior floor finishes include wax-polished concrete surfaces in the offices and packed clay bricks with a sand bed in the exhibition hall and lecture room. Both floor types have high thermal mass and absorb body heat via radiation; they are hardwearing, inexpensive, and easy to maintain.

The HRDC's goals with respect to finishes are expressed by the philosophy that, wherever possible, it is ideal to leave building surfaces in their natural state to demonstrate the construction method and show the aesthetic potential of the material. Natural finishes and water-based coatings are used where needed for weather and corrosion protection.

Interior walls are lime-washed white to enhance daylighting distribution and for the lime's disinfectant properties. White road marking paint is used on tires to enhance daylighting possibilities. Secondhand and broken tiles are used for bathroom and kitchen wall applications.

Various methods of insulating the steel roofing were utilized. These include low-grade wool and lavender leaves packed into secondhand feed bags, waste polystyrene packaging, and waste brown corrugated cardboard. These materials are layered between the steel roof sheeting and a layer of invasive reeds removed from riverbeds.

Interior fittings consist of lampshades made from used car filters, waste-metal printing plates, and perforated metal tubes. The shades are placed over energy-saving compact fluorescent lamps. The chandelier in the exhibition hall is made from compact discs, which reflect the light from compact fluorescents. Exterior fittings include the work of a local artist who used recycled metal oil drum lids and rods to make security gates and burglar bars for the reception area. Soda cans are strung together

5.63 Rubble filled wire gabions help retain the earth and shade nearby walls. NINA MARITZ

to make an infill screen for the main gate. Secondhand windows and doors recovered from demolition sites and junkyards were reconditioned and used in the building.

How Is It Working?

The HRDC reaches into the community through educational outreach programs including schoolchildren participating in educational programs (such as a tire house project). Other educational programs put on by the Centre include a recycle yard program, sponsored studies for school dormitories, and housing studies. Through publication of various magazine and newspaper articles, and presentations by the director and architect at international conferences, the HRDC is also reaching out to a larger community.

5.64 Open-plan office space with cross ventilation. NINA MARITZ

The Centre offers skills training for local Namibians in the different construction methods incorporated in the HRDC. Many of the construction methods in the HRDC building are not new inventions, but were very new for the laborers and contractors on the project. Learning these techniques provides a valuable skill for unskilled workers in the city and country to take with them into the local community (and to implement in other regions of the country). Throughout the design process, many adjustments and variations to alternative techniques were discovered and applied in practice, helping make the HRDC an open environment for local and international visitors to learn from and explore.

Further Information

Anon. 2003. "Ground Broken for Habitat Research & Development Centre." www.windhoekcc.org.na/Repository/News&Publications/ Aloe/ALOEMay2003PMK.pdf. (*Aloe*: City of Windhoek. Issue 5, May 2003)

Habitat Research and Development Centre of Namibia. www.interact. com.na/hrdc/

Korrubel, J. 2005. "Lessons Learned in Building Sustainably in a Developing Country by the Habitat Research and Development Centre, Namibia." Presented at the 2005 World Sustainable Building Conference, Tokyo, Japan. September 2005.

NOTES

Background and Context

The Helena is a high-rise residential apartment tower located at 11th Avenue and West 57th Street in the Clinton neighborhood of Manhattan, New York City. Designed by FXFOWLE for the Durst Organization (with Rose Associates), this 38-story, 580-unit apartment building is the first private-sector green building of its type in New York City. Several other green high-rise residential buildings in New York City are following in the footsteps of the Helena. The Helena is projected to provide a 33% reduction in energy costs (and similar reductions in water usage) compared to comparable properties. The energy reductions are equivalent to a 65% reduction in energy budget according to LEED methodologies. These savings are the result of an aggressive green design and an estimated 3–5% increase in the first cost of the project.

The Helena is located on a site previously used for industrial purposes and currently planned for ongoing mixed-use development. The target market is young urban professionals—although the building has both market-rate and affordable housing units. The affordable housing units (of the same layout as market units) are located throughout the building and comprise 20% of the total units. The affordable housing unit component allowed the project to receive funding via tax-exempt bonds. Retail street-level elements contribute to the realization of the mixed-use master plan for the larger site.

5.66 The Helena Apartment Tower is the first phase of a full-block redevelopment on the west side of Manhattan. FXFOWLE ARCHITECTS, PC

The Affordable Housing Design Advisor, in citing the Helena as a Jury Selection in its Green Housing Projects Gallery (established to

5.65 The Helena Apartment Tower. FXFOWLE ARCHITECTS, PC

LOCATION
New York City, NY, USA
Latitude 40.8 °N
Longitude 74.0 °W

HEATING DEGREE DAYS
4744 65 °F base
[2636 18 °C base]

COOLING DEGREE DAYS
1160 65 °F base
[644 18 °C base]

SOLAR RADIATION
Jul 1940 Btu/ft^2/day
[6.12 kWh/m^2/day]
Jan 610 Btu/ft^2/day
[1.92 kWh/m^2/day]

ANNUAL PRECIPITATION
50 in. [1270 mm]

BUILDING TYPE
Hi-Rise Residential

AREA
550,000 ft^2 [51,095 m^2]

CLIENT
Durst Organization/Rose Associates

DESIGN TEAM
Architect, FXFOWLE; Consulting Engineers, Flack + Kurtz; Structural Engineer, Severud Associates; Contractor, Kreisler Borg Florman

COMPLETION
2005

demonstrate that green design can be achieved in affordable housing) notes several design features of merit. These features are grouped in six focus categories: Site Design, Green Building Design Strategies, Energy Efficiency, Water Conservation and Management, Green Materials, and Other. The specific features cited include: access to public transportation, a compact development, use of daylighting, a green roof, high-performance windows, energy-efficient HVAC systems, Energy Star appliances and lighting, the use of renewable energy, stormwater management strategies, the treatment of grey and/or blackwater, water-conserving landscaping elements, water-saving appliances, the use of green materials (local materials, materials with recycled content, and materials with low-VOC emissions), and other innovations.

5.67 The massing of the 38-story building creates 7 corner apartments on each floor. FXFOWLE ARCHITECTS, PC

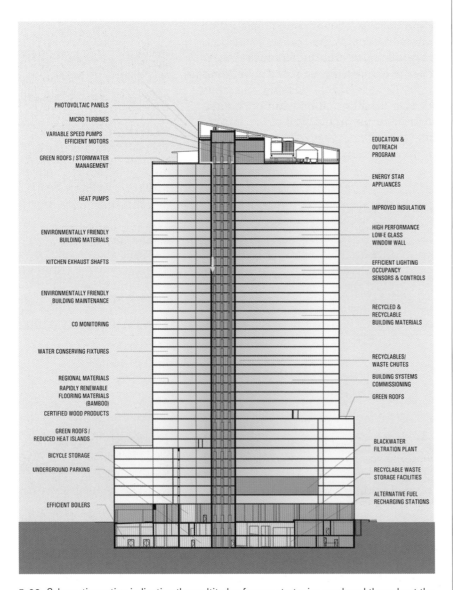

5.68 Schematic section indicating the multitude of green strategies employed throughout the Helena Apartment Tower. FXFOWLE ARCHITECTS, PC

Design Intent and Validation

The developer's intent was to obtain a U.S. Green Building Council LEED Gold certification for the apartment building—while meeting the demands of the New York City market and providing a substantial number of affordable housing units. This intent was accepted and embraced by the design team, to the extent that the Helena was viewed as a demonstration project for green design. An application for LEED certification was submitted and the project was awarded a Gold certification. As noted above, the Helena is a featured Jury Selection in the American Institute of Architects' Affordable Housing Design Advisor and a recipient of a Green Building Design Award from Global Green USA.

Strategies

Site. This particular project fits into the master planning for the urban Manhattan site. A view to the Hudson River was maintained by setting the building back along an existing visual access corridor. The north (least environmentally desirable) side of the site was used for building support services (including the blackwater treatment plant). There is ready access to public transportation from the site, including a compressed natural gas shuttle running from the Helena to the subway station during peak hours. Green roofs (approximately 12,000 ft^2 [1200 m^2]) reduce stormwater runoff and urban heat island effects.

5.69 One of the green roofs used to mitigate stormwater runoff and the urban heat island effect.
FXFOWLE ARCHITECTS, PC

5.70 Blackwater treatment plant under construction. FXFOWLE ARCHITECTS, PC

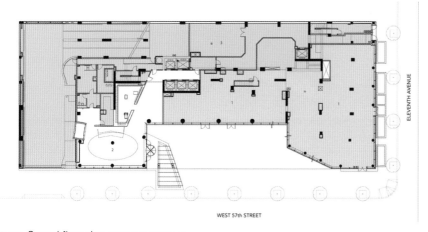

ELEVENTH AVENUE

WEST 57th STREET

5.71 Ground floor plan. FXFOWLE ARCHITECTS, PC

Water efficiency. Aggressive application of water efficiency strategies is anticipated to reduce potable water usage by about a third, compared to a comparable non-green building. The on-site blackwater treatment plant conditions three-quarters of the building's wastewater for subsequent reuse in low-flow water closets, the HVAC system cooling tower, and for landscape irrigation.

Energy and indoor environmental quality. Numerous strategies to reduce the consumption of non-renewable energy resources and improve indoor environmental quality were implemented. Building integrated photovoltaics (BIPV; some enclosing the mechanical penthouse, but also including a very public array on the entry canopy) are a visible

5.72 Polycrystalline photovoltaics laminated in the glass canopy over the entry.
FXFOWLE ARCHITECTS, PC

representation of this effort. The PV system is 13.1 kW peak and, along with cogeneration, is expected to contribute 10% of the building's baseline electrical requirements. The on-site cogeneration plant employs two 70 kW microturbines—with "waste" heat being used to heat domestic hot water. A master switch in each apartment can be used to turn off all built-in lighting and the top half of convenience receptacles, and place the HVAC system in sleep mode. The Helena is intended to use 50% green power—under a two-year contract with Community Energy, Inc., a for-profit company marketing (through ConEdison Solutions) NewWind Energy® supplies energy from a 30-megawatt wind power project located near Syracuse in upstate New York.

The HVAC system employs water-source heat pumps. All appliances bear the Energy Star label and the Helena is Energy Star qualified. The Durst Organization is an Energy Star Partner. Excellent air quality was a key design intent. Trickle vents provide outdoor air to each apartment unit, and operable windows allow for occupant participation in climate control decisions.

5.73 BIPVs on the entry canopy (and on the penthouse) generate 13.1 kW (peak) of electricity.
FXFOWLE ARCHITECTS, PC

Materials and resources. Wood floors from Forest Stewardship Council (FSC) certified suppliers are used in the Helena. Cabinetry and bifold doors are made of wheatboard. Wood products using urea-formaldehyde binders were avoided. Paints, carpets, and adhesives are all low-VOC products. Drywall (gypsum wall board) was a 100% recycled product. More than 80% of the construction waste from the project was diverted from landfills by construction management practices.

Beyond design. Green guidelines will be distributed to building occupants. Each floor of the building has a recycling chute to encourage tenant recycling. Interestingly, FXFOWLE was commissioned by the Battery Park City Authority to prepare sustainable design guidelines for residential buildings. These guidelines show their influence in the design of the Helena and several other New York City green apartment buildings.

5.74 Typical apartment with floor-to-ceiling low-ε glass for views and daylighting. FXFOWLE ARCHITECTS, PC

5.76 Efficient kitchen and dining areas are a classic New York apartment typology. FXFOWLE ARCHITECTS, PC

5.75 Trash room with one chute for trash and one for recycling (prior to signage). FXFOWLE ARCHITECTS, PC

5.77 Expansive view from an apartment unit. FXFOWLE ARCHITECTS, PC

How Is It Working?

No post-occupancy studies have been performed on this recently completed project to evaluate building performance in place and over time. Validation of design intent and execution has come from external organizations in the form of several prestigious design awards and a LEED Gold certification.

Further Information

Affordable Housing Design Advisor, Green Housing Projects:
www.designadvisor.org/green/helena.php

FXFOWLE: www.fxfowle.com/

GreenHome: www.greenhomenyc.org/ (select What is Green Building, then NYC Green Building profiles)

Logan, K. 2005. "High-Metal Tower," *Architecture Week* (online). www.architectureweek.com/2005/0928/design_1-1.html

Background and Context

The University of Oregon's Lundquist College of Business needed to replace an aging building that connected three existing smaller buildings. The building's site, along an axis between the historic entrance to the college and the main library, gives it a high profile. The university had in place a campus-wide sustainable development plan and Lundquist College had a commitment to certain sustainability goals—as a result both parties had a mutual desire to aim for the greenest building possible.

The University engaged a Construction Manager/General Contractor who was brought into the project early in the design process. This enabled the design team to work closely with the CM/GC as the design developed, ensuring that the design was feasible and within the established financial parameters. Lillis was a complex project—to be built in the middle of an active campus, while minimally disrupting classes.

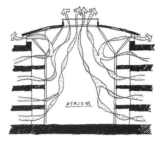

5.78 Conceptual sketch of the Lillis ventilation strategy. SRG PARTNERSHIP

LOCATION
Eugene, Oregon, USA
Latitude 44.1 °N
Longitude 123.2 °W

HEATING DEGREE DAYS
4546 base 65 °F
[2529 base 18.3 °C]

COOLING DEGREE DAYS
247 base 65 °F
[137 base 18.3 °C]

SOLAR RADIATION
Jan 368 Btu/ft^2/day
[1.16 kWh/m^2/day]
Jun 1975 Btu/ft^2/day
[6.23 kWh/m^2/day]

ANNUAL PRECIPITATION
52 in. [1321 mm]

BUILDING TYPE
Institutional—classrooms, offices, common areas

AREA
196,500 ft^2 [18,255 m^2]; four occupied stories; 40,000 ft^2 [3716 m^2] of pre-existing buildings

CLIENT
Lundquist College of Business, University of Oregon

DESIGN TEAM
Architect: SRG Partnership; PV: Solar Design Associates and New Path Renewables; Construction Manager/General Contractor: Lease Crutcher Lewis

COMPLETION
October 2003

5.79 Entry plaza fronting the Lillis Business Complex; the entry facade is of laminated glass with integrated photovoltaics. LARA SWIMMER PHOTOGRAPHY

Design Intent and Validation

The client and designers began with a goal to achieve a building that would be at least 40% more efficient than required by the Oregon Energy Code. The designers were also asked to follow a process that could result in a solution with the performance of a LEED (the U.S. Green Building Council's Leadership in Energy and Environmental Design program) certified building (the decision to pay for the formal LEED process, however, was not made until after the designers had finished working drawings). To make these goals a reality, the design team developed complementing strategies involving daylighting, solar control, natural ventilation, electricity generation using photovoltaic arrays, expanding the thermal comfort zone (by occupant cooling with ceiling fans), night

ventilation of thermal mass, and wiring half of all the plug load receptacles and lighting circuits in faculty offices on occupancy sensors. A
team of consultants, including energy engineers and daylighting
experts, modeled various designs to determine how well design concepts were meeting project goals. The CM/GC agreed to recycle 95%
of the demolition waste from the existing buildings (related to LEED
Materials & Resources credits).

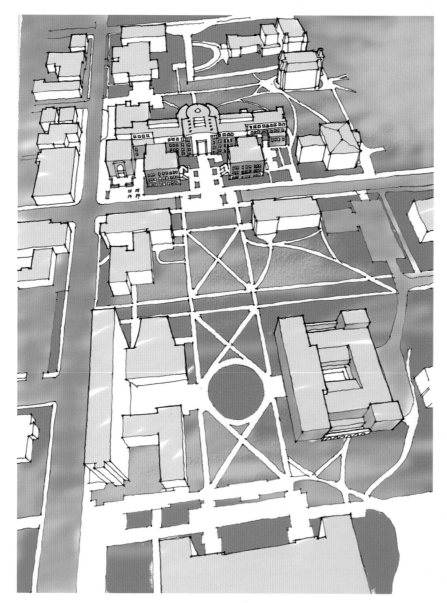

5.80 Birds-eye sketch of the Lillis Business Complex showing the new building (top center)
relative to existing buildings on site and a long narrow east–west form. SRG PARTNERSHIP

Strategies

Orientation and form. The designers conceived of the building as a
long and thin building running along an east-west axis. This configuration

is essential to the success of the various green strategies. Not only are north- and south-facing windows easier to control for daylighting and solar gain, they also take advantage of the prevailing seasonal wind directions (from the north and south). This long, east-west configuration yields a sizable south-facing facade capable of incorporating photovoltaics and substantial daylight apertures.

Natural ventilation. In addition to the long and thin form, the auditorium and lecture hall push out beyond the primary edge of the building (see plan, Figure 5.80). This gives these rooms more building skin, meaning more opportunity for clerestory windows and skylights as inlets/outlets for natural ventilation. The main part of the building rises to four stories while the auditorium/lecture hall is only two stories tall. The lecture hall is toplit with louvered skylights. A four-story atrium organizes the building spatially and provides a means for stack ventilation (Figure 5.81). Concrete floors provide enough thermal mass for night ventilation to be a viable cooling strategy.

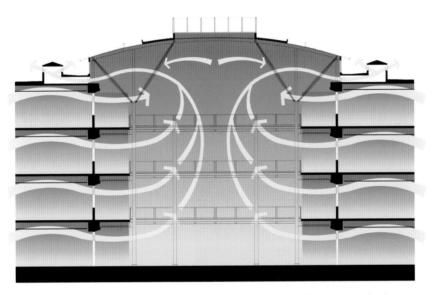

5.81 Natural ventilation strategy. Air enters through inlets in the classrooms and exits through outlets at the sides of the atrium. SRG PARTNERSHIP

Solar control and daylighting. As the design progressed from schematic to design development, the designers worked to weave the various strategies together into complementary building systems, always with the goal of reducing internal loads while providing a pleasing and functional environment for the occupants. The solar control and daylighting systems are closely related in Lillis. When the building is in cooling mode, computers automatically close shades or skylight louvers in unoccupied rooms to minimize solar gains. When people enter a room and turn on the light switch, the computer opens the shades/louvers as far as necessary to reach a targeted illuminance for the activity at hand. Instructors can choose lecture versus video projector light settings, etc. If the shades are completely open and more light is needed, the computer will turn on dimmable electric lamps and increase luminaire output until the targeted illuminance is met. Using daylight not only makes people happy and more productive, it is a "free" source of light and produces less heat for a given illuminance than electric lighting.

Light shelves. Light shelves on the south-facing windows are another feature with a beneficial impact on solar gains as well as daylighting. External overhangs shade the windows, especially from the high summer sun, and effectively reduce cooling loads. In addition, they reflect light deeper into the interior of the building allowing for better daylight distribution. Internal light shelves reduce daylight illuminance immediately adjacent to the windows, while increasing illuminance deeper in the space. This provides a more even distribution of daylight in the room and also helps to reduce glare (see Figures 5.82, 5.83, and 5.84).

South-facing offices have exterior and interior light shelves just like the classrooms. The daylight window, however, always remains unshaded. The shallow depth of the offices and the light shelf prevent direct radiation from the daylight window from striking any work surfaces in the office. The view window can be shaded when necessary. North-facing offices have no light shelves because they rarely see direct sun. Light interior finishes allow for a higher reflectance to enhance daylight distribution. Efficient electric lighting systems, controlled by daylight and occupancy sensors, allow for minimal electricity use, thereby saving resources.

5.82 External shading on south-facing classrooms.

5.83 Light shelves made of metal screen bounce light up to the ceiling plane in the classrooms. SRG PARTNERSHIP

5.84 Light shelves in a south-facing Lillis classroom. EMILY J. WRIGHT

Integrated cooling systems. Outside air is used to cool the building and the occupants as much as possible before relying on mechanically-cooled air. A mixed-mode cooling system, as well as night ventilation of mass, provides for a high-efficiency cooling approach.

Hybrid ventilation. Classrooms have raised concrete floors, arranged into risers for seating areas. Air is drawn in from the outdoors, passes under the floor slab and enters the room through outlets in the risers. If the outdoor air is too warm to effectively cool a space, it can be mixed in a plenum with mechanically-conditioned air. The air from the classroom is drawn through a grille in the ceiling into ducts that exhaust the air into the atrium. In the atrium, the air rises to the top and exits through gravity ventilators. The process is assisted, when necessitated by loads, by the smoke evacuation system (using a variable speed drive and fans) at the top of the atrium.

The auditorium and lecture hall utilize natural ventilation through the stack effect whenever possible. These rooms have low air inlets and their own stack with an outlet near the roof of the fourth floor (as shown in Figure 5.81). An HVAC system—separate from the one used in the rest of the building—kicks in to provide extra heating or cooling when necessary.

5.85 Light finishes provide high reflectances to enhance daylighting. EMILY J. WRIGHT

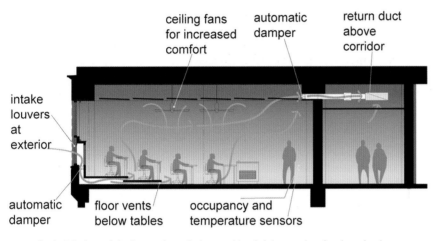

5.86 Cool nighttime air is drawn through the outside air inlets and under the raised concrete floors, cooling the slabs at night so they can absorb heat during the day. SRG PARTNERSHIP

The concrete floors and Eugene's cool nighttime temperatures make night ventilation of mass a viable strategy. Nighttime ventilation of mass works best in climates with large diurnal temperature swings. In Eugene, summertime temperatures often range from 90 °F [32 °C] by day to 45 °F [7°C] at night. The raised concrete floor and outside air inlets in the classrooms permit air to be drawn in at night (when it is coolest), precooling the slab. This slab will absorb heat during the day as the outside temperature rises and the sun and occupants add heat to the space. The cooling and warming patterns of the thermal mass were evaluated through simulation studies.

The offices on the north side of the building see very little direct solar radiation during the warm summer months. As a result, these offices can be cooled entirely through natural ventilation. Windows are operable, so when the outdoor air temperature is cool enough the windows can be opened to cool an office. The offices also have louvers underneath the windows. These louvers can be opened to introduce a limited flow of outdoor air while the windows remain shut. Ventilation air is exhausted through the top of the office into ducts and then exhausted through the atrium (Figure 5.87).

5.87 The Lillis atrium serves as an entry, circulation, and social space. Balconies along a circular stair provide study areas where students gather. The atrium also exhausts air from the classroom wings via stack ventilation. LARA SWIMMER PHOTOGRAPHY

In addition to immediate space cooling through natural ventilation, occupants in the north-facing offices can initiate night ventilation by setting a timer that leaves their louvers open for several hours during the night. While the building is in "night flush" mode, fans draw air through these louvers and into the office, cooling the concrete floor and ceiling. This precooled concrete will then absorb heat during the day, helping to keep the occupants cool.

Photovoltaics. The south-facing glass curtain wall with integrated polycrystalline photovoltaics comprises a 5.9 kW array. There are translucent PV panels in the skylights, which are equivalent to a 2.7 kW array. Roof panels on the mechanical room produce 6.2 kW, and other roof sub-arrays provide 29.9 kW—for a grand projected total of 45 kW of PV power. See Figures 5.88, 5.89 and 5.90. By agreeing to purchase the electricity thus produced at $0.25 per kWh for the next ten years, the local utility played a key role in providing financial incentives for this signature renewable energy feature.

How Is It Working?

As of this writing, the building has been occupied for two years. Post-occupancy studies are ongoing, and preliminary results have yielded some interesting findings.

The University of Oregon Planning Office continues to fine-tune the building systems through user surveys and close communication with facility managers. In a recent survey, users indicated that they did not fully understand the building controls and wanted more posted instructions—underscoring the importance of education and communication with building users, particularly in buildings with complex systems. Other post-occupancy studies have found substantial thermal variation within offices when ceiling fans were not used, and thermostats that were located some distance from where building occupants were likely to sit. In addition, one study points to evidence that the stack effect through the atrium does not always work as intended, and that, on occasion, air-flow from the atrium is reversed back into the hallways instead of being directed through the top of the atrium. Overall, however, the ventilation system is functioning well. The facility manager said, "Everyone expected the glazed 65 ft [20 m] atrium to have oven-like temperatures and it is comfortable!"

An extensive study of the lighting system found that the system provided the targeted illuminances for the tasks. One investigation examined whether faculty were overriding the automated lighting presets, and found that this rarely, if ever, occurred. Most faculty use the preset lighting levels as designed.

A user survey found people generally happy with the building, perceiving conditions to be somewhat "bright" on the south side (this may or may not have negative connotations) and perceiving the north first floor classrooms to be cold, even though dry bulb temperatures are usually around 70 °F [21 °C].

5.88 South-facing glass curtain wall has a 5.9 kW photovoltaic array. The PV cells are spaced farther apart at lower levels for better views and daylighting and closer together higher on the wall to produce more energy.

5.89 Glazing panel with embedded polycrystalline PV cells and interconnecting conductor strips.

5.90 Photovoltaic panels on the roof, comprising one of several Lillis PV arrays.

Further Information

Bohm, M., W. Henderson and A. Swain. 2005. "It's Hot Up Here! A Study of Thermal Comfort in the Lillis Business Complex 4th Floor Office." darkwing.uoregon.edu/%7Eakwok/VSCS/lillis/index.htm

Brown, G.Z. et al. 2004. "A Lesson in Green." *Solar Today*, March/April.

Brown, G.Z. et al. 2004. *Natural Ventilation in Northwest Buildings.* Energy Studies in Building Laboratory, University of Oregon, Eugene, OR.

Chapin, S. and J. Chen. 2005. "Illuminating Lillis: Light Levels and Patterns of Use of the Daylighting Integrated Lighting Systems in the Lillis Business Complex." darkwing.uoregon.edu/%7Eakwok/VSCS/lillis/index.htm

Docker, F. 2005. "Lillis Business Complex: The Question of Perception." darkwing.uoregon.edu/%7Eakwok/VSCS/lillis/index.htm

McKelvey, A. 2005. "Lecture Hall Comfort at the Lillis Business School." darkwing.uoregon.edu/%7Eakwok/VSCS/lillis/index.htm

University of Oregon Planning Office. 2004. "Post-Occupancy Evaluation of Lillis Business Complex." University of Oregon, Eugene, OR.

Background and Context

The National Association of Realtors (NAR) Headquarters is the first green office building in downtown Washington, DC to be built from the ground up (not as a retrofit or remodel). Sited in a very prominent location near the U.S. Capitol, the 12-story, 133,000 ft² [12,356 m²] building has a substantial presence in the heart of the nation's capital. The NAR Headquarters has received a Silver ranking in the U.S. Green Building Council's LEED-NC Version 2 certification program.

The intention of the design team was to develop a building that, in the words of NAR spokesperson Lucien Salvant, represented "our lobbying power, our prestige and our financial success." At the same time: "We wanted to make a statement that Realtors do care about the environment." This is an interesting juxtaposition of intents that bodes well for the future of green buildings. The National Association of Realtors invested an additional $2 million (about 5% of construction costs) to go green—and hopes that the investment will pay back in lowered utility bills and improved ease of leasing space to other tenants. A representative of another DC-based organization opined that the NAR Headquarters is "a very glitzy building." Green and glitzy may make for a viable mix in the urban context.

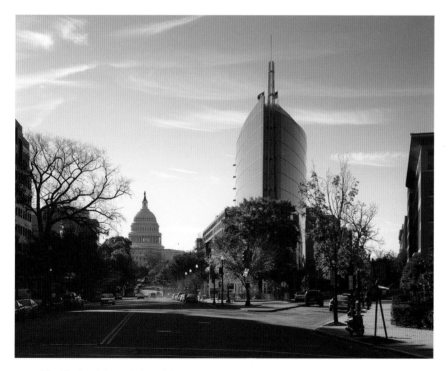

5.92 The National Association of Realtors headquarters building, Washington, DC.
© ALAN KARCHMER

The NAR Headquarters building is located on a triangular site that evolved from L'Enfant's planning for the capital—with many streets intersecting at odd angles as parallel streets meet radial streets. The site was last occupied by a defunct service station and a small disheveled

NATIONAL ASSOCIATION OF REALTORS HEADQUARTERS

5.91 Early conceptual gesture sketch. GUND PARTNERSHIP

LOCATION
Washington, DC, USA
Latitude 38.54 °N
Longitude 77.2 °W

HEATING DEGREE DAYS
3999 65 °F base
[2222 18 °C base]

COOLING DEGREE DAYS
1560 65 °F base
[867 18 °C base]

SOLAR RADIATION
Jul 1990 Btu/ft²/day
[6.28 kWh/m²/day]
Jan 670 Btu/ft²/day
[2.11 kWh/m²/day]
Sterling, VA data

ANNUAL PRECIPITATION
35 in. [884 mm]

BUILDING TYPE
Offices, commercial

AREA
133,000 ft² [12,356 m²]

CLIENT
National Association of Realtors

DESIGN TEAM
Design Architect, Gund Partnership; Architect of Record, SMB Architects; Consulting Engineers, E.K. Fox & Associates; Structural Engineer, Fernandez & Associates; Project Management, CarrAmerica

COMPLETION
October 2004

park. Brownfield site mitigation played an important role in project development and LEED certification. Nine of the project's 33 LEED points (roughly 25%) relate to Sustainable Sites; these strategies include: Site Selection, Urban Redevelopment, Brownfield Redevelopment (involving excavation and disposal of contaminated soil), three elements of Alternative Transportation, roof and non-roof Heat Island Reductions, and Light Pollution Reduction.

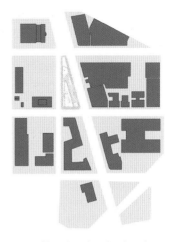

5.93 Site plan showing location of the NAR headquarters on a triangular site near the U.S. Capitol. GUND PARTNERSHIP

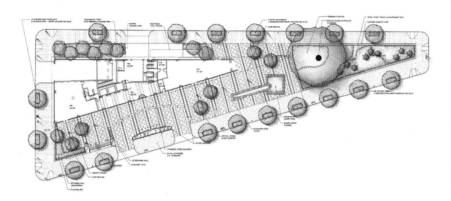

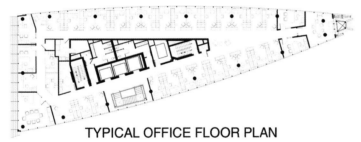

TYPICAL OFFICE FLOOR PLAN

5.94 Ground floor and typical office floor plan show maximization of figure-ground relationship on a triangular site. A portion of the site is given to native and adaptive plants that have low water needs. GUND PARTNERSHIP

Design Intent and Validation

The NAR Headquarters building has received numerous awards, including: a Bronze Award from *Building Design and Construction* magazine; a *Washington Business Journal* Best Architecture Award; an American Architecture Award from the Chicago Athenaeum: Museum of Architecture & Design; and a Sustainable Design Award from the Boston Society of Architects/NYC American Institute of Architects Chapter.

The client and design team intent to produce a green project was validated by the building's LEED Silver certification. Because of the LEED certification process, a detailed sense of "green" design intent can be inferred from the strategies adopted for the project.

Strategies

Site. The site-related design strategies were discussed above. These were of great importance to the project as a whole. Although a brownfield site, the NAR project also occupies a highly-visible site with location, location, location. Synergies among design intents are possible and delightful.

Water efficiency. Water-efficient landscaping, coupled with water-use reduction, were the strategies adopted to address this area of concern. Native and adaptive plant species were selected for landscaping to reduce the need for irrigation. In addition, a 8500 gal [32,175 L] cistern stores collected rainwater for landscape irrigation. Waterless urinals and low-flow faucets with motion activation are projected to reduce potable water consumption by 30% compared to a just-meets-code design.

5.95 The north end of the building expressed by a steel frame tower. © ALAN KARCHMER

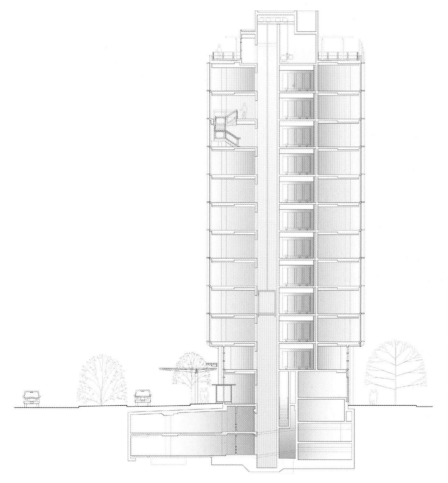

5.96 Building section showing 12 stories above ground with below-ground areas for mechanical equipment, parking, and a cistern to store rainwater. GUND PARTNERSHIP

Energy and atmosphere. The strategies (above and beyond the LEED prerequisites) enacted in this area of design include: increasing Energy Efficiency (to 30% greater than code minimum) and utilization of Green Power. The energy efficiency improvements were obtained through design of a high-performance, low-ε glass curtain wall and selection of efficient HVAC systems. Green power involves the purchase of at least 50% of the building's electricity from sources employing renewable energy resources—in this case from a Green-e (a renewable electricity certification program) wind energy supplier.

Indoor environmental quality. LEED strategies to improve occupant experiences in the building include: Low-Emitting Paints, Low-Emitting Carpets, Indoor Chemical & Pollutant Source Control, Thermal Comfort, and Daylight & Views. Materials selection addressed low-VOC paints, carpets, sealants, and adhesives. A CO_2 monitoring system is used to ensure appropriate indoor air quality.

Thermal comfort conditions meet the requirements of ASHRAE Standard 55—which surprisingly is not a code requirement for buildings in general. The electric lighting load is less than $1 \, W/ft^2$ [$10.8 \, W/m^2$] as a result of aggressive daylighting. Electric lighting is controlled by photocell dimming and occupancy sensors. Ninety percent of all building spaces are daylit.

5.97 Shaded outdoor spaces provide break areas for occupants and a respite above the city. The trellis shades 30% of the roof area; container gardens and the white-colored roof reduce the urban heat island effect. ROBERT C. LAUTMAN

Materials and resources. Recycled Content and Local/Regional Materials strategies were employed. Structural and finish materials with a high recycled content were selected. At least 20% of materials were locally manufactured; of these materials, 50% were locally harvested.

5.98 Expansive views from a conference room which has carpet tiles with recycled content and low VOC. Ceilings are of mineral fiber acoustical tiles with more than 65% recycled material. © ALAN KARCHMER

Beyond design. Several strategies that reach beyond the design stage were also implemented. A public education program is intended to educate visitors (and occupants) about the building's "green" aspects. Two ongoing management plans were developed: one that addresses housekeeping practices (non-toxic chemicals, recycled-content supplies) and another that addresses tenant improvements (via guidelines to maintain the green character of the building).

5.99 Conference room tables and paneling use a fast-growing eucalyptus veneer. © ALAN KARCHMER

5.100 Daylit entrance and elevator lobby. © ALAN KARCHMER

5.101 Reception seating area takes advantage of daylight and views via a double-glazed, high-performance curtain wall. © ALAN KARCHMER

5.102 The narrow plan of the building allows daylight penetration to open stairways (left) and corridors (right). © ALAN KARCHMER

How Is It Working?

No post-occupancy studies have been performed to evaluate building performance in place and over time. Validation of design intent and execution has come from external organizations in the form of design awards and a LEED Silver certification.

Further Information

Birnbaum, J. 2004. "Realtors Wield the Power of Intimidating Views." *washingtonpost.com*, October 4; p. E01.

5.103 A 100-year-old tree at the northern end of the site is habitat for many nesting birds. The area was expanded and restored with native plants tolerant of drought, cold, heat, and urban conditions.
ROBERT C. LAUTMAN

The Gund Partnership. www.gundpartnership.com/

Hedgpeth, D. 2004. "Hoping Benefits Bloom by Going Green," *The Washington Post*, May 17. Available through U.S. Green Building Council. www.usgbc.org/(select News, then USGBC in the News)

National Association of Realtors, "500 New Jersey Avenue, NW Grand Preview Brochure." www.realtor.org/VLibrary.nsf/files/500NJBrochure.pdf/

National Association of Realtors, "The Construction of NAR's New Washington Building." www.realtor.org/vlibrary.nsf/pages/newdc/

U.S. Green Building Council, LEED Project List: www.usgbc.org/(select LEED, then Project List, then search for project)

NOTES

Background and Context

The development of the project at One Peking Road followed a new approach for Hong Kong—placing a green, landmark commercial building in the middle of one of the most highly sought-after real estate sites in the area. With a location inland from the waterfront, along Peking Road in Tsim Sha Tsui on Kowloon Peninsula, it is conveniently located within walking distance of famous hotels and shopping streets, and is linked with public transportation (Figure 5.105). The location of the building, situated behind the two-story former Marine Police Headquarters building, allows the primary facade of the building an unobstructed south-facing orientation. The design is a strong contrast between old and new and sets a model of green design for high-rise construction.

The intention of the design team was to provide users and tenants of the building with a direct relationship to the surroundings through a transparent curtain wall that uses a triple-glazed, low-ε, high-visibility transmission glazing system with a ventilated cavity. Another design intention was to integrate, visually and spatially, the former Marine Police Headquarters on the adjacent site. Although the One Peking Road building towers over its two-story neighbor, homage is given by a 24-ft [7.3 m] high glazed lobby wall—with views to the historic facade of the headquarters and providing a possible extension to the city's public space.

5.105 The One Peking Road office building amidst low-rise buildings in the prime tourist area of the Kowloon Peninsula. ROCCO DESIGN LTD.

The sail-like, curved building profile allows for a larger floor plate for offices in the mid-level zone and narrower floor plates for two restaurants on the uppermost floors. The array of photovoltaic panels at the top of the building gives subtle reference to the numerous boats in Hong Kong harbor and the curvilinear roof of the Cultural Center nearby. One Peking Road utilizes numerous green strategies to conserve resources and energy: an "active facade" (the glass curtain wall), daylighting, water-saving devices, heat recovery systems, and the recycling of materials during the construction process.

5.104 One Peking Road tower.

LOCATION
Hong Kong, China
Latitude 22.18 °N
Longitude 114.10 °E

HEATING DEGREE DAYS
425 65 °F base
[236 18 °C base]

COOLING DEGREE DAYS
8284 50 °F base
[4602 10 °C base]

SOLAR RADIATION
Feb 964 Btu/ft^2/day
[3.04 kWh/m^2/day]
Jul 1677 Btu/ft^2/day
[5.29 kWh/m^2/day]

ANNUAL PRECIPITATION
88 in. [2225 mm]

BUILDING TYPE
Offices, commercial

AREA
284,200 ft^2 [26,400 m^2]

CLIENT
Glory Star Investments Ltd

DESIGN TEAM
Architect, Rocco Design Ltd;
Project Manager, DTZ Debenham
Tie Leung Project Services Ltd;
Project Architect and Structural
Engineer, WMKY Architects and
Engineers Ltd; Electrical and
Mechanical Engineer, J. Roger
Preston Ltd; Contractor, Gammon
Skanska Construction Co. Ltd;

OFFICE

N

0 3 6 9 12m

5.107 Typical floor plan shows elongated east-west form to maximize solar access to the south facade and provide for views to the Hong Kong harbor. ROCCO DESIGN LTD.

Curtain Wall Contractor, Permasteelisa Hong Kong Ltd.

COMPLETION
April 2003

5.106 Site plan showing building location on the corner of the block with the 2-story former Marine Police Headquarters in foreground. ROCCO DESIGN LTD.

Design Intent and Validation

The client and designer began with the intent to create a high-rise building that favorably integrates with the eclectic combination of surrounding buildings. The team took an approach that considered the integrated design of energy-efficient building systems that could provide occupants with thermal comfort and also maximize views of the harbor.

In 2004, the building design received the Hong Kong Institute of Architects (HKIA) highest Medal of the Year for its architectural expression and the integration of shading and envelope technologies; a Quality Building Award for the collaboration of the project team; and the Joint Structural Division Award by the Hong Kong Institute of Engineers (HKIE) for structural innovation.

Strategies

Building form and orientation. Positioned on a small and narrow site measuring 90 ft by 263 ft [27.5 by 80 m], the longer facade of the building faces south which fortuitously provides a view to the harbor. Such orientation provides clear solar access (for photovoltaics) and simplifies solar control (for shading devices and the glazing system). The curvilinear form of the southern facade breaks from traditional rectilinear building forms by tapering the building and consequently shortening the floor plates on the upper floors. Retail establishments and pedestrian connections to public transportation are situated on the ground floor; 19 floors of multi-tenant office space comprise the mid-level zone, and three levels in the upper zone offer a narrow floor plate, yielding daylight penetration (and views) from all sides for the restaurants. The sky court at the top of the building houses the photovoltaic array.

A triple-glazed, active wall system combines three layers of clear glass and a ventilated cavity which channels return room air to a heat exchanger. Between the glazing panels on the east and west facades, perforated motorized blinds operate automatically using energy produced by the photovoltaics. Deflected heat from impinging solar radiation is dissipated into the ventilated cavity.

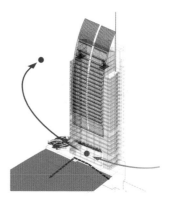

5.108 Diagram of facade designed to work with the path of the sun to enhance the performance of shading devices and photovoltaic panels.
ROCCO DESIGN LTD.

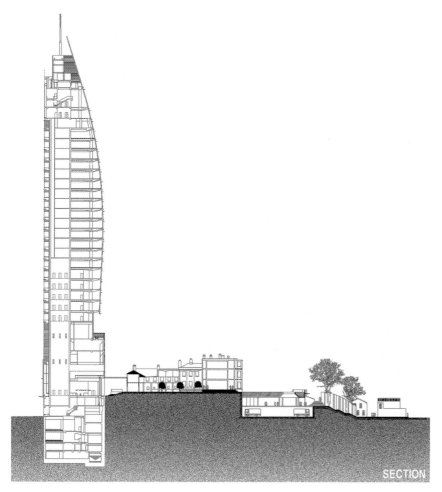

5.109 Site section shows a thin building allowing for daylight penetration from both the north and south facades. ROCCO DESIGN LTD.

Heat recovery system. An air-to-air heat exchanger recovers heat (coolth) from the exhaust air from the office areas. Heat wheels are linked with the fresh air intake to absorb the residual cooling load of the packaged air-conditioning units providing the make-up air supply.

Recycling of materials during construction. Steel formwork systems were reused from other projects, rather than wood forms, to reduce waste timber and reduce construction costs (as they are then used for other projects). During construction, building contractors segregated inert (e.g. metal and timber) waste materials for recycling and non-inert materials for landfill disposal.

Water conservation. Toilets, urinals, and lavatories on the office and restaurant floors use motion sensors for water conservation.

Shading and daylighting. East, west and south building facades call for a different approach to solar control. The high summer sun is partially blocked by horizontal aluminum shading devices on the south facade (Figures 5.110 and 5.111).

5.110 A ventilated cavity with modest aluminum shading devices and triple glazing with a low-ε coating allows cool air exhausted from the building interior to pass upwards through the space between the glass panes. ROCCO DESIGN LTD.

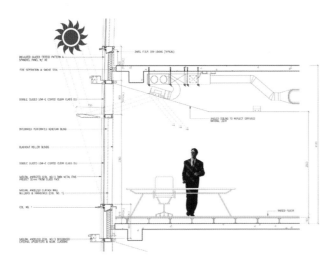

5.111 Shading on the south facade prevents direct solar radiation from high altitude sun from penetrating the building envelope during critical times of the day. ROCCO DESIGN LTD.

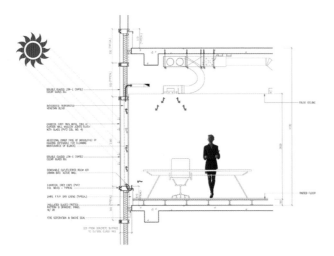

5.112 East and west facades use a perforated Venetian blind within the glazing cavity to provide needed shading. ROCCO DESIGN LTD.

The shading device also serves as an external light shelf by reflecting light onto the ceiling near the window. The standard ceiling height is 9 ft [2.8 m] and the ceiling in office areas near the window angles up toward the window to maximize daylight in the work zone. The low altitude of the sun on the east and west facades during the early morning and late afternoon demands almost 100% blockage. In response, motorized blinds are installed within the triple-glazing system on the east and west facades and are controlled by light sensors (Figure 5.112).

Building integrated photovoltaics. Positioned at a tilt of approximately 67°, 144 modules of polycrystalline silicone photovoltaic cells cover approximately 2150 ft^2 [200 m^2], making use of the renewable solar energy resource to produce an average 10,344 kWh/year of electricity (Figures 5.113 and 5.114). The currently installed PV array represents coverage of approximately 25% of the total area that could potentially be used for PV installations.

5.113 Interior catwalks at the photovoltaic glazing provide access to the panels. ROCCO DESIGN LTD.

5.114 Building integrated photovoltaic cells laminated within the glazing are framed by a steel truss on the roof of the building. ROCCO DESIGN LTD.

How Is It Working?

To date no post-occupancy evaluation studies have been performed. Several full-scale performance tests and simulations for various strategies, such as lateral wind tests, were performed on the curtain wall during design development.

Further Information

Business Environment Council, Environmental and Sustainability Case Studies Initiative, Hong Kong-Beam Society, "Case Studies: 1 Peking

Commercial Building." www.hk-beam.org.hk/fileLibrary/
One%20Peking_GCPL_C1071.pdf

Hui, S.C.M., Hong Kong University, Case Studies on Sustainable
Design. www.hku.hk/mech/sbe/case_study/case/hk/pek/top.htm

Youngs, T. 2003. "One Peking, Tsim Tsia Tsui Landmark Contrasts,"
Building Journal Hong Kong China, May.
www.building.com.hk/feature/10_03peking.pdf

Youngs, T. 2004. "HKIA Annual Awards 2003," *Building Journal Hong
Kong China*, March/April. www.building.com.hk/feature/2004_
06hkia2003.pdf

absorption refrigeration system—a chemical cooling device that transfers heat from an evaporator to a condenser by means of the cyclical condensation and vaporization of a water-salt solution; driven by heat input.

active facade—a facade that responds to changing weather conditions by modifying its performance (by varying apertures, shading, etc.).

airflow rate—a measure of the quantity of air that passes through a defined area (window, duct) in a unit of time; expressed in cfm (cubic feet per minute) [L/s (liters per second)].

alternating current (AC)—the flow of electricity from high potential to low potential in a stream that varies sinusoidally in amplitude and direction over time; grid or mains electricity is AC.

altitude angle—a solar angle that indicates the height of the sun in the sky.

ambient—referring to conditions in the immediate surroundings; sometimes used to describe naturally-occurring (or unaltered) conditions; in lighting, usually referring to general or area-wide conditions.

amorphous PV—a photovoltaic module manufactured using a thin film of silicon; amorphous modules do not have the circular structure characteristic of mono-crystalline PV modules.

anidolic zenithal collector—a toplighting device that collects daylight from a view of the north sky and delivers the daylight into a space via a diffusing element; the daylight is reflected and redirected as it passes through the device.

anode side—the negatively charged side of a fuel cell.

array—an assemblage of photovoltaic modules; PV manufacturers sell modules that are assembled on site into larger capacity units called arrays.

ASHRAE—American Society of Heating, Refrigerating and Air-Conditioning Engineers.

azimuth angle—a solar angle that indicates the position of the sun relative to a reference orientation (typically solar south).

balance of system—describes the components of a photovoltaic system beyond the PV modules themselves (this usually includes batteries, inverters, controllers).

base load—a "typical" average electrical load for a building or generating system.

berm—an earthen construction rising above the surrounding ground plane; typically built to block views; channel wind, water, or circulation; or partially earth shelter a building.

bilateral (daylighting)—a daylighting system that introduces light into a space from two (generally opposite) directions.

biodegradable—a material (organic) that will degrade under the action of microorganisms; generally describes a material that will decompose in nature in a reasonable time period.

biodiversity—the existence of a large number and variety of species in a given geographic area; often used as an indicator of ecological health.

biofuel—a fuel derived from unfossilized plant material (such as wood, garbage, rapeseed, manure, soybeans).

biomass—unfossilized biological matter (wood, straw, dung) that can be processed (burned, decomposed) to produce energy (typically heat).

bioregional development—development consistent with the constraints of a bioregion (a geographical area with common ecological processes and systems).

bioremediation—a process that uses microorganisms to break down environmental pollution.

boiler—active mechanical equipment that heats water (or steam) for space heating or domestic hot water.

brownfield—an unused/underused former industrial or commercial site that is environmentally contaminated, with the contamination limiting its potential reuse.

building integrated photovoltaics (BIPV)—photovoltaics modules that are integrated into a building enclosure element (such as a roof shingle, glazing unit, spandrel panel).

Building Use Survey—a formal means of obtaining information regarding building performance from occupants (see www.usable-buildings.co.uk/).

cathode side—the positively charged side of a fuel cell.

cell—a unit of a photovoltaic collector panel; PV cells are assembled into modules by the manufacturer, modules are then assembled into arrays by the design team.

CFD—computational fluid dynamics; refers to numerical simulation of the motion of a fluid (typically air) in a space; typically used to predict the performance of natural ventilation and active air distribution systems.

charge controller—a device that regulates the flow of electric voltage and current.

chiller—active mechanical equipment that cools water for space cooling.

cistern—a storage container for rainwater.

clarifier—a settling tank that separates residual solids from treated wastewater.

CO_2 emissions—the release of carbon dioxide into the atmosphere; identified as a principal cause of global warming and a focus of many green design efforts.

coefficient of performance (COP)—a dimensionless number used to express the efficiency of chillers (and heat pumps); COP is the ratio of the cooling output to the energy input (in consistent units).

coefficient of utilization (CU)—a measure of the ability of a lighting fixture and space to deliver light from a lamp to a task plane; the delivery efficiency of a fixture/space combination; expressed as a decimal value.

cogeneration—an electrical generation process that produces useful (versus waste) heat as a by-product; the process of co-producing electricity and heat on site.

coincident loads—loads that occur at the same time; used to describe thermal loads that contribute to system capacity requirements; used to describe thermal and electrical load patterns (for cogeneration systems).

color rendering index (CRI)—a measure of the ability of a given light source to accurately present object color; expressed as a whole number value.

commissioning—a process that ensures that the owner's project requirements have been met; this involves design validation, testing of equipment and systems, and training and documentation.

compact fluorescent—a small fluorescent lamp, marketed primarily as a replacement for less efficient incandescent lamps.

conduction—the transfer of heat through direct molecular contact within or between solid objects.

contrast—a measure of the difference in luminance (brightness) between two objects within the field of view; contrast enables vision, but too much contrast can cause glare.

convection—the transfer of heat through the action of a fluid (typically air in building design situations); natural convection occurs without mechanical assist while forced convection involves mechanical assist.

cooling capacity—a measure of the cooling load that can be met by a given system; expressed in Btu/h [Watts].

cooling degree day (CDD)—a measure of the summer severity of a climate (or current weather); the CDDs for a day equal the average daily temperature minus a reference temperature (often 65 °F [18 °C]) that represents the balance point temperature of a building.

coolth—a term used to describe a beneficial flow of heat during the cooling season, as in "the roof pond provides a source of coolth during the morning hours."

daily heat gain—the amount of heat from various sources gained during the course of a 24-hour period.

daylight factor (DF)—the ratio of daylight illuminance at a given point within a building to the horizontal illuminance at an exterior reference point; daylight factor represents the efficiency of a daylighting system in delivering daylight to a specified location; expressed as a decimal or percentage.

Decibel—a dimensionless unit used to express sound pressure level or sound power level.

deconstruction—the philosophy and practice of designing a building to facilitate ease of disassembly to encourage reuse of components.

deforestation—the large-scale and long-term removal of trees from a region, typically due to over-cutting for fuel or building materials.

desiccant—a material with a high affinity for water vapor; used as a dehumidifying compound; used as a coating on an energy (enthalpy) wheel.

design cooling load—a statistically significant cooling load (heat gain) that serves as the basis for system design and equipment sizing; expressed in Btu/h [Watts].

design development—a phase in the design process where design decisions are finalized; equipment and materials are selected, detailed and specified; and construction documents are begun or prepared; design development follows schematic design.

diffuse reflection—a reflection from a matte (non-specular) surface, in which light (or solar radiation) leaves a surface in generally random directions not directly related to the angle of incidence; no clear image can be seen via diffuse reflection.

direct current (DC)—the flow of electricity from high potential to low potential in a continuous, unidirectional stream; electricity from a battery or directly from a PV module is DC.

diurnal—referring to a 24-hour (daily) cycle.

diurnal temperature range—the daily range of temperature; the daily maximum temperature minus the daily minimum temperature; expressed in degrees F [C].

dry-bulb temperature—a temperature measurement taken using a dry-bulb thermometer; an indicator of sensible heat density; expressed in degrees F [C].

earthship—a building design approach that relies upon passive heating/cooling and renewable energy, rainwater harvesting, on-site sewage treatment, food production, and the use of societal by-products as building materials.

ecological footprint—a measure of the land area required to sustain an individual, community, or country; typically expressed in acres [ha] per capita.

electrochemical—a chemical process that results in an electrical charge.

embodied energy—the energy required to produce a product (from extraction of raw materials, through manufacturing, and including transportation to the point of use); expressed as Btu/lb [kJ/kg].

energy recovery ventilator (ERV)—a device (usually self-contained) that transfers heat and moisture between incoming and outgoing air streams as part of a building ventilation system.

Energy Star—a certification system for energy-efficient appliances.

enthalpy—a measure of the total (sensible and latent) energy content of air; expressed as Btu/lb [kJ/kg].

enthalpy wheel—a type of rotary heat exchanger that transfers both heat and moisture.

equinox—when day and night are of equal length (approximately March 21 and September 21).

evaporation—the process of changing from the liquid to the vapor phase (or state); evaporation can be an effective cooling process because of the amount of heat required to break molecular bonds to effect this change.

extensive green roof—a vegetated roof with fairly short plantings and a limited depth of soil.

external daylight illuminance—the daylight illuminance at a reference point outside of a building.

extruded expanded polystyrene (XEPS)—a form of thermal insulation manufactured by extruding expanded polystyrene; XEPS has a higher R-value and higher compressive strength than MEPS.

first cost—the cost to acquire a facility, not including operating, maintenance, and repair costs.

flow—the volume of fluid that passes a given point per unit of time; a factor in determining the potential power generation of a wind or hydro system; airflow is a key factor in the design of natural ventilation and most HVAC systems.

fluorescent—a low-pressure gaseous discharge electric lamp that operates on the basis of electron flow through an arc tube.

footcandles—I-P unit of illuminance; lumens per square foot.

Forest Stewardship Council (FSC)—an international non-profit organization that promotes sustainable forestry and timber use practices.

glare—a negative visual sensation caused by excessive brightness or contrast; glare may be classified as direct or reflected and as discomforting, disabling, or blinding.

green—a building, project, or philosophy based upon reducing environmental impacts related to energy, water, and materials use; green buildings respect building occupants as well as those indirectly affected by building construction/operation.

green travel plan—a management policy to encourage environmentally-friendly travel for employees.

grid-connected—an on-site power generation system that is linked to the local utility system.

ground source heat pump—a heat pump that transfers heat to/from the below-ground environment rather than to/from the ambient air; more energy-efficient than a conventional heat pump.

halogen—a relatively small, long-life incandescent lamp; the terms quartz-halogen or tungsten-halogen are also used.

head—the vertical height (depth) of water that exerts pressure on a turbine; a factor in determining the potential power generation of a hydro system.

heat exchanger—a device that transfers heat from one medium (air, water, steam) to another without mixing of the media.

heat gain—a flow of heat that will increase the temperature of a building or space; heat gains include radiant, convective, and conductive heat flows through the building envelope and the flow of heat from lights, people, and equipment within a building; cooling load is heat gain that directly affects air temperature (excluding stored radiation gains).

heat loss—a flow of heat that will decrease the temperature of a building or space; heat losses include radiant, convective, and conductive heat flows through the building envelope and/or heat flows due to evaporation.

heat pipe heat exchanger—a heat exchanger that employs refrigerant-filled tubes to exchange heat between two media through the cyclic vaporization and condensation of the refrigerant in the tubes.

heat pump—a mechanical-electrical heating/cooling device that transfers heat from a condenser to an evaporator by means of the cyclical condensation and vaporization of a refrigerant circulated by a compressor.

heat recovery system—a system that captures "waste" heat (which would otherwise be rejected) as a means of increasing building energy efficiency.

heat recovery ventilator (HRV)—a device (usually self-contained) that transfers heat between incoming and outgoing air streams as part of a building ventilation system.

heat sink—a location with a lower temperature that will accept heat flow from a location with a higher temperature; a place to dump heat from a building being cooled.

heating degree day (HDD)—a measure of the winter severity of a climate (or current weather); the HDDs for a day equal a reference temperature (often 65 °F [18 °C]) that represents the balance point temperature of a building minus the average daily temperature.

high pressure sodium—a high-intensity gaseous discharge electric lamp that operates on the basis of electron flow through an arc tube.

horizontal axis wind turbine (HAWT)—a wind machine with the axis of rotation parallel to the ground (as opposed to a vertical axis machine with the axis of rotation perpendicular to the ground).

humus—an organic substance consisting of decayed vegetable or animal matter; the output of a composting toilet; humus can provide nutrients for plants.

HVAC system—heating, ventilating, and air-conditioning; an active climate control system.

hybrid system—an on-site power generation system that includes alternative devices (such as PV, wind, or fuel cells) as well as conventional devices (such as a diesel generator).

hydrocarbon fuel—any fuel that is principally composed of molecules containing hydrogen and carbon; fossil fuels are hydrocarbons.

hydrogen fuel cell—a device that generates electricity via the chemical reaction of hydrogen with oxygen.

hydroponic reactor—an element in a wastewater treatment system in which aquatic plants floating atop liquid in a tank provide aquatic-root-zone treatment of the wastewater.

hypothesis—a formal statement that predicts the behavior of a system; a testable statement.

IESNA—Illuminating Engineering Society of North America.

illuminance—the density of light falling on a given surface; expressed as fc [lux], which are lumens per unit area.

impervious (surface)—a material that prevents the passage or diffusion of a fluid (such as water).

impulse turbine—a type of microhydro turbine that relies on the kinetic energy of water jets to rotate the turbine; the turbine can be open and not fully immersed in water.

indoor air quality—the collective condition of air within a building relative to occupant health and olfactory comfort; acceptable indoor air quality is typically a baseline design intent.

infrared radiation—radiation bordering the visible spectrum (light) but with longer wavelengths; radiation emitted by objects near room temperature.

inlet area—the collective size of opening(s) through which air is admitted for natural ventilation; typically net area (less the effects of mullions, screens, etc.) is of interest; expressed in square feet or square meters.

insolation—the intensity of solar radiation that reaches a given surface (wall, ground, solar collector) at a specific time; typically expressed as W/ft^2 [W/m^2].

intensive green roof—a vegetated roof with some tall plantings and a fairly deep soil cover.

internal daylight illuminance—the illuminance caused solely by daylight at a defined location within a building.

interreflections—light reflected from surface to surface.

inverter—a device that converts direct current (DC) to alternating current (AC); used with on-site power generation systems such as wind or photovoltaics.

isolux—a line connecting points of equal illuminance (or equal daylight factors).

kinetic energy—energy embodied in an object or fluid due to its motion.

lamp—any manufactured source of light.

latent heat—heat that is connected to an increase or decrease in the moisture content of air in a building; heat is absorbed by the evaporation of moisture and released by the condensation of moisture; the heat required to change the phase (state) of a material; the latent heat of vaporization is related to a change from the liquid to the vapor state, the latent heat of condensation is related to the opposite phase change; in buildings, latent heat is typically experienced as an increase or decrease in the moisture content of air.

life-cycle analysis—in building design, an analysis of the energy and environmental implications of a material from "cradle to grave."

life-cycle cost—the cost to obtain, operate, repair, and decommission (or salvage) a building over a defined period of time.

light—radiation that is visible (can be seen by the human eye).

light scoop—an architectural device used to collect and bring light into a building.

light shelf—a device that is installed at the building facade to more evenly introduce daylight into a space to improve daylight distribution; light shelves may be external to the daylight aperture, internal, or both.

low-ε—low emissivity; a coating applied to glass to improve its thermal performance by reducing radiation heat transfer through the glass.

lowest mass temperature—the minimum temperature reached by thermal mass in a passive cooling system; an indicator of the feasibility and capacity of the night ventilation of mass strategy.

lumen maintenance—a measure of the consistency of luminous flux over time; used to describe lamp performance or lighting system output.

luminaire—a lighting fixture.

luminance—the density of light leaving a surface or source; expressed in lumens per square foot or candelas (lumens per steradian) per square meter; the qualitative evaluation of luminance is termed brightness.

luminous efficacy—a measure of the efficiency of a light source; the ratio of light output by the source to energy (electric) input; expressed in lumens per Watt.

luminous flux—a flow of light; expressed in lumens.

lux—SI unit of illuminance; lumens per square meter.

maintenance factor—an adjustment factor that accounts for the loss of illuminance (in electric lighting or daylighting systems) due to the deterioration of reflective surfaces and lamps, and the collection of dirt on glazing; expressed as a decimal value.

mercury vapor—a high-intensity gaseous discharge electric lamp that operates on the basis of electron flow through an arc tube; this lamp has generally been displaced by metal halide lamps.

metal halide—a high-intensity gaseous discharge electric lamp that operates on the basis of electron flow through an arc tube.

microclimate—a localized area of differential climate relative to the larger surrounding macroclimate; examples include the climate under a shade tree (versus in the open), the climate on a south-facing slope (versus a north-facing one), the climate at an airport (versus a downtown location in the same city).

mixed-mode cooling system—a cooling solution that employs both active and passive strategies to achieve comfort (e.g. natural ventilation and an active HVAC system).

module (PV)—a photovoltaic panel; modules are assembled on site into PV arrays.

molded expanded polystyrene (MEPS)—a form of thermal insulation manufactured by molding expanded polystyrene; commonly called beadboard.

natural ventilation—the flow of outdoor air through a building in a passive system, using naturally occurring forces (wind, stratification, pressure differences); natural ventilation can provide cooling and/or improve indoor air quality.

net metering—an arrangement whereby a utility customer with an on-site power generation system is billed based upon a "net" electrical meter reading that represents the difference between site draws from the grid ("purchases") and site input to the grid ("sales").

non-potable water—water that is not fit for human consumption.

optimization—a design process that attempts to determine the most beneficial size of a system or component based upon a balancing of costs and savings.

overcast sky—a design sky (with complete cloud cover, no direct solar radiation, and fully diffuse light distribution) that is used as the basis for much daylighting design; an overcast sky is brighter at the zenith than at the horizon (making a unit of horizontal aperture more effective than a unit of vertical aperture).

parasitic energy—energy "losses" from a system due to components necessary for the system operation (such as pumping energy in a solar thermal system); parasitic energy demands decrease system efficiency.

passive downdraft evaporative cooling (PDEC)—an alternative name for a cool tower.

payback—the time that it takes for a system (investment) to pay for itself through accrued savings (often energy cost savings); both economic and energy payback may be of interest in green design; energy payback is the time it takes for a device or system to save or generate the amount of energy required to produce and install the device or system.

peak load—the maximum electrical load for a building or generating system in a given time period.

peak oil—a term used to describe the occurrence of maximum oil production as a function of resource availability; once peak oil has been reached, production (and oil availability) will necessarily decrease.

penstock—valve or gate that controls the flow of water in a microhydro system; sometimes this term is also used to describe the channel connected with this control device.

permeable medium heat exchanger—a heat exchanger that permits the transfer of moisture as well as heat.

pervious (surface)—a material that readily permits the passage or diffusion of a fluid (such as water).

phantom load—an electrical load that appears to occur without explanation, typically due to background power draw by appliances and equipment that are seemingly not in use (such as power consumed by instant start lamps and televisions).

phosphoric acid fuel cell (PAFC)—a fuel cell that uses phosphoric acid as the electrolyte (which acts as a differential barrier allowing positive charge to pass through, while inhibiting negative charge) thereby creating current.

photosensor—a light-sensitive sensor used to control the operation of an electric lighting system; often used in daylight-integrated electric lighting systems and to control exterior lighting elements.

plate heat exchanger—a heat exchanger that uses flat plates to separate and transfer heat between two media.

post-occupancy evaluation—a formal investigation into some aspect of building performance conducted after a building has been placed into normal use.

potable water—water fit for human consumption.

prevailing wind—the predominant direction from which wind blows; this is often seasonal and sometimes changes diurnally.

profile angle—an angle that relates the position of the sun to the plane of glazing; defined as the angle between a plane perpendicular to the plane of the glass and the rays of the sun traced in a plane parallel to the window plane; profile angle is used in the design of shading devices.

proton exchange fuel cell (PEM)—a fuel cell that uses a plastic polymer as the electrolyte (which acts as a differential barrier allowing positive charge to pass through, while inhibiting negative charge) thereby creating current.

psychrometric process—one of several processes that change the condition of moist air; the psychrometric processes include sensible heating, sensible and latent cooling, evaporative cooling, and dehumidification (among others).

Radiance—software used to model lighting conditions; provides high-end simulation capabilities.

radiation—the transfer of heat between two objects not in contact (but within view of each other) through the action of electromagnetic radiation.

rammed earth—a building construction technique that produces walls by compressing soil (and additives) in forms on site.

reaction turbine—a type of microhydro turbine that relies on the pressure difference between inlet and outlet to rotate the turbine; the turbine must be encased and immersed in water.

reclaimed materials—materials that are being reused, but have not been significantly altered from their physical form in a previous application.

reflectance—the characteristic property of a material (or surface coating) that allows it to redirect incident radiation without changing the nature of the radiation; expressed as a percentage of incident radiation.

relative humidity—a measure of the moisture content of the air; the amount of moisture actually held by the air compared to the maximum amount that could be held at the same temperature; expressed as a percentage.

renewable energy—energy produced by a resource that is rapidly replaceable by a natural process (examples include wood, biofuels, wind, and solar radiation)

room surface dirt depreciation factor—an adjustment factor that accounts for the negative impact of dirt, dust, and aging on room surfaces that results in lowered reflectance over time; expressed as a decimal value.

rotary heat exchanger—a heat exchanger that employs a rotating wheel to transfer heat between two adjacent air streams; heat wheel (sensible only) and enthalpy wheel (sensible and latent exchange) options are available.

runaround coil—connected coils that are used to exchange heat between two air streams located some distance apart through the action of a water loop that connects the coils.

R-value—a measure of thermal resistance; the inverse of the thermal conductance of a material; expressed as ft^2 h °F/Btu [m^2 K/W].

sanitary drainage—building wastewater that contains biological pollutants and must be treated before discharge into the environment.

selective surface—a surface coating applied to solar collectors to increase absorptivity and decrease emissivity, thereby increasing the effectiveness of the absorber surface.

sensible heat—heat that is connected to an increase or decrease in the temperature of air or objects in a building.

shading coefficient (SC)—the ratio of solar radiation (heat) transferred by the transparent portion of a window or skylight to the radiation incident on the window/skylight; expressed as a decimal value; solar heat gain coefficient (SHGC) is replacing SC for many applications.

skin-load-dominated building—a building the climate control needs of which are determined principally by exterior climate conditions acting through the building envelope; also termed "envelope-load dominated."

soil moisture content—a measure of the water content of soil; affects the conductivity of the soil and impacts the performance of earth tubes, earth sheltering, and ground-source heat pumps.

solar chimney—an architectural device that collects solar radiation to enhance the stack effect (typically as part of a natural ventilation system).

solar loads—cooling loads resulting from the impact of solar radiation on a building.

solar transit—a device used to sight and make angular measurements of obstructions to the direct solar radiation on a site.

specific heat—a fundamental thermo-physical property of a material; the amount of heat required to raise the temperature of a unit mass of a material by one degree relative to the amount of heat required to raise the temperature of a similar mass of water by one degree; specific heat (along with material density) is a factor in thermal capacity.

specular reflection—a reflection from a specular (mirror-like) surface, in which light (or solar radiation) leaves a surface at an angle equal to the angle of incidence; specular reflection can produce a viable image of a source or object.

stack effect—a naturally occurring phenomenon wherein hot air rises establishing a vertical circulation of air; employed in some natural ventilation systems.

stand-alone—an on-site power generation system that is not linked to the local utility system; also known as "off-the-grid."

standard incandescent—an electric lamp that operates on the basis of a heated filament that glows; "standard" distinguishes this type lamp from a quartz-halogen incandescent.

stick-framing—a construction method that predominates in the North American single-family housing market, using small-dimension wood members assembled on site into a structural frame.

stormwater—rainwater that is not immediately absorbed on site and must be dealt with through on-site or off-site means.

stratification—the naturally occurring separation of a vertical volume of fluid (for example, an atrium or water storage tank) into temperature zones (hot high, cool low).

Sun Angle Calculator—a proprietary product that presents horizontal projection sun angle charts for a range of latitudes.

sun angle chart—a two-dimensional plot that represents the position of the sun in the sky vault over the course of a year; horizontal and vertical projection charts are readily available; the Sun Angle Calculator is a form of sun angle chart.

sunpeg chart—a type of sun angle chart used with physical model shading studies; a gnomon on the chart projects a shadow corresponding to a selected date and time of day.

sun-tracking photovoltaics—a photovoltaic module mounted on a movable frame that rotates to follow the sun's path, maximizing total insolation and thereby electrical energy production.

superinsulation—the use of extensive insulation in the building envelope (substantially beyond code minimums) such that the building becomes an internal-load-dominated building.

sustainable—a building, project, or philosophy that is based upon allowing this generation to meet its needs without impeding the ability of future generations to meet their needs; in essence a project with no net negative environmental impacts.

swept area—area delineated by the rotation of the propeller of a wind turbine; equal to $(\pi)(r^2)$, where r is the radius of the propeller.

task lighting—lighting for a specific use or area (as opposed to ambient lighting).

temperature—a measure of the density of heat in a substance (not the absolute quantity of heat); heat flow is proportional to temperature difference; expressed in degrees F [C].

temperature stratification—the layering of a fluid, due to differential density, that results in a measurable vertical temperature gradient (e.g. hot air high, cool air low).

thermal capacity—the heat storing capability of a material; the amount of heat stored by a thermal mass.

thermal mass—a material that is selected and/or used based upon its ability to store heat; good thermal mass will have high thermal capacity (density times specific heat).

throat area—the smallest unobstructed cross-sectional area through which air passes on its way from inlet to outlet in a natural ventilation system.

time lag—a delay in the flow of heat through a material caused by the thermal capacity of the material; time lag can be used to shift loads across time.

tower exiting airflow rate—the volume of air leaving a cool tower per unit of time; a partial measure of tower capacity.

transmittance—the amount of light (or solar radiation) that passes through a substance; expressed as a percentage of incident light (or solar radiation).

trickle vent—an opening in a building envelope that allows a steady and controlled flow of outdoor air to enter the building.

U-factor—the overall coefficient of heat transfer; a measure of the thermal conductance of a building assembly; the inverse of the sum of the thermal resistances of an assembly; expressed as Btu/h ft^2°F [W/m^2 K].

ultraviolet radiation—radiation bordering the visible spectrum (light) but with shorter wavelengths; ultraviolet radiation is part of the solar radiation spectrum.

unilateral (daylighting)—a daylighting system that introduces light into a space from only one direction.

urban heat island effect—the tendency for urban areas to maintain a higher ambient temperature than surrounding suburbs or rural areas; caused by the absorption of solar radiation by built surfaces and heat emissions from buildings.

vapor compression refrigeration system—a mechanical-electrical cooling device that transfers heat from an evaporator to a condenser by means of the cyclical condensation and vaporization of a refrigerant circulated by a compressor; driven by electrical input to the compressor.

vertical axis wind turbine (VAWT)—a wind machine with the axis of rotation perpendicular to the ground (as opposed to a horizontal axis machine with the axis of rotation parallel to the ground).

visible transmittance (VT)—the transmittance of a glazing relative to radiation in the visible portion of the spectrum (excluding infrared and ultraviolet radiation); visible transmittance may differ from solar transmittance for some glazings.

volatile organic compounds (VOCs)—compounds that vaporize (evaporate) at room temperature; VOCs are produced by many building materials and furnishings; an indoor air pollutant; low- or no-VOC options are available for many products.

waste heat—heat produced as a generally unusable by-product of some process.

wastewater—water that must be treated for proper disposal; sanitary drainage.

wet-bulb depression—the difference between coincident wet-bulb and dry-bulb temperatures.

wet-bulb temperature—a temperature measurement taken using a wet-bulb thermometer; an indicator of sensible heat density and air moisture content; wet-bulb and dry-bulb temperatures are identical at saturation (100% relative humidity); expressed in degrees F [C].

wind farm—a grouping of wind turbines used to generate electricity; usually for commercial purposes.

windward—in the direction (or on the side) from which the wind is blowing.

zone—an area of a building with characteristics or needs that substantively differ from those of other areas; for example a daylighting, thermal, or fire zone.

GLOSSARY OF BUILDINGS

The buildings described in the strategies and case studies are included here with their geographic location and the primary design architect.

BUILDING	LOCATION	ARCHITECT
1 Finsbury Square	London, UK	Arup Associates
Adam J. Lewis Center For Environmental Studies	Oberlin, OH, USA	William McDonough + Partners
Arup Campus Solihull	Blythe Valley Park, Solihull, England, UK	Arup Associates
Ash Creek Intermediate School	Independence, OR, USA	BOORA Architects
Bayerische Vereinsbank	Stuttgart, Germany	Behnisch, Behnisch & Partner
Beddington Zero Energy Development	Beddington, Sutton, England, UK	Bill Dunster Architects
British Research Establishment (BRE) Offices	Garston, Hertfordshire, England, UK	Feilden Clegg Architects
British Museum of London—Glass Shell	London, UK	Foster and Partners with Buro Happold
Bundy Brown Residence	Ketchum, ID, USA	Rebecca F. Bundy Architectural Design
Burton Barr Central Library	Phoenix, AZ, USA	will bruder architects, ltd
California Polytechnic University-San Luis Obispo Solar Decathlon House 2005	San Luis Obispo, CA, USA	California Polytechnic University-San Luis Obispo
Casa Nueva, Santa Barbara County Office Building	Santa Barbara, CA, USA	Blackbird Architects, Inc.
Chesapeake Bay Foundation	Annapolis, MD, USA	SmithGroup
Christopher Center, Valparaiso University	Valparaiso, IN, USA	EHDD
Clackamas High School	Clackamas, OR, USA	BOORA Architects
Cornell Solar Decathlon House 2005	Ithaca, NY, USA	Cornell University
Coventry University Lanchester Library	Coventry, England, UK	Short and Associates
Domaine Carneros Winery (Pinot Noir Facility)	Napa, CA, USA	Valley Architects of St. Helena
Druk White Lotus School	Shey, Ladakh, India	ARUP + ARUP Associates
EcoHouse	Oxford, England, UK	Susan Roaf
Eden Project	Outside St. Austell, Cornwall, England, UK	Sir Nicholas Grimshaw
Emerald People's Utility District Headquarters	Eugene, OR, USA	Equinox Design, Inc.

BUILDING	LOCATION	ARCHITECT
Ford Premier Automotive Group Headquarters	Irvine, CA, USA	LPA with William McDonough + Partners
Fisher Pavilion	Seattle, WA, USA	Miller/Hull Partnership
GAAG Architecture Gallery	Gelsenkirchen, Germany	Pfeiffer, Ellermann und Partner
Genzyme Center	Cambridge, MA, USA	Behnisch Architekten
Global Ecology Research Center, Stanford University	Palo Alto, CA, USA	EHDD
Guangdong Pei Zheng Commercial College	Huadi, China	Mui Ho Architect
Habitat Research and Development Centre	Windhoek, Namibia	Nina Maritz Architect
Hearst Memorial Gym, University of California Berkeley	Berkeley, CA, USA	Julia Morgan and Bernard Maybeck
The Helena Apartment Tower	New York, NY, USA	FXFOWLE Architects, PC
Hong Kong and Shanghai Bank	Hong Kong, China	Foster and Partners
Honolulu Academy of Arts	Honolulu, HI, USA	John Hara & Associates
Hood River Public Library	Hood River, OR, USA	Fletcher, Farr, Ayotte
IBN-DLO Institute for Forestry and Nature Research	Wageningen, The Netherlands	Behnisch, Behnisch & Partner Architects
IslandWood Campus	Bainbridge Island, WA, USA	Mithūn Architects
Jean Vollum Natural Capital Center (The Ecotrust Building)	Portland, OR, USA	Holst Architecture PC
Kuntshaus Bregenz	Bregenz, Austria	Peter Zumthor
Laban Centre	London, UK	Herzog and de Meuron
Lady Bird Johnson Wildflower Center	Austin, TX, USA	Overland Partners Architects
Lillis Business Complex	Eugene, OR, USA	SRG Partnership
Logan House	Tampa, FL, USA	Rowe Holmes Associates
Martin Luther King Jr. Student Union	Berkeley, CA, USA	Vernon DeMars
Menara Mesiniaga	Subang Jaya, Malaysia	T.R. Hamzah & Yeang International
Mt. Angel Abbey Library	St. Benedict, OR, USA	Alvar Aalto
National Association of Realtors Headquarters	Washington, DC, USA	Gund Partnership
The Not So Big House	Orlando, FL, USA	Sarah Susanka

BUILDING	LOCATION	ARCHITECT
New York Institute of Technology Solar Decathlon House 2005	New York, NY, USA	New York Institute of Technology
One Peking Road	Hong Kong, China	Rocco Design Ltd
Patagonia Headquarters, Ventura	Ventura, CA, USA	Miller/Hull Partnership
Quayside Village Cohousing Community	Vancouver, BC, Canada	Cohousing Development Center
Queen's Building at De Montfort University	Coventry, England, UK	Short and Associates
Raffles Hotel	Singapore	Rennovation: Fredrick Gibberd and Partners
Rhode Island School of Design Solar Decathlon House 2005	Providence, RI, USA	Rhode Island School of Design
Ridge Vineyard—Lytton Springs Winery	Healdsburg, CA, USA	Freebairn-Smith & Crane
Roddy/Bale Garage/Studio	Seattle, WA, USA	Miller/Hull Partnership
Ronald Reagan Library	Simi Valley, CA, USA	Pei Cobb Freed & Partners
Royal Danish Embassy	Berlin, Germany	Nielsen, Nielsen & Nielsen A/S
Ryan Library, Point Loma Nazarene University	San Diego, CA, USA	Architects MDWF and Lareau and Associates
Sabre Holdings Headquarters	Southlake, TX, USA	HKS, Inc.
San Francisco Public Library	San Francisco, CA, USA	Pei Cobb Freed & Partners
Seattle City Hall	Seattle, WA, USA	Bassetti Architects with Bohlin Cywinski Jackson
Shaw Residence	Taos, NM, USA	John Shaw
Sokol Blosser Winery	Dundee, OR, USA	SERA Architects
St. Ignatius Chapel at Seattle University	Seattle, WA, USA	Steven Holl Architects
The William and Flora Hewlett Foundation	Menlo Park, CA, USA	BH Bocook Architects
Water Pollution Control Laboratory	Portland, OR, USA	Miller/Hull Partnership
Westhaven Tower	Frankfurt, Germany	Schneider + Schumacher
Woods Hole Research Center	Falmouth, MA, USA	William McDonough + Partners
University of Texas-Austin Solar Decathlon House 2005	Austin, TX, USA	University of Texas-Austin
Zion National Park Visitor's Center	Springdale, UT, USA	James Crockett, AIA

NOTES

Insulation Materials

Air Krete, Inc. www.airkrete.com/
Allen, E. and J. Iano. 2003. *Fundamentals of Building Construction,* 4th
    ed. John Wiley & Sons, New York.
Bonded Logic, Inc. www.bondedlogic.com/
BREEAM EcoHomes Developer Sheets (Building Research
    Establishment, Garston, Watford, UK). Available at: www.breeam.
    org/pdf/EcoHomes2005DeveloperSheets_v1_1.pdf
Building Green. www.buildinggreen.com/
Icynene Inc. www.icynene.com/
Johns Manville. www.johnsmanville.com/
Mendler, S., W. Odell and M. Lazarus. 2005. *The HOK Guidebook to
    Sustainable Design*, 2nd ed. John Wiley & Sons, Hoboken, NJ.
North American Insulation Manufacturer's Association.
    www. naima.org/
Structural Insulated Panel Association. www.sips.org/
Wilson, A. 2005. "Insulation: Thermal Performance is Just the
    Beginning." *Environmental Building News*, Vol. 14, No. 1, Jan.

Strawbale Construction

California Straw Building Association. www.strawbuilding.org/
Commonwealth of Australia. Technical Manual: *Design for Lifestyle and
    the Future*. Available at: www.greenhouse.gov.au/yourhome/
    technical/fs34e.htm
Jones, B. 2002. *Building With Straw Bales—A Practical Guide for the UK
    and Ireland*. Green Books, Totnes, Devon, UK.
Magwood, C. and P. Mack. 2000. *Straw Bale Building—How to Plan, Design
    and Build with Straw*. New Society Publishers, Gabriola Island, BC.
Steen, A. 1994. *The Straw Bale House*. Chelsea Green Publishing
    Company, White River Junction, VT.
The Straw Bale Building Association (for Wales, Ireland, Scotland, and
    England). strawbalebuildingassociation.org.uk/

Structural Insulated Panels

Build It Green Structural Insulated Panel. www.buildit-
    green.co.uk/about-SIPs.html
Little, J.C. and A.T. Hodgson. *Structural Insulated Panels: Sustainable
    Design Incorporating Impact on Indoor Quality.* Available at:
    www. pathnet.org/si.asp?id=1081
Morley, M. 2000. *Building with Structural Insulated Panels (SIPS)*. The
    Taunton Press, Newtown, MA.
Sarah Susanka's Not So Big Showhouse 2005.
    www.notsobigshowhouse.com/2005/
Structural Insulated Panel Association. www.sips.org/

Double Envelopes

Boake, T.M. 2003. "Doubling Up." *Canadian Architect*, Vol. 48, No. 7, July.

Boake, T. M. 2003. "Doubling Up II." *Canadian Architect*, Vol. 48, No. 8, August.

Diprose, P. and G. Robertson. 1996. "Towards a Fourth Skin? Sustainability and Double-Envelope Buildings." www.diprose.co.nz/WREC/WREC.htm

Herzog, T., R. Krippner and W. Lang. 2004. *Facade Construction Manual*. Birkhauser, Basel, Switzerland.

Oesterle, E. et al. 2001. *Double-Skin Facades: Integrated Planning*. Prestel, Munich.

Green Roofs

British Council for Offices. 2003. Research Advice Note: "Green Roofs." Available at: www.bco.org.uk/

Centre for the Advancement of Green Roof Technology. commons. bcit.ca/greenroof/

Earth Pledge. 2004. *Green Roofs: Ecological Design and Construction*. Schiffer Publishing, Atglen, PA.

Green Roofs for Healthy Cities. www.greenroofs.net/

Harris, C. and N. Dines. 1997. *Time-Saver Standards for Landscape Architecture,* 2nd ed. McGraw-Hill, New York.

Oberlander, C.H., E. Whitelaw and E. Matsuzaki. 2002. *Introductory Manual for Greening Roofs for Public Works and Government Services Canada*, Version 1.1. Available at: ftp://ftp.tech-env.com/ pub/SERVICE_LIFE_ASSET_MANAGEMENT/PWGSC_Greening Roofs_wLinks.pdf

Osmundson, T. 1997. *Roof Gardens: History, Design, and Construction*. W.W. Norton, New York.

Velazquez, L. 2005. "Organic Greenroof Architecture: Design Consideration and System Components." *Environmental Quality Management*, Summer.

Velazquez, L. 2005. "Organic Greenroof Architecture: Sustainable Design for the New Millennium." *Environmental Quality Management*, Summer.

Daylight Factor

British Standards. 1992. *Lighting for Buildings: Code of Practice for Daylighting* (BS 8206-2). BSI British Standards, London.

Brown, G.Z. and M. DeKay. 2001. *Sun, Wind & Light: Architectural Design Strategies*, 2nd ed. John Wiley & Sons, New York.

IESNA. 1999. *Recommended Practice of Daylighting* (RP-5-99). Illuminating Engineering Society of North America, New York.

Moore, F. 1993. *Environmental Control Systems: Heating, Cooling, Lighting*. McGraw-Hill, Inc. New York.

Square One Research (Daylight Factor). www.squ1.com/daylight/daylight-factor.html

Stein, B. et al. 2006. *Mechanical and Electrical Equipment for Buildings*, 10th ed. John Wiley & Sons, Hoboken, NJ.

Daylight Zoning

Ander, G. D. 2003. *Daylighting Performance and Design*, 2nd ed. John Wiley & Sons, New York.

Baker, N., A. Fanchiotti and K. Steemers (eds). 1993. *Daylighting in Architecture: A European Reference Book.* Earthscan/James & James, London.

Bell, J. and W. Burt. 1996. *Designing Buildings for Daylight*, BRE Press, Bracknell, Berkshire, UK.

Brown, G.Z. and M. DeKay. 2001. *Sun, Wind & Light: Architectural Design Strategies*, 2nd ed. John Wiley & Sons, New York.

CIBSE. 1999. *Daylighting and Window Design.* The Chartered Institution of Building Services Engineers, London.

CIBSE. 2004. *Code for Lighting.* The Chartered Institution of Building Services Engineers, London.

Guzowski, M. 2000. *Daylighting for Sustainable Design*, McGraw-Hill, New York.

Moore, F. 1985. *Concepts and Practice of Architectural Daylighting*, Van Nostrand Reinhold, New York.

Rea, M.S. (ed.). *IESNA Lighting Handbook*, 9th ed. Illuminating Engineering Society of North America, New York.

Toplighting

Evans, B. 1981. *Daylight in Architecture.* Architectural Record Books, New York.

International Energy Agency. 2000. *Daylight in Buildings.* Lawrence Berkeley National Laboratory, Berkeley, CA.

Millet, M. and J. Bedrick. 1980. *Graphic Daylighting Design Method.* U.S. Department of Energy/Lawrence Berkeley National Laboratory, Washington, DC.

Moore, F. 1985. *Concepts and Practice of Architectural Daylighting.* Van Nostrand Reinhold, New York.

Stein, B. et al. 2006. *Mechanical and Electrical Equipment for Buildings*, 10th ed. John Wiley & Sons, Hoboken, NJ.

Whole Building Design Guide, "Daylighting." www.wbdg.org/design/daylighting.php

Sidelighting

Evans, B. 1981. *Daylight in Architecture.* Architectural Record Books, New York.

International Energy Agency. 2000. *Daylight in Buildings.* Lawrence Berkeley National Laboratory, Berkeley, CA.

Millet, M. and J. Bedrick. 1980. *Graphic Daylighting Design Method.* U.S. Department of Energy/Lawrence Berkeley National Laboratory, Washington, DC.

Moore, F. 1985. *Concepts and Practice of Architectural Daylighting.* Van Nostrand Reinhold, New York.

Stein, B. et al. 2006. *Mechanical and Electrical Equipment for Buildings*, 10th ed. John Wiley & Sons, Hoboken, NJ.

Whole Building Design Guide, "Daylighting." www.wbdg.org/design/daylighting.php

Light Shelves

Evans, B. 1981. *Daylight in Architecture.* Architectural Record Books, New York.

IEA. 2000. *Daylight in Buildings: A Source Book on Daylighting Systems and Components.* International Energy Agency. Available at: gaia.lbl.gov/iea21/ieapubc.htm

LBL. 1997. "Section 3: Envelope and Room Decisions," in *Tips for Daylighting With Windows.* Building Technologies Program, Lawrence Berkeley National Laboratory. Available at: windows.lbl.gov/daylighting/designguide/designguide.html

LRC. 2004. "Guide for Daylighting Schools," developed by Innovative Design for Daylight Dividends, Lighting Research Center, Rensselaer Polytechnic Institute, Troy, NY. Available at: www.lrc.rpi.edu/programs/daylightdividends/pdf/guidelines.pdf

Moore, F. 1985. *Concepts and Practice of Architectural Daylighting.* Van Nostrand Reinhold Company, New York.

NREL. 2003. "Laboratories for the 21st Century: Best Practices" (NREL Report No. BR-710-33938; DOE/GO-102003-1766). National Renewable Energy Laboratory, U.S. Environmental Protection Agency/U.S. Department of Energy. Available at: www.nrel.gov/docs/fy04osti/33938.pdf

Internal Reflectances

Brown, G.Z. and M. DeKay. 2001. *Sun, Wind and Light: Architectural Design Strategies,* 2nd ed. John Wiley & Sons, New York.

Hopkinson, R., P. Petherbridge and J. Longmore. 1966. *Daylighting.* Heinemann, London.

Rea, M. (ed.). 2000. *The IESNA Lighting Handbook*, 9th ed. Illuminating Engineering Society of North America, New York.

Robbins, C. 1986. *Daylighting: Design and Analysis.* Van Nostrand Reinhold, New York.

Stein, B. et al. 2006. *Mechanical and Electrical Equipment for Buildings,* 10th ed. John Wiley & Sons, Hoboken, NJ.

Shading Devices

Olgyay, V. 1963. *Design with Climate.* Princeton University Press, Princeton, NJ.

Olgyay, A. and V. Olgyay. 1957. *Solar Control & Shading Devices.* Princeton University Press, Princeton, NJ.

Pacific Energy Center, Application Notes for Site Analysis, "Taking a Fisheye Photo." www.pge.com/pec/ (search on "fisheye")

Pilkington Sun Angle Calculator. Available through the Society of Building Science Educators: www.sbse.org/resources/index.htm

Solar Transit Template. Available through the Agents of Change Project, University of Oregon: aoc.uoregon.edu/loaner_kits/index.shtml

Electric Lighting

The European Greenlight Programme. www.eu-greenlight.org/
International Organization for Energy-Efficient Lighting.
    www.iaeel.org/
Rea, M. (ed.). 2000. *The IESNA Lighting Handbook*, 9th ed. Illuminating
    Engineering Society of North America, New York.
U.S. Department of Energy, Energy Efficiency and Renewable Energy,
    Lighting. www.eere.energy.gov/EE/buildings_lighting.html
Waide, P. 2006. "Light's Labour Lost." International Energy Agency,
    Paris.
Whole Building Design Guide, "Energy Efficient Lighting."
    www.wbdg.org/design/efficientlighting.php

Direct Gain

Balcomb, J.D. et al. 1980. *Passive Solar Design Handbook, Vol. 2, Passive
    Solar Design Analysis*. U.S. Department of Energy, Washington, DC.
Fosdick, J. 2006. Whole Building Design Guide, "Passive Solar Heating."
    www.wbdg.org/design/psheating.php
Greenbuilder.com. A Sourcebook for Green and Sustainable Building,
    "Passive Solar Guidelines." www.greenbuilder.com/
    sourcebook/PassSolGuide1-2.html
Mazria, E. 1979. *The Passive Solar Energy Book*. Rodale Press, Emmaus, PA.
Stein, B. et al. 2006. *Mechanical and Electrical Equipment for Buildings*,
    10th ed. John Wiley & Sons, Hoboken, NJ.

Indirect Gain

Balcomb, J.D. et al. 1980. *Passive Solar Design Handbook, Vol. 2, Passive
    Solar Design Analysis*. U.S. Department of Energy, Washington, DC.
Brown, G.Z. and M. DeKay. 2001. *Sun, Wind & Light: Architectural Design
    Strategies*, 2nd ed. John Wiley & Sons, New York.
Mazria, E. 1979. *The Passive Solar Energy Book*. Rodale Press, Emmaus, PA.
Stein, B. et al. 2006. *Mechanical and Electrical Equipment for Buildings*,
    10th ed. John Wiley & Sons, Hoboken, NJ.

Isolated Gain

Balcomb, J.D. et al. 1980. *Passive Solar Design Handbook, Vol. 2, Passive
    Solar Design Analysis*. U.S. Department of Energy, Washington, DC.
Brown, G.Z. and M. DeKay. 2001. *Sun, Wind & Light: Architectural Design
    Strategies*, 2nd ed. John Wiley & Sons, New York.
Mazria, E. 1979. *The Passive Solar Energy Book*. Rodale Press, Emmaus, PA.
Stein, B. et al. 2006. *Mechanical and Electrical Equipment for Buildings*,
    10th ed. John Wiley & Sons, Hoboken, NJ.
U.S. Department of Energy, Energy Efficiency and Renewable Energy,
    "Isolated Gain (sunspaces)." www.eere.energy.gov/consumer/
    your_home/designing_remodeling/index.cfm?mytopic=10310

Active Solar Thermal Systems

Brown, G.Z. et al. 1992. *Inside Out: Design Procedures for Passive Environmental Technologies*, 2nd ed. John Wiley & Sons, New York.
Grumman, D. L. (ed.). 2003. *ASHRAE GreenGuide.* American Society of Heating, Refrigerating and Air-Conditioning Engineers, Atlanta, GA.
U.S. Department of Energy, Energy Efficiency and Renewable Energy, "Water Heating." www.eere.energy.gov/consumer/your_ home/ water_heating/index.cfm/mytopic=12760
U.S. Department of Energy, Energy Efficiency and Renewable Energy, "Solar Hot Water and Space Heating & Cooling." www.eere.energy. gov/RE/solar_hotwater.html

Ground Source Heat Pumps

ASHRAE. 1997. *Ground Source Heat Pumps: Design of Geothermal Systems for Commercial & Institutional Buildings.* American Society of Heating, Refrigerating and Air-Conditioning Engineers, Atlanta, GA.
Econar Energy Systems. 1993. *GeoSource Heat Pump Handbook* (on Whole Building Design Guide site). www.wbdg.org/ccb/DOE/ TECH/geo.pdf
Geothermal Heat Pump Consortium. www.geoexchange.org/
Hydro-Temp Corporation. www.hydro-temp.com/
International Ground Source Heat Pump Association. www.igshpa.okstate.edu/
Oregon Institute of Technology, Geo-Heat Center. geoheat.oit.edu/
Stein, B. et al. 2006. *Mechanical and Electrical Equipment for Buildings*, 10th ed. John Wiley & Sons, Hoboken, NJ.
Water Furnace International. www.wfiglobal.com/

Cross Ventilation

Brown, G.Z. and M. DeKay. 2001. *Sun, Wind & Light: Architectural Design Strategies*, 2nd ed. John Wiley & Sons, New York.
National Climatic Data Center. www.ncdc.noaa.gov/oa/ncdc.html
Olgyay, V. 1963. *Design with Climate*. Princeton University Press. Princeton, NJ.
Royle, K. and C. Terry. 1990. *Hawaiian Design: Strategies for Energy Efficient Architecture*. Diane Publishing Co., Collingdale, PA.
Square One. www.squ1.com/site.html
Stein, B. et al. 2006. *Mechanical and Electrical Equipment for Buildings*, 10th ed. John Wiley & Sons, Hoboken, NJ.

Stack Ventilation

Grondzik, W. 2000. "Natural Ventilation in the FAMU School of Architecture Building: Intent Meets Reality," *Proceedings of the 2000 Conference of ASES* (Madison, WI). American Solar Energy Society, Boulder, CO.

Grondzik, W. et al. 2002. "The Logan House: Signing Off," *Proceedings of 27th National Passive Solar Conference—Solar 2002* (Reno, NV). American Solar Energy Society, Boulder, CO.

Kwok, A. and W. Grondzik. 1999. "The Logan House: Measuring Air Movement," *Proceedings of 24th National Passive Solar Conference* (Portland, ME). American Solar Energy Society, Boulder, CO.

Kwok, A. and W. Grondzik. 2000. "The Logan House: Stack Effect Effectiveness," *Proceedings of 25th National Passive Solar Conference* (Madison, WI). American Solar Energy Society, Boulder, CO.

Stein, B. et al. 2006. *Mechanical and Electrical Equipment for Buildings*, 10th ed. John Wiley & Sons, Hoboken, NJ.

Whole Building Design Guide, "Natural Ventilation." www.wbdg.org/design/naturalventilation.php

Evaporative Cool Towers

Chalfoun, N. 1997. "Design and Application of Natural Down-Draft Evaporative Cooling Devices," *Proceedings 1997 Conference of ASES*. American Solar Energy Society, Boulder, CO.

Givoni, B. 1994. *Passive and Low Energy Cooling of Buildings*. Van Nostrand Reinhold, New York.

Givoni, B. 1998. *Climate Considerations in Building and Urban Design*. Van Nostrand Reinhold, New York.

Global Ecology Research Center, Stanford University. globalecology. stanford.edu/DGE/CIWDGE/CIWDGE.HTML

Thompson, T., N. Chalfoun and M. Yoklic. 1994. "Estimating the Thermal Performance of Natural Draft Evaporative Coolers," *Energy Conversion and Management*, Vol. 35, No. 11, pp. 909–915.

U.S. Department of Energy, Office of Energy Efficiency and Renewable Energy, High Performance Buildings, Zion National Park Visitor Center. www.eere.energy.gov/buildings/highperformance/zion/

Night Ventilation of Thermal Mass

Brown, G.Z. and M. DeKay. 2001. *Sun, Wind & Light: Architectural Design Strategies*, 2nd ed. John Wiley & Sons, New York.

Haglund, B. "Thermal Mass in Passive Solar Buildings," a Vital Signs Resource Package. Available at: arch.ced.berkeley. edu/vitalsigns/res/downloads/rp/thermal_mass/mass-big.pdf

Moore, F. 1993. *Environmental Control Systems: Heating, Cooling, Lighting*. McGraw-Hill, New York.

Stein, B. et al. 2006. *Mechanical and Electrical Equipment for Buildings*, 10th ed. John Wiley & Sons, Hoboken, NJ.

Earth Cooling Tubes

Abrams, D., J. Akridge and C. Benton. 1980. "Simulated and Measured Performance of Earth Cooling Tubes," *Proceedings of the 5th National Passive Solar Conference* (Amherst, MA). American Solar Energy Society, Boulder, CO.

Brown, G.Z. and M. DeKay. 2001. *Sun, Wind & Light: Architectural Design Strategies,* 2nd ed. John Wiley & Sons, New York.

Givoni, B. 1994. *Passive and Low Energy Cooling of Buildings.* Van Nostrand Reinhold, New York.

Lee, T. G. 2004. "Preheating Ventilation Air Using Earth Tubes," *Proceedings of the 29th Passive Solar Conference* (Portland, OR). American Solar Energy Society, Boulder, CO.

Solar.org Earth Tubes Exhibit. www.solar.org/solar/earthtubes/

Stein, B. et al. 2006. *Mechanical and Electrical Equipment for Buildings,* 10th ed. John Wiley & Sons, Hoboken, NJ.

USDOE. 2006. *A Consumer's Guide to Energy Efficiency and Renewable Energy: Earth Cooling Tubes.* Office of Energy Efficiency and Renewable Energy, U.S. Department of Energy, Washington, DC.

Earth Sheltering

Baum, G. 1980. *Earth Shelter Handbook,* Technical Data Publications, Peoria, AZ.

Boyer, L. and W. Grondzik. 1987. *Earth Shelter Technology.* Texas A&M University Press, College Station, TX.

Carmody, J. and R. Sterling. 1983. *Underground Building Design: Commercial and Institutional Structures,* Van Nostrand Reinhold, New York.

Sokol Blosser Winery. www.sokolblosser.com/

Sterling, R., W. Farnan and J. Carmody. 1982. *Earth Sheltered Residential Design Manual,* Van Nostrand Reinhold, New York.

Underground Buildings: Architecture & Environment. www.subsurfacebuildings.com/

Absorption Chillers

Allen, E. and J. Iano. 2001. *The Architect's Studio Companion,* 3rd ed. John Wiley & Sons, New York.

Hoke, J. R. (ed.). 2000. *Ramsey/Sleeper Architectural Graphic Standards,* 10th ed. John Wiley & Sons, New York.

Rafferty, K. D. 2005. "Absorption Refrigeration." *Geo-Heat Bulletin,* Vol. 19, No. 1. Geo-Heat Center, Klamath Falls, OR.

Rosaler, R.C. 2004. *The HVAC Handbook.* McGraw-Hill, New York.

Southern California Gas Co., New Buildings Institute. 1998. *Guideline: Absorption Chillers.* Available at: www.newbuildings.org/ downloads/guidelines/AbsorptionChillerGuideline.pdf

USDOE. 2003. *Energy Matters Newsletter* (Fall 2003). U.S. Department of Energy. Washington, DC. Available at: www.oit.doe.gov/ bestpractices/energymatters/fall2003_absorption shtml

Plug Loads

American Council for an Energy-Efficient Economy. www.aceee.org/

Federal Trade Commission. www.ftc.gov/bcp/conline/pubs/ products/ffclight.htm

International Energy Agency. www.iea.org/

Oxford Brookes University, Electronic Appliances and Energy Labels. www.brookes.ac.uk/eie/ecolabels.htm#3

Plug Loads. www.plugloads.com/

Stein, B. et al. 2006. *Mechanical and Electrical Equipment for Buildings*, 10th ed. John Wiley & Sons, Hoboken, NJ.

Suozzo, M. 2000. *Guide to Energy-Efficient Commercial Equipment*, 2nd ed. American Council for an Energy-Efficient Economy, Washington, DC.

USDOE. 2005. *Buildings Energy Databook*. Office of Energy Efficiency and Renewable Energy, U.S. Department of Energy, Washington, DC.

U.S. Environmental Protection Agency, Energy Star program. www.energystar.gov/

Air-to-Air Heat Exchangers

ASHRAE. 2004. *2004 ASHRAE Handbook – HVAC Systems and Equipment*. American Society of Heating, Refrigerating and Air-Conditioning Engineers, Atlanta, GA.

ASHRAE. 2004. Standard 62.2-2004: "Ventilation and Acceptable Indoor Air Quality in Low-Rise Residential Buildings." American Society of Heating, Refrigerating and Air-Conditioning Engineers, Atlanta, GA.

Dausch, M., D. Pinnix and J. Fischer. "Labs for the 21st Century: Applying 3Å Molecular Sieve Total Energy Recovery Wheels to Laboratory Environments." Available at: www.labs21century. gov/conf/past/2003/abstracts/a3_dausch.htm

Grumman, D.L. (ed.). 2003. *ASHRAE GreenGuide.* American Society of Heating, Refrigerating and Air-Conditioning Engineers, Atlanta, GA.

State of Oregon. "Demand-Controlled Ventilation: A Design Guide." Oregon Department of Energy. Available at: egov.oregon.gov/ ENERGY/CONS/BUS/DCV/docs/DCVGuide.pdf

Energy Recovery Systems

"BetterBricks Case Study: Hot Lips Pizza." Available at: www.betterbricks.com/

Goldstick, R. 1983. *The Waste Heat Recovery Handbook*. Fairmont Press, Atlanta, GA.

Goldstick, R. and A. Thumann. 1986. *Principles of Waste Heat Recovery*. Fairmont Press, Atlanta, GA.

Grumman, D.L. (ed.). 2003. *ASHRAE GreenGuide.* American Society of Heating, Refrigerating and Air-Conditioning Engineers, Atlanta, GA.

Photovoltaics

Florida Solar Energy Center, Photovoltaics. www.fsec.ucf.edu/pvt/

IEA Photovoltaic Power Systems Programme. www.iea-pvps.org/

National Renewable Energy Laboratory, Solar Radiation Data. rredc.nrel.gov/solar/old_data/nsrdb/redbook/atlas/

U.S. Department of Energy, National Center for Photovoltaics.
    www.nrel.gov/ncpv/
Whole Building Design Guide, "Building Integrated Photovoltaics
    (BIPV)." Available at: www.wbdg.org/design/bipv.php
Whole Building Design Guide, "Distributed Energy Resources (DER)."
    Available at: www.wbdg.org/design/der.php

Wind Turbines

American Wind Energy Association, "The Wind Energy Fact Sheet."
    Available at: www.awea.org/
U.S. Department of Energy, Energy Efficiency and Renewable Energy,
    *A Consumer's Guide to Energy Efficiency and Renewable Energy:
    Sizing Small Wind Turbines.* Available at: www.eere.energy.gov/
    consumer/your_home/electricity/index.cfm/mytopic=11010
U.S. Department of Energy. *Wind Energy Resource Atlas of the United
    States.* Available at: www.nrel.gov/wind/
U.S. Department of Energy, Wind Powering America.
    www. windpoweringamerica.gov/

Microhydro Turbines

Harvey, A. et al. 1993. *Micro-Hydro Design Manual: A Guide to
    Small-Scale Water Power Schemes.* ITDG Publishing, Rugby,
    Warwickshire, UK.
Masters, G. 2004. *Renewable and Efficient Electric Power Systems.*
    Wiley-IEEE Press, New York.
U.S. Department of Energy, Microhydropower Systems.
    www.eere. energy.gov/consumer/your_home/electricity/
    index.cfm/mytopic=11050

Hydrogen Fuel Cells

Fuel Cells 2000. www.fuelcells.org/
U.S. Department of Energy, Hydrogen Program.
    www.hydrogen.energy.gov/fuel_cells.html
UTC Power. www.utcfuelcells.com/
Whole Building Design Guide, "Fuel Cell Technology."
    www.wbdg.org/design/fuelcell.php

Combined Heat and Power

Case studies of CHP systems, UTC Power. www.utcpower.com/
Grumman, D.L. (ed.). 2003. *ASHRAE GreenGuide.* American Society
    of Heating, Refrigerating and Air-Conditioning Engineers,
    Atlanta, GA.
United States Combined Heat and Power Association.
    uschpa.admgt.com/

United States Environmental Protection Agency, Combined Heat and
    Power Partnership. www.epa.gov/chp/
USEPA. 2002. *Catalogue of CHP Technologies*. United States
    Environmental Protection Agency, Combined Heat and Power
    Partnership, Washington, DC. Available at: www.epa.gov/chp/
    project_resources/catalogue.htm

Composting Toilets

Clivus Multrum Inc. www.clivusmultrum.com/
DeaTech Inc. www.deatech.com/natural/waste/toilet.html
Del Porto, D. and C. Steinfield. 2000. *Composting Toilet System Book: A
    Practical Guide to Choosing, Planning and Maintaining Composting
    Toilet Systems*. The Center for Ecological Pollution. Concord, MA.
Ecochem Inc. www.ecochem.com/
Envirolet. www.envirolet.com/
Environmental and Renewable Energy Information Center.
    www. solareco.com/
Jenkins, J. 1999. *The Humanure Handbook: A Guide to Composting
    Human Manure*. Jenkins Publishing. Grove City, PA.
Joseph Jenkins, Inc. www.jenkinspublishing.com/compost-links.html
Michigan Tech Peacecorps. peacecorps.mtu.edu/
Oikos-Green Building Source, "What is a Composting Toilet System
    and How Does it Compost?" Available at: oikos.com/library/
    compostingtoilet/
Reed, R., J. Pickford and R. Franceys. 1992. *A Guide to the Development
    of On-Site Sanitation*. World Health Organization, Geneva.

Water Reuse/Recycling

Brown and Caldwell Consultants. 1990. *Case Studies of Industrial Water
    Conservation in the San Jose Area*. Report prepared for the City of
    San Jose, CA and the California Department of Water Resources.
California Department of Water Resources. 2004. *Water Facts: Water
    Recycling*, No. 23. Available at:
    www.owue.water.ca.gov/recycle/docs/WaterFact23.pdf
The Chartered Institution of Water and Environmental Management,
    "Water Reuse." www.ciwem.org/resources/water/
Greywater Irrigation. www.greywater.com/
Ludwig, A. 2000. *Create an Oasis with Greywater*, 4th ed. Oasis Design,
    Santa Barbara, CA.
Oasis Design, "Greywater Central." www.greywater.net/
Quayside Village Cohousing Community.
    www.cohousingconsulting.ca/subpages/projects_quay.html
State of California, Office of Water Use Efficiency. 1995. "Graywater
    Guide: Using Graywater in Your Home Landscape." Available at:
    www.owue.water.ca.gov/docs/graywater_guide_book.pdf
State of Florida, Department of Environmental Protection. 2003 "Water
    Reuse for Florida: Strategies for Effective Use of Reclaimed Water."
    Available at: www.dep.state.fl.us/water/reuse/techdocs.htm

Stein, B. et al. 2006. *Mechanical and Electrical Equipment for Buildings*, 10th ed. John Wiley & Sons, Hoboken, NJ.

U.S. Environmental Protection Agency (Region 9). "Water Recycling and Reuse: The Environmental Benefits." Available at: www.epa.gov/region9/water/recycling/

Living Machines

Corkskrew Swamp Sanctuary (Living Machine). www.audubon.org/local/sanctuary/corkscrew/Information/Living Machine.html

Living Designs Group (Living Machines). www.livingmachines.com/

Oberlin College, Adam Joseph Lewis Center, Living Machine. www.oberlin.edu/ajlc/systems_lm_1.html

Todd, J. and B. Josephson. 1994. "Living Machines: Theoretical Foundations & Design Precepts." *Annals of Earth*, Vol. 12, No. 1, pp. 16–24.

Todd, N.J. and J. Todd. 1994. *From Eco-Cities to Living Machines: Principles of Ecological Design.* North Atlantic Books, Berkeley, CA.

USEPA. 2001. *The "Living Machine" Wastewater Treatment Technology: An Evaluation of Performance and System Cost.* EPA 832-R-01-004. U.S. Environmental Protection Agency, Washington, DC.

USEPA. 2002. *Wastewater Technology Fact Sheet: The Living Machine®.* U.S. Environmental Protection Agency, Washington, DC.

Water Catchment Systems

Iowa State University. 1979. *Private Water Systems Handbook*, 4th ed. Midwest Plan Service, Ames, IA.

Montana State University Extension Service, "Rainwater Harvesting Systems for Montana." www.montana.edu/wwwpb/pubs/mt9707.html

Stein, B. et al. 2006. *Mechanical and Electrical Equipment for Buildings*, 10th ed. John Wiley & Sons, Hoboken, NJ.

USEPA. 1991. *Manual of Individual and Non-Public Water Supply Systems.* U.S. Environmental Protection Agency, Washington, DC.

WaterAid International, Rainwater Harvesting. www.wateraid.org/international/what_we_do/how_we_work/sustainable_technologies/technology_notes/2055.asp

Young. E. 1989. "Rainwater Cisterns: Design, Construction and Water Treatment" (Circular 277). Pennsylvania State University, Agriculture Cooperative Extension, University Park, PA.

Pervious Surfaces

Partnership for Advancing Technology in Housing, Toolbase, "Permeable Pavement." www.toolbase.org/techinv/techDetails.aspx?technologyID=98

Sustainable Sources. 2004. "Pervious Paving Materials." Available at: www.greenbuilder.com/sourcebook/PerviousMaterials.html

USEPA. 1980. *Porous Pavement Phase I—Design and Operational Criteria* (EPA 600-2-80-135). Urban Watershed Management Research, U.S. Environmental Protection Agency, Washington, DC.

USEPA. 1999. *Storm Water Technology Fact Sheet: Porous Pavement* (EPA 832-F-99-023). Office of Water, U.S. Environmental Protection Agency, Washington, DC.

Bioswales

California Stormwater Quality Association. 2003. "Vegetated Swale," in *California Stormwater BMP Handbook*. Available at: www.cabmphandbooks.org/Development.asp

Center for Watershed Protection. 1996. *Design of Stormwater Filtering Systems*. Ellicott City, MD.

Spokane County Division of Utilities, "Stormwater Utility - Grassy Swale Construction." Available at: www.spokanecounty.org/utilities/stormwtr/swale.asp

Spokane County Division of Utilities, "Grassy Drainage Swales in Residential Developments." Available at: www.spokanecounty.org/utilities/stormwtr/data/sw-2.pdf

The Stormwater Manager's Resource Center. www.stormwatercenter.net/

USEPA. 2004. *Stormwater Best Management Practice Design Guide, Vol. 2, Vegetative Biofilters*. U.S. Environmental Protection Agency, Washington, DC. Available at: www.epa.gov/ORD/NRMRL/pubs/600r04121/600r04121asect6.pdf

Retention Ponds

Center for Watershed Protection, 1996. *Design of Stormwater Filtering Systems*, Ellicott City, MD.

LMNO Engineering, Research, and Software, Ltd. "Rational Equation Calculator" (an online tool to calculate drainage basin peak discharge rate). Available at: www.lmnoeng.com/Hydrology/rational.htm

McCuen, R. H. 2005. *Hydrologic Analysis and Design*, 3rd ed. Pearson Prentice Hall, Upper Saddle River, NJ.

The Stormwater Manager's Resource Center. www.stormwatercenter.net/

USEPA. 1999. *Storm Water Technology Fact Sheet: Bioretention* (EPA 832-F-99-012). U.S. Environmental Protection Agency, Washington, DC.

Arup Campus Solihull

Arup Associates. www.arupassociates.com/

Austin, B. et al. 2003. "Design for Workplace Performance—Fact or Fiction—Sustainability and Profit." www.cibse.org/pdfs/7caustin.pdf

Haddlesey, P. 2001. "Shedding the Light," *Light and Lighting* 23: 8–10.

Hawkes, D. and W. Forster. 2002. "Arup Campus," *Architecture, Engineering, and Environment,* Lawrence King Publishing, London.

Long, K. 2000. "Health Resort," *Building Design* 1453: 15–17.

Long, K. 2001. "A Job Well Done," *Surface* 26–27, 29–30.

Powell, K. 2001. "Candid Campus;" *Architects' Journal* 215/7: 24–35.

Wong, D. J. and C. Perkins. 2002. "The Integrated Arup Campus," *New Steel Construction* 10/1: 21–3.

Beddington Zero Energy Development

Bill Dunster Architects/ZEDfactory. www.zedfactory.com/

Bioregional Development Group. www.bioregional.co.uk/

BRE. 2001. Case Study: "BedZED-Beddington Zero Energy Development, Sutton" (General Information Report 89). Building Research Establishment, Ltd, Garston, Watford.

Dunster, B. 2003. *From A to ZED: Realising Zero (fossil) Energy Developments.* Bill Dunster Architects/ZEDfactory Ltd, Wallington, Surrey.

Hawkes, D. and W. Forster. 2002. "BedZED Sustainable Development," in *Architecture, Engineering, and Environment,* Lawrence King Publishing, London.

Ove Arup & Partners. www.arup.com/

Smith, P.F. 2001. *Architecture in a Climate of Change: A Guide to Sustainable Design,* Architectural Press, Oxford.

Twinn, C. 2003 "BedZED," *The Arup Journal* 1/2003.

2005 Cornell University Solar Decathlon House

Bonaventura-Sparagna, J., E. Chin-Dickey and N. Rajkovich. 2005. "The Cornell University Solar Decathlon Team: Learning Through Practice." *Proceedings of the ASES/ISES 2005 Solar World Congress* (Orlando, FL). American Solar Energy Society, Boulder, CO.

Cornell University Solar Decathlon. www.cusd.cornell.edu/

Northeast Regional Climate Center. www.nrcc.cornell.edu/

PVWatts: A Performance Calculator for Grid-Connected PV Systems. rredc.nrel.gov/solar/codes_algs/PVWATTS/

U.S. Department of Energy, Solar Decathlon. www.eere.energy.gov/solar_decathlon/

Druk White Lotus School

Arup Associates. www.arupassociates.com/

Barker, D. 2002. "Building a School in India," *Architecture Week* 31 July.

Druk White Lotus School. www.dwls.org/

Fleming, J. et al. 2002. "Druk White Lotus School, Ladakh, Northern India," *The Arup Journal* 2/2002.

Habitat Research and Development Centre

Anon. 2003. "Ground Broken for Habitat Research & Development Centre." Available at: www.windhoekcc.org.na/Repository/News& Publications/Aloe/ALOEMay2003PMK.pdf (*Aloe*: City of Windhoek. Issue 5, May 2003).

Habitat Research and Development Centre of Namibia. www.interact.com.na/hrdc/

Korrubel, J. 2005. "Lessons Learned in Building Sustainably in a Developing Country by the Habitat Research and Development Centre, Namibia." Presented at the 2005 World Sustainable Building Conference, Tokyo, Japan. September 2005.

The Helena Apartment Tower

Affordable Housing Design Advisor, Green Housing Projects. www.designadvisor.org/green/helena.php

FXFOWLE. www.fxfowle.com/

GreenHome. www.greenhomenyc.org/ (select What is Green Building, then NYC Green Building profiles)

Logan, K. 2005. "High-Metal Tower," *Architecture Week* (online). www.architectureweek.com/2005/0928/design_1-1.html

Lillis Business Complex

Bohm, M., W. Henderson and A. Swain. 2005. "It's Hot Up Here! A Study of Thermal Comfort in the Lillis Business Complex 4th Floor Office." www.uoregon.edu/%7Eakwok/VSCS/lillis/index.htm

Brown, G.Z. et al. 2004. "A Lesson in Green." *Solar Today* March/April.

Brown, G.Z. et al. 2004. *Natural Ventilation in Northwest Buildings.* Energy Studies in Buildings Laboratory, University of Oregon, Eugene, OR.

Chapin, S. and J. Chen. 2005. "Illuminating Lillis: Light Levels and Patterns of Use of the Daylighting Integrated Lighting Systems in the Lillis Business Complex." www.uoregon.edu/%7Eakwok/VSCS/lillis/index.htm

Docker, F. 2005. "Lillis Business Complex: The Question of Perception." www.uoregon.edu/%7Eakwok/VSCS/lillis/index.htm

McKelvey, A. 2005. "Lecture Hall Comfort at the Lillis Business School." www.uoregon.edu/%7Eakwok/VSCS/lillis/index.htm

University of Oregon Planning Office. 2004. "Post-Occupancy Evaluation of Lillis Business Complex." University of Oregon, Eugene, OR.

National Association of Realtors Headquarters

Birnbaum, J. 2004. "Realtors Wield the Power of Intimidating Views." *washingtonpost.com*, October 4; p. E01.

The Gund Partnership. www.gundpartnership.com/

Hedgpeth, D. 2004. "Hoping Benefits Bloom by Going Green." *The Washington Post*, May 17. Available through U.S. Green Building Council www.usgbc.org/(select News, then USGBC in the News).

National Association of Realtors, "500 New Jersey Avenue, NW Grand Preview Brochure." Available at: www.realtor.org/VLibrary.nsf/files/500NJBrochure.pdf

National Association of Realtors, "The Construction of NAR's New Washington Building." Available at: www.realtor.org/vlibrary.nsf/pages/newdc

U.S. Green Building Council, LEED Project List. www.usgbc.org/(select LEED, then Project List, then search for project).

One Peking Road

Business Environment Council, Environmental and Sustainability Case Studies Initiative, Hong Kong-Beam Society, "Case Studies: 1 Peking Commercial Building." www.hk-beam.org.hk/fileLibrary/One%20Peking_GCPL_C1071.pdf

Hui, S.C.M. Hong Kong University, Case Studies on Sustainable Design. www.hku.hk/mech/sbe/case_study/case/hk/pek/top.htm

Youngs, T. 2003. "One Peking, Tsim Tsia Tsui Landmark Contrasts," *Building Journal Hong Kong China* May. www.building.com.hk/feature/10_03peking.pdf

Youngs, T. 2004. "HKIA Annual Awards 2003." *Building Journal Hong Kong China* March/April. www.building.com.hk/feature/2004_06hkia2003.pdf

INDEX